Life is a Beach

Life is

A Vacationer's

McGraw-Hill Book Company

a Beach

Guide to the West Coast

Parke Puterbaugh and
Alan Bisbort

NEW YORK   ST. LOUIS   SAN FRANCISCO   BOGOTÁ   HAMBURG   MADRID
MEXICO   MILAN   MONTREAL   PANAMA   PARIS   SAN JUAN
SÃO PAULO   TOKYO   TORONTO

1 2 3 4 5 6 7 8 9 SEM SEM 8 9 2 1 0 9 8

ISBN 0-07-050983-2

LIBRARY OF CONGRESS CATALOGING-IN-PUBLICATION DATA

Puterbaugh, Parke.
    Life is a beach: a vacationer's guide to the West Coast / Parke Puterbaugh and Alan Bisbort.
        p. cm.
    ISBN 0-07-050983-2
    1. Pacific States—Description and travel—1981– —Guide-books.
    2. Pacific Coast (U.S.)—Description and travel—Guide-books.
    I. Bisbort,Alan, 1953–   . II. Title.
    F852.3.P88   1988
    917.9'0433—dc19   87-35349
                                                                 CIP

Book design by Kathryn Parise
Maps rendered by Paul Pugliese

Acknowledgments

Because the West Coast is thousands of miles away from our natural habitat, we could not rely on what sportswriters call the home-field advantage. That is to say, we could not—as was the case on the East Coast—come and go at a leisurely pace or expect an open door and a warm meal to be waiting for us around the next bend. For part of the spring and all of the summer of 1987, our world was defined by the four doors of a rented car and the four walls of an endless string of motel rooms. We had an entire coast to explore, much of it new to us, and an ironclad itinerary that left no time for viruses or hangovers or even relaxing on the weekend, as almost everyone else in the civilized world does. Although this certainly added to the excitement and spontaneity of the trip (and, we hope, of the writing), it also made for some anxious moments.

Once again, a world of friendly strangers came through for us, as did our loved ones back on the home front. All along the Pacific Coast Highway we met and were befriended by kind souls whose help made our road a lot easier. These folks include Patrick Hennessey (in Coronado); Shirley McMahill (in La Jolla); Chris Hill, David Anderson and Pam Criddle (in Pacific Beach); Nancy Bell (in San Clemente); Curtis Harris and Bob Roubian (in Newport Beach); Dan Williams and Duane Johnson (in Long Beach); Larry Birkett (in Redondo Beach); John Patrick Longfellow (in Santa Barbara); Robert E. Bussinger (in Big Sur); Donna Wikstad (in Santa Cruz); Bill Gillespie (in Half Moon Bay); Breck and Ann Hitz (in San Francisco); Julia Bartlett (in Point Reyes); Jeff and Joan Stanford (in Mendocino); and John and Margot Thompson

v

(in Klamath). Across the Washington state line, we'd like to thank Gene and Darlene Caldwell (in Westport); Sera and Larry Lesley (in Kalaloch); and Brian R. Peterson and Carolyn Gibbons (in Blaine).

On the home front, we'd like to thank those who looked after our affairs while we were away and also served as an emotional conduit to the lives we knew back East—namely, Carol Hill, Abbie Miller, Mark Mattucci, Lois Korzendorfer, John Dunlap, and Mark and Anne Puterbaugh. Special thanks to Carol for helping with the index again—and for keeping the home fires burning for four long months. Finally, we'd like to thank our parents—Harold ("Biz") and Penny Bisbort, and Helen Puterbaugh—for their continued and seemingly boundless help and encouragement.

We feel privileged to be working with some special people at McGraw-Hill. Our editor, Lisa Frost, has hung tough through two books with us and deserves a long vacation (on Nantucket). She's not yet drowned in the seas of paper we've thrown at her, and her enthusiasm for the series keeps our own spirits high. We'd also like to thank Terrence Fehr, whose cover illustrations have captured the spirit of our venture; Paul Pugliese, whose maps have made everything perfectly clear; Hilah Anne Selleck, our sharp-eyed and sympathetic copyedditor [sic]; and Kathryn Parise and Eve Kirch for their splendid book design.

Contents

Introduction

Several years ago, when we were putting the finishing touches on our book about the beaches of the East Coast, the idea of writing a similar volume about the West Coast came quite naturally to us. Perhaps it was the paralyzing fear of having to go out and look for real jobs again that had us thinking "sequel." Maybe it was a massive case of culture shock: we had suntans and our friends had mortgages. Whatever the case may be, the West Coast—as it had for the Dust Bowl farmers—suddenly became our way out, our land of opportunity, our hedge against spiritual recession.

It made perfect sense. We had already spent two summers and logged 20,000 miles in a cramped Toyota without so much as a fist fight. Along the way, we had devised a collaborative method of combing the coastline that worked well for us. Traveling alone certainly has its rewards, but if you want to travel *and* meet a publication deadline, it takes two to tango. Besides, how much fun can one person have at the beach, shuffling past the happy, chattering crowds like a solitary phantom?

After the East Coast had succumbed to our portable Smith-Corona—which, in the course of two coastlines and 1,200 typed pages has needed only one minor repair—our thoughts began to drift westward. This, we reasoned, was a normal reaction for any American. Go West, Young Man. Westward Ho! Manifest Destiny. The Gold Rush. California or Bust. The only thing Lewis and Clark had over us was their names. They were easier to pronounce.

Having both been raised, for the most part, on the East Coast, we'd spent our summers building sand castles in such idyllic spots as Cape Cod, Hatteras Island, Myrtle Beach, Jekyll Island and Fort Lauderdale. Still, we'd always been fascinated by the *promise* of the West Coast. We longed to see how the other half lived. The East Coast has a sunny paradise known as Florida, but the West has Southern California, a place that seems larger than life to almost all Americans. Stoking the myth, the Beach Boys celebrated their home turf in five-part harmony. In one of their most popular songs, the group politely dismissed the girls of the east, the midwest and the north in favor of the tanned goddesses from California. Taking note of this in our wide-eyed early adolescence, we made a pact to head west at some future date to check it out for ourselves. Easterners generally being more cautious and less impulsive than westerners, it took us 20 years to act on our plan.

In the meantime, we got to make a few trial runs—both business and pleasure winging us west on occasion—so that we weren't unfamiliar with the lay of the land when it came time to embark on the official odyssey that resulted in this book. Lugging a couple of suitcases and a trunk full of preliminary research, we flew the friendly skies, soaring high above the 3,000 miles of fruited plains and purple mountains' majesty between the two coastlines. Our destination was Los Angeles and then the open highway north and south of it. Our objective was another Endless Summer. If you recall, there was a mid-sixties movie with that title about a couple of guys carrying surfboards on their heads who followed the sun around the world in search of the perfect wave. Our aim was not dissimilar. We were just looking for a few more things than they were: good scenery, nice beaches, a touch of history, interesting places to stay and eat and have fun after the sun goes down. And we didn't carry surfboards on our heads. We carried notebooks in our hands.

Basically, we described what we saw and experienced at each stop without preconceptions or prejudice. Candor is one of the virtues of this series, we believe, and honesty is our stock in trade. In other words, we are unafraid to be opinionated. Fortunately, the West Coast is blessed in so many ways—the rugged natural beauty of the coastline, the sunny temperament of the people—that we found ourselves dispensing lots of praise.

We did wind up dispelling—for ourselves, anyway—a few myths about the West Coast. It is not, for instance, one big, thousand-mile sand beach dotted with the bodies of millions of blond, attractive, scantily clad sunbathers. On the contrary, the water north of Los Angeles is frigid and the surf is often hazardous. If the sharks or currents don't get you, the kelp beds will. A heavy-gauge wetsuit is a lot less sexy than an itsy-bitsy teenie-weenie yellow polka-dot bikini, but we saw a lot more of the former than the latter on many beaches. Then there are natural hazards to contend with. Sandstone bluffs crumble into the ocean, the wind blows sand in your face, and the land sometimes quakes beneath your feet. To top it off, the sun doesn't shine every day, either. Even in Southern California, they are subjected to a late-spring, early-summer phenomenon known as the "June gloom."

Still, we found ample cause for celebration out where the sun sets on America, including sand, sky, surf, daunting headlands and breathtaking scenery. Although we were surprised to discover how much of the coast is rural and sparsely populated, Southern California lived up to its reputation as the most sociable and wide-open place in the universe. We were exposed to the West Coast in all of its moods: cold and hot, sunny and overcast, quiet and rowdy. We experienced flat sand beaches and plunging coastal mountains, nouvelle cuisine and Jack-in-the-Box, wine coolers and draft beer, yin and yang and yoga on the rocks.

Starting out in May, just about the time school lets out and the bodies begin hitting the beaches, we chased the sun north through a long summer. From Southern California all the way up to the icy waters of Puget Sound, we hugged the shore, arriving in the far northwest at the height of its warm season. When we complete this series—and we are only one Gulf Coast volume shy of doing so—we will have traced a clockwise circuit around the perimeter of America: from Maine to Florida, up the Gulf of Mexico and across the Florida panhandle to Texas, then north from California to Washington.

This particular book is meant to be read as a guidebook and travelogue about the West Coast, from the Mexican border to the Canadian border. We visited every beach, bay and coastal settlement in between—be it a city of millions or an unincorporated hamlet of a few dozen—that could be feasibly reached by car, by ferry or on foot. The format is the same as our East Coast book. We wrote anecdotal general essays about each locale, discussing everything from history to what you'll find there now: things to do, what the people and the environment are like, whether or not you are likely to have a good time. Then we described accommodations, restaurants and nightlife, making general observations and specific recommendations.

Should your curiosity be stirred by a particular entry, we've included addresses and phone numbers for local chambers of commerce and visitors bureaus, which are good sources for further information. At the back of the book is a directory of hotels, motels, inns and restaurants mentioned in the text. *You* can take it from there.

One final thing we'd like to clarify about this book is the subtitle: *A Vacationer's Guide to the West Coast*. Our definition of "vacationer" is a generous one. To us, a vacationer is anyone who travels for the sheer joy of discovery. That he or she is required, by the nature of employment, to confine their traveling to a week or two each summer makes no difference. If you love the ocean, it doesn't matter what time of year you come to pay your respects or how long you stay. Our ideal vacationer, generally speaking, can abide crowds and boardwalks as well as solitude and natural beauty. Most important, he or she gets a certain feeling when standing at the shore's edge, looking out at the setting sun or just watching the waves roll in, that can be experienced nowhere else.

On that note, we will assume that if you've read this far, you're ready to turn the page and travel up the coast with us.

Parke Puterbaugh
Alan Bisbort
March 1988

California

Were California to break away from the North American continent, as the more pessimistic earthquake forecasters insist will happen, it would be the seventh richest country in the world. It is, with 25 million people, the most populous American state and easily the most well-off, both financially and in terms of natural beauty. It has given the United States two of its last four presidents and sends the largest congressional delegation, numbering 45, to Washington, D.C. The statistics and superlatives glibly roll out of the books and off the tongue, and the genial Californians take comfort in them. After all, how else are they to rebut the highfalutin scorn of provincial East Coast aristocrats who think the universe began somewhere in the vicinity of Plymouth Rock?

The tendency with places as large in body and spirit as California is to try to diminish them by falling back on stereotypes. There's no denying that California has given rise to a raft of cartoonish characters: the muscular blond surfer boy; the curvaceous, air-headed beach girl; the playboy yachtsman and his doting ingenue; the wine-sipping matron of the arts; the crackpot land speculator; the sleazy movie mogul; the sleek would-be actress or model; the mohawked suburban teen nihilist; the gum-chomping, jive-talking Valley Girl; the New Age cultist; the hip, the laid-back and the burned-out. Toss in Charles Manson and Jim Jones, and you have a good idea of how the Golden State is seen by out-of-staters.

Fortunately, the stereotypes don't hold. After spending any time in California and allowing its physical environment and psychic ambience to spin a spider web around your perceptions, the clichés are quickly jettisoned. The next step is conversion. It is tempting to swallow the myth that Californians have created for themselves—a load of sun and fun and money to burn, where never is heard a discouraging word and the skies are not cloudy all day. A person can easily go from skeptical disbeliever to religious convert in one fell swoop. It happens all the time—which is only to say that it's difficult to find a rational middle ground. Therefore, we can state without fear of contradiction, after many months of traveling and objective assessment, that California is, well, California.

Even before its discovery, California was shrouded in myth. Spanish explorers had long heard tales of an exotic island where dark-skinned women enslaved unsuspecting sailors for their pleasure. Thus, it was only natural for the Spaniards to assume that the land they came upon in the 1500s—the one with the majestic, mountainous shoreline—was the isle of their dreams. One can imagine a boatload of titillated Spanish deckhands giddily hopping ashore and stepping forward to receive their punishment.

We hopped ashore—landed at LAX, actually—in much the same spirit, eagerly stepping forward to receive our punishment from the nearest car-rental agency. Soon enough, we were taking a crash course (no pun intended) in Southern California freeway etiquette. Our rite-of-passage consisted of several trial heats between Los Angeles and San Diego. It is this sun-baked, overdeveloped jungle of asphalt and stucco from which many visitors form their impressions of California. But this 150-mile corridor is only a small fraction of the whole story. A thousand more miles of California lie north of Los Angeles County.

We quickly learned, on the first leg of our journey, that the culture of California has its roots in the Middle East: in Detroit, Michigan, where they make the cars, and in Saudi Arabia, where they drill the oil. Without the ocean, California would go batty. But without the car, it would shrivel up like a raisin in the sun. (And without Colorado's rivers, it would die of thirst.) Flying down the freeways, braking only for the Border Patrol and the inevitable rush-hour traffic snarls, Southern Californians subsist on a diet of sun, sand, surf and speed. (You can add sushi, sprouts, salad and smoothies to this list, if you like.) It is an intoxicating blend for a first-time visitor and a veritable love potion to a native—that is, anyone who's been here for over six months.

In Southern California people never stop moving, beginning and ending every quest for fun with the pedal pressed to the floor. Theirs is a civilization in perpetual motion: flying by in cars, jeeps, dune buggies, motorcycles, mopeds, bicycles, skateboards, surfboards, sailboats, roller skates and running shoes. Though we were initially overwhelmed by the bustle of a state that is perceived by the rest of the world as being laid-back, we quickly realized we'd better get in there and start moving with them or we'd never figure out what was going on. All we can say is that we gave it our best shot. In the end, we passed the Electric Kool-Aid Acid Test. The proof of our successful assimilation: a group of surfers who adopted the two of us proclaimed us to be, upon our mutual parting, "a couple of party dudes." We never learned how to surf, but we learned how to hang ten (beers, that is) with the best of them. We're no great shakes on the volleyball court either, but we spiked every bottle of Corona we were served like true Olympic champs.

California is an accommodating place. We could have easily made it our home, when our travels were over. And why not? It's a hospitable state filled with people who have themselves arrived from somewhere else. Unlike other states, they don't hold this against you. California is accustomed to a steady migratory influx, welcoming newcomers all the time. Forget about New York City; from all we've seen and read, the Statue of Liberty really belongs in Los Angeles Harbor.

If you've lost track of someone in your life, chances are good he or she has wound up in California. It's been the last stop for gold diggers, hard-luck Okies, real-estate wheeler-dealers, homesteaders, squatters, up-and-comers, down-and-outers, the old and rich, the young and hopeful. People chase their dreams westward. In the sixties, the musical counterculture of San Francisco and Los Angeles played Pied Piper to a whole generation of musk-scented gypsies. In the eighties, neatly groomed entrepreneurs with microchips on the brain have been drawn to Silicon Valley. What-

ever the latest trend—be it scientific, cultural or supernatural—
California sings the siren's song. As has been observed, it's as if
the country lists after you cross the Mississippi River, and everything that isn't bolted down rolls out to the West Coast.

The coast is exactly where they come, too. Not the desertlike
interior nor the blazing valleys, but the edge of the continent—
and the southern edge, at that. Although the California coastline
is 1,200 miles long, over half the state's population chooses to live
in the bottom sixth of the state, the land of warm temperatures
and scant rainfall known as Southern California. Generally, Southern California is considered to run from San Diego to Los Angeles,
but Santa Barbara is sometimes said to be the roof on this funhouse.
The reasons everyone comes here are obvious enough. This is
where the beaches are, where the sun shines most brightly, where
the good times roll.

When you get down to it, each California county could pass for
a state in itself. San Diego County alone has 70 miles of beaches.
Its endless shores took us weeks to canvass. Orange County is another state-within-a-state, boasting 45 miles of coastline and such
archetypal beach towns as Newport Beach, Long Beach and Laguna Beach. Then there's Los Angeles County ... we hardly know
where to begin with this one.

Essentially, the state of California breaks down into three distinct regions: Southern California, the Central Coast (from Santa
Barbara to San Francisco) and Northern California (from Marin
County to the Oregon state line). The last two share a more understated appeal, particularly as far as the human element is concerned.
Spiritually and scenically, however, their rewards are bountiful:
endless stretches of coastline that, in their untarnished majesty,
rival any in the world. Big Sur, for instance, must be seen to be
believed—and not just seen but driven, with your wheels mere
inches from a thousand-foot drop into the raging Pacific. And
what of the unheralded beauty of the north coast—the Marin
headlands, Point Reyes, Sonoma County, the village of Mendocino?

California is, if one word can be pinned upon it, abundant.
Abundant in nature, abundant in people, abundant in energy, abun-

dant in destinations. While we were traveling, it became a running joke: the state without an end. We were not bothered, however, because we were having a good time rhapsodizing around every blessed curve in the Coast Highway and exclaiming at the sights and sounds on the beach. We hope we're fortunate enough to do it again sometime.

Southern Coast

Border Field State Park

America officially begins at a place called Border Field State Park. It slams right up against Mexico in a large wave of sand and steep hills. Depending on how you look at it, Border Field is either the beginning or the end of the road. For us, it was the beginning.

The park serves double duty as a guarded international border and public park. It is a mist-shrouded, breezy stretch of beach with a surrounding wildlife area, blanketed with wildflowers, marshlands and jagged cliffs. Border Field is patrolled by lizards, birds and uniformed officials of the U.S. Immigration Service, which makes for an interesting dichotomy.

This border was established on October 10, 1849, the date California was officially wrangled away from the Mexicans to become part of the United States. A cement monument stands nearby, commemorating our friendship with this vast Latin giant. Some informative placards recount the history of both nations, while others describe the ancient natural history of geologic uplift and erosion that created the beach at Border Field. Unfortunately, the words on many of these have been chiseled away by salty sea breezes, sand, sun and rust and are nearly illegible now. That's all right, though, because nearly everything else between the two nations seems to have blurred in modern times as well.

Construction and land development, for instance, know no borders. The city of Tijuana nestles right up to the 10-foot fence. Posh, new, Mexican homes line the far hills. Closer to the beach, a more familiar third-world aesthetic is firmly entrenched. Scorched, eroding dirt, trash and graffiti follow a straight line downhill to the ocean's edge. The first commercial venture on the Mexican side, the Hotel Martin, is a sad, crumbling adobe block that looks like it might fall off its cliff-side perch at any moment and, like a clay teardrop, land in the ocean. Across the bedraggled street sits Tijuana's "modern" new bullring. Looking like a fifties version of a flying saucer, it is already liberally covered with colorful graffiti *en español*. The bullring looms less than a hundred yards from Border

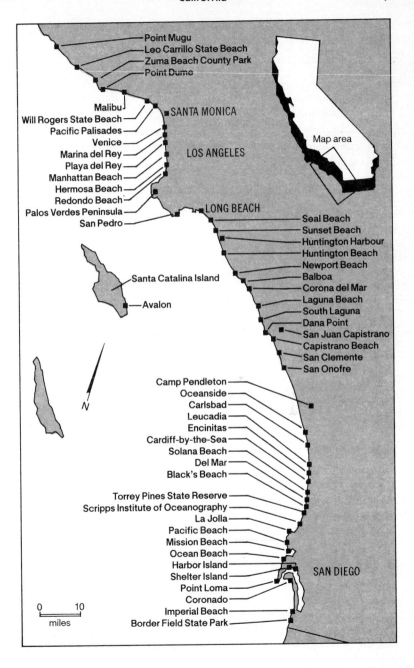

Point Mugu
Leo Carrillo State Beach
Zuma Beach County Park
Point Dume

Malibu
Will Rogers State Beach
Pacific Palisades
Venice
Marina del Rey
Playa del Rey
Manhattan Beach
Hermosa Beach
Redondo Beach
Palos Verdes Peninsula
San Pedro

SANTA MONICA

LOS ANGELES

LONG BEACH

Seal Beach
Sunset Beach
Huntington Harbour
Huntington Beach
Newport Beach
Balboa
Corona del Mar
Laguna Beach
South Laguna
Dana Point
San Juan Capistrano
Capistrano Beach
San Clemente
San Onofre

Santa Catalina Island

Avalon

Map area

Camp Pendleton
Oceanside
Carlsbad
Leucadia
Encinitas
Cardiff-by-the-Sea
Solana Beach
Del Mar
Black's Beach

Torrey Pines State Reserve
Scripps Institute of Oceanography
La Jolla
Pacific Beach
Mission Beach
Ocean Beach
Harbor Island
Shelter Island
Point Loma
Coronado
Imperial Beach
Border Field State Park

SAN DIEGO

N

0   10
miles

Field, and the Saturday afternoon "olés!" easily cross the international border. A large number of flesh-and-blood aliens make the passage with little difficulty, too.

There are more intimidating fences between suburban homes than the one that separates the United States from Mexico. The portliest Mexican could scale the border fence with a bellyful of burritos and one hand tied behind his back. Further inland, we noticed, the fence is in some places no taller than a tennis net, with a few strands of rusty, easily clipped barbed wire on top. Toward the beach, the fence simply ends about 20 feet shy of the water. The remaining stretch of open sand is watched from above by a gaggle of border cops who loiter around their lime-green patrol cars like teenagers in a McDonald's parking lot. At night, who knows what goes on.

The United States–Mexico border is 1,952 miles long, yet the San Diego end of the line accounts for over a third of all illegal-alien arrests. During the month of April 1986, no fewer than 71,908 illegal immigrants were arrested here. (April is traditionally a busy month, due to seasonal employment opportunities in the fields.) During April 1987, however, "only" 34,962 Mexicans were arrested. The 50 percent drop was due largely to a tough new immigration law.

All in all, a side trip to this out-of-the-way state park is worthwhile if you're in the vicinity. To get here, take Hollister Street south out of Imperial Beach for two miles, then turn right on Monument Street and follow the winding road to the park entrance. The scrub grass–covered cliffs of old Mexico rise on the left, while the green, irrigated fields of the United States lie on the right. As you draw closer to the ocean, you will notice a change in air temperature. The dry swelter of Imperial Beach yields to the cool mists of Border Field Wildlife Refuge, one of the last remaining salt marshes in Southern California. The surf is rough, whipped to a froth by the winds. Signs advise visitors not to swim, not only because the surf is hazardous but because the waters are contaminated with Tijuana sewage. And so you simply stare at the ocean and contemplate the strangeness of the scene at the far southwestern corner of America. The first beach in California is, indeed, an experience unlike any other.

Imperial Beach

Although Border Field serves as her Mexican buffer, America really and truly begins at Imperial Beach. Here you will find the southernmost condominiums on the West Coast, the southernmost shopping malls and franchise burger stands and the southernmost "Born in the U.S.A." T-shirts. You will also find a small community (pop. 22,000) whose mostly middle-class and mostly legal citizens try to keep the problems that plague Tijuana from spilling over the border.

Considering Imperial Beach's proximity to Mexico—on clear days you can see Tijuana's bullring from the beach—it is surprising that the shantytown presence isn't stronger. Imperial Beach is unabashedly suburban, with running and bike paths, skateboard tracks, baseball fields, public libraries, modest houses and pricey condos. It is not a resort town, but it is growing. On the few plots of land where the bulldozer has not roamed, development appears imminent, heralded by signs that say "Coming Soon" with artists' conceptions of the impending architectural leviathans. One such sign served as a portent of what lay ahead on the road to Los Angeles. It bore the silhouette of Don Quixote rearing back, as if wounded by the accompanying words, "La Mancha Development/ For Lease/Shopping Center."

Though Imperial Beach might entertain boomtown fantasies, its boom is destined to be no louder than a firecracker. It is built on the flatlands between the Tia Juana River and the San Diego Bay, which ensures that it can grow only so far. Much of what remains undeveloped is a federally protected estuary—the northern end of the Border Field Wildlife Refuge. Until someone figures out a way to build condos on the water, Imperial Beach will remain a small city.

The Mexican presence in Imperial Beach is large, though not as overwhelming as in Los Angeles, where the jobs are. For obvious geographic reasons, a large Chicano community has settled in Imperial Beach and Chula Vista, its inland neighbor. The issue of immigration is particularly sensitive here due to the constant presence of the border patrol. There are random immigration checkpoints throughout the area, not just on the border. Like speed traps, they exist all the way to Los Angeles. The hot issue during our visit was a tragic traffic accident involving the border patrol and a van full of illegal aliens. A squad car gave chase to a smuggler's van ferrying 28 undocumented migrant laborers. During the high-speed pursuit, the van overturned, killing a four-month-old baby and sending 18 Mexicans to area hospitals. To add to an already volatile situation, a California congressman was simultaneously petitioning the U.S. House of Representatives to pass his anti-immigration legislation, which would construct a 15-mile-long wall of concrete, chain-link and barbed-wire fence along the Mexican border in San Diego County.

But enough of this no-win scenario; let's hit the beach. Either of the two main drags, Palm and Coronado Avenues, leads to the water from busy Interstate 5. Along these parallel routes lies the only real evidence of Imperial Beach's bordertown taint: mobile-home parks, seedy pool halls, shacklike bars and liquor stores (with an anomalous "Seacoast Natural Foods" store thrown in to confuse you). Eventually, you will reach Seacoast Drive, which runs along the ocean.

The beach was extended a few years back by a massive infusion of sand from nearby San Diego Bay. The dredgings were deposited in front of what was once a seawall and a few rocks, leaving Imperial Beach with a wide, sandy swatch of brown gold suitable for framing a beach towel (with you as the reclining seminude). At the center of the beach is the town pier. Surfers line up to crack their crania on the underpinnings of this huge structure, where sizable waves break loud and hard. Sections of the pier have periodically been destroyed by rough surf. Swimming can be dangerous, due to unpredictable rip currents and the distribution of imported sand. (The ocean floor drops off dramatically where the pile of dredge ends.) Lifeguards are on duty and swimming advisories are issued daily.

There's one more hazard as well. Ponder this sign, hammered into the sand along the southern part of the beach: "Contaminated with Sewage. Keep Out. Avoid All Contact. No Swimming, Wading, Surfing or Water Skiing." This, we learned, was due to neighboring Tijuana's inadequate sewage-treatment program. Apparently, untreated refuse is dumped into the ocean and floats north with the current. *¡Gracias, mis amigos!* Be that as it may, Imperial Beach is worth a once-over. At least the setting—given the protected marshland behind it and the foreign nation beside it—is intriguing.

Accommodations

The *Surfside Motel*, located on the beach three blocks from the pier, is the very essence of what we conceive a beach motel to be. It faces a wide beach, and if the ocean's too rough or cold, there's a baby lima–shaped pool ringed with palm trees out front. Beyond this, a string of budget motels lines the I-5 off-ramps. Imperial Beach is a buyer's market, and you can often score a bargain room. We, for instance, stayed at a *TraveLodge* for under $30.

Restaurants

The best seafood restaurant in town, touted by tourists and natives alike, is *Anthony's Fish Grotto*. Okay, fine. Seafood would normally suffice at the beach (and in this book), but when you're in the very first beach town in America, one taco toss away from the bullrings of Tijuana, you feel almost duty-bound to track down the best Mexican dinner in town. Our find was a place called *Manuel's*. Its calling card reads "Foot to Go" (with a "d" added in ballpoint pen over the errant "t"), but their screen-door walk-in joint was just what we had in mind. For under $4 we each had a combination plate with a beef taco and burrito, rice and beans, chips and soda. While we waited for our "foot," we studied the artwork: black velvet paintings of matadors, desperados and a giant bear that looked like it was rendered by a nine-year-old. Spanish conversations flowed freely and melodiously throughout the restaurant, giving us the unmistakable impression that this might indeed be authentic Mexican food. It was. The tacos and burritos were stuffed with shredded (not ground) beef, and the hot sauce was fiery enough to make us weep in gratitude and not in pain.

Nightlife

There are so many pool halls and beer joints along Palm and Coronado Avenues that if the United States ever wants to field an Olympic billiards team, they should recruit heavily in Imperial Beach. Oh, yes, there's also a live-music club in town called, ahem, the *Country Bumpkin*. Y'all come!

FOR FURTHER INFORMATION

Imperial Beach Chamber of Commerce
825 Imperial Beach Boulevard
Imperial Beach, CA 92032
(619) 424-3151

Coronado

Driving north from Imperial Beach along Route 75, you pass from a land of no money to a land of new money. First, you notice the yachts, pressed close together in neat rows. They fill the Glorietta Bay Marina, their long masts standing straight like a fistful of pencils jammed in a cup. Then you realize that the price of gas, in the space of 10 miles, has jumped 25 cents a gallon. Finally, as you turn off the highway onto Orange Avenue, which leads into downtown Coronado, you pass by a palatial old hotel and opulent private homes fronted by lawns that are better tended than country-club putting greens.

Coronado is a wealthy bedroom community of 20,000 residents, most of whom work in nearby San Diego, just a short hop over the Coronado Bay Bridge. The town's only industry is tourism, and the largest employer is the Hotel del Coronado. Built in 1887, the "Del" is one of the most identifiable landmarks on the Southern California coast. This grand old palace is among the last of a dying breed of elegant seaside hotels. It is itself very much alive, however, and doing a land-office business on the spot it has occupied for a century. Several presidents have signed the guest register, not to mention notables from the Duke and Duchess of Windsor to John Wayne and Marilyn Monroe. *Some Like It Hot* was filmed here.

The hotel's Victorian grandeur lords over the beachfront like a rich aunt whose bearing will intimidate you into minding your manners without her having to say a word. Of course, there are some spoiled brats who won't behave for anybody. Just down the beach, like a rebellious nephew who's run off out of reach, sits a garish, skyscraping condominium complex executed in an architectural style that can only be described as Modern Bad Taste. Known as La Playa, it comprises six towers' worth of overpriced real estate at surf's edge. It was the only eyesore on Coronado's otherwise attractive beach.

If you continue up Orange Street from the Hotel del Coronado, you'll follow a graceful S curve through a shopping district lined with cafés and stores that service the recreational needs of the community (mostly swimwear and surfboards). Curiosity drove us to study the bulletin board in the window of a local real estate agency, to which were pinned fading snapshots of houses and condos with short exhortations ("This beauty has everything!") and unbelievable prices scrawled underneath. Nothing could be touched for under $160,000. Condos were outpricing houses, with the three-bedroom units at La Playa leading the way at $399,000. While we gawked in disbelief, a maroon Rolls pulled up to the curb, discharging a fur-clad matron who swept into the office with a determined stride.

There's lots of beach to go around in Coronado, even for those who can't afford to live on it. *Coronado City Beach* runs for about a mile from the Hotel del Coronado up to the airstrip at the North Island Naval Air Station. The beach is wide, the sand fine. A wall of rock lines Ocean Boulevard, where parking is plentiful. Of course, this being the Pacific Ocean, the water is so cold that even on a balmy May afternoon waves rolling over our ankles made our knees buckle. The locals didn't seem to mind the ocean's late-spring frigidity, though. The knot of surfers bouncing around in the waves included a couple of girls. No one was wearing wet suits, and no one was screaming, either. The water warms up in late summer, topping off at about 70 degrees. All around us, Spanish was spoken at rapid tempo. Most of the people on the beach don't vacation here; rather, they come here at the end of the day, after work or school. It's part of the daily routine, a vital element of the Southern California lifestyle.

From the beach, you gaze out at the bluffs of Point Loma, which juts into the ocean north of here. At sundown, a deep rosy orange envelopes everything—ocean, beach, peninsula—in a phantasmagoric haze that intensifies until nightfall finally closes the curtain. It's a display best witnessed from a balcony at the Hotel del Coronado, with a bottle of rich, red California wine to fire the imagination.

On a more earthbound note, the naval presence is everywhere. Planes land all day and most of the night at the North Island Naval Air Station. Often the shadow of a returning aircraft will pass over your supine form as you lie on the beach. The North Island base enjoys the distinction of being the birthplace of naval aviation (in 1911). From here, Charles Lindbergh took off for New York, where he embarked upon his famous transatlantic flight in 1927. A few miles south, recruits are trained at the U.S. Naval Amphibious Base, along the San Diego Bay.

The other beach worth mentioning is *Silver Strand State Beach*, off Silver Strand Boulevard between Coronado and Imperial Beach. It runs along the narrow peninsular midsection for 2½ miles. You can swim in the beach or the bay, and the surf fishing's good, too. Like most state parks, this one comes with rest rooms, picnic tables and fire rings. The only deterrent is the fairly stiff fee exacted at the front gate: $4 per car. This, we quickly learned, is the standard California state park charge—at least in the crowded southland. A high fee, yes, but it's put to good use.

Accommodations

There are 689 rooms in the *Hotel del Coronado*, and every one is different. Built in 11 months according to plans that were not written down but improvised day by day, the "Del" is one of the architectural wonders of the western world. At the time of its construction, it was the largest electrically lighted structure outside of New York City. Four hundred of the rooms are originals, dating from 1888; the others are in a wing added on a few decades back. Try to stay in the main part of the hotel. This four-story marvel rambles around in a rectangle that surrounds a green courtyard filled with palm trees and bright flowers. The on-premises amenities include two Olympic-size pools, six tennis courts, a pair of volleyball nets and a croquet green.

More important than the statistics is the feeling of informal old-world elegance that fills the place. It's not in the least stuffy. Rambling around the "Del" is like exploring a rich old relative's mansion. If you come here, you'll be living above your station but will be made to feel right at home. "You've stayed with us before?" the bellhops ask as you arrive, as if assuming you've come back to renew an old friendship. You'll have no difficulty spotting the Hotel del Coronado. Its brick-red turrets and gleaming white Victorian exterior make it look less like a hotel than a castle. The Hotel del Coronado is a vacation oasis and a bona fide National Landmark, too. Long may it stand.

Across the street from the Hotel del Coronado is a more modestly scaled but no less commodious hotel, the *El Cordova*. The 40 rooms are actually small apartments, tucked into stairwells around a brick-floor courtyard of ground-level shops and a Mexican restaurant. Birds chirp outside the windows, breezes billow through the curtains, and as you amble from kitchen to bedroom you'll feel like you're padding about in your own home. The rooms come with kitchenettes, and you are steps away from downtown Coronado.

Restaurants

The *Crown Room* in the Hotel del Coronado has served presidents, movie stars, kings, sheiks and tycoons from all over the world, so it's certainly good enough for you. The question is, are you good enough for it? The Crown Room is the largest of six restaurants on the premises. It is as long as a football field, and the ceiling is 60 feet high—one of the largest free-standing wood structures in North America. There is not a single nail in it; wooden pegs hold the vaulted sugar-pine ceiling together. The food's not bad at ground level, either, tending toward traditional surf-and-turf fare like prime rib, filet mignon, poached salmon and catch of the day. The most formal dining room at the hotel is the *Prince of Wales Room*. We were advised of the dress code by our bellhop: "California formal—which means coat and tie and shoes." It seems that if you don't spell it out, some folks might show up for dinner in bare feet.

For Mexican food, we followed the crowds into *Miguel's Cocina*, in the mall surrounded by the El Cordova. The $1.25 blackboard specials included margaritas, Corona beer and fish tacos. We chowed down on chimichangas and burritos stuffed with top sirloin, amply flanked by piles of rice and beans.

One more place merits a word: *S&M Submarine Sandwiches*, a sub shop that has been dishing out grinders on Orange Avenue for 17 years. The prices are low (two or three dollars for a sub that could launch missiles), and they make everything from tuna-and-avocado subs to gourmet chili dogs. A great place to grab a quick lunch.

Nightlife

Don't come to Coronado expecting big-city nightlife. That can be found over the bay in San Diego. Your choices on the Coronado side of the bridge are pretty much limited to a trio of Irish bars along Orange Avenue. At the busiest of these, *McP's Irish Pub*, a satin-voiced soul singer was emoting Stevie Wonder ballads. Coming attractions included a band called Null and Void. The rest rooms were identified by a sign that read, "Mc Pee-Pee Room." There was a crowd on hand, however, making the atmosphere cozy and preppie-ish. Down the street, we poked our heads into a shamrock-festooned saloon called *Danny's* and saw three pub-crawlers and a silent jukebox. Presumably, things perk up on weekends.

good. On that red-letter date, the town of San Diego de Alcalá
was created by the Franciscan mystic-priest Father Junípero Serra.
More a visionary than a humble padre, Serra launched the first
European settlement on the West Coast with a game plan that General Sherman would have envied. Serra's town consisted of a military battalion and Catholic mission, the latter being the religious
equivalent of a plantation. It was this mission system, devised by
the charismatic Serra, that eventually subjugated the native population of California, reducing their numbers and turning the survivors into veritable slaves. The recruitment method employed by
the 21 missions in this network was known as "the cross or the
sword"—a religious conversion policy not unlike that used by marauding Muslims during their invasion of North Africa. In fact,
by the time the Spanish overlords were finished, the people of the
Kumeyaay tribe, as well as many others in the territory, were either dead by the sword or totally dependent on the mercy of the
cross. Today, Serra's original settlement, prosaically called *Old
Town*, stands in reconstructed salute to this and other colonial
achievements. Old Town is predominantly a shopping mall set
among adobe buildings, but Serra's first mission still stands, and
worship services are held in the original chapel every Sunday.

A century ago, gold was discovered in the mountains east of San
Diego and the town really started booming. Both crime and land
prices soared overnight. The railroad arrived, helping to further
the cause of rampant land speculation. A fast-talking operator from
back east named Alonzo Horton had the foresight to buy up the
entire waterfront of San Diego and then lay out a grid of streets
upon which the downtown business district would one day be built.
He called his venture New Town. Even today, it looks brand-new,
perhaps because it is dominated by nondescript modern skyscrapers, most of which bear bank logos. A further testament to the
man can be found at nearby Horton Plaza, which, like Old Town,
is primarily a shopping plaza with little historical significance.
There is, however, a decent art museum attached to the complex.

Eighty years ago, the U.S. Navy landed in San Diego, building
shipyards and installations on every available piece of land and creating a gray military sprawl of its own. Soon enough, because of
its near-perfect natural harbor, San Diego became the permanent

base for our largest West Coast fleet. Today, well over 100,000 naval personnel are stationed here, not to mention the thousands of employees who work for private military contractors like General Dynamics.

Forty years ago, despite all the massive facelifts and dramatic changes, San Diego was considered just another backwater Navy town, ranking 43rd in population among U.S. cities. Today, it is still a Navy town, but it is not sleepy. Its population has passed the one million mark, and it is the seventh largest city in the country. In the intervening four decades, the area has swelled like a dry sea sponge tossed into a tidepool. Every year brings 30,000 new arrivals to San Diego, while 29 million more pay a visit. Countless others are planning to move here as corporate headquarters around the country play musical chairs with their serf-like employees.

There is a reason for this sudden migration. The weather in San Diego is ideal for anyone who doesn't crave variety. It seldom rains, and when it does, according to a local citizen, people stare at the heavens as if witnessing a solar eclipse. Temperatures rarely stray from the 70- to 80-degree range all year long. San Diego offers mountains to explore, zoos, museums, theaters and, of course, 70 miles of beach in the surrounding county. This breeds an atmosphere of almost insufferable self-satisfaction. Sandy Ego, we took to calling it.

Okay, let's toss the colorful brochures aside for a second and look at what really and truly happens when a million relative newcomers get together in one lovely place and 30,000 more people a year start muscling in on the paradise. For one thing, a smog-shrouded maze of superhighways is created. They intertwine all over the terrain like seaweed, giving the freeway novice a headache and a pair of watery eyes. (You may be told otherwise, but there *is* smog in San Diego.) The land boom in San Diego has spawned a religion of development. No fewer than 29 pages of listings in the Yellow Pages are devoted to real estate. The result is a sprawl of apartment complexes and fake adobe homes that stretches toward the horizon in every direction. And even this is not enough to accommodate the new arrivals. According to the local media, a housing shortage is threatening to reach crisis proportions.

The pace of life in San Diego is deceptive. Though leisurely on the surface, the city positively throbs with an undercurrent of manic activity, with the main culprit in the high-stress sweepstakes being the automobile. Cars are in constant motion, glittering like metallic bugs in the dry heat. Bicycles, roller skates and skateboards hound the heels of the more sedate pedestrians. Joggers blip past the proud waterfront developments. Mostly these are young businesspeople, the new blood of rootless San Diego. Sailboats and yachts cut through the bay like stilettos. The race is on, and you can't figure out where the finish line is or what you get if you win. Perhaps an eternal game of golf.

It cannot go unrecorded that San Diego suffers from a chronic hang-up about Los Angeles. You can't walk 10 feet without someone telling you how much greater Sandy Ego is than Los Angeles. One local publication actually stated, "San Diego is a city that plans its growth, careful to avoid 'Los Angelization.'" (Won't somebody wake them up and tell them it's already happened?) It is a self-image upheld by denigration, which betrays an ounce or two of inferiority.

Okay, we could rail on about the shameless boosterism of San Diego. Everyone we spoke to sounded like a hireling of the chamber of commerce, ticking off local attractions like an auctioneer calling out tobacco prices. But this sort of thing begins to wear thin after a few days. Here are but a few of the titles the city claims: "Sports Town USA," "Golfland USA," "America's Finest City," "California's Oldest City," "The Place Where California Began," "California's Plymouth Rock." Do these names not bug you, too?

We could go on about all the tourist attractions you are endlessly beseeched to visit, most of which are glorified shopping malls based around Disney-esque themes: Seaport Village, Gaslamp Quarter, Horton Plaza, Old Town, New Town, rah-rah-rah. But instead we'll bluntly tell you the only attractions worth going out of your way to see are the museums and theaters of *Balboa Park*, the *San Diego Zoo* (although at $7.50 a head, you've got to see a lot of monkeys to break even), and the ocean beaches of San Diego County.

FOR FURTHER INFORMATION

San Diego Convention and Visitors Bureau
1200 Third Avenue, Suite 824
San Diego, CA 92101
(619) 232-3101

Greater San Diego Chamber of Commerce
110 West C Street, Suite 1600
San Diego, CA 92101
(619) 232-0124

Ocean Beach

If you can somehow wrest your car from the jaws of the San Diego
Freeway (I-5) and turn onto the Ocean Beach Freeway (I-8), you'll
soon be at the water. Before you get there, however, the road will
fork. The right fork, Mission Bay Drive, steers off toward Mission
Beach, Pacific Beach, La Jolla and the beaches of north San Diego
County. The left fork, the Ocean Beach Freeway, quickly becomes
Sunset Cliffs Boulevard and deposits you in Ocean Beach before
charting a cliff-hugging course along the Point Loma peninsula.

Ocean Beach is the designated beach town along the peninsula.
Its downtown and oceanfront areas look like a party that somebody forgot to clean up after. To put it bluntly, Ocean Beach is a
sub-Coney Island maze of dirty streets, litter-strewn parking lots,
sun-faded storefronts and rough-looking bars. Let us take you on
a tour of Ocean Beach, as seen through our sunglasses one breezy
May afternoon.

The first commercial establishment we encountered in Ocean
Beach was a cinder-block cycle shop called Dago Choppers. On the
front was painted a huge grinning skull; beside it, the words "Come
in." No thanks. Rounding a corner onto Newport Avenue, we
passed a large wooden structure, painted two shades of pink, that
at first glance looked like an abandoned POW barracks. It didn't
appear to have a name, being identified as, simply, "Motel." The
public parking lot across the street was scented with urine and rot-

ting trash. A few disabled ex-bikers and/or vets jangled around like mad dogs policing an auto-salvage yard. Some shirtless, long-haired reprobates and their girlfriends spilled out the back of a parked van, carrying on like unrepentant remnants of the Manson clan. "Right on, dude," one hoarsely bellowed at a companion, hoisting her lunchtime Budweiser in salute. Huge unemptied garbage cans lined the sidewalk every 10 feet, but there was more garbage on the sand than in the cans. A car rumbled up, loudly blaring a cassette tape in defiance of a sign that read: "Noise or Music Audible More Than Fifty Feet From Its Source Is Prohibited."

Out on the pier, some scuzzball skateboard clowns whizzed past the occasional fishers, frozen with boredom on a day when nothing was biting. The concrete pier is long, aged and sturdy. Midway out, a small food stand called the *Sea Dawg* sells fish 'n' chips and beer. In the water, displaying the same patience as the fishers, a group of surfers wait for the right wave. They bob up and down on the swells, making small talk until...here comes a monster. Just before it starts to curl, they steer into it. You think they've missed it, but then they emerge astride their boards in a shower of flying foam, negotiating the sloping face of the spilling wave with perfect body English. The wave angles in at Ocean Beach's quarter-mile of sand, then rolls ashore. And the surfer, who has U-turned out of it, is belly-down on the board again, paddling back out toward the break.

Watching surfers in action is nearly as fun as surfing itself—especially to a pair of board-shy easterners who have equilibrium problems on dry land. After witnessing one particularly thrilling ride, we headed off the pier—taking in the sight of a guy asleep on the beach with a boom box for a pillow and a woman the size of the John Waters character Divine shoveling food out of a brown bag—and browsed the shopping district. This was not as pleasurable a pastime as the word "browse" might suggest. Few stores were doing what could be termed a healthy business. The prevailing retail motif was Southern California schizophrenic: natural-food emporiums and fast-food grease pits; T-shirt shops that cater to brain-damaged AC/DC fans and upscale boutiques that sell glorified T-shirts for $40. The intellectual bent of the community could be read in the contents of a purported bookstore: two racks of paperback romances dwarfed by shelves of greeting cards and magazines. Outside the store, a pair of punks ambling by stopped to hump the cardboard standup of Vanna White that advertised her book.

On a corner, while we waited for a girl in a Fotomat booth to stop jawing with her boyfriend and sell us some film, we saw what appeared to be a street gang forming a circle. On closer inspection, it turned out to be 10 guys kicking a hackey-sack ball around. It was two o'clock on a Wednesday afternoon. Don't they go to school? Work? What is this? Pondering this epidemic of idleness as we made our way back to the car, we were passed by a middle-aged man with orange-brown hair and purple splotches on his face who was grinning just a little too broadly. We picked up the pace and floored it out of Ocean Beach.

A final image: the local giveaway newspaper, *The Beacon*, contained an ad for a man who was running for city council. This was not your average paid political advertisement, however. On it, said candidate was pictured in a straitjacket. "City Council Candidate (district two) Loch David Crane will attempt a SUSPENDED STRAIGHT JACKET ESCAPE on MAY 30, 3 p.m. at the Belmont Coaster. If he survives this dangerous act, you can VOTE FOR LOCH DAVID CRANE on September 15!" To this ad was tagged a final line: "He must be crazy." Could be they're all crazy.

FOR FURTHER INFORMATION

San Diego Peninsula Chamber of Commerce
P.O. Box 7018
San Diego, CA 92107
(619) 223-9767

Point Loma

Once out of the madness of Ocean Beach, the land rises—first gently, then steeply—until you're high above the water, looking down on beach and bay from a ridge of ruddy-brown sandstone. Sunset Cliffs Boulevard leads partway out the peninsula, edging along cliffs that are succumbing to lapping waves at an alarming rate. Several parking turnouts have been closed, and signs warn you to stay back at others. Still, this two-mile stretch along Sunset Cliffs before the road peters out is the most memorable stretch of the peninsula. A dirt path follows the cliffs, and you can scuttle like a crab to the edge of a heart-stopping dropoff and look straight down. The ocean glitters like a diamond necklace, and the cliffs, particularly at dusk, take on a beautiful deep-red hue. Divers and surfers frequent the pocket beaches shoehorned into coves, but swimming is out of the question.

To traverse the full length of Point Loma, turn off Sunset Cliffs Boulevard onto Hill Street. After ascending a vertical grade that'll make your engine sputter and whine, turn right onto Catalina Boulevard (Route 209). This becomes Cabrillo Memorial Drive and leads all the way out to *Cabrillo National Monument* at the tip of the peninsula. Along the way, miles of naval installation fly by. In San Diego, the naval presence is overwhelming. You're never far from the barbed wire gates of a military base, the whoosh of planes taking off and landing, jeeps whizzing by, mile-long defense contractor plants, barracks, barbed wire, barracks, barbed wire...ugh!!

But meanwhile, the peninsula narrows as you pass an endless military graveyard à la Arlington National Cemetery. Beyond this lies Cabrillo National Monument. For $3 per car, you can look at a stone monument, an old lighthouse and a visitors center, plus hiking trails that lead to tide pools.

All things considered, Point Loma looks better at a distance from the beach at Coronado than at close range. As it absorbs more and more of the overflow from the 30,000 new bodies a year arriving in San Diego, Point Loma might just sink into the ocean under all the new weight long before the ocean erodes it away naturally.

FOR FURTHER INFORMATION

San Diego Peninsula Chamber of Commerce
P.O. Box 7018
San Diego, CA 92107
(619) 223-9767

Shelter Island
Harbor Island

In the sixties, sand dredged from the bottom of San Diego Bay was dumped on a mud bank inside the armpit where the Point Loma peninsula bends back toward downtown San Diego. The resulting sandbanks were christened Shelter Island and Harbor Island, and private investors poured millions into developing them, building high-rise hotels, restaurants and marinas. Familiar corporate hotels, such as the *Sheraton Grand*, perch upon this artificial paradise like watchtowers. You'll pay no less than $100 a night to sleep here, and $150 to $500 is a more accurate range. Unless you own a boat or your Fortune 500 employer is springing for convention expenses, prospective vacationers might want to point their rudders elsewhere. For boaters, however, there's extensive berthing on both islands. Shelter Island can accommodate 2,000 small craft, and Harbor Island about half that.

Pacific Beach
Mission Beach

Pacific Beach and its smaller, poorer cousin, Mission Beach, are two like-minded party towns just up the coast from the DMZ of Ocean Beach. Luckily, the thin mouth of Mission Bay separates them from the latter, ensuring that their all-American brand of fun does not verge on low-rent nihilism.

A 2¾-mile paved boardwalk links Mission Beach with Pacific Beach, and it is upon this cement stage, the long beach in front of it and the plethora of great bars nearby that the nonstop party is thrown. Without a doubt, Pacific Beach and Mission Beach exhibit the first real signs of life on the coastal cardiogram of Southern California. It is not until you walk down Garnet Avenue toward the Crystal Pier and then turn onto the boardwalk that you actually feel like you are entering the pumping aorta of a true California beach town. You know, the kind you always read about: skateboards, roller skates, volleyball on the beach, surfboards, surf shops, surf bars and surf bunnies.

Although both towns are, as their signs proclaim, "communities of San Diego," they have more in common with the monkey cages at the San Diego Zoo than any of the neighborhoods in that booming metropolis. Besides, they're sizable communities in their own right. Pacific Beach has a population of over 40,000, and though Mission Beach is limited by its peninsular space, it's nothing but wall-to-wall real estate. You see all types here—families, college kids, beach bums, businesspeople, old folks, tiny tots, preppies, punks, hippies, health nuts, Hare Krishnas, girl watchers and boy watchers. The community profile is a mysterious blend—and, sometimes, clash—of these divergent elements.

Lately, a lot of landmarks in old Pacific Beach have been displaced by enterprises like Haagen-Dazs ice cream and Mrs. Field's Cookies, heralding the arrival of a seriously upscale developmental agenda. Longtime residents lovingly refer to their town as "PB" but also disparagingly call it "Baja La Jolla," mocking the preppies who drive down the hill from much wealthier La Jolla to party.

Mission Beach is the raunchier of the two towns. Some real dead-enders galumph along the boardwalk, lurching uncertainly among all the healthy blond youths who move as fast as their wheels will spin. One lowlife, a Gregg Allman lookalike wearing a T-shirt that read "Get It Up and Keep It Up," could not even stand up. So intoxicated was he by two in the afternoon that he kept dropping to one knee in order to save himself from falling facedown on the sidewalk. An out-of-commission roller coaster sits nearby, and attempts are underway to make it operational again. It is an apt metaphor for Mission Beach.

The lowlife element is counterbalanced by the college kids who populate Mission Beach. Strolling through here on any day is like walking along fraternity or sorority row during Rush Week. Shirtless guys clutching tall Buds lean off balconies, passing vocal judgment on the human parade, while bikini-clad beauties casually sit back and toy with drinks and suntan oil. On the boardwalk, they jog, bike and skate past all the staggering residue, paying them no heed. One sun-bronzed guy calmly stood atop his skateboard while two leashed, panting lapdogs gamely pulled him along like miniature huskies. Only in California.

There's a pretty public beach with a landscaped picnic area north of Crystal Pier in Pacific Beach. The largest stretch of sand in the area belongs to Mission Beach, which is narrow but long. It runs the entire three-mile length of the boardwalk and has designated areas for board surfing, bodysurfing and swimming. The water conditions are updated on a blackboard outside the lifeguard station. (For instance, "Lots of rip currents and deep holes on the inside of the surf zone. Ask us where to swim.") During the summer season, parking for cars as well as beach blankets is at a premium, as the town floods with young Californians.

No matter what time of year it is, though, the surfers rise with the sun in this town, heading out at dawn to catch the waves. Part of the reason is that surfing is off-limits on many local beaches after 11 a.m. The other explanation is that surfers are masochistic. One ex-surfer we met was now into "body whomping." Body whomping is a variation on bodysurfing that requires the practitioner to roll into the hollow tube of a large wave—he called it "entering the green room"—and then allow the force of the breaking wave to pound him senseless onto the ocean floor. He described that one last moment before the wave collapsed as "magical." He also confessed he had back problems.

North of town, surfers gather at Tourmaline Surf Park, a rocky stretch of shoreline off-limits to swimmers. The waves are notoriously large here and break a good distance out from shore. The old guard of the surfing scene congregates here. The purists are distinguishable from the come-latelies because they steadfastly adhere to the dying tradition of long boards with single fins and no leg-lines. "A good surfer never loses his board," a good surfer informed us.

Accommodations

A relatively new addition to Pacific Beach's oceanfront is the *Pacific Terrace Inn*. This pinkish-brown hotel blends its three stories into the sand as unobtrusively as a 73-room inn possibly can. It is a modern luxury hotel, but there's no sense of stuffiness about the place. It's built on the site of what used to be a transient hotel. The transients moved down to Mission Beach, and the Pacific Terrace rose from the ashes. It's quite a leap upward, an indication of the money that has been flowing into the local economy. Many rooms have balconies overlooking the ocean and the hotel's large, heated pool. The staff is young and friendly. Most of them hail from the community and can tell you everything you need to know about Pacific Beach, and then some.

A complete contrast to the Pacific Terrace, the *Crystal Pier Motel* is set front and center in the heart of Pacific Beach. The name does not lie. It is situated directly on the short, historic Crystal Pier (dating from 1927). The rooms are actually separate cottages affixed like a row of white boxes to both sides of the weather-beaten pier. Each cottage has a different type of sea creature carved into the cute blue shutters. The Crystal Pier Motel is popular with fishers, who can toss their lines in the water without leaving home.

Restaurants

Restaurant-wise, Pacific Beach is a standoff between fast-food mediocrity and moderately up-and-coming new restaurants. Italian and Mexican cuisines do battle with fish 'n' chips and cheeseburgers, and nobody's a clear winner yet. This much we know for sure: *Cass Street Bar and Grill*, the locals' hangout of choice, serves the best burgers in town. That was the unanimous claim of everyone we talked to, all of whom eat there so often it's like an extension of their refrigerators. Alternatively, you can get a solid Mexican dinner at *Club Diego's* as a prelude to an evening of dancing and drinking there.

Nightlife

In the immortal words of a Beastie Boys song that was just getting popular as we were traveling up the West Coast, "You've got to fight for your right to PARRR-TY!" In the immortal words of a local Pacific Beach party animal, "For me there's living at the beach and then there's middle age. And then there's death." We could continue to quote immortal words till our mortal bodies keeled over, but even that would not adequately capture the transcendent wildness of the nightlife in Pacific Beach and Mission Beach. You simply have to take the drinking tour with us. In the immortal words of Franklin Delano Roosevelt, "You have nothing to fear but fear itself."

To see everything in a night or two is nearly impossible, but with the assistance of a volunteer welcoming committee—consisting of a local ex-surfer and ski bum, a self-proclaimed truant champion, a Marin County transplant and his cocktail-waitress girl-friend—we gave it the old college try. At the end of the evening, we got the thumbs-up from our much younger hosts. ("You guys are real party dudes," one noted approvingly.) The town of Pacific Beach gets our unqualified thumbs-up as well.

We drank in enough places to fill a scorecard. We even managed to get pulled over by the cops, the result of making a rolling "California stop" at a four-way intersection. The officer turned on his blue and red flashers, and when we didn't stop ("Honestly, sir, we had no idea you wanted us"), he got on the bullhorn, yelling "Pull over, goddamn it," loud enough to be heard in La Jolla. After the driver offered a believable alibi and passed the coordination test with Baryshnikov-like grace, the officer was all sweetness and light, shaking hands and praising us for having the good sense to appoint a designated driver. But enough about that; let's get on with the tour.

The place to go for what our guides called a "prelude to partying" is the *Lahaina Beach Club*. It's located over the boardwalk and ocean, midway between Pacific and Mission beaches. At sunset, locals head there in droves to toast the end of another day in paradise. It gets crowded, but there's always room for one more at the bar.

After the ritual sunset stop at the Lahaina, we headed to Mission Beach to check out two pleasantly seedy beer joints—the *Beachcomber* and the *Pennant*—located next door to each other on Mission

Boulevard. They are almost indistinguishable, with wooden bars and booths, plastic cups of draft, boisterous and sometimes slurred conversations and a clientele that would not pass the dress code at a sock hop. Out front, we noticed a wide-tired beach bike leaning against a lamppost. It had a makeshift beer holder mounted on the handlebars: a Campbell's Soup can held in place by electrician's tape. Nothing like having one for the road, especially if your driver's license has been revoked.

Next, it was time to return to Pacific Beach for a quick perusal of the live-entertainment scene. *Jose Murphy's*, *Mary's* and the *Old Pacific Beach Café* are the best of the lot—the former two for rock and roll (but come expecting "300 guys and 2 girls," our guides warned us), the latter for jazz and blues. If listening to long-haired boogie monsters isn't your cup of brew, then maybe a few of the local saloons would be more to your liking. It was to ours. We quickly quaffed a Bass ale at *Hennessey's*, an upscale chain bar popular in Southern California, ignoring the acoustic duo picking and singing quietly beneath the din of the crowd. Hennessey's is big with the natives only because it was built on the site of a late, lamented Mexican restaurant and bar.

Up the street and around the corner is the *Cass Street Bar and Grill* (although "Grail" would be more like it). A pool table in the middle, open windows all around, stuffed marlin on the wall, cold Pacific beer in long-necked bottles on the bar top...Cass Street is Southern California personified. The old gang sits around and talks about "PB" the way it used to be. Don't worry, though. They don't get maudlin about it.

Kahuna's might as well be your final stop. It was quite nearly ours. Kahuna's is a surf bar, plain and simple, perhaps *the* surf bar on the Southern California coast. Like the pipeline of a wave, only dauntless surfers venture inside. Surf music plays on the jukebox (lots of Beach Boys, Jan and Dean and instrumental surf hits like "Wipeout"); long, macho surfboards hang from the ceiling; footage of surfing feats plays continuously on video monitors; and surfers pack the place, especially on the "rage nights" of Friday and Saturday. Kahuna's is headquarters for the Mission Beach Surf Club and sponsors an annual surfing contest. Its credentials are in order, in other words.

The place is run by the head Kahuna, a scary-looking guy with a graying beard and baggy, soiled surfer's trunks. Throughout the evening, he taunts and regales the crowd over a microphone, and at closing time his monologue can get pretty intense. He offered a free shot of Jose Cuervo Gold to any woman who bared her breasts for him. He leapt over the bar to referee a fistfight he helped instigate. The fight was over in a flurry of punches and shoving, and the offending party was taken outside to be summarily disciplined. The throng inside, meanwhile, began chanting, "Kahuna! Kahuna! Kahuna!" Needless to say, only the most fearless female ventures into Kahuna's lair, especially with him muttering lewdly into the microphone while pacing behind the bar like a trapped panther.

Despite all the mayhem, Kahuna's is a much-beloved institution, sort of a frat house for the surfing cult. It was also a great place for us to end our evening in PB. Cowabunga, whatever that means.

Oh yes, one other place you might want to visit is *Club Diego's*—if you can get in, that is. In season, the line wraps around the block. Diego's is a dress-coded "new-wave disco" for the young, the restless and the fashionable of Pacific Beach. Generally unpopular with locals—again, it occupies the site of a beloved and bygone Mexican restaurant—Diego's nevertheless brings a lot of warm bodies into Pacific Beach. Like a glitzy magnet, it lures people from La Jolla and San Diego. The majority of women sport the latest fad attire seen hanging in the swank shops of La Jolla, and for them, the dance floor becomes an extension of their team-fitness aerobics classes. Suffice it to say, this is a very healthy, athletic and good-looking young crowd.

FOR FURTHER INFORMATION

Pacific Beach Chamber of Commerce
P.O. Box 99183
San Diego, CA 92109
(619) 272-4300

La Jolla

It is widely and incorrectly assumed that La Jolla (pronounced, *la hoya*) means "the jewel" in Spanish. In truth, it translates as "the hollow." But the townspeople of this Croesus-rich community can be forgiven for this etymological error. La Jolla does indeed look like a jewel—maybe the prize bauble on the marble-topped vanity of Southern California. Not even the Hope diamond can boast a setting quite so splendid as this village of millionaires nestled in the bluffs overlooking the Pacific north of San Diego.

Technically, La Jolla is a community belonging to San Diego, but in every imaginable way, it is removed. The freeway cacophony of downtown San Diego is miles to the east. La Jolla is set on a hill, distanced by altitude and attitude from rabble-rousing Pacific Beach and Mission Beach, which lie below. Despite an ongoing real-estate boom, every attempt is made to cultivate a village atmosphere. Much like the villages of the Hamptons, way back east on Long Island, a combination of money, refinement and righteous civic pride creates a rarefied small-town atmosphere. It is a small town with as many brokerage firms as Wall Street, but a small town nonetheless.

The average price tag on a La Jolla home is $450,000. To be a homeowner here involves more than simply keeping your lawns mowed and hedges trimmed. Yard maintenance and landscaping are, like so many things in the sun-kissed wonderland of Southern California, pursued with a fervor bordering on the fanatical. The entire town looks like a botanical garden, with more types of flowers filling side gardens and rimming front lawns than can be cataloged in a field guide. The houses themselves are splendid realizations of architectural fantasy, each a potential page out of *Architectural Digest*. The prevailing style is a creative merger between traditional and Mission-style architecture, with modern elaborations upon these themes, the principal end being harmony with the environment. The sun and the ocean play starring roles. Picture windows and sun decks are positioned to catch the golden rays and courtyards face the Pacific, while trees and flowers embower the premises.

The ocean exerts a near-mystical pull upon all who live in La Jolla, many of whom begin and end their day with a pilgrimage to its edge. People gravitate to the beaches with the same sense of holy mission that drives Muslims to stop what they're doing and pray to Mecca five times a day. Early morning and sunset attract devotional throngs. They watch the sun and the sea from porches and balconies. They come in cars and vans with surfboards jammed in back or tethered on top. They jog along Coast Boulevard, the girls looking like beauty-pageant winners, the guys resembling Mr. Universe contestants. Some bring picnic baskets with them, crawling out onto sandstone shelves to toast the rosy sun as it slides into the crystal goblet of the Pacific.

Yes, they work hard and play hard in La Jolla. In their leisure hours, they don't rest or relax. Their hobbies are physically demanding activities like surfing, scuba diving and spike-or-get-spiked volleyball. Before eight and after five the whole town gyrates like the pumping pistons of a giant engine. Legs bounce up and down, balls are tossed or batted to and fro, helmeted bicyclists fly around curves, surfers paddle out or streak in on a big wave. It's enough to give a sedentary observer motion sickness.

The town's prosperity is predicated largely upon real-estate transactions, stock-market investments and other it-takes-money-to-make-money schemes. The heart of La Jolla is the Prospect and Fay Street intersection, which looks like a reduced-scale model of New York's financial district. Outside the offices of Paine Webber and Merrill Lynch sit rows of gleaming BMWs and Mercedes—foreign cars for patriotic free-enterprise capitalists who've earned their money the old-fashioned way: spitting figures into a telephone all day long while their pile of gold gets bigger. For lunch, they march single file into a place called the Soup Exchange. Presumably, the price of minestrone rises or falls on a daily basis.

The high-pressure lifestyle of making and spending money is bound to take a toll that no amount of scuba diving or tennis can adequately soothe. This perhaps explains why a village of 30,000 can list five pages of state-licensed psychiatrists in its Yellow Pages, not to mention a psychic consultant who accepts gift certificates. Stress is a hot topic of conversation. Relationships, right down to the most intimate detail, are discussed as casually as the weather. At dinner one night, we were seated next to a medical professional and his date. Both were in their early forties. Both were divorced. And both talked of nothing else, barely pausing to swallow their food. The male interrogated his partner with highly personal questions whose premises were incredibly silly. "Did you ever get to the point where you dug each other on a soul level, or was it all fantasy?" he queried earnestly while nibbling on a calamari strip. "Did you giggle together?" he asked with deep concern. By this time, *we* were giggling together, but the best was yet to come. Of his own marriage, dissolved after nearly two decades, he allowed that "we weren't right for each other from day one, and I knew it." The conversation accelerated into a lengthy analysis of an apparent put-down at the hands of a psychic nutritionist, which was generously interpreted as "a loving gesture."

Before this turns into the sequel to *The Serial* that is crying to be written, we should redirect our gaze, like all good La Jollans, to the beaches. Set into cloistered coves against a sandstone backdrop, open to the full force of the churning sea, here are some of the finest surfing beaches in California. The foremost of these is *Windansea Beach*, forever immortalized in Tom Wolfe's treatise on the surfing cult, *The Pump House Gang*. To find the legendary Windansea, you have to know what you're looking for. Turn off La Jolla Boulevard onto Nautilus Street and follow it till it dead-ends into Neptune Place. In the late afternoon, you'll find a knot of surfers numbering about 30 bobbing up and down on their boards like seals clinging to driftwood. Just offshore, the surf funnels through an underwater canyon, making for 8- to 10-foot waves on good days. The surfing is so radical (better get used to the lingo) that competition is keen for wave space. Novices and outsiders are not welcome. Surfers are territorial, here and everywhere, and we heard stories about arguments degenerating into fisticuffs, with the local boys ejecting unwanted "valleys" (a disparaging term for inlanders) attempting to encroach on their waves.

But on this particular afternoon we saw nothing but the serenity of the setting sun, the hypnotic whoosh of the ocean and peace and goodwill in the water and on the shore. This scene was so emblematic of the California experience that it merits some elaboration. A trio of middle-aged divers, yellow tanks strapped to their backs, waded into the water, caucusing briefly before disappearing beneath the surface. An apple-cheeked beauty with blond hair jogged by in a turquoise sweatshirt and coral sweat pants. Vans lined the streets, with doors slid open to reveal fur-covered seats, carpeted floors and knee-high card tables at which cross-legged blue-jean boys cracked jokes and sipped beer. A guy in a wet suit came jogging down a side street, surfboard under his arm, anxiously scanning the waves. People assumed meditation poses on rock ledges, hands shielding eyes from the sun's orange glare as they gazed seaward. A girl in a bulky sweater, guitar slung over her shoulder, strummed and strolled out onto the rocks, as if serenading the sea. One of the surfers caught an amazing ride, tunneling through the foam and down the wave face until he was shooting the curl. And, moment by moment, the setting sun turned the buff-colored sandstone to honey.

If you keep walking, you'll pass beach after beach shoehorned into the rocky, ear-shaped protrusion of land upon which La Jolla sits. Some of the more popular beaches are *Bird Rock* (a promontory covered with guano and seals); *Children's Pool Beach* (which, its name to the contrary, is plagued with dangerous rip currents); and *Marine Street* and *La Jolla Strand* (in-town favorites that draw surfers, fishers, swimmers and divers in nearly equal numbers). Parking abounds along the beach, particularly on Coast Boulevard, which follows the curving coastline from *Whispering Sands Beach* all the way around to *La Jolla Cove*. Here, at a place called Alligator Head, a breakwater curves outward. Anyone can walk out on it, though at risk of getting showered by waves exploding onto its cement base. The fury of the sea is readily apparent here, as breakers rebound off the wall and collide with incoming swells in a noisy geyser.

Just above the cove, the shoreline assumes a more regular course. The area north of the bend in the bay is known as *La Jolla Shores*. Behind a broad beach lies a large, grassy public park with picnic tables, dressing facilities and dirt pathways that meander beneath scrubby pines and tall, spindly palms.

Accommodations

On May 3, 1987, the town of La Jolla celebrated its centennial. The local newspaper, in its coverage of the event, recounted that glorious spring afternoon in 1887 when La Jolla sprang into existence. The first line of the story said it all: "It could not have been a better day for selling real estate." It was boom time in California, and settlers scurried westward like ants to a picnic to join in the land grab. One historical account claims they were sold a false bill of goods: "The plots were touted as having water mains and convenient telephone and rail service, none of which was true." But it didn't matter. The setting was so much like paradise, who was going to quibble over telephone service?

If you're visiting La Jolla, you basically have two options: stay in the heart of the village or out on the beach at La Jolla Shores. Should you decide on the former, a luxury hotel called the *Empress* is conveniently located in the business district. The rooms are extra large, appointed with marble-tiled baths and stocked minibars. Thick terrycloth robes hang inside mirrored closet doors. Mauve cloth napkins sit next to a gilt-edged ice bucket. On the lobby level is a gourmet Italian restaurant called *Manhattan;* in the basement, an exercise room, spa, sauna and shower. The atmosphere at the Empress is graciously formal, with a dash of continental flair.

The best place on the beach is the *Sea Lodge,* adjacent to the *La Jolla Shores–Kellogg Park Beach.* The feeling here is more outdoorsy, rustic and recreational. Each room at the Sea Lodge is like a private ski lodge. Wood-planked ceilings meet in an arch high over your head. Flowers and semitropical vegetation fill an airy courtyard in the center of the complex. The Sea Lodge also has its own on-premises restaurant and heated pool, not to mention the broadest, sandiest beach for miles around. Highly recommended.

Restaurants

For a moneyed community, La Jolla has some surprisingly affordable places to eat. A large pizza at *Carino's Italian Restaurant and*

Pizza House was going for only eight bucks. Down the street, combination platters at *Don Juan's Mexican Restaurant* were being given away for $3.95. Both were overflowing with happy, chattering natives, who know a good cheap feed as well as the next person. Of course, it goes up from here, and you can pretty much name your price. On the high end, *George's at the Cove* gets the overall nod for best view, service and food, which ranges from elegantly prepared seafood dishes to beef, poultry and pasta.

We're fond of *Hartley's*, a seafood restaurant whose mesquite-grilled fish is exceptionally good. Among the choices are locally caught sea bass, as well as ahi and mahimahi. These can be combined with items like Malaysian tiger prawns to create a sumptuous platter that'll send you home happier than a fisherman with a full net.

Nightlife

At night, La Jolla becomes a promenade for window shoppers and after-dinner strollers. Mingled in among the banks and office buildings are numerous small shops, galleries and bistros. If you're after nothing rowdier than a walk down store-lined streets, La Jolla will do just fine. The best we could come up with beyond this, however, was a disco at the new *Marriott* and a lounge pianist at *Avanti*, a restaurant-cocktail bar. Eventually, we gave up and rolled down La Jolla Boulevard's long incline into the almost numberless bars, clubs and dives of Pacific Beach. Apparently, a lot of La Jollans do likewise.

FOR FURTHER INFORMATION

La Jolla Town Council
1055 Wall Street, Suite 1010
P.O. Box 1101
La Jolla, CA 92038
(619) 454-1444

Scripps Institute of Oceanography

About a mile north of La Jolla Shores, the Scripps Institute Pier juts into the water. Here, on land and buildings donated by philanthropist and town guardian angel Ellen Browning Scripps, is the world's most sophisticated marine biologic research center. The grounds of the Scripps Institute of Oceanography include an aquarium that's open to the public free of charge (though a $2 donation is suggested). The glass tanks hold everything from a 12-foot spiny lobster to an old gray grouper who cowers in a corner, avoiding eye contact. Highlights include the display of rainbow-hued exotics from Micronesia and the frozen-in-glass coelacanth, a nearly extinct biological curiosity that looks like a battered piece of luggage. On a more sobering note, this bit of wisdom from one of the exhibits bears repeating, as we'd seen evidence of its veracity on every coast we'd traveled: "Man has interfered with nature's supply of sand to our beaches, thus compounding the erosion problem, and we are now seeing the results of this intervention. Putting it bluntly, we are losing our beaches."

Torrey Pines State Reserve

A few miles north of Scripps is Torrey Pines State Reserve. Still technically in San Diego, it's located in so peaceful a setting you'll easily forget it brushes against a city of one million. Trails lead into stands of the rare Torrey pine, which grows only in this park and on an island 175 miles northwest of here. Several overlooks offer breathtaking views of the beach 300 feet below. An old lodge, built in 1902, serves as a visitors center. The peace and tranquility of the park are interrupted only by rustling breezes and the occasional sight of a gopher breaking open a Hottentot fig. This is nature's own therapy, the most soul-satisfying medicine of all: an oasis of calm set beneath an awesome canopy of *Pinus torreyana*.

Black's Beach
Torrey Pines State Beach

Black's Beach is the most famous nude beach in the country. This notorious "clothing optional" beach, set at the base of the high bluffs in between the Scripps Pier and Torrey Pines State Beach, is as controversial as it is hard to reach. It is so out of the way we wondered why anyone gets upset that people enjoy the sun and the beach *au naturel*. Who's going to see them?

The dimensions of the feud have occasionally plunged Black's Beach into the national news. The citizens of San Diego, none too comfortable with the idea of an army of nudists descending on one of their beaches, voted in October 1977 to ban nudity at Black's Beach. But the naked sun worshipers were not about to be stopped. In defiance of the law, nudity still prevails at Black's Beach. It has become a custom that won't be denied.

The upshot is that the community, perhaps in retaliation, ignores the area. At least it appeared that way to us. Seldom have we seen a beach with so much litter blowing about. Heaps of refuse choked the high-tide line. Trash cans overflowed with uncollected garbage. They might be righteously adamant about their freedom to disrobe, but these nudists sure leave a mess behind. Either that or the city never empties the trash cans.

In any case, here is a list of items we saw piled up along beautiful, natural Black's Beach on a May weekend: plastic jugs, Styrofoam cups, beer and pop cans, juice containers, plastic spoons, the webbing that holds six-packs together, countless straws, milk cartons, a piece of a broom, a lampshade, a flashlight, spent birth-control devices, a length of rope, carry-out food containers and balloons, both full and deflated.

Like we said, it's not an easy beach to get to. You either scramble down treacherous paths cut into the cliffside from La Jolla Farms Road or hike in from two miles away in either direction. Although 5,000 frolicsome nudists reportedly partied here on July 4th, 1977, all we saw on Mother's Day 1987 were half a dozen bare-assed men wandering the beach in white socks and tennis shoes. In order to glimpse this sad spectacle, we'd scrambled over rocks, edged along cliffs and were very nearly stranded in a cove or two by an advancing tide. The walk up from Scripps Pier looks shorter and easier than the hike down from the Torrey Pines end of the beach. The Torrey Pines route, though, offers more dramatic scenery: enormous toppled boulders and giant piles of debris that give the beach the appearance of a prehistoric landscape, plus bulbous, rounded formations and huge sheets of blackboard-smooth rock.

The less adventurous will prefer to stay put on "clothing mandatory" Torrey Pines State Beach, an adequate day-use beach. An ample parking area abuts the Los Penasquitos Lagoon and Salt Marsh. A midmorning arrival is recommended if you want a summertime parking spot. From the lot, you pass under a bridge to get to the beach, where the sand is streaked black and rounded stones and seaweed roll ashore.

Del Mar

Every town worth its chamber of commerce has a slogan, and most of them are meaningless, but Del Mar's has a basis in fact. "Where the Turf Meets the Surf" is the calling card in this picture-postcard village of 5,000 in north San Diego County. The turf in question is the *Del Mar Racetrack*, which lies inside a triangle formed by Via de la Valle, Camino Del Mar and Jimmy Durante Way. The surf, of course, is the Pacific Ocean, just a stone's throw from the track.

Del Mar is known for thoroughbred racing. The brief season runs from mid-July through mid-September, packing the town with racing buffs, especially Los Angelinos with a yen for the track. Little has changed at Del Mar since Bing Crosby and Pat O'Brien presided over the opening-day festivities back in 1937. To this day, a scratchy recording of Crosby crooning his ode to Del Mar plays before the first race with all the reverence of a national anthem. The Del Mar Racetrack is rated one of the top five in the country. The other 10 months of the year, the track and grounds host the annual Del Mar Fair (mid-June through early July), as well as

Grand Prix auto racing, horse shows, antique and exotic car exhibitions, flea markets and so on.

Before the first "...and they're off" echoed around the track, Del Mar was already off and running on an initially shaky but eventually well-heeled course. In 1885, a developer named Taylor acquired 338 acres and began building a seaside spa—including the 30-room Casa Del Mar Hotel, a dance pavilion, bathhouse, natatorium and railroad depot—which thrived briefly before succumbing to bankruptcy, flood and fire (in that order) by 1890. The town foundered and nearly died until it received a roaring twenties facelift: a renovated luxury hotel, rebuilt pier and new highways to get there. The fairgrounds came in '36, the track a year later, and Del Mar has grown so steadily ever since that there's scarcely a square foot to build on today. Now Del Mar suffers from the opposite problem: too much development and congestion to suit those who remember the days before Cinzano umbrellas took over.

Like La Jolla just down the road, Del Mar values and guards its village atmosphere. Still, there's only so much you can do when a determined developer pulls into town with a pile of loot and a savage pack of lawyers in tow. When we passed through, the entire community was up in arms over some miscreant who wanted to build multistory hotels, shops and freeway access ramps on the fragile, protected San Dieguito Lagoon. Environmentalists, worried that he'd figure out a way to circumvent the Lagoon Enhancement Act (finding loopholes is seldom a problem in the world of high finance), were tearing what was left of their hair out. Citizens were alarmed that more suburban blight was headed their way. Along Camino Del Mar, a banner reading, "Hotel or Lagoon? It's Up to You!" was slung overhead. "We do not want you meddling in our local land-use problems," a Del Mar councilman angrily told an agent from the Department of Commerce at a public hearing.

So it goes all over America. Conservationists and ordinary people have to win every battle just to maintain the status quo in a peaceful community or nature preserve, while the other side only needs to win one time. It's a dangerous game we're playing with our land and, particularly, our beaches.

The beach at Del Mar, by the way, is a pure delight. To get there, you must move a few blocks west of the town center. This is easily done by turning off Camino Del Mar onto 15th Street and following it to the water. Here, extending all the way up to 29th Street, is a broad, low-angle beach that's ideal for swimming, surfing and fishing. A lifeguard station at 17th Street is manned year round, while those at 20th and 25th streets are staffed in summer only. *Del Mar City Beach* is so popular and parking so limited that you must get here by 8 a.m. on an average summer morning if you hope to find a space. Often, town residents find themselves squeezed off their own beach by inlanders during the peak months of July and August.

Del Mar City Beach is bounded at the south end by *Seagrove Park*, a grassy area frequented by schoolchildren. As you walk north along the glittering sand, the beach narrows drastically. A wall of rocks is the homeowners' slim defense against a sea that tiptoes like a trespasser perilously close to their back doors. Beyond the city beach lies the mouth of the San Dieguito River, dry at low tide, and Del Mar Bluffs City Park. A steep wooden staircase inundated with sand leads to a spectacular overlook from the top of the bluff. The 360-degree panorama from this vantage point encompasses the ocean, the town of Del Mar and its racetrack.

Accommodations

Though traffic roars along overtaxed Camino Del Mar at all hours, Del Mar is still best described, as a *Newsweek* article put it 17 years ago, as "a sleepy little seacoast town." You mosey from cafés to shops, much as you would along some Parisian side street, spending part of the day at the beach or soaking up rays by a pool.

The only motel on the beach is, appropriately, the *Del Mar Motel on the Beach*. It's a charmingly unpretentious place that has been around since 1946. There aren't a lot of fancy extras, but it's got everything you need for a stay at the beach. Moreover, it's smack-dab on Del Mar City Beach, across the street from the train station and next door to two good restaurants.

In toward town, a few paces from the tony shops and outdoor cafés, is the *Stratford Inn of Del Mar*. Named after a famous old hostelry that was a Del Mar landmark in the first half of this century, the Stratford Inn is an architectural curiosity. It burrows low into a hillside off Camino Del Mar. Rooms are set into cul-de-sacs off a main catwalk that winds around the building. Constructed of gray, weathered wood, the Stratford Inn definitely blends into the environment. The air is fragrant with honeysuckle, the grounds are invitingly quiet and the large rooms come with kitchenettes and balconies.

Restaurants

Down on Coast Boulevard, next to the Del Mar Motel, a pair of restaurants do a brisk summertime business. *Jake's Oceanfront Restaurant* offers a menu of seafood prepared any number of ethnically diverse ways—e.g., Chinese (Fresh Fish Szechuan, broiled with soy, ginger and peppers), New Orleans (Fresh Fish Cajun Style, blackened with Cajun spices) and Spanish (Shrimp and Scallops Valencia, sautéed with tarragon, orange zest and beurre blanc). Next door, the *Poseidon* serves a varied menu of seafood, beef and poultry; an added plus is the outdoor patio, which faces the ocean.

When it comes to seafood, though, you can't beat the *Fish Market*. Del Mar's Fish Market is the main link in a chain of restaurants with franchises in San Mateo, Santa Clara, Palo Alto and Phoenix, Arizona. They own a two-boat fishing fleet, which sails in every afternoon with a fresh catch of swordfish, albacore, wahoo, thresher shark and Pacific red snapper. This combination fish market and restaurant is close by the racetrack. The menu is enormous and the prices moderate, ranging from $6.95 for a snapper dinner to $13 for a Troll Chinook salmon steak. A smoked fish appetizer is a must: the Salmon/Albacore Combo ($5.25) is a a moist and meaty masterpiece with a subtly smoky taste. Other interesting fare includes sashimi (fresh Hawaiian Ahi) and squid (Panko Calimari Steak).

The Fish Market is large and noisy, its cavernous dining rooms overflowing with families out for a happy feed. If you're in a quandary about what to order, walk up to the fresh-fish counter, decide what looks good to you and order it back at your table. Some like it hot, and if you're one of them, shake a few drops of Trappey's Good'n Hot Mexi-Pep Louisiana Hot Sauce on your food. Bottles of this spicy condiment are part of the table setting at the Fish Market.

Nightlife

As is the case in most self-professedly quiet towns, you won't find much to do beyond eating well and bedding down early in Del Mar. If you want nightlife, roll up to Solana Beach, which has plenty of it. If you just want a drink or two in decent surroundings, stroll into *Bully's*—either the surf-and-turf restaurant on Camino Del Mar or its around-the-corner Mexican counterpart.

FOR FURTHER INFORMATION

Greater Del Mar Chamber of Commerce
1401 Camino Del Mar, Suite 101
Del Mar, CA 92014
(619) 755-4844

Solana Beach

It's hard to tell where Del Mar ends and Solana Beach begins, but we think it has more to do with nightclubs than jurisdictional boundaries. Solana Beach (*solana* means "sunny spot") is party headquarters for north San Diego County, and the townspeople, whose per capita income is even greater than those of Del Mar, are apparently not thrilled that their community plays Pied Piper to a hip-hopping party crowd seven nights a week.

By our count, Solana Beach has seven sizable nightclubs. One of these, the Distillery West, is a nonalcoholic bar that sells juice, near beer and soda pop to kids "from 9 to 40" along with a hearty helping of Top Forty hits blaring high above four dance floors from an enormous PA. This fairly benign enterprise keeps the kids out of range of drugs and alcohol in a safe environment, and yet the Distillery's owner claimed to be waist-deep in litigation with the town council over permits. It sounded like bureaucratic harassment, with the council making life difficult for club owners by insisting they post permits that are all but impossible to obtain.

Up the road, Club Diego's (a sister enterprise of the Pacific Beach Diego's) underwent a 22-month paper chase with the city. All this seems to stem from paranoia over the wrong element being drawn into Solana Beach, as well as a justifiable concern about overcrowding. As one person put it, Solana Beach gets "buried" in the summer with day-trippers from all over the county. This inundation has its darker side. Kids flock here, drawing the usual lot of unsavory transients "who come out at night to do their hunting, if you know what I mean," in the words of a native who looked none too savory himself.

Be that as it may, it's easy to see why the beach gets packed. It's a small beach, entered by a cement ramp and set like an amphitheater between tall, crumbling bluffs. The grounds of *Solana Beach County Park* include a community center, lifeguard station and shuffleboard courts.

We don't want to bad-rap Solana Beach ourselves, because the beach looked fine and we had a terrific evening carousing from club to club. The whole of San Diego County is undergoing so much growth that it's hard to say how the smaller communities are going to keep it all under control and maintain their identity. Suffice it to say that Solana Beach and the adjoining towns to the north—Cardiff, Encinitas and Leucadia—are growing rapidly. Collectively, these four burgs are known as San Dieguitos, or "Little San Diego." They may not remain little for long. In fact, they do not seem little now.

Accommodations

Most people come to Solana Beach for the day or evening, but don't sleep over—at least not in a motel room. If you're an exception, the *Casa Blanca Motel* is right on Highway 101, a few doors down from Club Diego's.

Restaurants

The *Fish Market Restaurant* posts a Solana Beach address, though it sits hard by the Del Mar Racetrack and Fairgrounds. Let that suffice, then, for a primary recommendation. Second choice is *Club Diego's*, where you can eat a square Mexican meal, then shake off the fat on the dance floor.

Nightlife

The nightlife in Solana Beach is—what's the word—*bitchin'*. Those too young to drink have a viable option of an evening out at the *Distillery West*. The legal drinkers head for *Club Diego's*, the *Tight End* or the *Belly Up Tavern*. The last of these was packed to the rafters on a Monday night—no small feat, as anyone who's ever tried to find something to do on a Monday night can attest. A roomy club with a well-groomed clientele, the Belly Up draws live performers as diverse as Wendy O. Williams and Sun Ra, throwing in reggae, folk, fifties and blues. We saw a local band who covered oldies as if they'd written 'em themselves. They were called the Mar-Dells (a pun on Del Mar). It was a pleasant evening of rock and roll and crowd-watching that culminated in our winning a music trivia quiz. The prize? The Mar-Dells' double album! Now, if we only had a turntable in the car....

FOR FURTHER INFORMATION

Solana Beach Chamber of Commerce
210 West Plaza
Solana Beach, CA 92075
(619) 755-4775

Cardiff-by-the-Sea

Cardiff is the most unassuming and easily missed of the quartet of communities known as San Dieguitos. It lies between Solana Beach and Encinitas. The chief attractions are a couple of state park beaches on opposite sides of town.

Cardiff Beach State Park is west of the San Elijo Lagoon and south of town along the Pacific Coast Highway. The large beach is entered from a dusty, bumpy, pothole-ridden parking lot. At the south end, a pathway leads to tide pools.

If you're traveling north along Highway 101, keep your eyes peeled for *San Elijo State Park*, because the two left turns you'll need to make come up suddenly and are real whammer-jammers. The first left will deposit you in a day-use lot where you can stash your car and walk straight out to the long, lifeguarded beach. The second left is actually an elongated U-turn around the highway median that eventually leads to the park's campground. Set high atop a jagged cliff, San Elijo is the southernmost campground in the state park system, and during the summer its 171 sites fill up quickly.

The campground is nicely laid out, with scraggly hedges providing some shade and privacy. The sites closest to the cliff's edge are the ones to shoot for. From these sites you can hear the waves at night and not the traffic that runs by the highway side of the campground. You're also nearer the wooden stairs that lead to the beach. It costs $12 a night to camp and $4 for day-use parking. San Elijo is one of 18 state parks along the California coastline, all of which charge roughly comparable camping and day-use fees.

FOR FURTHER INFORMATION

Cardiff-by-the-Sea Chamber of Commerce
2179 San Elijo`Avenue
Cardiff-by-the-Sea, CA 92007
(619) 436-0431

Encinitas

There was a lot of crap on the beach at Encinitas. By that, we don't mean the usual residue of litter, lean-to pizza joints and ramshackle hot-dog stands. No, we mean human excrement. As unpleasant as it might be to write or think about, the evidence lay right before our eyes, noses and toes. It was spread among the smooth, round stones just outside the twin cement culverts that empty, like large shotgun barrels, onto the far end of *Moonlight Beach*. Fortunately, it seemed far enough from the swimmers not to pose an immediate health hazard.

Moonlight Beach, for the record, is the largest and most popular beach in Encinitas. It's a half-mile swath of sand that lies between a rare break in the city's dominating cliffs. On the beach is a fine, multipurpose park with lifeguards, volleyball nets, tennis courts, a baseball diamond, snack bar, picnic tables and rest rooms. The overwhelming stench coming from the drainpipes seemed incongruous in a town desperate to lure vacationers off the nearby freeway with the promise of clean, uncrowded beaches.

We followed the flow from the pipes back toward Highway 101, tracing it to what seemed like its logical source. Three blocks up Encinitas Boulevard, on a direct axis with the beachfront drainpipes, sat the Encinitas Sanitary District sewage-treatment plant. A call to district headquarters netted a typically congenial Californian who informed us that the runoff we saw actually came from a local underground creek and not from the sewage-treatment plant. He allowed that a few sewer lines run alongside the creek but "typically do not" spill over into it. We must have caught Encinitas on an atypical day, because the brown muck lying on the beach did not look like creek water. The friendly fellow at the Sanitary District office, meanwhile, said he'd look into the matter right away.

Sewage treatment—like parking, freeway snarls, illegal immigration and drinkable water—is an ongoing, almost unsolvable problem in Southern California, especially as more folks jam-pack their way in every day. Rich or poor, skinny or fat, tan or pale, everyone has basic human functions. They eat, drink, digest and . . . you get the picture. Where does it all go? According to the *California Coastal Access Guide*,* "Sewage treatment plants use the ocean as a location for the disposal of treated effluent." Like many other towns, Encinitas occasionally has problems with the effluent.

Encinitas has another problem worth mentioning: cliff erosion.

---

*California Coastal Commission. Berkeley: University of California Press, 1981.

Unfortunately, this one will never be solved. There was at one time a Sixth Street and most of a Fifth Street in Encinitas. Maps clearly show they existed. They do not exist now, having become the property of the Pacific Ocean. A local geologist, using old surveys and maps, has determined that 800 feet of Encinitas' shoreline has disappeared in the last hundred years. Much of this growing city sits on the edge of cliffs overlooking the ocean. The cliffs are made of sandstone, shale and siltstone, and constant assault by waves opens up cracks and fissures underneath that eventually cause the cliff tops to pitch forward.

In 1938, for example, the Self-Realization Fellowship, under the aegis of Swami Paramahansa Yogananda, built its temple on a cliff south of town. At the time, it was the largest building on the Southern California coast, a four-story marvel complete with swimming pools and landscaped gardens. In the stormy winter of 1941, however, the cliff gave way and the temple had no choice but to go with the flow.

Next to the grounds of the Self-Realization Fellowship is *Sea Cliff County Park*, a suitably meditative bluff-top spot from which to ponder the ocean and the town of Encinitas. The beach lies 128 steps down from a tiny parking lot. It, too, is small but quite popular with surfers, who've given it the nickname "Swami's." As you tread the winding steps to the beach, pay close attention to the cliffs. Held in place by a blanket of metal fencing, they've been reduced to a wet claylike consistency by the relentless pounding of the waves and are slowly but surely disappearing.

Despite the obvious folly, homes are still being built on the cliffs in Encinitas. Some of them are already listing noticeably. An inordinate number of "For Sale" signs have sprouted on the lawns of the otherwise well-scrubbed suburban neighborhoods that line Neptune Avenue just a hop and a plop away from the ocean. The city council has addressed the problem, ordering all beachfront property deeds to include the disclaimer, "This property subject to loss due to cliff erosion." A few public access points along Neptune Avenue have washed out, and their precipitous stairways are now off-limits. The state beach access at *Sea Bluffs* in neighboring Leucadia, for instance, washed out in 1983 and hasn't been reopened.

This is especially tough on an unspectacular place like Encinitas, which is looking for a way to capitalize on its location in sunny Southern California. In October 1986, Encinitas grew by annexation, incorporating the surrounding communities of Leucadia, Cardiff-by-the-Sea and Olivenhain to become the "big-time city of North [San Diego] County." All told, 44,000 people live in the "new" Encinitas. To bolster its image, the city now refers to itself as the "Flower Capital of the World." Back in the brown hills an enormous nursery and greenhouse industry grows most of the carnations dyed and sold on city streets around the world. Encinitas also boasts the Quail Botanical Gardens, a self-guided chaparral grove and bird sanctuary that covers 31 lovely acres. Then there are the landscaped grounds of the Self-Realization Fellowship, where flowers have been known to blossom. Other than that, though, Encinitas is pretty short in the flower department. A window box here, a rock garden there, a drainage ditch full of wildflowers—not the sort of preponderance of floral growth you'd associate with the Flower Capital of the World. In fact, much of Encinitas, away from the well-groomed residential lawns along the cliffs, has a brown, almost scorched coloration, the result of dry, hot weather and the bulldozing of lot after lot.

We are not picking on Encinitas. To those who call it home, it doubtless has its appeal. New money has begun to trickle in—evident in the rapid upscaling of the downtown shopping district. Perhaps the new city government will be able to satisfactorily address the growth problems facing Encinitas. Don't hold your breath about the cliffs.

Accommodations

Just inside the Encinitas city limits sign, on the north end of town, an entire motel—the faded and ill-fated Gold Coast—was up for rent. The most expensive hotel in Encinitas, *Sanderling Place*, bills itself as "by the sea," but in actuality it overlooks the sewage-treatment plant, Highway 101, Interstate 5 and a billboard for Michelob Lite. It's also four unsidewalked blocks from Moonlight

Beach. You can pay $75 to $95 at the Sanderling for a comfortable room, heated pool, jacuzzi, complimentary continental breakfast and cable TV. Or you can stay next door at the *Budget Motel* (that's the actual name) and pay half that for approximately half the comforts. A *TraveLodge* between Encinitas and Leucadia is closer to the beach. Priced between these extremes, it may be a better choice than either. However, your best bet in Encinitas might be to camp in *San Elijo State Park*, to convert to an Eastern religion and wander the tranquil grounds of the Self-Realization Fellowship, or to keep moving up the Ocean Highway.

Restaurants

Encinitas is suddenly top-heavy with semifancy Italian and Mexican cafés that look out on Highway 101, which cuts through town. These halfway houses for the upwardly mobile are bedecked with carved wooden signs that try to give their shopping-plaza backdrops a classy image. Sometimes it works, but usually it only seems to render them more sterile and inauthentic. One place it works is the *Old Town Mexican Café*, located in Lumberyard Center, where they post reasonably priced daily specials on a blackboard outside. *Lupita's*, on the other side of the highway, is a lower-priced and -scaled Mexican eatery with authentic Mexican artifacts lying around the premises.

The most intriguing menu in the area was posted by *Costamar Mex Seafood*. Stuffing the usual tortillas and taco shells with seafood makes for some interesting possibilities, such as Lobster Burritos, Shrimp Tacos and Crab Enchiladas. The entrées were even more tempting: Seafood Paella, Mexican Abalone and Shrimp Vallarta, for starters. Dinner prices run from $7 to $10.

Nightlife

Your options include an Irish pub, a fern bar and a roadhouse saloon or two on the other side of the tracks (literally—the Atchison,

Topeka and Santa Fe Railroad runs right through town). Most folks who want to rock more than a chair head down to Solana Beach to belly up.

FOR FURTHER INFORMATION

Encinitas-Leucadia Chamber of Commerce
930 First Street
Encinitas, CA 92024
(619) 753-6041

Leucadia

Despite its new municipal attachment to Encinitas, the community of Leucadia retains a separate and more appealing identity of its own. It is a place where alternative lifestyles (read: vegetarian restaurants and old Volkswagen bugs) go to roost.

Founded in 1888 by a pack of English spiritualists, Leucadia is a congenial, funky and slightly rundown stretch of Highway 101 that runs along the crumbling sea cliffs. *Leucadia* means "isle of paradise" in Greek, and the streets here are named for Greek deities (Daphne, Diana, Phoebe, Glaucus). But as in the Elysian Fields, not much goes on here. People live and let live, work construction jobs when they're available, surf whenever they're not working, eat tacos and brown rice, and stare unconcerned as cars pass through town. They simply don't need vacationers in Leucadia. The beaches aren't big enough to attract them and the cliffs are eroding. The sign at *Leucadia State Beach* had this spray-painted addendum: "No tourists. Go home."

One local resident, a surfer, was seen staring wistfully at the rugged surf on the state beach. He'd suffered a shoulder injury in a nasty spill some weeks earlier and found himself beached until it healed. In the meantime, he pedaled a bike to stay in shape, but somehow it wasn't the same. Leucadia was his alternative to Pacific Beach, where he'd been living until he felt squeezed out by mounting crowds and rents. Pacific Beach, it turns out, had been his alternative to Ocean Beach, which had been his alternative to Imperial Beach. Gradually, he says, he will make his way north to the magic land of Santa Barbara. "I want to live at the beach forever," he announced with absolutely no solicitation. For now, Leucadia is his home. Relaxed, uncrowded and untrendy, it is his isle of paradise. Besides, he knows someone who has private access to the beach.

FOR FURTHER INFORMATION

Encinitas-Leucadia Chamber of Commerce
930 First Street
Encinitas, CA 92024
(619) 753-6041

Carlsbad

Carlsbad is an anomaly. Of all the towns that cling to the Southern California coast, it is the only one not founded by a Spaniard or profoundly shaped by Latin influences. Instead, Carlsbad was the brainstorm of Gerhard Schutte, a German who came west via Nebraska to found a town of "small farms and gracious homes." His dream was made possible in 1883, when the Arizona Eastern Railway was completed, linking Southern California with the rest of civilization. This line also opened up the land between Los Angeles and San Diego to homesteaders. Schutte headed up the list and moved on out.

Spanish and Indian influences are not entirely absent from the historical record. For centuries prior to Schutte's arrival, the Luseiño Indian tribe lived on the land between the two lagoons that form the approximate boundaries of Carlsbad. The Indians, however, were quickly run off or placed under the subjugation of the missions when, in 1769, the conquistador Gaspar de Portolá arrived with his faithful sidekick, Father Juan Crespi. Even though the entire area was under Spanish rule, the only lingering trace of their influence today is Agua Hedionda, the name given to one of the local lagoons. It means "stinking waters."

By 1886, when Schutte arrived, the mission system had been destroyed and the land grab was on. Schutte and his like-minded gang purchased a chunk of land and began planting eucalyptus trees and squaring off lots for their dream town. In the process, they discovered that the mineral water from their wells was chemically identical to that found at the renowned Ninth Spa in Karlsbad, Bohemia (now Karlovy Vary, Czechoslovakia). The town now had a name and an identity. Carlsbad became Olde Europe set in the New World. When word got out about the water, settlers gradually began arriving. Mostly families of English stock, they were humble, no-nonsense folk and their town was built on old-country standards.

Surprisingly little has changed in that respect to this day. Original buildings have been restored, and the subsequent growth of the town stringently adheres to an established code. For this reason, Carlsbad can justifiably call itself the "Village by the Sea." Some of the local buildings—Magee House, Twin Inns, the Santa Fe Railway Station—have been designated National Historic Landmarks. In light of its geographical location, Carlsbad's preservationist bent is doubly striking. With its Victorian, Dutch and Bohemian architecture, Carlsbad has an appealingly antiquarian personality—remarkably when you consider it's next door to the huge military town of Oceanside and not so very far north of San Diego's urban jumble.

The best place to orient yourself in Carlsbad is the chamber of commerce office, located inside the original Sante Fe Railway Station on Elm Street. It is the oldest commercial building in town, dating back to 1887. Another must-visit is the Alt Karlsbad Haus, on Carlsbad Boulevard (the main street running parallel to the ocean). Built in 1964 on the site of the first mineral well, the house is rather oddball. It looks like something out of Monty Python's quest for the Holy Grail, but it's actually an exact replica of Antonín Dvořák's house in Prague. The great composer is honored by a plaque on one of the walls. On another wall, a separate plaque reads, "The formation of the Hanseatic League in the 13th Century gave birth to modern civilization and through commerce and trade lifted Europe out of the Dark Ages." Not the sort of plaque you expect to find in Southern California.

Today, Carlsbad seems to have everything going for it. Of the 37 square miles that fall within the city limits, only a third have been developed, and according to a respected older resident, "we're putting the screws on too much more growth." The public school system is one of the best in the country. The unemployment rate is the lowest in San Diego County. The public library is larger than most college libraries. The average temperature is a comfortable 59 degrees Fahrenheit. The young people look healthy and happy. ("Hey, John," one yells at another from a car, "your new haircut looks great.") The old folks look contented, too. After a while, you begin to wonder if this isn't the town Norman Rockwell was painting all those years. You also realize that Carlsbad is not just a place to vacation. It's a place to settle down in and attend the church of your choice.

Actually, a very fine beach visit can be had in Carlsbad, which has been blessed with a long, almost uninterrupted state beach. Part of it is backed by high bluffs, but you can park at the top for free and walk down to the beach. In addition, *South Carlsbad State Beach* has 226 campsites atop the bluffs.

Accommodations

It isn't cheap to stay in the "Village by the Sea." The village mentality does not abide anything that smacks of discounted cheapness, because it could mean just that—*anything*. Still, the danger is that the opposite can happen, too. To wit, in walks Mr. Corporate Big Bucks, turning the town into a premier luxury resort where, if you don't have a five-iron in your hand, you're suddenly Mr. Schmuck. Though Carlsbad is ripe for this sort of walling-in-with-hedges, such development has not yet been carried too far.

The *La Costa Resort Hotel and Spa* is an example of the far side. It is one of the most exclusive resort compounds in the country. They host major golf and tennis tournaments, and the rich and famous flock here. If you need to ask the price, you can't afford it.

One step down in price and a leap closer to the beach is the

Carlsbad Inn. It is a beach and tennis resort, built near the center of town under the watchful old-world architectural guidelines of the community. Rooms go for $85 to $125, which is competitive with the premium chain motels. One rung lower brings you, ironically, even closer to the beach. The *Ocean Manor Motel* is directly on the ocean. The 47 suites and studio rooms start at $40 out-of-season and $55 in-season.

Restaurants

If you like fried seafood, you can get it by the basket at *Harbor Fish South*, an outdoor-patio joint beside the ocean and next door to a surf shop. The clientele is younger and less discriminating than the crowd in the dining rooms at *La Costa*. The Surfer's Special, for instance, is a cheeseburger and fries. *Nieman's American Bar-Seagrill-Café-Brasserie* (hike!) is worth visiting because it's housed in the oldest Victorian structure in Carlsbad, formerly the Twin Inns. Several signs warn you to wear proper attire. If you're not inclined to do so, then you should at least enjoy the restored architecture from the vantage point of the yard.

Nightlife

Dooley McCluskey's Olde Ale House is an exact replica of an old European alehouse, right down to the wooden shingles on the roof. It is a very upscale, no-cover, full-service bar. Order some of the green-bottle beers and pretend you're in Merry Olde for a few rounds before slogging off to bed.

FOR FURTHER INFORMATION

Carlsbad Chamber of Commerce
P.O. Box 1605
Carlsbad, CA 92008
(619) 729-1786

Oceanside

Oceanside is the second largest city in San Diego County. No fewer than 103,000 people call it home. Because no real, abiding sense of history or restraint exists here, as it does in neighboring Carlsbad, Oceanside continues to grow like a balloon attached to a helium nozzle. According to the Oceanside Economic Development Council, the population will be 129,761 by the year 2000.

The main reason for Oceanside's rapid growth—and, when you get down to brass tacks, its very existence—is Camp Pendleton, the world's largest Marine base. Camp Pendleton is literally right next door to Oceanside, its back gate opening onto Oceanside Harbor. A total of 45,000 Marine personnel work and train at Camp Pendleton. Those who don't live on the base live in Oceanside with their families.

At first glance, Oceanside doesn't look like the stereotypical military town. Great pains have been taken to disguise what could be a counterproductive image, at least on the waterfront. The harbor area is slick and modern, with 800 pleasure craft—including luxury yachts—tethered in the marina. Two classy restaurants book-end the harbor front, along with a pack of red-roofed condominiums in the ubiquitous hacienda mold. A small shopping area—called, of all things, Cape Cod Village—thrives here, too.

Should you round the bend at the south end of the harbor, though, a sign warns, "Travel at Your Own Risk." We weren't sure how to take this. Perhaps the sign was intended to warn of flash floods or oncoming trucks on the steep, curvy street ahead, but it seemed to be conveying a second, unintended message. Oceanside, we repeat, is a military town. It may not be a bona fide war zone, as many landlocked military towns are. But as you pull away from the new-money harbor, you begin to notice the faded storefronts; broken-bulb saloons; ratty food stands; thrift shops full of military hand-me-downs; discount clothiers (one window display still featured Rambo T-shirts); and chockablock, flat-roofed duplex housing—telltale signs of the military lifestyle, which hasn't really changed since World War II.

Consider the options that pass for nightlife, for example. After a week of sweating and grunting back in the hot, dusty hills of

Camp Pendleton, a man can work up quite a thirst. But when the man's a Marine—one of a select few good men—his thirst isn't just heavy, it's profound. To quench it, he heads to Oceanside. Prides Inn, by the Oceanside Pier, is the sort of place he goes to drink. A faded onetime motel, its peeling sign beckons, "Welcoming Those Who Have Served and Those Serving." In other words, you are welcome at the Prides Inn if you look like Sergeant Carter or Ollie North, less so if you don't. The gift shop next door, incidentally, advertised something called Mr. Zog's Original Sex Wax.

Unless you are a veteran and like to be reminded of it, you might want to vacation elsewhere. Even the beach looks like it's reeling in the aftermath of a recent war. In some places, the shoreline is little more than a wall of rubble, all that's left of a beach that has apparently retreated for good. The Oceanside Pier, at the heart of *Oceanside City Beach*, could not even be walked on during our visit in 1987. Having been battered by stormy seas, it was then undergoing refurbishment as some sort of promenade. At 1,900 feet, it is the longest pier on the West Coast.

If in the area, you should definitely pay your respects to the ghosts of Mission San Luis Rey. Located four miles east of Interstate 5 on Route 76, this historic landmark has been dubbed the "King of the Missions." It was the largest of the Franciscan-run missions that helped the Spanish wrest control of the Alta California frontier from Native Americans. Mission San Luis Rey was founded in 1769 by Father Juan Crespi and quickly became the showcase of the elaborate mission system. Today, it houses an active order of Franciscan monks and is also open to the public for viewing and souvenir buying. Of particular interest are the original paintings by local Indians.

FOR FURTHER INFORMATION

Oceanside Chamber of Commerce
512 Fourth Street
Oceanside, CA 92054
(619) 722-1535

San Onofre State Beach
Camp Pendleton

San Onofre State Beach is the last stop in San Diego County, ushering you right to the Orange County line. There are north and south entrances to this four-mile beach, whose grounds include a 272-site campground. The beach faces a great wall of bluffs and is reached by descending trails. The surfing here is good, especially by San Mateo Point at the north end.

It seems unusually deserted out here along the San Diego Freeway (I-5) between Oceanside and San Clemente: quiet, rolling hills and beaches that run for 20 miles without so much as a hint of a resort condominium or shopping galleria. The longer you contemplate this virgin landscape, though, the more it becomes a case of "What's wrong with this picture?" You are, in reality, on the grounds of Camp Pendleton, a 125,000-acre Marine training installation. Even with 45,000 recruits running around the brushy hills, however, Camp Pendleton is considered an ecological preserve, since its extensive acreage is off-limits to commercial development. Still, you never know what might whiz by in this deceptively empty landscape. We were enjoying the view at a freeway overlook when an amphibious tank came roaring across the terrain, kicking up a cloud of dust.

There's more excitement than meets the eye on the drive through Camp Pendleton. Signs along the freeway warn, "Dust Clouds Next 17 Miles." Diamond-shaped signs by the "View Point" overlook caution of rattlesnakes. Furthermore, if you're traveling north, you can expect traffic to grind to a halt as the border patrol checks each vehicle for illegal aliens. But all this is small potatoes compared with the unease of swimming within sight of the San Onofre Nuclear Generating Station, also on the grounds of Camp Pendleton, overlooking the state beach. The foreboding twin generators are rounded half-globes, each topped with a nipple-shaped stack and pulsing red lights—and we know all about the poisoned milk of nuclear power they yield.

This controversial and much-protested facility reportedly sits along a fault line. Although serious doubts about nuclear power have been raised in the wake of Three-Mile Island and Chernobyl, they desperately need all the energy they can lay their hands on in overcrowded Southern California, where the population in some cities has doubled in a decade. Splitting atoms is the only way to keep the lights on and the VCRs rolling.

Anyone swimming, surfing or sunning at San Onofre is forgiven the odd wave of trepidation occasioned by the inevitable glance at the power plant on the bluff. The parking lot for the north end of the state beach literally butts against Southern California Edison's employee parking lot. It's easy to mistake one lot for another— and we did. After gazing at the beach from the correct lot (a dusty field reached by a sidewinding asphalt track), we pushed on to our next stop: the visitors center at the power station. Although a modern, informative visitors center was mentioned in the literature— and the guards at two different Checkpoint Charlies told us how to get there—we were finally informed that it had been shut down two years before. "Is there someone in particular you want to visit?" we were asked by a woman at the badge-issuing site. We did pick up a pamphlet entitled "About Cocaine," wondering why it needed to be stocked there.

If you're staying nearby, you will not lose sight of the fact that you're in a potential danger zone. Our motel in San Clemente provided a color brochure on emergency preparedness. (Really, a few sheets of motel stationery would have made us just as happy.) The brochure discussed the four emergency alert levels, listed the radio stations to tune to for news bulletins and evacuation procedures in the event of a general alert, and instructed what to pack should evacuation become necessary. "Plan for two days away from home," it read. "Lock your doors and turn things off as you would if you were going on a weekend vacation." Presumably, you won't be packing a swimsuit.

San Clemente

An Italian explorer named it, a Scandinavian developer founded a town here, but it took a president from California to really put San Clemente on the map. Yes, it was Richard Nixon who made every newspaper reader in the country aware of this small city of 30,000 in southern Orange County. For the one and a half terms of the Nixon administration, a red-roofed estate known as Casa Pacifica served as the Western White House.

It's easy to see why the president chose San Clemente as his home away from home. The town is set right on a striking beach, with weathered bluffs and chaparral-covered hills rising behind it. Maybe Dick Nixon knew a secret all the smart local surfers have tried to keep to themselves: that the best surfing spot in the area is the beach spread out before Casa Pacifica, a place known as Cotton Point. Although Nixon was flown directly to San Clemente after his resignation speech, he did not stick around to shoot the curl at Cotton's. The Nixons vacated Casa Pacifica not long after clearing out of the White House and moved to New Jersey.

Since Nixon left office in 1974, the pace of life in San Clemente has slowed considerably. The eyes of the nation have in recent years been focused farther up the California coast, on Ronald Reagan's ranch in the hills above Santa Barbara. The return to pre-presidential calm has suited San Clemente just fine. It's a lovely, unassuming little town, looking much as it did when it was advertised to prospective buyers in 1925 as "a village done in the fashion of old Spain." Incorporated in 1928, the town has maintained a comely architectural consistency. The Spanish style of white stucco and red tile was mandated in the city building code for a long time.

The streets of San Clemente are not laid out in the usual perpendicular grid. They meander, following the contours of the land. To get to the town pier and municipal beach, turn west off El Camino Real (the main drag) onto practically any street and follow it downhill and around curves until you wind up at the water. Call it slalom driving. *San Clemente City Beach* has picnic tables, swing sets, fire rings and lifeguard stations spread out on its soft brown sand. A small cement Amtrak hut sits next to railroad tracks not more than 50 feet from the water. The surf is strong here, drawing an enthusiastic brace of surfing regulars. At high tide, large breakers slam into the pier pilings, turning the frothing water a milky green. The pier is the focal point of what little social life exists in San Clemente. An indoor/outdoor bar and seafood restaurant draw a mixed bag of panting surfers, contemplative fishers and curious tourists. All of them are tickled to be served drinks and appetizers by some of the best-looking mermaids in Orange County.

Immediately south of the city beach is *San Clemente State Beach*, which has a very different character. Whereas the municipal beach is wide and hospitable to swimmers and surfers, the state beach is narrow, prone to rip currents and almost primevally wild. A 156-site campground spreads out above the beach, and a pathway leads down a steep ravine to the ocean. Near water's edge, the sand suddenly slopes sharply down to the water. Breakers try to run up the slope, but only an occasional tongue of foam licks the dry sand above it. Swimming is discouraged here, and most surfers choose to hotfoot it to more southerly beaches like *Cotton's* and *Trestles*. These two primo surf spots are not reachable by car; you must hike a mile with a board on your head to get there. If you happen to see a handful of surfers studying the distant ocean from a freeway exit ramp south of town, they're trying to decide whether the day's waves are worth the long walk in.

By the way, Richard Nixon may attract crowds to San Clemente again in the near future. Plans are afoot to establish a presidential library, and a site on a bluff north of town has been chosen. Eventually, 40 million pages of documents—no doubt containing 40,000 undeleted expletives—will be cataloged and stored here. As for the old homestead, you can catch a perfectly clear view of the former Western White House from San Clemente State Beach, or from Avenida del Presidente before it crosses over the San Diego Freeway.

Accommodations

Back in the Nixon years, helicopters and Air Force jets chauffeuring politicians, dignitaries, friends and the prized Nixon canines to Casa Pacifica turned little San Clemente into a major air-traffic hub. Many visitors put up at the *San Clemente Inn*, the closest and most amenable inn in the area. According to a faded newspaper clipping, "During the Nixon presidency, the San Clemente Inn orbited to the point of international celebrity as the administrative vortex for the nearby Western White House."

The San Clemente Inn now operates as a hotel condominium, offering homey apartment-style suites with dish-filled kitchen cabinets, additional Murphy beds in the living-room wall and all the comforts of home for between $55 and $115 a night. The grounds include a pool and spa, shuffleboard courts, a thick green mat of grass and gargantuan pineapple palm trees. The inn borders San Clemente State Beach, and the restaurant contains some Nixon memorabilia.

Restaurants

Look no further than the San Clemente Municipal Pier for dinner. You have two choices—three, really, if you count catching your own. On the left is the *Fisherman's Restaurant*, which serves full seafood dinners. On the right is the *Fisherman's Lounge*. Guess which side we wound up on. Fortunately, the bar serves heavy appetizers that can pass for dinner. The appetizer menu includes smoked fish (albacore or halibut); chicken leg–sized prawns in cocktail sauce; and a thick fisherman's chowder of fresh fish, bay shrimp and snow crab in a tomato and vegetable base. The Fisherman's Lounge also has a happy hour from three to six, during which time you can munch on beef ribs (25 cents per), refried beans and chips, raw veggies and dip, plus dessert. All but the ribs are free, as long as you're drinking.

The San Clemente Inn has an on-premises restaurant called *Swallow's Cove*, whose menu includes a house-special bouillabaisse, Sea Bass Capistrano and Seafood Fettucine.

Nightlife

After sunset, San Clemente gets quieter than an orange grove. A few whoops were spilling out of a bar-lounge called *DJ's* on El Camino Real, but this was about as wild as it got. Laguna Beach, 10 miles north, is the closest party outpost. We were directed to a club there by a San Clemente cocktail waitress who told us this was reggae night. "Have you ever heard of reggae music?" she asked, as if she were an elementary school teacher introducing a new vowel sound. "It's really coming on strong," she added. (This, 10 years after the death of Bob Marley.) Instead of trying to fashion our bangs into dreadlocks and driving to Laguna, we held tight to our bar-side perches at the Fisherman's Lounge and learned all about surfers and their wayward lifestyle from a garrulous bartender.

FOR FURTHER INFORMATION

San Clemente Chamber of Commerce
1100 North El Camino Real
P.O. Box 338
San Clemente, CA 92672
(714) 492-1131

Capistrano Beach
San Juan Capistrano

The two-mile beachfront along Capistrano Bight is known as "California's Riviera." Though force of habit makes us recoil from such gratuitous titles, this one seems justifiable enough. The San Diego Freeway passes close by, giving those driving south from Los Angeles their earliest glimpse of the Pacific. At first glance, Capistrano Beach looks like a mirage of white sand and emerald water gleaming beneath a bright blue sky. But this vision is for real.

Tiny Capistrano Beach's vacation industry is growing as the demand for unblighted beach and room to build pushes upward from San Diego and down from Los Angeles. It is one of Southern California's prettiest beach communities. A few miles inland, the legendary swallows still flock to San Juan Capistrano. On or about March 19th (St. Joseph's Day), the mission here becomes the nation's busiest birdhouse, as thousands of cliff swallows complete their migration north from Argentina. San Juan Capistrano is their home from March to October, when they return to Argentina. The swallows come and go like clockwork, although the ceaseless construction in the area has reduced their nesting grounds—and their numbers.

Down on the shoreline, Capistrano Beach boasts a wide, unblemished public beach. A road called the Palisades drops down from steep residential hills to meet the Coast Highway. The entrance to *Capistrano City Beach* is near this intersection. A large lot with metered parking (25 cents an hour, no small bargain for a California beach) faces the ocean. The beach is popular but seldom overrun. At 7 a.m. on a drizzly May morning, a group of girls were enthusiastically engaged in a little pre-school volleyball practice. Meanwhile, the usual array of cars was parked along the lip of the lot, their drivers impassively contemplating the sea before a hard day of making deals or hammering nails. By midmorning, a furious full-court basketball game was in progress. In the distance, surfers were congregating off *Doheny Point*, one of the most renowned surfing spots in Southern California.

Yes, with its near-constant ocean breeze, bountiful sunshine and idyllic beach, Capistrano delivers on its "California Riviera" sobriquet.

Accommodations

Out here, along Capistrano Beach (or anywhere in Southern California where a view of the ocean can be had), the average price of a home is a cool million, and the lot it sits on will set you back $850,000 or so. The garden-variety tourist flying down the Coast Highway can enter this fantasy world for a night or week without having to pay through the nose by staying at the *Capistrano Surfside Inn*. It's a time-sharing private-ownership resort whose unoccupied suites are rented out just like those in a hotel. But what you get here would put most hotels to shame: a fully equipped kitchen, a private jacuzzi, glass-topped dining-room table, comfortable designer furniture in peach and cream tones, track lighting, mirrored closet doors...you get the picture. The Capistrano

Surfside Inn faces the long Capistrano City Beach/Doheny State Beach strand, and a pedestrian overpass will lead you from the front door over the Coast Highway onto the warm sands before you can say, "Surf's up!" The rates range from $100 to $185 a night, depending on the size of the suite and the season, and are generally competitive with nearby hotels and motels of far less luster.

Restaurants

A Mexican restaurant called *Olamendi's* does a land-office business out on the Coast Highway, across the street from the beach. Its popularity was easy to gauge from the full lot on a midweek afternoon. Inside, around semicircular booths, moderately priced Mexican food is served. The tacos, burritos and enchiladas are made every conceivable way (stuffed with shredded beef, sirloin steak, chicken, fish, pork, cheese—you name it). The gold menu carries a one-word endorsement from Richard Nixon on the back: "Excellent." Up by the cash register hangs a picture of El Presidente, nervously posing with the kitchen staff.

Nightlife

No nightlife can be found in Capistrano Beach, but you might catch a national act at the *Coach House* in nearby San Juan Capistrano. During our time in the area, the bookings tilted toward old hands working the club circuit (e.g., Edgar Winter, Leon Russell, Gary Puckett, BTO, Hot Tuna and Doc Severinson).

San Juan Cap (as it's known in native shorthand) is a formerly quaint, mission-style community now beset with endless corridors of malls whose acreage rivals that of a cattle ranch. The train station is the hub of weekend nightlife. Everyone from wandering minstrels on down performs for the assembled multitude, some of whom even ride the rails from L.A. just to be part of the crowd. All aboard!

FOR FURTHER INFORMATION

Capistrano Beach Chamber of Commerce
P.O. Box 2335
Capistrano Beach, CA 92624
(714) 496-1017

San Juan Capistrano Chamber of Commerce
31882 Camino Capistrano, Suite 218
San Juan Capistrano, CA 92675
(714) 493-4700

Dana Point

Dana Point merits a footnote in American literary history. A young sailor, Richard Henry Dana, Jr., came here in the 1830s aboard the Boston brig *Pilgrim*. His experiences as a naïf on the high seas were recorded in the autobiographical narrative *Two Years Before the Mast*, which reads something like Herman Melville's seafaring odysseys minus the metaphoric white whale.

Nowadays, if Dana were able to return to the jutting headland named after him, he'd almost certainly be piloting a yacht with a name like *Fancy Dancer*, sipping cognac from a crystal snifter, and squeezing an attractive, bikini-clad girlfriend half his age. The Dana Point jetty has become a haven for pleasure vessels here in the nouveau riche southland. Its protected harbor can accommodate 2,500 yachts. The bad news is that the surfing at Dana Point (known as "Killer Dana" before they walled out the waves) has been ruined. Oh well, there's always *Doheny State Beach*, just a mile or so down the road, between Capistrano Beach and Dana Point.

The surf at Doheny just south of the jetty is a crusher, earning it the nickname "the Boneyard." Below this point, the beach is wide and safe for swimming. (Eventually, it connects with Capistrano City Beach.) A shaded, 115-site campground sits back from the beach, and there are plenty of day-use facilities as well. The

park was named after Edward L. Doheny, Jr., a wildcatting oil-
man who bought land around here in the late twenties.

The Dana Point Harbor development is unfortunately so exclusive that it seems unreal to ordinary people and looks like an imitation New England yachting center. To the wallet, it can be as
hazardous as the 25-foot waves that used to bombard Dana Point.
Amid a sea of pricey gift shops, orange and blue Sarpellegrino umbrellas and expensive restaurants with names like *Picasso*, we felt
as lost as a square rigger in a heavy squall. On the other hand, if
retail usury masquerading as a "shopping experience" appeals to
you, then Dana Point ought to be a suitable port in which to drop
anchor.

FOR FURTHER INFORMATION

Dana Point Chamber of Commerce
24671 La Plaza
Dana Point, CA 92629
(714) 496-1555

Laguna Beach

When people hear the name Laguna Beach, they think of far-off
places: the French Riviera, the Greek Isles, the coast of Italy. Anywhere but Orange County, California, where it is something of an
anomaly—a pastel watercolor fantasy in a land of mall and freeway blueprints and archconservatism. Laguna Beach is, first and
foremost, an artists colony. Numberless small galleries line the
Coast Highway through town, and intimations of art are everywhere. While every other beach town in Southern California hosts
lifeguard races and volleyball tournaments, Laguna sponsors art
festivals and an event called the Pageant of the Masters. Easels and
tripods are as plentiful as palm trees, especially around sunset,
when artists with an empathy for nature work to capture the gold
fire that illuminates the coves and beaches.

People who live in Laguna Beach love everything about it: the intellectual camaraderie that encourages self-expression and abides eccentricity; the cool, even climate and striking beauty of cliffs that plunge to a dramatic shoreline; the European manners of the place, with its emphasis on high culture and old (for California) money. There's even room for surfers and skateboarders and all the less intellectual flotsam that washes ashore on California's coastline. Their presence keeps the community from getting swamped by its own pretensions. This balance between extremes in lifestyle, each of which has more or less the same end (nature nourishing the body and/or soul), makes Laguna Beach one of the most interesting communities on either coast—right up there with Provincetown, Massachusetts, or Key West, Florida.

Laguna Beach has always marched to the beat of a different drummer. Unlike much of the rest of California, which was parceled out in the form of land grants from the rulers of Spain and Mexico to friends of the throne, Laguna was homesteaded by tree-planting pioneers following American annexation. It was initially called Lagonas, from the Shoshone word for "lakes," because of several freshwater lagoons situated where creeks pour into the ocean from the canyon lands behind it. The first arrivals were Mormons, followed by Methodists, who erected a tent city. The first hotel opened in 1886 and has been operating in various shapes and forms ever since as the Laguna Hotel.

"Lagonas" was changed to "Laguna Beach" in 1904. Artists began making an enclave there in the early years of the century, following the lead of one Norman St. Claire. Gradually, a style known as California impressionism began to evolve, after an artist named Lewis Botts painted his famous *Girl of the Golden West* here in 1914. Much like the plein air artists of Monet's French impressionist school, they painted the natural surroundings with rapid brushstrokes and an eye for the way the golden sunlight bathed the natural landscape.

The Laguna Beach Art Association was founded in 1918, and thereafter art galleries began popping up all over. The tiny town has enjoyed a wide reputation as an artists colony for most of the century. Today, you can walk down the street and see signs such as this one hanging in the front windows of small galleries: "We buy old Laguna and Old European paintings." Yes, there is a difference between the two. While there's certainly a great deal of validity to California impressionism, much of what passes for art in Laguna Beach these days is the sort of pastel-tinted renderings of sunny vistas, birds in flight and vases spilling with flowers that decorate dentists' offices in Des Moines. As for the Pageant of the Masters, this highly touted mid-July theatrical event finds actors and artists re-creating famous paintings (*Whistler's Mother, Blue Boy*), culminating in a grand tableaux vivant sitting of Da Vinci's *Last Supper*.

Where there's arts, there's... you guessed it, crafts, and Laguna's streets are chockablock with jewelers, potters and antique dealers hawking their pricey wares. The cultural imperative extends all the way to the waterline. Down by the boardwalk at Main Beach, a beautiful art deco chess table, done in a colorful mosaic of ceramic tile and flanked by two small benches, sits on the grassy picnic area.

Main Beach is just that. In a town of tiny coves and pocket beaches, this is the big enchilada. It's located at the center of town, where Broadway meets the Coast Highway. Two gas stations—a Mobil and a Union 76—face the beach like beefeaters at the gates of Buckingham Palace. Main Beach, with its volleyball and basketball courts, picnicking green and long, sandy beach bordered by a winding boardwalk, is a buzzing hive of aerobic activity. Amid this blur of bodies in motion, don't be surprised to see New York–class fashion models posing and preening on a professional shoot. A lot of those models live in Laguna Beach, as does a sizable population of gay men. For that matter, plenty of big-time film-industry types burrow here as well. The former estate of Bette Davis, for example, is a local landmark. With its rugged terrain and distinctly Mediterranean look and feel, considerable movie footage has been shot in and around Laguna Beach.

Beyond Main Beach, plenty of smaller beaches exist in both directions along the Coast Highway. Seemingly every side street ends on the cliffs, with a public access stairway leading to a small, fan-shaped cove. There are upward of 25 such beaches within the town limits of Laguna; we'll survey the more noteworthy ones.

Starting in the apparently independent community of South Laguna (just above Dana Point) is *Salt Creek Beach Park*. This county-operated beach offers some of the best surfing in southern

Orange County, and the park fills quickly, even at $4 a car. *Aliso Beach County Park* lies a few miles up the Coast Highway, in the heart of the motel/burger stand/gas station corridor of South Laguna. Ample, inexpensive metered parking draws the summertime masses here, as does the fine surfing. Waves taller than the people playing in them, pushed along by impressive south swells, break with a thundercrack and a cascade of foam along the brown, sandy beach. A short, modern pier and the lagoon where Aliso Creek empties into the ocean—a popular bird-bathing spot, for all you gull watchers—are the unofficial beach boundaries.

Ah, here's a fun one. It's called *1,000 Steps Beach* and is located where Ninth Street meets the Coast Highway in South Laguna. You'll have to park a few blocks away on the highway's asphalt shoulder, since all the curbs are red in the immediate vicinity, but the walk from your car to the top of the stairs will warm up your calf muscles for the trek down the lengthy cement staircase to the sea. At the bottom, you'll find a small beach pinned against steep cliffs, Gibraltar-sized rocks that delineate the cove and huge waves that run up on the beach with great force. Houses cling precariously to the cliffs, each with its own set of stairs that looks more like a ladder. Climbing out of this grotto is the real acid test (and this is actually an apt choice of words, since Timothy Leary and his sugar-cube-swallowing gang frequented this beach in the sixties). The ascent numbers 219 steps, not 1,000. It only feels like a thousand. Incidentally, you can amuse yourself on the return trip by reading the obscene graffiti that has been scrawled, Burma Shave–style, onto the vertical face of each step.

The prettiest beach in Laguna, *Victoria Beach*, is also one of the hardest to find. Given the lack of signs, it would appear the locals want to keep it that way. The beach is entered at several points along Victoria Drive, a street off the Coast Highway that's lined with homes built as close together as any block of brownstones in New York City. They've sacrificed space and acreage in exchange for easy access to a common, sandy front yard along the Pacific Ocean. Hiking down from the walkway and stairs at the north end, you pass private homes set behind a yellow cinder-block wall. A final curve deposits you on one of the nicest beaches in Southern California. The bodysurfing is awesome. But Victoria Beach is an attractive beach to hang around even if you're doing nothing but enjoying the sun.

North of Main Beach, Heisler Park serves as a point of entry to *Picnic Beach* and *Rockpile Beach*. A path meanders along the gentle, grassy bluffs above the beach, and steps lead down to both. Picnic tables are nestled among the trees of Heisler Park, giving Picnic Beach its name. Rockpile, meanwhile, is strictly a surfing beach. (Here, as everywhere in Laguna Beach, metered on-street parking is the rule.) Finally, *Crescent Bay* takes us to the north edge of town. Large, tubular waves make Crescent Bay a prime bodysurfing spot.

If you want to discover some of the unmentioned and mostly unnamed beaches reachable from the many street ends in Laguna Beach, you're on your own. Everyone in Laguna has a favorite beach tucked away they don't tell strangers about. But there's plenty to go around, and you might stumble onto an unpeopled cove with any luck. You're reminded and beseeched, however, to respect private property (i.e., don't throw full cans of beer at picture windows, build bonfires or holler "yee haw" every time you catch a wave).

The main artery through Laguna Beach is the Coast Highway, which unfortunately snakes right through the center of town. The otherwise genteel village atmosphere is constantly harassed by the stream of traffic that races through it. There is simply no other way to get from Dana Point to Newport Beach, though there ought to be a bypass. (A proposed freeway set a few miles inland was nixed years ago.) And so the four-lane Coast Highway sends an endless stream of traffic whizzing through, making getting in and out of your parked car a sport more hazardous than surfing. With the steel nerves of a matador waving a red flag at an angry bull, you must step into the path of snorting, fuming traffic and enter your car before being beheaded by a truck driver's side mirror. If traffic were rerouted away from town, Laguna Beach would be a more pleasant place.

As it is, though, Laguna has atmosphere, culture and scenic beauty in abundance. Renowned for its village friendliness, the town even used to have an unofficial greeter—Eiler Larson, by name. A veritable mountain man, with a shaggy beard and a neighborly grin, Larson used to stand at the city limits, shouting "How are you?" to those coming and "Leaving so soon?" to those going, for eight hours a day. After he died, numerous tributary wood likenesses began appearing on the town's sidewalks.

You've got to love a community that has its own active beautification council, which successfully battled outside business interests that wanted to refashion Laguna into a "convention center" in the seventies. Instead, the would-be developers were sent packing, and the threatened town center was fashioned into the landscaped, open-air Main Beach park. Along the coastline, such happy endings are few and far between. This one deserves a standing ovation.

Accommodations

Expect to pay three figures a night for European inn–style lodgings in Laguna Beach. The old *Hotel Laguna* still is the hostelry of first choice, while the *Hotel San Maarten* makes up in amenities what it lacks in history. A string of park-at-your-door motels cut from plainer cloth runs from South Laguna to Dana Point. The *Laguna Reef Motel*, near Aliso Beach, looked to be the most habitable of these. If you want to go straight to the top, however, try the *Aliso Creek Inn*, a five-star golf resort on the beach.

Restaurants

"Fine dining on the waterfront." How often have you heard those words, only to find yourself in a warehouse-sized fried fish camp across the street from the ocean, stranded in a gravel parking lot like a beached whale? Well, in Laguna Beach, it's hard to find anything but genuine fine dining on the waterfront.

Topping the list is the *Beach House Inn*, which sits at the end of a street with the evocative name of Sleepy Hollow Lane. A wall of glass faces the water, and the ocean view is available to all. The menu selections tend toward creative, California-style nouvelle cuisine. The broiled filet of sole, for example, is accompanied by bananas sauteed in butter and brown sugar, plus chutney and grated coconut. The Beach House Fish Kabob consists of shrimp, bacon-wrapped scallops and bell peppers impaled on a skewer and placed atop a bed of brown rice, with a pair of spiny lobster tails rounding out the platter. Set in an old house that used to belong to actor Slim Summerville (a comedic film actor and one of the original Keystone Kops), the Beach House has not altered the original architecture, and a relaxed air pervades the dining room. Try coming at sunset, when a spectacular view will complement your dinnertime spread.

As a footnote, if you're driving north of Laguna, make a point of stopping at a little yellow lean-to called the *Sunshine Cove* for one of their fabled, healthy date shakes.

Nightlife

As the dinner hour wanes, several of Laguna's more popular restaurants metamorphose into nightspots. The *White House Tavern*, built in 1918, is filled with Tiffany lamps, varnished wood tables and the sounds of reggae music, which is locally very popular. Bar bands on weekends, reggae during the week seems to be the lay of the land at the White House. *Las Brisas*, along Cliff Drive, serves authentic Mexican Riviera cuisine but also attracts a sizable crowd who come to the bar to meet and mingle.

FOR FURTHER INFORMATION

Laguna Beach Chamber of Commerce
357 Glenneyre Street
P.O. Box 396
Laguna Beach, CA 92652
(714) 494-1018

Corona del Mar

Corona del Mar is a small but well-heeled suburb attached to the southern end of Newport Beach on the Ocean Highway. It has the mixed blessing of a popular state beach that is more accessible, during the crowded summer season, than Newport Beach's lengthy strand. Located at the end of Marguerite Avenue, *Corona del Mar State Beach* is a gigantic sandbox, wider at the north end, where no fewer than eight volleyball nets have been set up. All year round, like some kind of fertility rite, tanned bruisers and their svelte, aerobicized sweethearts get physical with the volleyball. Many folks, however, prefer to encamp comfortably on beach towels, readying their tans for unveiling at happy hour. We were content to sit and stare at what looked like a real-life rerun of *Beach Blanket Bingo*.

Climbing the rocks at the north end of the beach, in defiance of the "Don't Climb on Rocks" sign, will net you a nifty vantage point from which to study Newport Harbor. Corona del Mar forms one side of the harbor's mouth, and if you scramble down the protective rocks to the sandy cove below, you can watch the boats come and go in relative solitude. Corona del Mar State Beach also has a decent snack bar, clean rest rooms and outdoor showers. It costs $4 to park for the day, but there's no charge for pedestrians. Thus, many people park on the streets (if they can find spaces) and walk in for free. The traffic must be a headache to local residents, but all in all, it could be worse.

FOR FURTHER INFORMATION

Corona del Mar Chamber of Commerce
2855 East Coast Highway
P.O. Box 72
Corona del Mar, CA 92625
(714) 673-4050

Newport Beach

Newport Beach has been mislabeled. The goods are in order, but the writing on the can is all wrong. Everything we read beforehand had us believing Newport Beach was going to be "Nouveau Beach," a land of big-time conspicuous consumption. Oh, it is that, but then all of Southern California is the same way—nouveau as

Dove Bars and as conspicuous a bunch of consumers as have ever toted plastic.

We came to Newport Beach expecting the *ne plus ultra* of manic wheeler-dealer entrepreneurs and bored, wealthy women dripping with jewels and designer outfits. After all, wasn't it modeled after Newport, Rhode Island—an exclusive community of yachts and mansions for jet-age millionaires? To be sure, some of this is true. Ten thousand pleasure craft are docked at Newport Harbor, the second largest in the country (after the other Newport). But there's a viable side of Newport Beach accessible to anyone, regardless of whether he or she owns a boat and an American Express Gold Card. After we'd spent nearly a week in the area, it dawned on us that Newport Beach has been called nearly everything but what it truly is: a fun and funky beach town.

So let's open the can and spoon out the goods. First of all, Newport Beach is not exactly a town. It's a city of 65,000 people, many of whom admittedly drive expensive European automobiles. Newport Beach has, in the last decade, been spreading away from the harbor toward the hills, where walled-in, armed retirement camps and planned condo civilizations have been erected. Like separate nations, each hoists its own flag, and signs saying "now selling" and "models open" quickly come to acquire an annoyingly overfamiliar ring, like a phone you don't want to answer.

Still, the bulk of the money—and the ragtag heart and soul of the city—is out on the Balboa Peninsula, a thin finger of land that reaches into the Pacific and then bends around to protect the large, beautiful harbor. Backbays and waterways have been dug into the peninsula and several small, inhabited islands sit close by, like Balboa Island and Lido Island (the latter an exclusive enclave reachable only by boat). From the vantage point of the harbor, Newport Beach looks and feels like a casual, fun place, almost always sunny and dominated by watery pastimes. As in Fort Lauderdale, Florida— to which Newport Beach bears more than a fleeting resemblance— boats are docked right up against the back doors of houses. ("Hey, Dad, can I *please* have the keys to the *Lorba Lynda* tonight, I promise I'll have it back by eleven. . . .")

The fun and funky beach town begins when you turn off the Coast Highway onto Balboa Boulevard (a.k.a. Route 55 South).

The turn is a sharp one, but chances are you'll recognize it by the line of traffic. Balboa Boulevard is the only way out onto the peninsula, running for six miles from the Coast Highway turnoff to a harbor jetty called the *Wedge*. This jetty forms one side of Newport Harbor's mouth and looks across the water at Corona del Mar State Beach on the other side. The Wedge is a notorious surfing spot, treacherous and unsafe to all but the most accomplished surfing diehards.

To oversimplify a bit, the money is on the harbor side of the peninsula and the fun is on the ocean. The beach runs for the full six-mile length of the peninsula. Most beachgoers assemble in the vicinity of the two piers—one in Newport Beach, one in Balboa on the tip. Both are buzzing beehives of activity, but more boisterous is the three-block neighborhood around the Newport Pier. This pier was originally known as McFadden Pier, after a pair of brothers who built their first pier in 1888 on this site, then began laying out a seaside community. History still lingers around the pier in the form of the Dory Fleet. Since 1891, the Dory Fleet has launched their wooden boats into the Pacific before dawn every morning, returning to the same spot beside the pier by 9:30 a.m. to sell their fresh catch in the sand. Undaunted by the sort of creeping (and creepy) modernity that has made them obsolete elsewhere, the Dory Fleet pushes off every morning. Their presence is the kind of touch that made us look fondly on Newport Beach. The word on the street, though, is that the country-club set that runs this town wants to do away with the Dory Fleet because it's so, so, so... who really knows why these people do what they do? In this case, though, the Dory Fleet will surely prevail, because they are enormously popular with locals and visitors alike.

The piers—and the bars and restaurants around them—are the main source of Newport Beach's fun and funk. People of all ages and persuasions flock to these streets and jam the peninsula with traffic. In season, it's not unusual to find traffic slowed to a bumper-to-bumper standstill on Balboa Boulevard, all the way out to the Ocean Highway, which has its own gridlock problems. Traffic is a thorn in Newport Beach's side—and in a sense, they have themselves to blame for it. They voted years ago not to have the San Diego Freeway (I-5) built closer to the coast, in order to preserve

the peace and quiet of their community. Their good judgment back-
fired, as the Coast Highway has proved inadequate for the increased
traffic burden from Newport Beach's spurting growth. Consequently, the sought-after quaintness has been buried under a haze
of car fumes.

Once you get to the beach, you'll quickly forget the ride. Newport is a quintessential California beach by day and a rocking, rolling party zone at night. Some of the best clubs and bars are within
easy walking distance of the pier, and the human parade on the
sidewalk along the oceanfront is intoxicating in and of itself. Despite the nonstop crunch of humanity, Newport Beach is an amazingly friendly place. The most violent blows result from hands
pounding affectionately on backs, and the loudest shouts are those
approving of the minuscule size of some promenading bikini.

Balboa Pier is two miles farther out the peninsula. Things are
only a little less crazy out here. On the harbor side, just across
from the pier, is the Balboa Pavilion, a Victorian landmark dating
from 1906. A renowned hotspot back in the Big Band days, the
pavilion still hosts big events in the present day. You can also board
a harbor-cruise tour boat here and see the homes of John Wayne,
King Gillette, the estate of the guy who invented the "pocket fisherman," and so on. Whale-watching expeditions and passenger ferries to Catalina Island also depart from Balboa docks.

Okay, so Newport Beach has been mislabeled. No doubt an in-
flated emphasis on money has a lot to do with it, as does a run-
away real-estate market, fueled by rapid population growth. Such
"planned communities" as Santa Ana, Irvine, Orange and Costa
Mesa didn't exist twenty years ago. Now they are big cities. The
same thing happened in Newport Beach, a once-quiet seaside haven for fishers and rich folks who considered it a less hectic alternative to Los Angeles. All that changed when the sixties generation
began making piles of money and then came down with that movie-
fied form of midlife crisis known as the Big Chill.

One mecca for the nouveau riche in Newport Beach is a place
called Fashion Island. It is definitely not an island, nor does it look
very fashionable, unless gray concrete qualifies as a fashion statement. Fashion Island is an enormous landlocked hub of shopping,

business and finance that was built far from the harbor on land belonging to the Irvine Company. The latter is a mysterious entity that owns much of the land in Orange County, selling it off a hundred acres at a time to the highest bidder. (Actually, they only lease it in 99-year blocks.)

Fashion Island is the perfect symbol of soulless corporate might thrilled with itself, unabashedly flexing its muscles more grotesquely than a Mr. Universe contestant. At the empty heart of Fashion Island is a posh shopping mall, the visual symbol of which is a huge outdoor sculpture titled *Joining Hands*. The similarities to Michelangelo's Sistine Chapel ceiling are embarrassingly obvious, even to a pair of amateur art buffs like ourselves. Three figures swirl around in the air, reaching out for each other but not quite extending their hands far enough. Perhaps they should be extending American Express cards, because soon enough, the shoppers who stroll by here will be extending theirs in the direction of the sales clerks at Nieman-Marcus, Pierre Deux, Caswell-Massey, Ylang-Ylang, Fiorucci, Forty Love and the Posh Potato. At Fashion Island, shopping is indeed a religious experience, the ultimate act of faith being to plunk down a wad of money for a totally useless piece of merchandise—say, fifty or sixty bucks for a miniature rag doll stuffed inside a plastic egg.

Girdling the shopping mall in a perfect circle are the various corporate headquarters that make all this buying possible. The buildings are done in a numbingly unimaginative skyscraper style, causing a deadening pang in the soul when looked at for too long. No, if Fashion Island is an island at all, it is a desert one, surrounded by an asphalt ocean, with Mercedes for sand dunes, sidewalks for beaches and valets for horseflies. Ultimately, the most disturbing thing about Fashion Island is that it disguises the fact that Newport Beach is, essentially, a fun and funky beach town.

Accommodations

If you find yourself shipwrecked on Fashion Island, or merely arriving on business, two of the mightiest fortresses in the hotel industry will gladly haul you in for the evening. The mightiest is the *Four Seasons Hotel*, arguably the most prestigious hotel chain in the country. Each of the 296 plush, well-appointed rooms in Newport Beach's $75 million, 19-story Four Seasons is the very pinnacle of graceful corporate style. No detail has been overlooked to make your stay a successful one, from the baskets of complimentary soap and shampoo to the exquisite Italian marble and heavy wood furniture throughout the spacious rooms and suites. There are telephones in the living room, at your bedside and even in the bathroom—presumably for those inopportune moments when nature and New York call at the same time. With fresh flowers on the table, original artwork on the walls (the Four Seasons must have had every artist in Laguna Beach working overtime), fully stocked minibars, tennis courts, a spa, a large pool, basement-level health club, 24-hour concierge service and a squadron of valets who literally sprint to meet your every whim, the Four Seasons is the kind of place King Tut would have wished to stay when he traveled on business.

Marriott also has a hotel on Fashion Island with an even sportier resort flavor. It is double-billed as a hotel and tennis club. Larger than the Four Seasons, its 603 rooms are spread out over two buildings. There are eight lighted tennis courts on the grounds, and guests enjoy golfing privileges on the course behind the hotel. (Four Seasons guests are extended golfing privileges as well.) The Marriott is also a bit more casual than the Four Seasons, giving you the option of parking your own car. This is a seemingly small thing but one that makes you feel less like a prisoner in a luxurious cell than a guest who can come and go at will. In addition, there are restaurants and nightclubs galore on the premises.

Down by the beach, the accommodations, ironically, are scarcer than gulls' teeth. The Balboa Peninsula is largely residential. Many overnight visitors arrive by boat and simply stay on them. The beach is assaulted by day-trippers who hail from the prefab inland towns as well as the inundated L.A. suburbs. For the record, there are a handful of bed-and-breakfast inns near the Newport Pier. One, the *Portofino Beach Hotel*, is a former surf shop remodeled in the Italian Riviera style. "We would preserve more of our history," the manager drily explained, "but we don't really have any out here to preserve."

Restaurants

In Newport Beach we met a restaurateur who became a combination culinary and intellectual hero to us. Bob Roubian is his name, and he is the owner-guru of the *Crab Cooker*. He is an expert on the subject of fish. More than that, he is obsessed with them. He thinks about fish, night and day. He dreams about fish. He poeticizes about fish. He sculpts fish. He writes songs about them, even recording a song, "Who Hears the Fishes When They Cry," that he sells as a 45 in his restaurant. Music and fish have a lot in common, he tells us, in that both have scales. He likes to "eat lots a fish." (That is his motto.) He also runs the best seafood restaurant in Newport Beach and maybe the universe.

Located near the pier on Newport Boulevard, the Crab Cooker is a local institution that's been operating on this spot for 37 years. Roubian is an easygoing, likable kind of guy, but he enforces strict standards when it comes to seafood. For instance, he will only buy fish that have been caught by the hook-and-line method (no net-caught schools for him; it depletes the population in an already overfished sea, and besides, it's impossible to eviscerate them properly). He insists that the fish be eviscerated (bled and cleaned) and packed on ice within five minutes of being pulled from the water. This ensures total freshness. Fresh fish never smells fishy, swears Roubian. If anything, it smells a little sweet, like watermelon.

His wonderful, ramshackle restaurant is packed every evening, his claims seemingly verified by an army of loyal customers. The Crab Cooker doesn't take credit cards and you can't make a reservation. You must show up, get in line and wait your turn. To Roubian, this is democracy at work, and he'll make no exceptions— not for a U.S. president, not for his own grandmother, not even for himself. Even John Wayne, a longtime Crab Cooker regular, had to wait his turn. Sometimes the wait can be a long one, so you might as well settle back on the wooden benches outside with a paper cup of the Crab Cooker's famous seafood chowder until your name is called.

Fresh fish, shrimp, crab and scallops are cooked on wooden skewers over a charcoal grill, because that's the way Roubian saw his mother do it when he was a child. The food is served on paper plates and the beer and wine in plastic cups, almost like a picnic. Chairs don't match, the walls are wildly decorated with bric-a-brac, and there's little standing on ceremony. The result is an inspiring slap in the face of conformity. All dinners arrive with homemade bread, coleslaw and Romano potatoes. The food is beyond compare. The combination plate ($8.50) is probably the best way to get a feel for the method in Roubian's madness, although you won't want to pass up the smoked salmon appetizer, either.

Newport Beach is doubly blessed in the seafood department. Another top-notch restaurant, the *Cannery*, is just down the street from the Crab Cooker, on the placid harborside. It is a historic re-creation of an old canning company, with original machinery displayed throughout the restaurant: wheels, pulleys, conveyer lines, boilers, autoclaves and processing machines. Have no fear, though. They aren't plugged in, nor are they just another gimmick to distract you from mediocre seafood. The Cannery serves strictly fresh fish, shrimp, lobster and abalone. The latter is a rare, disappearing delicacy that looks like conch, tastes like chicken and commands upward of $30 when you can find it on a menu. Unlike the Crab Cooker, the Cannery serves nonseafood items as well. But by this time, our motto had become "eat lots a fish," and we did. Thumbs up to the Cannery.

Nightlife

As we've said, most of the action on the Balboa Peninsula is by the piers. At the Balboa Pier, set your time machine to the fifties and step into the wonderful world of flirtatious adolescent kids on parade. Around and around the bayside Balboa Pavilion buzzes an army of new Annettes and Fabians who are too young to drink and so must swarm on the streets instead. Dressed to kill, they walk around until a group comes together like a log jam. Then the blond, athletic cops arrive on the scene to disperse them for loitering. A few innocuous groans are heard, the Barbie Doll girls standing on the fringe chomping gum and looking convincingly air-headed. At the end of another night of mindless cruising, they head out to the end of the Balboa Pier for a hot dog at *Ruby's*, an authentic neon-fringed diner. You should stop there, too, if just to witness California's fifties resurgence firsthand.

The crowd gets a bit older and noisier at the Newport Pier. Motorcycles and muscleman T-shirts replace high fashion, and the raised voices are a tad more menacing. The same blond, athletic cops survey the scene and think twice about intervening. Mostly, though, the chaos has an order to it that only a Californian can understand. Handshakes, high-fives and backslaps are the order of the day. No big deal in a beach town.

The bars around Newport Beach are as good as they get in Southern California. *Blackie's*, for instance, is the archetypal beach bar: mounted hammerhead shark, more team pennants than there are flags at the U.N., three televisions, each tuned to a different baseball game, pool tables, a jukebox, friendly bragging about sexual prowess and arguing about favorite teams or players. It's actually more of a daytime drinking oasis than a hub of Newport Beach's nightlife.

For live rock and roll, head around the corner to *Rumplestiltskin's*. It's got all the right ingredients for a good time—no cover, no dress code (well, you do have to wear shoes) and reasonably priced beer. The music is catch as catch can, usually one of a million L.A. bar bands that make their living playing up and down the coast. They sport outmoded shag haircuts and boogie proficiently and loudly enough to get people dancing. Just down the street is *Woody's Wharf*, another wild rock and roll club set on the bayside. A seafood restaurant by day, this mild-mannered establishment metamorphoses into a hotbed of rock at night and is nearly always packed.

The Warehouse, on the Lido Peninsula, also has live rock bands, showcased in a darker restaurant setting without benefit of a dance floor. The dress code is more stringent and the atmosphere somewhat tame, but the prettier women seemed to be smitten with the place, and there were lots of them. If you like jazz—real jazz, not mood muzak or new-age drivel—then the *Studio Café*, near the

Balboa Pier, is your spot. On the weekends, it gets mighty crowded, with the line extending out the door.

FOR FURTHER INFORMATION

Newport Beach Convention and Visitors Bureau
1470 Jamboree Road
Newport Beach, CA 92660
(714) 644-8460

Huntington Beach

A small bust, oxidized green by the salt air, stands at the foot of
the Huntington Beach Municipal Pier. A Hawaiian surfer with a
cracked, friendly smile and a lei around his neck, he is Duke Kahanamoku, a legend around these parts. More than anyone else, he
spread the word about Huntington Beach, turning a withering,
would-be resort into a bustling beach mecca sought out by millions.

Duke was an Olympic swimmer and world-class surfer—one of
the first, in fact, to make a living at these things. Way back at the
turn of the century, this Hawaiian-born Pied Piper of the waves
publicly promoted the sport, skiing the sloping surf on his favorite
plank like a happy-go-lucky Macadamia nut. His salary was paid
by a railroad mogul who wanted to give the public a good reason
to travel his freshly laid stretch of track, which ran from Los
Angeles to Huntington Beach.

The surf at Huntington is some of the best in California. Following Duke's lead, a small but growing surfing cult began pointing their longboards toward Huntington Beach. In the early sixties,
surfing went national. When the Beach Boys and Jan and Dean
took the sport into the Top 40, writing and singing a string of
catchy surfing anthems, the entire nation suddenly grew desirous
of coastal access.

Surfing spread up and down the Pacific coast, but it was Huntington Beach that became known as "Surf City," after a number
one song by Jan and Dean. The first major surfing competition,

the Pacific Coast Surfboard Championships, was held here. Since the early seventies, the United States Surfboard Championships have drawn hundreds of thousands to the brown-sugar beach at Huntington over Labor Day. Surfers tend to get a far-off look in their eyes when they ponder the unobstructed south swells that spill forward in perfect curls of wave and foam (known as "rooster tails") at Huntington. Today, Duke Kahanamoku's spiritual godchildren expertly mount waves all day long before his beneficent gaze.

It's lucky for Duke that his eyes are turned seaward, for if he were to look over his shoulder, his smile would fade as rapidly as a Hawaiian shirt in a hot wash. Huntington Beach is not the city it used to be. Currently, it's caught in the viselike grip of what is cheerfully termed "downtown redevelopment." "The forecast for business is sunny," spouts the chamber of commerce, pointing with misbegotten pride to plans to obliterate everything on the oceanfront that doesn't fit in with the long-term corporate game plan. The upshot is that Huntington Beach will barely be recognizable in a few years and generally unaffordable to anyone not on an expense account.

Ground is being cleared even as we write. "Another safe, quality demolition," read a sign hooked to a fence surrounding a block of scorched earth. The old Huntington Beach—a motley but likable assortment of surf shops, dive bars and taco shacks along the Pacific Coast Highway and Main Street—is falling brick by brick like ducks in a shooting arcade. We have no delusions here: we're not lamenting the passing of great architectural landmarks, by any means. No, it's just sad to see something so typically unimaginative and, by design, exclusive go up in their place—to wit, the usual blundering blobs of concrete and glass that block the beach, arrogant monuments to the almighty dollar.

Here's what to expect at Huntington Beach in the coming years. The modest strip of merchants and motels along Huntington City Beach will be cleared to make room for the "Waterfront": a $345-million, 50-acre "mixed use project" consisting of four towering hotels and a gated residential community. Room rates on the beach will double and triple. Since surfers live on a shoestring and bring little money into a community, surf culture will inevitably wane.

The town will play down the surfing championships, citing obscure or hastily passed ordinances to make life difficult for anyone under 25. The beach will primarily become a playpen for those flashing plastic at the Waterfront.

Huntington Beach, in this period of rapid transition, defies easy summarization. In fact, it appeared to us to abound in contradictions. Its beach is gorgeous—wide and long, it runs for more than eight miles, encompassing *Huntington State Beach, Huntington City Beach* and *Bolsa Chica State Beach*. On the other hand, ugly oil derricks blight the landscape everywhere you look: along the highway, in back yards, on the beach and on offshore platforms. Nine million gallons of crude a year are pumped out of Huntington Beach. The derricks rise and fall as far as the eye can see, like an aerobics class of giant black magpies. Derricks have been around since the twenties, when the first big Huntington Beach well blew with a roar that could be heard for miles. Although they're as common as sea gulls, you won't see oil derricks pictured or mentioned much in the literature about Huntington Beach. That wouldn't be good for tourism.

In 1986, the same year Huntington Beach was declared the safest city in the United States, a major riot erupted on the beach over Labor Day, making national news. Hundreds of thousands of kids had flocked to Huntington for the annual surfing championships. The crowd was thick, the day hot, and the beer flowed like a geyser of Huntington Beach crude. A few bozos tried to remove some girls' bikini tops. Their boyfriends took offense. Fists started flying, the crowd began chanting and, like an earthquake, the tremors spread across the beach. Cars were overturned and burned. The police arrived on the scene, dispersing the rampaging mob with brute force and billy clubs, herding them off the beach and down Main Street. Innocent people on both sides were injured, much private property was destroyed, and lawsuits are still flying around in the wake. As a result, the surfing championships have been moved back from Labor Day to late August to stem the crowds somewhat.

Because of incidents like the Labor Day riot, and because a small, unsavory element jangles around the beach like a fistful of bad pennies, Huntington Beach has been saddled with bad press. "They accuse us of having crime, but I never see them walking down the streets and finding out just how nice Huntington Beach really is," complained an elderly gift shop owner. She has a point. Huntington Beach certainly is pleasant enough from all outward appearances—a city of 165,000 (the tenth largest in California) whose residents live in well-tended suburbs. From the beach, the town fans east, merging like mating paramecia with an adjacent 'burb called Fountain Valley. The seedy bungalows and soon-to-be-razed mobile-home parks near the beach give way to neat rows of white stucco homes in quiet, palm-shaded neighborhoods.

People flock to Huntington Beach on summer weekends from the surrounding valley towns, as well as from surf-deprived Long Beach, with boards strapped to the roofs of everything from boat-sized woodies to old VWs with whooping cough. A word of advice to all who come for the day: park on the side streets, where a dime in the meter is good for one hour, instead of by the beach, where a quarter buys only 20 minutes. Or you can park all day at city and state beach lots for a reasonable $3.

All the action is centered around the 1,830-foot municipal pier. Folks fish off it, surf near it and skateboard like scuttling crabs in an asphalt lot underneath it. The beach is so extensive, sandy and clean and the tumbling waves that roll ashore so well-formed for surfing that Huntington was voted the sixth best beach in the world in a poll conducted by (of all things) *Lifestyles of the Rich and Famous*.

Roll over, Kahanamoku, and tell Kahuna the news.

Accommodations

Huntington Beach is coming down, and the motels we write about today may be brick dust tomorrow. The forecast calls for four as yet unnamed and unbuilt luxury hotels. One will have 467 rooms, two will run at about 400 and one will be an all-suite hotel. Having duly delivered this bit of preconstruction propaganda, it's worth adding what will happen to those who currently live on the sites earmarked for municipal and corporate takeover. The residents of the 239-unit Driftwood Mobile Home Park, for example, will be washed inland like driftwood whether they like it or not. The moneybagged firms that rig these things tactfully refer to it in 1984 doublespeak as a "conversion procedure." So it goes in the land of the free.

The *Best Western Huntington Beach Inn* is the largest oceanfront motel between Laguna Beach and Redondo Beach. Although it will eventually come down to make way for the first of the new hotel monoliths, we were told it would be around a few seasons longer. (The owner of the Huntington Beach Inn is the prime mover behind the Waterfront, so he can do what he wants with it.) More like a small resort than a motel, it has a nine-hole golf course, restaurant, cafe, lounge, ballroom-disco and more. Grab it while you can.

Inland, a wide thoroughfare known as Beach Boulevard brings traffic from the valley to the shore. It's lined with motels, convenience marts and shopping centers as far as the eye can see (or the car can drive). The *Regency Inn*, a cut above your average roadside roost, offers bright, spacious rooms and a pool-jacuzzi combo. The location, though not exactly on the beach, is no more than five minutes from it.

Restaurants

Café Express is housed in a converted Amtrak passenger car from which a tent has been tethered outward, creating a kind of alfresco effect while sparing diners the direct punishment of the sun. The emphasis is Italian, and although the spaghetti and lasagna are house specialties, we settled on missile-sized sub sandwiches, each of which proved good for two meals. Café Express faces the beach, and with its glass-topped tables and Middle Eastern Muzak, the ambience is something like that of a New York sidewalk café.

There used to be another café in Huntington Beach, this one at the end of the municipal pier. Washed into the ocean, along with parts of the pier, by a huge storm in early 1983, the *End Café* was rebuilt, only to collapse again in a late–1987 storm. The sea giveth and the sea taketh away.

Generally, the Pacific Coast Highway (or P.C.H., as it's otherwise known) is lined with places you'd never think of stopping into. But being daring when it comes to road food, we wandered into one cement shack after another until we found what we were looking for at a place called *H.B. Charbroiled Chicken*. Charbroiled chicken is big in Southern California. At H.B., they charbroil their chicks in lemon, butter and garlic, serving it with rice or beans, fresh salsa and a few flour tortillas on the side. Also recommended are the Killer Burrito and the Yummy Chicken Quesadilla. While waiting for your order, take a look around. The place is decorated, if you can call it that, like a surfer's bungalow. In one corner stands a cardboard standup of Elvis Presley, a lei around his neck and a bumper sticker across his chest reading: "Greatest legs, firmest breasts." (That's the restaurant's motto, not Elvis's.) A black-and-white TV rests on a surfboard shelf. Glossies of celebrities from John Wayne to James Dean are falling off the wall. Meanwhile, a guy who looks like he's just ridden a big wave through the front door of the place cooks up the grub and shouts for you when its ready.

Back at the pier, a classier setting awaits you at *Maxwell's*. A seafood dinner isn't inexpensive ($12 to $18) but is arguably worth it for the view over the water. Maxwell's adjoins the pier, but you'll have no sense of the recreational havoc going on beside and below you from the plush interior, especially with a tuxedo-clad lounge pianist tinkling the ivories while the sun slowly sets in the west. Maxwell's generally offers half a dozen fresh fish a day and an equal number of different ways to prepare them, from Cajun spiced to smothered in Mexican sauce to a simple (and probably preferable) sautéing or broiling.

Nightlife

You can gauge your appetite for the nightlife of Huntington Beach from the code of etiquette posted at the door of a popular hangout

across from the beach: "No knives, backpacks, ragged clothes, bicycles, roller skates, surfboards or animals allowed inside." At least
one of these rules was being flagrantly violated, as we saw any
number of animals drinking at the bar.

There's no dearth of bars in the vicinity, bearing names like *Cag-
ney's*, *Perqs*, *Faces* and so forth. Most cater to a localized surfer–
beach bum clientele. If you're visiting on business from Duluth,
you might want to confine your imbibing to the hotel cocktail
lounge.

If you're after a night on the town in preppie-ish, fifties-kitsch
rock and roll surroundings, let's go to the *Hop*. Owned by the Righteous Brothers, the hit-making duo from the sixties ("You've Lost
That Lovin' Feelin'," et al.), the Hop is a pink-neon time machine
to happy days. The music is all oldies, spun by a deejay in a booth
whose front is the grille of a Thunderbird. This is probably the
only deejay booth in the country that comes equipped with a working set of car headlights and a horn. Located at a shopping mall in
Fountain Valley, about five miles inland, the Hop draws a bubbling crowd of all ages and dance steps. Basketball goals are posted
at opposite ends of the dance floor. Sloppy, fun tunes from Johnny
Rivers and the Swingin' Medallions play on the PA while vintage
rock and roll footage runs on video screens. Elvis Presley's life
flashed before our eyes one night at the Hop: bristling young stud,
crewcut GI Joe, love-struck groom, leather-clad comeback artist,
obese drug addict. The atmosphere at the Hop is looser than Ike
and Tina Turner's version of "Proud Mary," and the long tables
encourage mingling. They don't miss a trick at the Hop.

FOR FURTHER INFORMATION

Huntington Beach Chamber of Commerce
Seacliff Village #32
2213 Main Street
Huntington Beach, CA 92648
(714) 536-8888

Huntington Harbour
Sunset Beach

North of Huntington Beach, an ecological preserve covers some 500 acres of wetlands. Even here, though, the odd oil derrick nestles in the shrubbery about as inconspicuously as a drunk relieving himself behind a tree. Word is that developers are hungrily eyeing this rare patch of unobstructed greenery. (How nice it would be to place developers on the endangered species list!) But for now the Bolsa Chica Ecological Reserve, on the inland side of the Coast Highway, can be explored and enjoyed by anyone. You can also swim or pedal a bike along three-mile *Bolsa Chica State Beach*.

A motel-restaurant-liquor store morass begins in earnest as you pass out of the protected area. Huntington Harbour is a northern extension of Huntington Beach, with slightly more upscale establishments pressed close together. Sunset Beach is a bit funkier, with such restaurants as *Harpoon Harry's*, the *Stuf'd Chicken* and *Liquor Burger* flashing past the car windows like poles in a picket fence. Parking is hard to find everywhere in Sunset Beach. There isn't enough for those who live here, much less for outsiders who come to swim. In the summer, the crunch reaches crisis proportions.

We stopped for lunch at the *Harbor House Café* in Sunset Beach, where a line ran out the door and a big canteen of coffee was set up for those waiting their turn on the porch. The Harbor House has been around since 1939. With a choice of indoor or outdoor patio dining and a menu heavy on omelettes (28 kinds), seafood and burger variations, it offers something for everyone, in pleasant surroundings. Also worth mentioning is the *Sunset Pub*, a popular watering hole that draws a crowd from Huntington Beach and Long Beach.

Seal Beach

Seal Beach was named for that flappy little sea mammal once so popular with the garment trade. For Orange County, it is a modest little town in the best sense of the word. It could just as easily have been named for its good fortune at having been sealed off from its neighbors. Located at the very north end of Orange County, just a pogo hop over the San Gabriel River from Los Angeles County, Seal Beach is a small town among sprawling giants.

The Pacific Coast Highway passes wide of Seal Beach, sparing the town center the nonstop wall of traffic headed to and from Long Beach and Los Angeles. One must vigilantly search for the correct turnoff (Seal Beach Boulevard) or miss the little town completely. Like the fictional village of Mayberry, Seal Beach is a world unto itself that exists primarily to serve those who live here. It has a Main Street that looks like a Main Street should—shaded, bricked over and as civilized as one of grandma's bedtime stories. It has a grassy park named for an American president, Dwight D. Eisenhower. There's a tiny historical museum housed in an antique railroad car, an art deco movie house with a Wurlitzer organ, a trio of Irish bars, a couple of seafood restaurants, a municipal pier, a city beach—and that's about it for Seal Beach. The main intersection at the beachfront is not your typical surf-culture strip. On the corner sits Grandma's Ice Cream and Cookie Parlor. Whoa dude, let's get into some intensely radical oatmeal cookies!

This is not to imply that Seal Beach remains completely undiscovered. The surf here is middlingly popular, approaching the two jettied beaches at a southerly angle, unobstructed by a becalming seawall as in Long Beach. Sometimes this produces perfect waves, sometimes not. This unpredictability keeps the town from becoming another Huntington Beach. Even when the waves aren't rocking and rolling, though, the currents and crosswinds are swift and potentially treacherous. At all public access points between 1st Street and Electric Avenue, a posted sign warns: "Beware of Beach Hazards, Long Shore Currents, Rip Currents, Inshore Holes, Sand Bars, Underwater Objects, Pier Seawall and Rock Structures."

None of the above seems to bother the surfers who make the trek to Seal Beach. Many of these determined pipeliners are too young to drive, so they take the bus from Long Beach, surfboards tucked under their arms like briefcases. At 9:30 on a Monday morning, we counted 78 adolescent surfers on the north side of the Seal

Beach Pier. Like tropical fish clad in all manner of fluorescent wet suits, they sat passively on their shark's-tooth–shaped boards, staring west, bobbing up and down, not speaking to one another, just waiting waiting waiting for the...ah, here it comes. But no—just another wimpy little gully whomper. Surfing is done on the shorter north beach and the city-run *Surfside Beach*, on the far side of the town's south jetty. The longest stretch of beach, between the pier and south jetty, is reserved for swimmers and sunbathers, all of whom behave in accordance with the family-oriented tone of the town.

The 1,885-foot pier dividing the beaches was destroyed on January 22, 1983, by the same storm that leveled Huntington Beach's pier. The Seal Beach Pier was rebuilt a year later by the civic-minded community, with a placard to commemorate their industriousness and a cute bronze sculpture of a seal.

During our visit, Seal Beach was the unfortunate recipient of a not-so-cute oil spill. By oil-spill standards, it was a small one (only 420 gallons), but it did close the beach for a while. Seems that one of the offshore drilling platforms sprang a leak or something; we never found out for sure because the oil-company execs hemmed and hawed for a few days, trying to duck culpability for the mess. Meanwhile, the civic-minded little town mobilized bulldozers and volunteers to clean up the crap. As we were leaving, the beach was reopened and clean. Meanwhile, the usual angry letters to the editor were beginning to appear. "The rigs not only besmirch the coastline," said one letter writer, "they pose a constant threat to our beaches and sea life." Let us guess: next comes the press release from the oil company, reassuring the townsfolk just how goshdarn environmentally conscientious they are. Then the mayor reminds the local citizens about the money and jobs the oil rigs bring the community. Then another offshore oil platform is built. Eventually, there's another spill....

One can only hope this scenario doesn't plague the good folks of Seal Beach again.

Accommodations

In this homey little town, there's really only one large motel—the *Radisson Inn Seal Beach*. Set far enough away from the town center so as not to detract from the Main Street atmosphere, the Radisson is still within easy walking distance of the beach and pier. It's a relatively new place, with 71 neatly appointed rooms and two small swimming pools. The room rate ($80 to $90) includes a free continental breakfast, brought to your door in the morning.

Restaurants

Of all the seafood places in Seal Beach, *Walt's Wharf* attracts the most devoted following. It's more upscale than the norm, drawing a large crowd of gregarious boat people in the late afternoon. There are nearly as many fish to choose from as there are types of imported beer on tap, and the seafood is as fresh as it comes. We accompanied our mugs of English ale with smoked fish and sashimi appetizers.

Nightlife

Three separate Irish bars are strung out along Main Street. They come in two flavors: funky and yukky (yuppie funky). The two funky ones, *Clancy's* and the *Irisher*, are almost identical—dark places with a pool table, rickety jukebox and moldy-oldie bar furnishings. "We don't have a town drunk," reads a sign in Clancy's. "We all take turns." *Hennessey's*, the yukky bar, draws the lion's share of the business. Clean, well-lighted and not the least bit like a true Dublin pub, this Irish-motif chain is on the cutting edge of trendy. It can't be denied, though, that Hennessey's is popular.

FOR FURTHER INFORMATION

Seal Beach City Hall
211 8th Street
Seal Beach, CA 90740
(213) 431-2527

Long Beach

It's hard to know exactly what to say about an American city that needed a British ocean liner to revive its sagging economy, but such is the saga of Long Beach, California. In 1967, the ailing city of Long Beach purchased the *Queen Mary*, the world's largest ocean liner, which had itself fallen on hard times. (By then, far more people wanted to fly than make the passage by water.) The *Queen Mary* was refurbished and turned into a tourist attraction. More important, perhaps, was the symbolism represented by the luxury liner. Laid to rest in Long Beach after 1,001 transatlantic crossings, the *Queen Mary* became the city's beacon for a hopeful future.

But the main draw is and will probably continue to be the *Queen Mary*. The historic vessel, more than 1,000 feet long, serves as a combination tourist attraction and hotel. The Queen of the High Seas saw action both as a first-class luxury liner "where the rich and famous took their ease" and a troop carrier dodging German subs in World War II. Now it's safely docked in Long Beach Harbor, protected by its own breakwater. Next door is the *Spruce Goose*, the world's largest airplane, housed under the world's largest aluminum geodesic dome. They charge what seems like the world's largest entrance fee ($13.95 for adults) to see them. Oh, and they hit you up for another $3 to park here.

Long Beach has rebounded from its midcentury decline to become a major center of industry, banking and convention business in the eighties. At least along the waterfront, it looks like a thriving, ultramodern all-American city. Freeways cloverleaf around towering glass-and-steel skyscrapers and skirt mast-filled marinas and landscaped lagoons. You won't find much greenery in Long Beach, at least not the kind associated with the outdoors. There is, however, an abundance of the sort of greenery that goes into seeding redevelopment. Since 1975, $1.3 billion has been pumped into the downtown area. The principal drawing card, to the business world at least, is the Long Beach Convention and Entertainment Center—192,000 square feet of meeting and exhibit space. More growth is on the drawing board: new hotels, a world trade center and themed shopping malls galore, all plotted in the millions. As for the *Queen Mary*, she is now owned and operated by an outfit known as the Wrather Corporation. What's good for business is good for Long Beach. You know how it goes.

What's good for business is not necessarily good for a prospective vacationer, though. Beyond a tour of the *Queen Mary* and the *Spruce Goose* there's not a heck of a lot to do here. For the beach lover especially, Long Beach is a dry well. The same breakwater that made Long Beach's artificial harbor the busiest port on the West Coast cuts the surf off completely. The ocean is calmer than a farm pond. No waves roll ashore here, forcing natives to head for beaches north or south to surf and swim. Besides, between the bilge pumped into the harbor by 4,000 cargo ships and not-infrequent oil spills from offshore derricks and tankers, water quality is a cloudy issue in Long Beach.

Long Beach's extensive city beach runs along Ocean Boulevard, from 1st Place to Alamitos Bay State Park. Over a Memorial Day weekend, it was all but empty. The 1,300-foot Belmont Pier was deserted except for a motley assortment of derelicts dressed in thrift-shop clothing who were fishing for their dinner. Those who could afford to had high-tailed it out of Long Beach for Catalina Island or the beaches of Mexico. The rest simply threw boards and wet suits into the back of the wagon and drove to Huntington Beach.

Long Beach is not entirely bereft of swimmable, sociable beaches. There's one that ranks with the best California has to offer. Though you won't find it mentioned by name in travel brochures, just ask anyone under 30 how to get to Horny Corners. It's not even an ocean beach but a strip of sand facing a calm lagoon on Bayshore Avenue between 1st and 2nd Streets in the Belmont Shores section of Long Beach.

Horny Corners came by its name and reputation honestly. Through the determined efforts of an army of nearly naked California girls who sunbathe and recreate on this spot all year long, Horny Corners has become one of the choicest bird-watching locales along the Pacific coast. They spread out on beach towels, glide down the street on roller skates and perch nonchalantly on a cement wall like crows on a telephone wire. The guys who come to ogle this pulchritudinous parade are the usual yellow-haired, scarlet-skinned, smooth-talking California surfboys who've made a career of starting up conversations with strange women. It's all part of the casual game of pick-up that's more popular out here than volleyball and surfing put together, when you get down to it (which they do, at the least provocation).

Back out in the rippled waters of Long Beach Harbor, one spies a number of what appear to be small resort islands with 10-story hotels built on them. Guess again, Sherlock: they're oil derricks, dressed up to be more appealing from the vantage point of Long Beach. These artificial islands received their designer look from the Walt Disney organization. Named after dead astronauts (e.g., Island Grissom, Island Chaffee), hidden behind high-rise hotel camouflage, bathed in peach and green lights, Long Beach's offshore oil industry is nothing if not innovative.

However, oil doesn't pump up the local economy nearly as much as it did earlier in the century. Black gold was first struck on Signal Hill in 1921. At that time, the Signal Hill Oil Field was the richest in terms of production per acre of any site in the world. It has since been pumped dry and has actually sunk like a fallen soufflé, but there's still oil to be found elsewhere in the area. The gussied-up derricks, we gathered, are something of a sore point in the community.

In the wake of redevelopment, Long Beach is scrambling to offer its sudden tide of credit card–carrying visitors more things to do. A Grand Prix is run on the city streets every April, drawing professional drivers and celebrities from Clint Eastwood down to Ted Nugent. You can float along the canals of *Naples Island*, fashioned after its Italian namesake, in a gondola. Long Beach is also the main gateway to *Catalina Island*. Ferries make the 22-mile trip on a nearly hourly basis, leaving from Catalina Landing in downtown Long Beach.

Though most visitors never see it, there's more to Long Beach than the revived waterfront. It's actually a sprawling city of 380,000, the fifth largest in California, much of which will never receive a monetary touch-up. Blocks and blocks of poor, ethnic and dangerous neighborhoods roll inland. One blighted ghetto bears the colorful name "Dogtown." It's safe to say that this side of Long Beach will not wind up on your vacation agenda.

On a brighter note, the whole *Belmont Shores* area, kind of an annexed residential community along the water in south Long Beach, is a peaceful, attractive neighborhood with excellent beach access along Ocean Boulevard and lively shopping and nightlife along 2nd Street. If you find yourself priced out of the high-rise hotels near the convention center, Belmont Shores is a reasonable alternative. Besides, it's the home of Horny Corners, with sights far more entertaining than anything on the *Queen Mary*.

Accommodations

The $58-million *Hyatt Regency* has become a landmark in the city's downtown renaissance. This 542-room tower is surrounded by glittering lagoons and walkways that lead to *Shoreline Park* and the downtown marina. On-premises features include several restaurants and bars, an exercise room, an outdoor pool and a sauna. From its airplane hangar–sized atrium lobby to the matchless view of the *Queen Mary* from many rooms, the Hyatt is first-class all the way.

Then there's the *Queen Mary* herself. After $20 million in renovations, the old dame reopened in 1981 as the *Hotel Queen Mary*. Her 390 staterooms are the largest ever built aboard a ship. Nowadays, you can sleep on a luxury liner without having to worry about seasickness. There's plenty of everything on this floating city: restaurants, bars, museums, shops, history. It has to rank as the most unusual form of overnight accommodations on the West Coast.

Vestiges of Long Beach's resort past survive at the *Breakers*, a sophisticated hotel built in the twenties and still doing business along Ocean Boulevard. The top floor of this massive, Spanish-revival hotel houses the *Skyroom Restaurant*, with its panoramic view of the harbor and coastline. The 242-room Breakers offers traditional elegance of a sort fast vanishing in Southern California, if it was ever prevalent to begin with. The Breakers, along with the *Villa Riviera* and the *Pacific Ocean Club* (both close by), are architectural landmarks in Long Beach—and a last glimpse at an older California, which is swiftly being swept aside by a new skyline of foreign banks and corporate headquarters executed in glass-and-steel *design moderne*.

Restaurants

Fine dining is a relatively new concept in Long Beach. The restaurant scene here has labored to keep pace with the city's fast-breaking redevelopment program, but these things take time. How do you convince a three-star chef to move to Long Beach? Tell him the oil derricks look like the Eiffel Tower? Nonetheless, it is possible to ante up for more than fish 'n' chips and saloon burgers here, thanks to places like *555 East Restaurant* (a New York–style gourmet eatery housed in a bank building) and *Parker's Lighthouse* (serving the best seafood in town). *Casa Sanchez* gets the locals' endorsement for Mexican food. And don't pass up breakfast or lunch at the *Potholder*, a favorite hangout where omelettes the size of surfboards are served to a drowsy crowd in the collective throes of a morning after.

Everything from Swedish to Turkish cuisine is available in Long Beach, but the most surprising find was a place that served real Southern-style barbecue. The down-home fare at *Johnny Reb's*—pit-cooked barbecue, crackling fried chicken, cole slaw, hushpuppies and home-made pies—had this pair of homesick southerners happier than cold hogs in warm mud.

We can't escape without mentioning *Joe Jost's*. It's the oldest continuously operating bar in California, run by three generations of Josts. Papa Joe, God rest his soul, invented a deli sandwich that has become a local institution. Called Joe's Special, it consists of a hunk of Polish sausage surrounded by a slice of Swiss cheese with a pickle spear stuck into a V-shaped slit, stuffed between mustard-slathered pieces of rye bread and wrapped in a waxed paper handle. Joe Jost's serves hundreds of specials every day for $1.55 each, and likewise for the other house specialty, a basket of pretzels, peppers and pickled eggs. As for the beer served at Joe Jost's—well, read on....

Nightlife

They pump ice-cold Blitz beer, brewed in Oregon, in 20-ounce schooners at *Joe Jost's* for $1.25. This is a deal worth driving across the country for. Joe's is an authentic roaring twenties bar, dating from 1924, that's still roaring in the eighties. The interior is virtually unchanged since those days. A huge back room houses six vintage, 100-year-old carved pool tables, which are nearly always filled. Businesspeople, working stiffs and beautiful losers elbow up to the stainless-steel bar to drink in an egalitarian environment that knows no class barriers. There's never any trouble here. One fight and you're banned for life, and no one wants to be blacklisted from Joe Jost's. What more can we tell you, except that every God-fearing American needs to hoist a goldfish-bowl–sized draft and munch a special at Joe Jost's at least once in his or her life. The original Joe's is on Anaheim Avenue, while a newer one has opened up on Pine Avenue.

From Joe's, if you feel like getting rowdy, Long Beach is your town. Just walk down 2nd Street and pick your spot: *Legends*, a sports bar owned by Dennis Harrah of the Rams; *Panama Joe's*, an upscale meet market that gets good bands on the weekends; or the *Acapulco Inn*, a college bar that's wilder than any toga party John Belushi ever went to. At the "AI," students from nearby Cal State Long Beach cut loose in a party environment so out of control that it's almost a movie-set caricature of hell-raising. The dress code forbids ties; they'll scissor it right off your neck and hang it behind the bar, alongside dozens of other sliced-off neck-wear. The computerized jukebox leans heavily on sixties party favorites, from "Louie, Louie" on down, while an assortment of games (pool, pinball, miniature basketball) keeps all hands busy that aren't squeezing dates or unattached members of the opposite sex. If you can keep up with this crowd, you deserve whatever you wake up with the next morning—a hangover, a fellow party animal, or both.

FOR FURTHER INFORMATION

Long Beach Area Chamber of Commerce
50 Oceangate Plaza
Long Beach, CA 90802
(213) 436-1251

Long Beach Area Convention and Visitors Council
180 East Ocean Boulevard, Suite 150
Long Beach, CA 90802
(213) 436-3645

Santa Catalina Island

To visit Catalina Island is to step back into the past—the prehistoric past, that is. Most of the island—86 percent of its 76 square miles—is owned by the Santa Catalina Island Conservancy, a nonprofit organization dedicated to maintaining it as a wilderness preserve. Consequently, Catalina looks pretty much the way it did when sun-worshiping Indians inhabited it 4,000 years ago. Even the Spaniards who arrived in 1542 with Cabrillo and again in 1602 with Vizcaíno, naming it after St. Catherine, didn't leave any scuff marks behind.

Santa Catalina is a rugged, rocky island 22 miles out to sea. Its dark, green hills rise straight out of the Pacific Ocean to heights of over 2,000 feet. Mount Oriaba, at 2,069 feet, is the highest point on the island. On days when the Santa Ana winds blow Southern California's smog away, Catalina can be clearly seen from Los Angeles Harbor.

Because the natural order has been allowed to prevail, Catalina is a different world from mainland California. The ecosystem is totally unique, with several species of plants and animals endemic only to the island. The most celebrated flora is the Catalina ironwood, a tree that has dwindled to the brink of extinction. Only two wild groves are left. A total of 395 species of plant life are native to the island, and a fascinating variety of animals make their home here as well. Catalina has its own subspecies of ground squirrel and fox, the latter a beautiful but elusive critter. Buffalo freely roam the island. Four hundred of them have grown from the original herd of 14, brought over in 1924 for the filming of *The Vanishing American*. Wild pigs, goats and deer also have the run of Catalina. Somewhere in the interior an actual working ranch, "El Rancho Escondido," raises some of the world's finest Arabian horses.

Okay, so how much can the average person see of these natural wonders if the island is such a tightly controlled conservancy? The answer is not much, really, because the only animal whose movements are restricted on Catalina Island is man. Hiking and backpacking on designated trails is permissible but requires a permit from the Los Angeles County Department of Parks and Recreation. The Catalina Island office is in Avalon, the island's only real population center. The permit costs nothing, but the trails aren't exactly an easy stroll through the clover. Camping requires an additional permit. Reservations are necessary because sites are limited, in order to keep the pristine interior of Catalina Island from becoming overrun. Unless you live here, driving a car on the island is out of the question. The ferries are for passengers only; no cars. And the island is too mountainous for bikes.

All these permits and prohibitions are certainly understandable and commendable. They keep the island free of roving bimbos and beer-gutted Jeep cowboys waving pistols at the mountain goats. The flip side is that you are off-loaded into a veritable encampment known as Avalon and expected to stay put. Avalon is on the eastern shore of Catalina, facing the mainland. Passenger ferries from San Pedro, Long Beach and Newport Beach dock here, making the town something of a tourist-oriented side pocket on the empty green billiard table of Catalina Island. If you arrive by ferry, as most folks do, you will be stuck in Avalon with the buffalo burger blues.

The first person we encountered after walking the ferry gangplank into Avalon was a bearded son of a gun with a sailor's cap on his gnarled web of red hair who pronounced himself our man.

Translated, this meant that for a modest fee he'd tote our bags to the hotel, which he warned was "all the way over on the other side of town." Be forewarned, folks: he is not your man. Avalon is all of 20 feet wide (actually, it covers one square mile), and if you can't walk to your hotel from the ferry landing, you've never been to a modest-sized shopping mall.

There are means by which one can see other parts of the island. Bus tours depart Avalon regularly. The most reasonable of these is the Skyline Drive, a 1¾-hour trip that takes you 10 miles into the heart of the conservancy. The Inland Motor Tour is a 3¾-hour expanded version of the same. Glass-bottomed boats display the prodigious underwater life in the clear, blue-green waters surrounding the island. Other boat tours explore the rougher, less-visited waters on the windward western side.

If you're boating over on a summer weekend, expect to be joined by a flood of traffic, as a flotilla of pleasure craft regularly turns the mainland-to-Catalina channel into a watery version of the Santa Ana Freeway. Some people even swim over from the mainland. Each year, they hold an Ocean Marathon, the record time for the passage being 7½ hours.

The salvation of our visit to Catalina Island was not a boat, a bus or even a buffalo burger. It was a golf cart. Everyone uses them on Catalina, and they can be rented for $15 an hour or $50 for all day. In two hours, we saw everything we needed to see, traveling the arrow-marked route into the hills behind Avalon. We probably saw some things we weren't supposed to see, too, but hey—it's hard to tell which roads are okay and which are restricted. We got enough of a feel for the natural riches that lay beyond Avalon to make us fantasize about a backpacking expedition at some later date. Perhaps another lifetime.

The most interesting course to steer your golf cart along is south out of Avalon on Pebbly Beach Road. This state route hugs the shoreline, revealing placid waters with a rocky bottom—perfect for snorkeling or skin-diving but not so hot for swimming. After two miles, the road turns inland, up a steep and winding grade that peaks at Mount Ada and the Wrigley Mansion. Incredible as it may seem, Catalina Island used to belong to William Wrigley

Jr., the chewing-gum magnate and owner of the Chicago Cubs. Upon his death, he deeded the island to the organization that maintains it as a nature conservancy.

If you keep your golf cart pointed along the roadway, you'll pass the second oldest golf course in the country (a nine-holer slapped into this rugged canyon in 1892) and the now-overgrown field where the Chicago Cubs held spring training for 26 years, from 1921 to 1951 (with four years off for war). A trivia note here: Ronald Reagan, the Cubs' radio announcer, often followed them to Catalina. Finally, just up Avalon Canyon Road from the golf course lies the William Wrigley, Jr., Memorial and Botanical Gardens.

The Wrigley Memorial, set at the top of the gardens, is an imposing structure. It took a year to build, and its 232-foot by 130-foot dimensions dwarf the surrounding canyon like an absurdly misplaced Lincoln Memorial. Plaques boast about its tonnage, craftsmanship and sturdiness. One hundred thirty-four thousand sacks of white cement met 9,900 sacks of gray cement head-on, the resulting block held together by 114 tons of steel. "The building is dedicated to William Wrigley, Jr.," reads a plaque at the courtyard entrance, "who in 1919 recognized the potential of Santa Catalina as a nature preserve." Set beside a nice prickly pear or a grove of ironwood, a plaque alone would probably have sufficed as an acknowledgment of Wrigley's generosity, don't you think?

The botanical gardens, though, are a pleasure to stroll through. Laid out in sections, they feature Catalina's endemics as well as oddities from around the world, like South Africa's red-hot poker. An entire area is given over to some of the strangest cacti ever collected in one place.

One other noteworthy attraction is the Casino, a Mediterranean-style structure built by Wrigley on Avalon's waterfront in 1929. It dominates the harbor the way his memorial overwhelms the Avalon Canyon. At one time, big bands blew hot and cool in the ballroom of this nongambling casino. Today, the Catalina Island Museum is housed in the basement, and first-run movies play on the main floor.

Accommodations

Our first night's lodging on Catalina Island reminded us of Paul Simon's song "Duncan," the one with the lines, "Couple in the next room bound to win a prize/They've been goin' at it all night long." We would therefore like to dedicate "Duncan" to the *Hotel Villa Portofino*, the Mediterranean "villa" we holed up in one night. The brochure had promised "a touch of Old World elegance and luxury." If this is what the old world was all about, we now understand the Boston Tea Party completely. At the Villa Portofino, "Old World" means a windowless room with cot-sized beds, tiny shower stalls and nothing to protect you from noisy neighbors. For this, you pay $80 and up per night. We're not wimps. We've been known to sleep in car seats and on top of picnic tables. But the noise level at the Villa Portofino kept us up all night. There's no excuse for this on Catalina Island.

A night later, we found sanctuary at the *Pavilion Lodge*, along Avalon's harbor front. The lodge spreads back from Crescent Street into a landscaped courtyard. The rooms are quiet and very comfortable. For curiosity seekers, the Pavilion Lodge owns a two-ton piece of redwood that drifted onto the island from the mainland and was placed in their courtyard garden with the help of several trucks, tractors and laborers.

Another outstanding hotel in town is the *Glenmore Plaza*. This pastel-tinted beauty is a century old, having hosted such eminences as Teddy Roosevelt and Clark Gable. The wicker-filled rooms are airy and large, and the room rate (which ranges from $70 to $120, more for suites) includes wine and cheese in the courtyard each afternoon and a continental breakfast. Incidentally, the crowds throng to Catalina from May through August, but the island is no less charming (and much less crowded) during the "undiscovered season," from September through April.

Restaurants

Around dinnertime one evening, an elderly gentleman with hearing aids attached to both ears stood wheezing in front of a seafood restaurant on Crescent Street, Avalon's waterfront thoroughfare.

Winded from his search for a suitable meal—a stroll that had covered three blocks and several posted menus—he turned on his wife
when she suggested they eat at a place with a "pot roast and potato pancake" special. "I'm not going to put that junk in my mouth!"
he cried in frustration. Propped up by a cane, he shuffled farther
down the street, determined to find something that wasn't both
overpriced and ordinary.

Most visitors who come to Catalina Island find themselves in
the, ahem, same boat. A hungry army, they wander the quaint
Mediterranean streets of Avalon, studying one menu after another
for some clue to its cuisine. Much of the seafood is, believe it or
not, brought over from the mainland. Even on the *Green Pleasure
Pier*, an open-air fish 'n' chips hut, *Avalon Seafood*, serves bland,
measly portions of fried seafood. They also offer an Abalone
Burger, a seemingly tragic waste of a vanishing animal. Speaking
of disappearing species, their competition on the pier sells Buffalo
Burgers, described by a distracted woman on a stool as "leaner
than beef." Even Avalon's finest restaurant proved a bit suspect.
The *Ristorante Villa Portofino*, an Italian restaurant in the aforemen-
tioned hotel, boasts real cloth tablecloths, a decent wine list and
an intricate menu. But on closer inspection, the posted review
proclaiming it Avalon's finest restaurant turned out to be a thinly
veiled pan.

In general, the cuisine of Avalon is stacked against the visitor.
We finally settled on *Antonio's Pizzeria*, simply because the sign in
the window said: "This restaurant has been declared a genuine
Catalina bomb shelter—come on in and bask in the ambience of
the decaying 50's while the world passes on." It's a fun, loosy-
goosy place with a fifties jukebox and a billion knickknacks on the
wall from that otherworldly era. Roasted peanuts are served as an
appetizer. You don't ask for them; they just shovel them out of a
barrel onto a paper plate and slap it on the table. The rest of the
menu is no more complicated than cold beer and pizza. Beats the
hell out of a buffalo burger.

Nightlife

Unless you know someone at the members-only *Catalina Yacht Club* or the members-only *Tuna Club* (the oldest sportfishing club in the world, founded in 1898 and featuring such diverse members as Zane Grey, Winston Churchill, Richard Nixon, King Olaf IV and Hal Roach), your nightlife could turn out to be as humble as the lonely buffalo's. The only live music we could scare up was someone named Tony Baloney, a self-professed human jukebox who knows 500 folk songs and takes requests. The best place to drink sans entertainment of Baloney's ilk is *J.L.'s Locker Room*, a sports bar that caters to a mixed crowd (i.e., it's not too macho for women). Rams, Angels and Dodgers photos adorn the wall, some inscribed to J.L. himself by players who've come all the way to Catalina Island to quaff a cold one at his bar.

FOR FURTHER INFORMATION

Avalon/Catalina Chamber of Commerce
P.O. Box 217
Avalon, CA 90704
(213) 510-1520

County of Los Angeles
Department of Parks and Recreation
P.O. Box 1133
Avalon, CA 90704
(213) 510-0688

San Pedro
Palos Verdes Peninsula

The enormous land area known as the Palos Verdes Peninsula, located in the southwest corner of Los Angeles County, is one that will, as Muhammad Ali used to say, shock and amaze ya. As is the case up in the northern part of the county—with the Santa Monica Mountains, the Malibu Peninsula and the Hollywood

Hills—the nearly empty Palos Verdes Peninsula is an example of the incredible diversity of land forms to be found in and around the City of Angels. The craggy, lunarlike peninsula rises out of the smog dish of the Los Angeles Basin and sticks into the fresh air of the Pacific just above the port town of San Pedro, site of Los Angeles Harbor. The latter is one of the world's largest artificial harbors, covering 7,000 acres and 28 miles of waterfront.

The Palos Verdes Peninsula is no party to this. Even though its jagged, cliff-lined shore embraces 15 miles of Pacific coastline, from San Pedro around the point to Torrance, the Coast Highway doesn't come near the peninsula. Instead, it moves inland, leaving the tough, shifting terrain of the peninsula to the hermitic wishes of the rich folks who live out here. If you want to drive around the peninsula, you must follow a series of small, winding back roads that pass through a quaking, unsettled landscape. Along this Jell-O-like terrain, a road sign warns of "Constant Land Movement Next 8 Miles." What could this mean, we wondered: Free souvenir earthquakes? A road that jiggles like the 25-cent "Magic Fingers" in old hotel rooms? What it means is that sections of the road, particularly in the vicinity of Portuguese Bend, look like they've just been removed from a waffle iron and have more dips in them than an amusement-park roller coaster.

The land here actually moves at the rate of one to six inches a month and has been doing so since the midfifties, when highway blasting caused the top layer of rock to separate from and slowly begin slipping over the lower (a phenomenon known as block-glide). However, you will find yourself holding your breath for reasons other than fear, as one beautiful panorama follows another until you work your way off the peninsula at Torrance. It is a completely unexpected and pleasurable way to enter the back door of Los Angeles.

At one time, the entire peninsula was the "rancho" of the Sepulveda family, until they sold it in 1914 to a company with plans to develop it as a "millionaire's colony." To that end, they called in the landscape firm of Olmstead and Olmstead (sons of Frederick Law Olmstead, the man responsible for New York's Central Park). Trees were planted on the barren lands, houses were built among them, and the millionaires dug in for the long haul. They're still dug in out here, although land movement has driven many to abandon the sloping Portuguese Bend area. The houses that didn't slip into the Pacific have been sold off for a song to intrepid souls unafraid to live in them. Yet the neighborhoods behind the falling ridge remain some of the most exclusive in Los Angeles.

The small, sandy coves that pass for beaches on the peninsula are difficult to get to. Still, where there's a beach, there's a way, even out on Palos Verdes. The most visited are *Malaga Cove* and *Abalone Cove County Beach*. Malaga Cove is the only true sand beach on the peninsula, and it's popular with surfers and swimmers who climb down with their boards and towels from the paved accessway. Abalone Cove, which straddles the legendary Portuguese Bend, is alleged to be popular with nudists.

Even if you don't take the plunge to the beaches, the cliff-hugging route along the outer rim of the peninsula makes for a worthwhile afternoon drive. The splendid architecture is something every developer should witness and learn from. Hidden among the trees and hills, the human habitations don't even try to compete with the grandeur of the landscape. This philosophy of architectural noninterference reaches a zenith with Wayfarers Chapel, located on the mainland side of the road just beyond Portuguese Bend. Built in 1946 by Lloyd Wright (son of Frank), the predominantly glass edifice makes worshipers feel as if they're outdoors. It is open to the public daily from eleven to four.

One last note to be sounded is an obituary for Marineland of the Pacific. Built on the peninsula in 1954, Marineland was once the home and playpen for a small population of Flippers, Orcas and Jaws. The three-ring aquatic circus is now, alas, closed down. The park's inaccessibility is the reason given for its financial demise. The property, at the time of our visit, was in the process of being sold—presumably to a multimillionaire with a penchant for very large swimming pools.

FOR FURTHER INFORMATION

San Pedro Chamber of Commerce
390 West 7th Street
P.O. Box 167
San Pedro, CA 90733
(213) 832-7272

Redondo Beach

Redondo is the Spanish word for "round," as in round and round it goes and where you wind up, nobody knows. Redondo Beach is a very confusing place to find your way around in because there is no single area you can point to as the center of town. There are instead several different pockets of retail and recreational activity, and in trying to find your way from one to another, "you can't get there from here" seems to apply.

A glance at a street map of Redondo Beach reveals a town shaped like a bow tie, arranged on a southwesterly diagonal and straddling both sides of the Pacific Coast Highway. The inland area, known as north Redondo, flares out toward the Los Angeles International Airport. It's a mostly middle-class neighborhood, parts of which are affordable to the surfers and sixties dropouts who grew up on the beach but can no longer keep pace with spiraling real-estate prices there.

South Redondo, on the water, is where the action is. Redondo Beach is the friendliest of the three beach towns that bunch up against the Palos Verdes Peninsula in the southwestern corner of Los Angeles. Unlike neighboring Hermosa Beach and Manhattan Beach, the residents of Redondo actually want you to come here. They are, in fact, waiting impatiently for streams of visitors to patronize the waterfront malls and plazas that have been constructed in anticipatory tribute to the tourist dollar.

In south Redondo are found all the hubs that keep Redondo Beach rolling: the yup-scale browsing and grazing district known as Riviera Village; the Redondo Municipal Pier, with its massive

Seaport Village and International Boardwalk, boasting row upon row of sit-down restaurants and stand-up food stalls; the King Harbor area, where the wealthy park their boats and cars and file into trendy restaurant-lounge complexes like the Red Onion and Charley Brown's. Then there is *Redondo City Beach*, which runs along a road called the Esplanade from the pier south to Torrance County Beach. The beach is very wide, the ocean a brilliant blue under nearly always sunny skies.

One of the features of the beachfront is the South Bay Bicycle Trail, a paved freeway for bikes, roller skates, skateboards and runners. Even the odd walker can be spotted on the trail, although mere strolling is generally too undemanding for the fitness-crazed Southern Californians. The 18-mile bike trail begins up in Malibu, winding through and around Redondo's King Harbor–Municipal Pier area before resuming a straight and steady course south along the city beach and finally terminating at the bluffs along the Palos Verdes Peninsula.

Cruising the strand on a single-speed bicycle is a popular pastime. In the South Bay area, climatic conditions almost mandate outdoor activity. The mercury rarely falls below 45 degrees in January or climbs above 75 degrees in July. Los Angeles' chronic halo of smog doesn't choke the beaches of the South Bay. Cooling offshore breezes ensure that the air is generally clean and skies blue in Redondo.

And so Redondo Beach sits, in all its gleaming Mediterranean splendor, waiting to be discovered. For the most part, everything you'd expect to find in a vacation destination is here, except the vacationers. Signs of underuse can be seen in such no-go developments as Pier Plaza, a promenade of octagonal wood shoppes trimmed in bright blue that look down on the horseshoe-shaped Municipal Pier and International Boardwalk. While the pier below bustles with tourists and fishers, Pier Plaza is a ghost town where even the Wendy's franchise seems doomed. At this point, it seems to be a case of too many shops and too few buyers (a variation on the too many condos, too few tenants theme we'd seen all over Southern California). But you can't expect miracles overnight. Things have only lately turned around for Redondo Beach, and the town is just now figuring out how to spread the word about itself.

Up until 10 years ago, Redondo was considered the ghetto of the South Bay. The town's real estate suddenly became desirable when rising property values forced longtime residents of wealthier Hermosa Beach and Manhattan Beach to move elsewhere. Redondo will itself surely become prohibitively expensive in due time, but for the present it's regarded as a friendly, attractive and relatively affordable village. This much is true: you don't have any sense of being near Los Angeles, even though you're rubbing right against its underside.

The history of Redondo Beach dates back to the late 1890s, when a trio of Spanish-heiress sisters sold the sand dunes they inherited to developers. Shipping was an important early industry, but after Redondo vied for and lost the fight to have the Port of Los Angeles established here, the town turned to tourism. A huge luxury hotel, along with tent cities for the less privileged, drew vacationers to the pristine beach. The Hotel Redondo—opened in 1890, stupidly torn down in 1926—was the sister establishment of the splendid Hotel del Coronado down the coast. During Redondo's heyday in the early decades of the century, folks would chuck tokens into the fabled Pacific Electric "red cars" and ride the rails from downtown Los Angeles to the beach.

Redondo Beach had it all: big-band ballrooms, offshore gambling ships reached by water taxis, and a huge, heated indoor saltwater pool called the Plunge. A Hawaiian named George Freeth was brought over to demonstrate the strange new sport of surfing to curious onlookers out behind the Hotel Redondo. He was tagged "the man who walked on water" (in a purely secular sense, of course), and a statue of him decorates the south end of the horseshoe pier.

Redondo's glory days are documented in the Redondo Beach Historical Museum, but really this is not a town obsessed with the past. To the contrary, modern Redondo Beach caters to and is built around the lifestyle of the New Californian who lives here. To generalize, this person works in real estate or the aerospace industry; runs, roller-skates, jazz dances, plays volleyball and lifts weights; and has decided not to raise a family in order to maximize the personal pleasures to be derived from making a lot of money and living at the beach. The only thing missing

from Redondo Beach's picture-postcard dreams of big-time afflu-
ence is a thriving tourist industry—and they're working on that
right now.

Accommodations

Back in the days of the Hotel Redondo, it was a major boon to
have a bathroom on every floor. Times have changed. Now we
have a bathroom in every room and a telephone in every bathroom.
The Hotel Redondo is long gone, but the *Palos Verdes Inn* is a suitable latter-day equivalent. The inn is about a half mile from
Redondo City Beach along a curve in the Pacific Coast Highway
where it begins to skirt the uplands of the Palos Verdes Peninsula.
Just a block away is Riviera Village, which has a neighborhood
atmosphere and plenty of shops, restaurants and bars. The inn itself is a self-contained city, with an excellent continental restaurant (*Chez Mélange*), gourmet deli (*Chez Allez*), big-band-revisited
supper club (the *Strand*) and a half-acre pool, spa and gardens on
the premises.

Additionally, some cheaper, older motels line the Coast Highway and a new high-rise *Sheraton* has appeared on the waterfront
in the King Harbor area. Building on the waterfront, though, is a
risky proposition. Witness the *Portofino*, an oceanfront hotel whose
first floor was destroyed by marauding waves during a freak winter storm in late 1987.

Restaurants

As befits a would-be tourist town, restaurants crowd Redondo
Beach from stem to stern, especially on the pier and around King
Harbor. There's little but restaurants on the Municipal Pier and
the International Boardwalk behind it. These range from coffee
shops to ethnic-cuisine stalls and long-established places like *Tony's
Fish Market Restaurant* and the *Cattleman*. Tony's has been around
since 1952, selling fresh seafood over the counter and at the table,
while the Cattleman deals in steaks.

A newer arrival on the pier, the *Breakers*, grills fish over mesquite wood. While waiting for your order, you can read the four-page *Breakers Seafood Journal*, a combination menu and collection of facts about fish. Did you know, for instance, that a female halibut can reach a weight of 800 pounds? By the way, the view over the water from any of the pier restaurants is terrific.

As for other parts of town, the *Blue Moon Saloon* in King Harbor is a good bet for seafood and is also a popular nightspot. Over in Riviera Village, the *Catalina Grill* serves healthy Cal-nouvelle cuisine in an atmosphere as pleasant as a beach cabana. Where else but in Southern California could you order something like "Mesquite Grilled Tequila Chicken with Avocado Butter"?

Nightlife

In Redondo Beach, as in so many California beach towns, franchise bars wind up commanding most of the business. *Hennessey's* in Riviera Village and the *Red Onion* in King Harbor draw the biggest crowds. Hennessey's is a pseudo-Irish bar with an informal atmosphere and happily buzzing crowd through which pert waitresses in khaki shorts circulate. The Red Onion is more of a get-down-and-party type of place. They don't mess around here: the deejay hurls relentless innuendos over the mike, even interrupting songs to heckle the crowd. Footage of bikini competitions plays on wall-mounted TVs, and there's some kind of amateur hot-bod contest every night of the week. The strip-off we witnessed was a drawn-out exercise in PG-rated voyeurism. The winner, who had her moves down to a science, was all of 19 years old—and, poor thing, was yawning all the way through it.

FOR FURTHER INFORMATION

Redondo Beach Chamber of Commerce
1215 North Catalina Avenue
Redondo Beach, CA 90277
(213) 376-6911

Hermosa Beach

The letter to the editor of *Easy Rider*, Hermosa Beach's giveaway paper, said it all: "The nemesis of Hermosa Beach that there's just no getting around [is] parking." Amen, sister. The complaint about parking holds true for those on both sides of the issue—the ones who live here and those just visiting for the afternoon. Hermosa Beach, a town of 22,000 occupying one square mile of prime L.A. beachfront real estate, does not take well to the summertime swarm that migrates seaward from such concrete-bunker wastelands as Torrance, Hawthorne and Compton. They get them right where it hurts: the car, the motorized pod that's vital component of every Angelino's life-support system.

In other words, they make it difficult as hell to park here. In all our many years of travel, we have never seen a town where parking-meter charges are enforced 24 hours a day. Welcome to Hermosa Beach. They are serious about this racket. No sooner had we pulled up to the curb, cut off the engine and taken two giant steps in the direction of a convenience store for change to feed the hungry meter when a meter maid (who was no Lovely Rita) began writing us a ticket—and was loath to stop writing it, even after we explained the situation. The private lots are costly. Some of the merchants, desperate for business, sling banners above their storefronts that read, "Free Validated Parking."

The other side of the coin is that often those who live here wind up losing the game of musical parking spaces. Consider this tale of woe from the letter writer quoted above: "Not long ago, my husband and I dared risk the parking fate when we returned [home] after picking up friends. Unfortunately, as expected, there wasn't a single parking space in sight for miles, so in lieu of driving in circles all night, we decided to park in our driveway. Now, if anyone has ever made a personal appearance to City Hall to pay for a parking ticket, you know this is the sin of all sins. We were *blocking the sidewalk*."

What's that line you always see on T-shirts in Southern California—"Another Shitty Day in Paradise"? Always a hassle, even under the best circumstances.

It's easy to understand why those who live here are so put out.

They pay a king's ransom and probably work 60-hour weeks to afford their yardless, boxlike stucco homes. These $150,000 cubes are pressed so close together that neighbors can shake hands without leaving their houses. The median income in this upper-crust-community is $50,000 (the highest in the South Bay), and many couples have chosen to go childless so they can continue to live in the manner to which they've grown accustomed. Hermosa Beach is a community of DINKs, in other words: Dual Income, No Kids.

For all their money, there's little the DINKs can do when the burger-and-brew rowdies from points east infiltrate Hermosa Beach on evenings and weekends. Somehow, these invaders find a way to keep the meters happy and, oblivious to the general tone of unwelcome, party hearty. As a result, Hermosa Beach is a curious collage of upscale and low-rent. Trendy Hermosa Avenue is lined with stores like the China Syndrome (dinnerware, of course), the Strawberry Patch Café and the Either/Or Bookstore. Down on Pier Avenue, on the other hand, a string of rock and roll bars faces a street patrolled by skateboard punks and bushy-haired bikers.

We are not complaining, mind you. A town is always more interesting when it partakes of both ends of the socioeconomic spectrum, and the underside gives Hermosa Beach a shot of character, much as it does in Newport Beach. Notably absent, though, are surf shops. That's because there isn't much surf in Hermosa. Apparently, the breakwater knocks the waves down to a size that only novices and locals have any fun with. Thus, the predominant activities on *Hermosa City Beach* are volleyball and roller-skating. Volleyball nets occupy a healthy corner of the broad, mile-long beach. The South Bay Bicycle Path—the paved marvel that runs from Malibu to Redondo—is sometimes the busiest thoroughfare in Hermosa Beach. A steady stream of joggers, roller skaters, skateboarders and cyclists flows in both directions in a more or less orderly fashion. Although everyone is moving at different speeds, this complex symphony of motion somehow plays through without a lot of spills or serious collisions.

Not that you won't be warned about watching it . After all, this is Hermosa Beach. In keeping with their fetish for regulations and ordinances, they've posted enough broadsides forbidding things on the beach to make you turn around and go home (that is, if you were able to find a parking space to begin with). But don't be deterred—there's plenty of beach to go around here. It's asphalt they're short on.

Accommodations

Because this is a residential community, there are few motels in Hermosa Beach—even along the Pacific Coast Highway, which is otherwise jammed with gas stations and restaurants—and only one directly on the beach. The *Sea Sprite Oceanfront Apartment Motel* is a welcome anomaly. First of all, it's so near the ocean that you couldn't be any closer except on a surfboard. The Sea Sprite goes against the prevailing winds of exclusivity, being an informal yet well-tended family motel. The prices are reasonable at $74 for a double room in season. They also rent apartment-style cottages, which cost approximately twice as much but can accommodate four or more. From the second-floor pool deck you can watch the world skate by on the bike path or just enjoy the ocean breeze. Incredibly enough, they've even managed to shoehorn in a parking space for every room. There's nothing fancy about the Sea Sprite, but when you're right on the ocean, who needs marble bathrooms and remote-control TV?

Restaurants

Hermosa Beach is sufficiently cosmopolitan to support a high-quality, ethnically diverse restaurant scene. You can ante up for Italian, French, Greek, Mexican, Arabian, Japanese, Korean, Thai, Chinese, Brazilian and even Albanian cuisine in this village. Nutrition is a prime consideration, and sushi just might be the favorite food of all. There are more sushi bars here than you can shake a chopstick at. One of these, *Paradise Sushi*, takes the unusual step of offering an "all you can eat" sushi dinner for $13.90. You've got 90 minutes to pack it in, so on your mark, get set...

Down on Pier Avenue, *Sushi Sei* offers sushi, soup, loud background music and an attempted comedy routine from the sushi chefs for under $10. It's hard to miss; just look for the enormous Japanese mural over the door. Around the corner on Hermosa Avenue, *California Beach Sushi* is yet another popular spot to eat it raw.

If you're on a budget, you can always duck into the *Fish Market Café* for a charbroiled fish sandwich or get a basket of fish 'n' chips at the funky-looking snack shed on the end of Hermosa's 1,320-foot municipal pier.

Nightlife

Like a stack of dominoes, four loud clubs line the south side of Pier Avenue in a row. It might be you, however, that's falling over by the end of the evening. This town rocks hard after dark. Every place books live bands, the music tending toward bar-band rock and roll, with blues-and-boogie duking it out with fifties and sixties cover acts. Your choices are *Hennessey's* (Irish-style chain bar that never fails to draw a crowd); the *Lighthouse* (former jazz club turned rock and roll bistro); the *End Zone* (a sports bar); and *Pier 52* (loose, cheap and rowdier than a Lynyrd Skynyrd concert). Beer is a bargain at the latter. You can buy a small pitcher at Pier 52 for the price of a single bottle at the Lighthouse. If you're on a budget, this may matter. If not, then do the Teaberry Shuffle down Pier Avenue until you hear a band you want to spend the night with. Then order up, have fun, and damn the parking meters.

Animal-house rock and roll isn't everyone's idea of a good time, and we're told the Hermosa Beach natives gravitate toward places like *Charley Brown's* and the *Red Onion* in Redondo Beach. Both places cater to a crowd characterized by a Hermosa Beach motel clerk as "full yuppie."

FOR FURTHER INFORMATION

Hermosa Beach Chamber of Commerce
323 Pier Avenue
P.O. Box 404
Hermosa Beach, CA 90254
(213) 376-0951

Manhattan Beach

The most salient event in Manhattan Beach's history was the naming of the town. The tale begins in 1902, when Stewart Merrill, a native New Yorker, acquired a portion of the 10-mile oceanfront land grant known as Rancho Sausal Redondo. When it came time to christen their sandy gold mine, Merrill and his business partner couldn't agree on a name. Merrill won the subsequent coin toss and, presumably homesick for the Big Apple, named it Manhattan Beach. This passes for history in Southern California.

You could almost flip a coin today attempting to discern the differences among the three beach towns—Redondo, Hermosa and Manhattan—strung out along the southern edge of Santa Monica Bay. The three have more similarities than differences. For starters, they're linked by the concrete South Bay Bicycle Trail, which does double duty as a boardwalk, and they all strive to cultivate as low-key a personality as possible, given their proximity to Los Angeles. Manhattan Beach is the most family-oriented and residential. Although its 2,300 acres are as developed as a gleaming suburb can be, Manhattan Beach seems to be in full control of its growth. The line of natural dunes hasn't been bulldozed away, and building heights have been held down to a bearable level. This fact, coupled with the town's sudden, San Francisco–like dip toward the ocean, allows those who live here a good, invigorating view of the Pacific. You feel the ocean, like a permanent drive-in movie whose purpose is to make you forget the freeway gridlock of Los Angeles.

Manhattan Beach's two-mile oceanfront is completely residential. The clean, sandy beach is bisected by a 900-foot pier and backed by a seawall adorned with tasteful murals. The remainder of Manhattan Beach's four square miles is packed crowbar-tight with tidy but not ostentatious homes. The typical front yard consists of a square foot of bleached pebbles and a dark green bush. The only real evidence of big-time development in Manhattan Beach is a 187-acre business park that sits, like an embarrassed Fashion Island, on the east end of town, five miles from Los Angeles International Airport and across the avenue from a smoke-belching power plant.

As the game of real-estate roulette picks up momentum, though, the family neighborhoods of Manhattan Beach are being seriously threatened by the specter of big bucks. The town's 33,500 residents do not want to be driven from Manhattan Beach by an army of wealthy come-latelies. Already, citizens are skirmishing with developers. The following was excerpted from a letter to the *Beach Reporter*, a local weekly:

Mr. Bush states that the current trend of residential development in the city is purely a matter of economics, that as land value increases, the longtime residents of Manhattan Beach should cash in their chips and move elsewhere, preferably to a place where land values are low....Once there, they could buy a larger house on several acres of wasteland where they could spend the rest of their days counting the profits derived from the sale of the home in which children grew up enjoying the beaches, the trees and the picturesque atmosphere that has made Manhattan Beach such a desirable place to live.

Indeed, it is a desirable little town. Inside the snug city limits are 13 churches, 2 libraries and 5 parks, one of which provides the setting for Sunday afternoon concerts during the summer. The businesses here are the sort of inconspicuous boutiques obsessive shoppers love to believe they've discovered for themselves. Even the local 7-Eleven goes the extra mile to make you feel well taken care of. Not only can you buy a cup of coffee, you're given a choice of three flavors: cinnamon, vanilla and amaretto. Ah, California.

Accommodations

There are no motels or hotels to be found on the beach in Manhattan Beach. The closest you can get is on the north side of town, three steep uphill blocks from the sea on Highland Avenue. The *Sea View Inn* is the most appealing of several choices. There are only eight rooms, but they encircle a swimming pool away from the noise of the busy street. Besides, prices are moderate for this neck of the woods.

The Radisson chain refers to its hotels as a "collection," like the abstract modern art that fills their hallways and lobbies. Lately, they've added another luxury aircraft carrier to their collection, the *Radisson Plaza Hotel* in Manhattan Beach. Presumably built to service the traveling execs who land at nearby LAX, the Radisson is shaped like a stack of after-dinner mints and fits the arid architectural mold of the adjoining business park. There's a golf course behind it and tennis courts beside it, but the hotel itself has about as much personality as a briefcase. It's also a three-mile drive to the beach, and double rooms start at $175—a stiff price made possible by our nation's tax laws, which allow corporations who stash their suited minions here to write it off.

Restaurants

Against our guiding principles, we succumbed to Mexican food again. We ended up at *El Macho Café* not because we heard its food was so much better than the seafood restaurants in town, but because they were running a special on Corona beer, *por favor*. Then, too, it was late, and most everything else was closed. Fortunately, the food was good, and we had the unique experience of visiting a salsa bar—sort of a salad bar offering different types of salsa, which vary in heat, color and flavor.

Nightlife

A local rag dubbed *La Paz* the "king of the beach bars" and "Animal House at the beach." It's a good one, no question about it. Located a volleyball serve away from the Manhattan Beach Pier, La Paz is chaotic in a friendly way, filled with a mixed beach crowd who have one thing, thirst, in common. Well, they're all Lakers fans, too. Every wooden surface in the place has been carved on, and the bar furnishings have seen better days. But this is exactly what you expect from a beach bar: pinball machines in one corner, sleeping dog in another, a game flickering on TV, beer sold by the pitcher.

The *Shellback Tavern*, just across the street, is no less friendly, and they serve food, too (mostly pizza, burgers and tacos). On the middle ground of Highland Avenue sits a franchise Irish pub, *Brennan's*, that's wild and crazy by franchise pub standards. They advertise "crab races" every Tuesday, for instance.

FOR FURTHER INFORMATION

Manhattan Beach Chamber of Commerce
P.O. Box 3007
Manhattan Beach, CA 90266
(213) 545-5313

Playa del Rey

Playa del Rey is a largely residential town built along streets that dead-end into a lagoon near the beach and on top of towering bluffs that look out over the beach. The chief calling card is *Dockweiler State Beach*, which runs from Manhattan Beach to the Del Rey Lagoon, a distance of about five miles. Across the lagoon lies Venice; behind it, along constructed waterways, Marina del Rey.

The word "wide" does not begin to describe the sandy expanse at Dockweiler. The beaches of Los Angeles County, extended shoreward with dredged-up sand and landfill, can handle lots of people. Even with all of Los Angeles knocking at the back door, such beaches as Dockweiler, Venice and Santa Monica seldom reach the saturation point. Parking in lots on the beach at Dockweiler costs $4 a day, and beware—you cannot make a U-turn once you approach the booth where they bag your four clams. Free parking can be found along the Pacific Coast Highway and on the side streets of Playa del Rey.

Marina del Rey

Like a hand with eight fingers, the yacht basin at Marina del Rey reaches inland, grabbing Los Angeles by the seat of the pants. It is the world's largest constructed small-craft basin, accommodating 5,878 boats in the water and another 3,000 in dry dock. The total number of boats in Marina del Rey is greater than the number of people who live here. Sails, sails everywhere and not a beach to swim on. Actually there is one, though it looks more like a lakeside than an ocean beach. At the end of Basin D a small, mushroom-shaped public beach faces the quiet waters of the lagoon, enabling calm-water swimming as well as wind-free sunbathing.

Admiralty Way runs in a great horseshoe around the harbor. It is along this royal boulevard that the moneyed heart of Marina del Rey can be heard to pound. Every boat slip is full, and there's a waiting list a nautical mile long. Posted in the window of the town's principal yacht broker are listings for used boats, ranging in price from a low of "only" $69,000 (for a Hatteras Sport Fisher with new engines) to $175,000 (for a 46-foot Venus ketch). A lot of boat owners rarely sail their prizes out of port. A small number live aboard their floating fortresses, but the vast majority own a boat simply to own a boat. They've got that kind of expendable income out here; we're afraid to ask where it comes from. (As an interesting footnote, Dennis Wilson of the Beach Boys drowned here.)

The story of how Marina del Rey was built is an intriguing one. As far back as 1887, a developer named M. C. Wicks proposed turning the Playa del Rey estuary and inlet into a major commercial harbor. His plans ultimately came to naught, as did all subsequent attempts at harbor development until 1954, when President Eisenhower authorized federal support of the Marina del Rey project. Serious construction of entrance channel jetties, under the joint auspices of the feds and the County of Los Angeles, began in 1957. It was not all smooth sailing, however. Storm damage to the harbor in the winter of 1962 necessitated the hasty construction of a $4.2 million offshore breakwater. The small-craft harbor was completed in 1965, but it's still not clear why so much federal money was spent constructing what is essentially a parking lot for rich folks' pleasure craft. Nevertheless, Marina del Rey has blossomed like a cactus flower out of its desertlike surroundings in only two decades. An impressive retail industry of waterfront restaurants, luxury hotels, big-city nightlife and specialty shops has grown around the harbor. In Marina del Rey you can, as a brochure proclaims, browse for everything "from socks to solid gold."

Marina del Rey is a community defined not by the collective personality of the people who live here (because many of the people you see *don't* live here), but by the multitude of services it offers boat owners. Signs heralding one's arrival in Marina del Rey offer this detailed list: "Apartments, Berths, Chandlery, Hotels, Launching, Maintenance, Moorings, Motels, Restaurants, Shops, Sportfishing, Town Houses, Yacht Sales." Yes, but where can a body go to get a simple cup of coffee? In Marina del Rey, we learned, you don't get a cup of coffee; you are served a steaming tankard of cappuccino, and it'll set you back $2 or so. If you're coming to Marina del Rey, scale your expectations and your expenses upward. Think mink.

From a distance, Marina del Rey looks as incongruous in its surroundings as Las Vegas, with two cube-shaped bank buildings rising from what appears to be barren desert. As you spiral closer to Admiralty Way—passing through the buffer zones that isolate Marina del Rey from the less glamorous neighboring communities of Culver City, Venice and Playa del Rey—an oasis of boats, buildings and greenery emerges seemingly out of nowhere. If you look and listen closely, you'll even hear ducks quacking and waddling around a large lake as if they owned the place—which they do, since it's a fenced-off nature preserve.

"Nowhere" is exactly what Marina del Rey was in the not so distant past. It's an instant community that came into being the way a packet of dry powder becomes a colorful pitcher of Kool-Aid when water is poured over it. Who's worried about history when you're living in a golden moment of recreational bliss? Step this way, and prepare to put on the ritz.

Accommodations

The Marina del Rey skyline is dominated by the *Marina Beach Hotel*, a 10-story, 300-room, 38-suite resort that looks like a giant sand dune. Appropriately, Marina Beach is directly across the street. The balcony views—of the Malibu coastline to the north, of the Palos Verdes Peninsula to the south—are majestic, especially around sunset. With a ninth-floor cocktail lounge, ground-floor gourmet restaurant and outdoor garden café and pool, you won't lack for pampering here. If you're not overwhelmed by the custom-designed furniture, etched glass and fine Italian marble that greets you in the lobby, then pull out the plastic and ready yourself for the high life.

If you're a man of means by no means, let us suggest two places that'll make you feel like a king of the road without costing you a royal fortune: the *Sea Lodge* (convenient to both Marina del Rey and the Venice Beach pier) and *Stern's Motel* (two miles away in Culver City, but very affordable, quiet and well-maintained). You won't be on Admiralty Way, but like the comedian says, you can't have everything—where would you put it?

Restaurants

Here's a bit of statistical trivia to try at your next cocktail party: There are more restaurant seats per square mile in Marina del Rey than in any other place except New York City. In this town of yachts and high rollers, you can dine well on Italian or continental cuisine at such fine and pricey restaurants as *Cyrano's* and *Fiasco's*, sipping wine and gazing contemplatively over the peaceful harbor.

Surprisingly, you don't have to drop large sums to get a decent meal in Marina del Rey. We landed the bargain to end all bargains at the *Todai Light House*. For only $10.95, we hungrily partook of an enormous, all-you-can-eat seafood and sushi buffet. The cafeteria-style troughs and trays were filled with good, fresh sushi—about eight different kinds, plus California rolls and quivering red hunks of raw tuna. On the hot side, you can choose from mahi-mahi, halibut, salmon, shrimp tempura, chicken teriyaki and more. The Todai Light House is a popular place, so you must sometimes take a number and wait your turn to be seated. The lunch-time buffet, by the way, is only $5.95.

On the waterfront, *Edie's Diner* does a big business in "burgers, chips and pie," which is what the sign out front advertises. Fifties chic is big in California. The diner of the eighties is a high-tech creation of neon swirls and ceramic tile, and the food is not as cheap as the authentic diners of yesteryear, but a well-cooked burger is always a wonderful thing. To find a place like Edie's on Marina del Rey's posh waterfront is proof positive that we've got a bona fide trend here.

Nightlife

A chain of restaurant-discos called the *Red Onion* has got the tiger of Southern California nightlife by the tail. Invariably, they are hot places to see and be seen, and Marina del Rey's Red Onion is no exception. The right half is a Mexican restaurant, while the door on the left leads to a downstairs discotheque. Which will it be—the lady or the taco? The place gets packed on a nightly basis with a mixed bag of Navy men, sailboat cowboys, brunettes, blonds and blacks, all sucking down Coronas and kamikazes (a vodka and lime concoction) and scoping the possibilities. On certain nights, you can drink all you want from the bar and gorge at the buffet table for a $5 cover charge. At this price, the drinks are not exactly loaded with liquor, so stick to beer if you're trying to cop a cost-effective buzz. As for the appetizers—well, you've got to like salsa and chips, fried potato skins and stuff like that. The smorgasbord of humanity is what really gets people's mouths watering at the Red Onion. Parking, incidentally, is by valet only. Leave the car over on Washington Street, a block away, if you want to do it yourself.

FOR FURTHER INFORMATION

Marina del Rey Chamber of Commerce
14014 Tahiti Way
Marina del Rey, CA 90292
(213) 821-0555

Venice

At the outset, Venice was just a dream. Almost 90 years later, it's still nothing but a dream—and something of a nightmare. Originally conceived with the express purpose of inaugurating a West Coast cultural renaissance, Venice is instead known far and wide as the home of $2 sunglasses, $3 T-shirts, $4 tarot readings and $5 stress massages. In Venice, New Age prophets walk shoulder to shoulder with the old-age homeless. In short, Venice has passed in less than a century from "visions of New Eden" to visions of New Jersey.

The original visionary was Abbot Kinney, a man who made his millions in cigarettes and spent them on 160 acres of marshland south of Santa Monica in 1900. For some reason, probably because of the haze of cigarette smoke, he saw similarities between his new property and the site on which Venice, Italy, was built. He commissioned two architects to design a "thoroughly equipped" city with streets, hotels, houses and, of course, canals. Fifteen miles of cement-bottomed canals. By June 1905, the canals were filled with water. All Kinney needed now were people to move to his Venice.

Like any good businessman, he lured folks to Venice with a gimmick—gondolas and gondoliers. He imported two dozen genuine gondoliers from old Venice, each with his own repertoire of Italian songs. They rowed potential buyers up and down the canals to look at the empty lots. Kinney then persuaded the newly arrived merchants to build their hotels, restaurants and shops in the architectural style of the Venetian Renaissance. He also oversaw the construction of a lecture hall, pavilion and theater. Provocative speakers were brought in, first-rate plays were put on, blue-ribbon orchestras performed, and the gondoliers sang themselves hoarse in an attempt to lure the culturally starved masses from their sunbaked contentment.

The experiment failed, culminating in a poorly attended run of *Camille*, starring Sarah Bernhardt, who at the time was packing houses back east. Visitors to Venice, it appeared, preferred the sand and sidewalks to the interior of a stuffy concert hall. To salvage his enormous venture, Kinney pulled an about face, filling in a number of his festering, plant-choked canals and bringing in side-show freaks, street theater and a roller coaster. Soon Venice be-came a veritable amusement park by the sea, complete with a miniature railroad and Ocean Front Walk. The conversion was aided when, in 1925, the little town became part of the growing glacier known as Los Angeles. By 1939, the process was complete, with Venice widely regarded as "the Coney Island of the West." Venice has since gone through many other transformations—cov-ered with oil wells, low-income housing and boarded-up slums, then adopted by the beatniks in the fifties, the hippies in the sixties, and artists and total-fitness freaks in the seventies. The town is trying desperately to avoid being adopted by yuppies in the eighties.

To get a handle on present-day Venice, all we had to do was observe the electoral process at work. We happened to pass through during a city-council race. The 6th District seat was up for grabs (the 6th District includes Venice as well as part of West Los Angeles). The incumbent was a woman named Pat Russell, who was portrayed by the dominant left-wing press as a shameless stooge for developers, bankers and every other nogoodnik imag-inable. Away from the beach, in the quiet neighborhoods along the six remaining canals, you could see Russell's posters and bump-er stickers proudly displayed, usually staked into the heart of a well-tended lawn. Russell's opponent, Ruth Galanter, was presum-ably against development and banking and for the poor and down-trodden. Her posters and bumper stickers were taped to the walls and windows along Ocean Front Walk (Venice's infamous cement boardwalk) or stapled to the boarded-up storefronts. We can only guess what Ruth Galanter stood for, because we never actually heard her views. That is because she spent the last month of the campaign in a hospital bed. She'd been stabbed in the throat and left for dead while asleep in her Venice home. Her suspected at-tacker was one of the dead-enders alleged to form her constitu-ency. Apparently, he didn't even know who she was.

The 6th District election made it clear that development has be-come a major political issue in Los Angeles. One looks around the city, which now spans over 460 square miles, and wonders what took them so long, and isn't it a little late. All our own doubts about development aside, Venice is in dire need of help. As it was in the beginning, the town still lives in a dream, perceiving itself as some sort of impervious Greenwich Village or Left Bank.

Granted, some parts of the dream are real enough, like the endless parade of entertaining oddballs who hang out, especially on weekends, along Ocean Front Walk. You are likely to see anything from a guy in a turban chewing glass to a legless, armless dwarf flailing his stumps to a loud tape of Latin disco music. You'll also see body builders working out at the Muscle Beach Recreation Area, freakish in their own way, as well as a motley assortment of sidewalk performers whose numbers include singers, strummers, piano players, violinists, mural artists, caricaturists, acrobats, chainsaw jugglers, comedians, animals performing stupid pet tricks, transvestites, leather freaks, punks, drunks, punch drunks and people who are truly insane. Venice also has a few bars and cafés along Ocean Front Walk; a great bookstore; a museum of Native American art; and a healthy disregard for chicness, big money and normal ways of doing things.

Venice is real, but it's in danger of falling asleep and dreaming itself out of existence. The canals that remain from Kinney's day are jokingly called water bird sanctuaries, but they are little more then smelly ditches, choked with old tires, broken glass and a thick skin of algae. The supporters of Pat Russell want to clean up the canals, a seemingly intelligent civic goal, but her opponents say this is just a ploy to jack up property values.

Plenty more is wrong with Venice. Its pier has been closed down. ("No admittance. Pier unsafe.") In the middle of the beach, the famous Pavilion is so thick with scatological graffiti you have to look closely to make out this sign: "Notice—Defacing Park Property May Result in a Maximum Penalty of $500 Fine and Six Months in Jail." At the south end of the beach, the gazebos along Ocean Front Walk have not been closed down but might as well be to anyone who doesn't routinely urinate outdoors. The lunatic fringe has taken over and set up a defiant beachhead—still smarting, apparently, from having the Pavilion taken away from them. Like a bad acid flashback, they loaf around in a demented, stinking rat pack, roasting like almonds in the sun while taking some measure of revenge by harassing curious passersby.

One scene sticks out above all the others we witnessed in three days (though everyone has his own stories to tell). A drunken gang of phony Rastafarians was holding court at one of the city's historic gazebos, passing a bagged bottle around at midday. An innocuous group of teenagers in white shorts and pink shirts happened by. "Look at duh preppies," the head Rasta jeered, his hairdo-hat combination taller than a wedding cake. "Look at duh m——f—— preps!" One of the kids got angry and cursed back at Mr. Haile Unlikely. Haile jeered at the kids again. The hot-blooded teen stepped forward. "If you're so bad, then come on," he shouted, his friends holding him back. The drunken Rastas had a race to see who could fall down laughing the fastest.

A Dutch fellow we met had a word for this side of Venice: *onguur*. Though he claimed it was untranslatable, his facial expression told us all we needed to know. Venice can be real *onguur* sometimes.

Lest we give the wrong impression, it's hard not to like certain aspects of Venice. The sights and sounds can be fascinating and endless, like in New York City on one of those rare, clear days when you think you just might be able to live there. *Venice City Beach* is spiked by three jetties and widened by sand dredged from the site of the Hyperion Power Plant down the coast. Venice isn't exactly a ghetto—at least it's not inexpensive to live here. A one-bedroom apartment on a rundown section of Ocean Front Walk goes for $650 a month.

No, we didn't despise Venice. It's just that when you see a place that has the setting, the brains and the free-spirited, laissez-faire attitude that Venice has, you want them to wake up from their fantasies and save what's left, before the next incarnation of Abbot Kinney walks in and tries to build another Venice. By the way, Ruth Galanter won the 6th District city-council seat in a close race.

Accommodations

You really don't want to stay in Venice, no matter how hip it might seem at the time. For one thing, it's dangerous after dark. For another, there's really nowhere to stay. Visit for the day, buy a T-shirt for $3, a hot dog and lemonade for another buck, watch the street performers breathe fire, and quietly take your leave. We stayed right in the middle of the madness, on Windward Avenue near the boarded-up pavilion. All things considered, we fared pretty well, because the room we found, forbidding though it looked from the outside, was at the *Venice Beach Cotel.* "Cotel" is short for "community hotel," and it is primarily run for international travelers on a tight budget—a hostel, if you will, but a notch better.

There's another cotel closer to the water, right on Ocean Front Walk. It's called the *Cadillac Hotel,* but it's more like a Yugo than a Cadillac. The rooms in both places are spartan but clean (no TV, no air conditioning, few private bathrooms), and security is tight (you must be buzzed in to see the place). Most of the foreigners we met at the Cotel claimed to be afraid to leave it. These weren't shrinking violets, either. Mostly hale and hearty Europeans in their twenties, they were veteran world travelers who'd seen it all. After seeing Venice, they preferred hanging out at the Cotel's hospitality room to combing the streets of Venice after dark. After a few night moves of our own up and down Ocean Front Walk, we saw their point and gladly joined them. A good time was had by all, as "the writers" helped promote world peace and unity by buying a group of Swedes and Aussies round after round of Mexican beer. Cheers, Tomas and Gunnard, wherever you are.

Restaurants

During the day, the *Sidewalk Café* is the best vantage point from which to observe the circus on Ocean Front Walk. You won't have to dodge roller skaters, skateboarders or the taunts of hung-over Rastas, either. The items on the menu have been given literary names, because the café adjoins the *Small World Bookstore.* Breakfast, for example, can be an omelette named after Gertrude Stein, Carlos Castenada, John O'Hara or Jack Kerouac. Lunch might be a burger bearing the name of Charles Dickens, Pablo Neruda or James Michener. (Logically, the latter features pineapple and ham.)

The best quick bite on the boardwalk can be had at *Del-Cor*, a pizza stand that also sells subs through its screen window. The New York–style pizza is good and thin-crusted—the kind you rarely find, even back east.

Nightlife

Aroma therapy is a new-age form of healing, hot off the California press. We first read about it in a Venice weekly devoted to "planetary health." This therapy is based on the belief that your nose takes in "essential oils" vital to your body's mental and physical health, and when unhealthy, you simply need to breathe in essential oils until you're as good as new. Sounds reasonable. Depression, for example, can be cured by inhaling the following herbs and spices: basil, bergamot, chamomile, clary, lavender, marjoram, rosemary and ylang-ylang.

Well, after sampling Venice both by day and by night, we have devised our own form of aroma therapy, which we'd like to share with anyone who's sick and tired of life in his or her hometown. Go to the south end of Venice City Beach at the end of a hot summer day. Stand anywhere along Ocean Front Walk and breathe deeply, keeping your mouth closed so as to maximize the amount of essential oils your nose takes in. We promise you'll be muttering "there's no place like home" in no time.

If, however, you wish to pick your way further through the olfactory mine field of Venice after dark, the *Townhouse* on Windward Avenue is the place to rock out. Large and loud enough for the rowdiest bike gang, the Townhouse features live rock and roll most nights in the summer.

FOR FURTHER INFORMATION

Venice Chamber of Commerce
P.O. Box 202
Venice, CA 90291
(213) 827-2366

Santa Monica

Santa Monica's beach is where the heart and soul of Los Angeles comes to have fun in the summer. It serves as the steam-release valve for L.A.'s vast and diverse population groups, a no-frills playland that attracts upward of 14 million visitors a year. That's about a quarter of the total load borne by all the beaches in Los Angeles County. Without Santa Monica in the summertime, Los Angeles would be one big smog-laced pressure cooker. In the process of serving as the much larger city's back door to the beach, Santa Monica (pop. 88,000) somehow manages to maintain a peculiar character and charm all its own.

There are many reasons for Santa Monica's popularity. The beach is a 3.3-mile-long strip of sand, dotted in the summer by a close-packed crowd of beach towels and picnic baskets. It is easily accessible from downtown Los Angeles via the Santa Monica Freeway (I-10), one of several main east-west boulevards (Pico, Wilshire, Santa Monica) or any number of bus lines.

The Santa Monica Pier, center of the action, rivals the best in the Golden State. A rickety wooden structure originally built in 1909, sections of it must regularly be rebuilt due to the beating it takes from the waves. Tiny arcades flare off from the main corridor, resulting in a cacophonous midway not unlike that of a state fair. All the ingredients are here for kids to have a good time and for parents to get nostalgic about their own gloriously misspent youth: Skee-Ball, basketball shoots, air hockey, Wedges/Hedges, bumper cars, rocking horses, an old antique wooden carousel and a gift shop where one can purchase a plaster cast of Elvis. The fast food on the pier is guaranteed to bring back memories, too—of indigestion. Step right up for tacos, hot dogs, cotton candy, deep-fried dough, fish 'n' chips and Alka Seltzer.

As far as swimming, the waves at Santa Monica are sufficient to excite the tiny tots on their styrofoam boards but not large enough to attract serious surfers in large numbers. Santa Monica is the home, however, of the real *Muscle Beach* (as opposed to the small weight lifting area down at Venice Beach). Conan-like men and women hoist barbells all day long while lesser mortals stand around in the sand and applaud.

The physical setting of the beach is almost as muscular as the weight lifters. Backed by a long, undeveloped bluff, Santa Monica's beach somehow seems tranquil even when thousands are jamming on the sand. Atop the bluff is *Palisades Park*, a shaded, 26-acre jewel that runs for 14 blocks, from Colorado Avenue to Adelaide Drive. This green buffer between the sand and the city is filled with benches and shuffleboard courts and is popular with Santa Monica's large contingent of senior citizens. Because it is a pleasant, un-patrolled area, though, a large number of the city's homeless can be seen in varying degrees of slumber and movement at all hours.

Santa Monica has a temperate, even climate—perfect for those who live outdoors and those who only come out to play. After the June gloom has run its course, the weather is dependably good year-round. Unfortunately, the same can't be said for the smog, which sometimes gets so thick you can't see across the street or breathe without smarting. But by and large, Santa Monica is a pleasant surprise. If it's possible for a beach this popular to be un-derrated, such is the case with Santa Monica. In order to hang out at a lot of other beach towns in Los Angeles County, you must either have money or "know" money. That is not the case in Santa Monica, which is accessible to all. Perhaps for this reason, it suf-fers in comparison to the more glittery L.A. beach towns. It does not pretend to have a style. It's just people having a good time at the beach, speaking Spanish as often as English.

Given a city the size of Los Angeles, there are bound to be prob-lems with its most popular beach. In recent years, Santa Monica has become the colostomy bag for the city's sometimes sick body. Waste and raw sewage are periodically piped directly into the ocean here, threatening the health of the community and the fish in the Santa Monica Bay. Local organizations have formed to put a stop to the dumping, and when the feces finally hits the fan, there will surely be political hell to pay.

Still, Santa Monica is special, and what makes it so is its year-round livability and unique personality. Grandeur and squalor are mixed in equal proportions. Paint peels from some of the old art deco buildings, but this slow decay is part of the appeal. It's no accident that Raymond Chandler was inspired by Santa Monica, modeling his fictional "Bay City" after the place. A rereading of any of the Philip Marlowe detective novels will reveal that not a whole lot has changed since Chandler cast his subterranean universe in the image of Santa Monica.

Accommodations

It is possible to stay near the beach in Santa Monica. Many hotels and motels, large and small, are strung out along Ocean Avenue a block or two from the Santa Monica Pier and just a pedestrian bridge away from the beach. Staying here also solves your beach parking problem, which in season can be a minor hassle as you do battle with the more experienced, have-you-hugged-my-bumper-today Los Angelinos. Still, there's one minor drawback to the location. Ocean Avenue can be loud, even at night. We learned this the hard way, by taking a room at the least expensive motel on the strip: $40 a night for two beds. It was priced so cheaply because it was a squalid four-walled cell, with rancid bedcovers and thin, lifeless pillows. If you want the cheapest bed on the block, then go for it: the *Pacific Sands Motel*. But you may wake up to regret it.

The Breakers is actually the best of the small motels on Ocean Avenue. Solid as a rock and set away from any other businesses, the Breakers is a bit more expensive but well worth it. If you're determined to go high-rise and/or name brand, then try the *Holiday Inn at the Pier*. The rooms are another hop up in price, but in a world where you never know what's going to greet you when you turn the key, Holiday Inn is at least dependable and consistent and often a lot more than that.

Restaurants

Overwhelmed by the choices, with all of Los Angeles spread out before us, we took the coward's way out and ate junk food on the pier. Later that night, we headed to *Ye Olde King's Head*, an authentic English alehouse close to the row of beachfront motels, one block up Santa Monica Boulevard. Here, you can get a large order of fish 'n' chips for $6.75 and then retire to the back-room pub for darts and draft beer.

Nightlife

Believe it or not, Santa Monica is only a boulevard away from Hollywood. Pick up an *L.A. Weekly* and comb the detailed listings for the lowdown on the local scene. You may not believe your eyes: *Club Lingerie*, the *Palace*, the *Palomino*, the *Whiskey a Go-Go* and the *Roxy* are just a few of the clubs in the Hollywood area. The last three of these are among the most venerable music venues in the country.

In Santa Monica, *Madame Wong's* and *McCabe's* are as hot as any clubs in the city, booking nationally known talent as well as a steady lineup drawn from the seemingly bottomless well of Los Angeles' native music scene: glam rockers, hard-core acts, neopsychedelics, speed-metal monsters, country punks and other flavor-of-the-month types out here in the land of the faddish abnormality.

It's actually quite difficult for us to comment on a music scene as extensive as L.A.'s, especially one within easy access to the beach. To a pair of beach bums who've been denied good music in more beach towns than we care to count, Los Angeles was almost too much of a good thing. If only they could space all this music out evenly along both American coasts, this would certainly be a better world to live in.

FOR FURTHER INFORMATION

Santa Monica Chamber of Commerce
1460 4th Street
Santa Monica, CA 90405
(213) 393-9825

Santa Monica Convention and Visitors Bureau
P.O. Box 5278
Santa Monica, CA 90405
(213) 393-7593

Pacific Palisades

This community, nestled in the Santa Monica foothills from Chau-tauqua Boulevard to Malibu, is not a beach town at all, even though it looks down upon one of the prettiest stretches of the Pacific coast. Originally populated in the twenties by Methodists who founded it as their "new Chautauqua," Pacific Palisades is now the exclusive domain of the rich, the very rich and the very, very rich. The streets, most of which branch off famed Sunset Boulevard, are winding, shaded routes, often ending in cul-de-sacs. If you get lost in Pacific Palisades, try to remember how you came. Chances are a knock on most doors will go unanswered, and the rest will be greeted by a house servant who has no idea what you want. Lovely yards, though, and very nice sprinkler systems. Parts of Pacific Palisades are included on the Hollywood celebrity bus tours.

Will Rogers State Beach

Just north of Santa Monica is a state beach named after our most famous cowboy philosopher. It is a three-mile swath worthy of the tribute. Will Rogers State Beach is a favorite of sun-bronzed locals who are serious about their volleyball and their tans. Its proximity to Hollywood makes it one of the more popular beaches in Los Angeles County. If you want to dig further into the life of the man who never met a man he didn't like, his 187-acre ranch is open to the public as *Will Rogers State Historical Park.* Tours of the main house and grounds are offered daily, year-round, and one can also hike through the vast natural area or ride on equestrian trails.

Malibu

The first thing one should know about Malibu is that there are two of them. The more famous Malibu is the "inner" Malibu—the film colony, the celebrity sandbox, the glamorous private world behind locked gates about which the rest of the world likes to gossip and wonder. The "outer" Malibu is a 27-mile stretch of winding shoreline and twisting canyons. Roughly, it runs from Coastline Drive at the Los Angeles city limits up to the Ventura County line. This side of Malibu, a wild corridor bounded by the Santa Monica Mountains and the ocean, is accessible to all.

The reality of Malibu is very different from popular conceptions of it. First of all, much of it is rugged and desolate. Steep mountains plunge to the sea, which crashes angrily against the rocks. The elements hang in precarious balance here, not infrequently tilting over into storm, flood, fire and chaos. One must drive through Malibu ever ready for rock slides and, in winter, mud slides. Some of the cliff faces along the Pacific Coast Highway are raw where mighty chunks have torn loose and fallen onto the road or into the ocean.

Narrow ridge tops zigzag northward. Houses are buried in the canyons between them. The hills are covered with dry, brown vegetation most of the year that turns green when the winter rains come. The threat of fire is constant in Malibu and the canyons behind it. Lightning, arson or a careless match can ignite a blaze that, propelled by hot desert winds, is capable of racing down the canyons toward the hapless seaside colony at speeds of 100 miles per hour. The other, opposite calamity is mud slides: slow, brown waves of muck, rock and debris that swallow up everything in their path.

Malibu is as staggering in some ways as Big Sur—just as capable of environmental temper tantrums and nearly as uninhabitable. Call it Little Big Sur. No matter what you label it, though, Malibu is a special place, above and beyond its pull as a magnet for Hollywood celebrities. The elements play no favorites here. Regardless of their purchasing power, the 20,000 people who live in Malibu have no more been able to tame it or claim it than the citizens of Tokyo could stop Godzilla. Nature does not obey directorial cues.

What the folks of Malibu *have* been able to do, for the most part, is keep other people out. The key tactic has been sewers—or rather, lack of them. There are no sewer lines in Malibu. Even the most vain, pampered celebrity must learn to live with a septic tank. And because lots are so small in Malibu, the tanks are often directly under the house. When the rains come or the ocean advances, the septic tanks runneth over, filling living areas with an unbecoming stench. Lifestyles of the rich and famous, eh?

Still, they're willing to live with fires, slides, their own excrement and nature's unfathomable fury in return for what they perceive to be privileged isolation from the ragtag masses. The homes in the gated, off-highway Malibu colony sit on lots so small that side walls practically touch. Meanwhile, the barracks-style residential blocks on the Coast Highway do, in fact, connect, looking from the perspective of the highway like rundown motel units. The highway comes so close to these homes you can practically knock on the doors as you drive by. Out back, the ocean is always running up to say how do you do.

As for the highway, it's another bane in Malibu. The Pacific Coast Highway is the only coast route connecting Los Angeles with Oxnard and Ventura to the north. Traffic tramples through Malibu on the four-lane P.C.H. like a stampede of heavy-footed cattle. On weekends, the road jams to a standstill with carloads of Angelinos headed to their favorite north county beaches or to play with the boats they keep in one of Ventura County's yacht basins. On summer weekdays, traffic is not awful. It's just bad.

In one of the most terrifying moments of the trip, we attempted to dash across the highway, only to find ourselves stymied in the middle turning lane while an unbroken line of cars and trucks whizzed by in both directions at high speeds. The thundering trucks and jeeploads of beach-bound brat packs hurling verbal abuse at us did not help our frayed nerves. But, as we learned, being a kamikaze pedestrian is unavoidable in Malibu. Parking lots at the state and private beaches up and down the Malibu coast fill up quickly, and the overflow lines the highway shoulders in both directions.

The beach access point we were attempting to reach was actually a cement walk between buildings—one of the narrow accessways the California Coast Commission has waged costly legal battles to establish, much to the chagrin of Malibu residents. Officially, it is known, thanks to *Doonesbury*, as the *Zonker Harris Accessway*. On either side lies private property. You're reminded not to trespass, although you do have the right to walk along the beach up to the high-tide line. We did just that, ambling in the direction of the Malibu Pier past all manner of sunbathers who paid us no mind (including a topless woman lying on her back, making not the least attempt to conceal her bronzed assets).

The pier at Malibu is an old, broad-planked affair, with the usual assortment of weather-beaten fishers grumbling about the fish not biting. North of it lies *Surfrider Beach*, one of the most popular in Los Angeles for surfing and swimming. The beach covers 35 acres, including nearly a mile of ocean frontage. On it, beautiful California blonds with electric eyes and minuscule swimsuits watch their boyfriends work out on the volleyball court or in the waves, which are fought over and claimed by the most skillful local surfers.

The pier is the modest commercial heart of Malibu. A string of restaurants, markets and small malls runs from the pier area north to Point Dume, where the coast takes a northwesterly turn and signs of humanity become markedly sparse. Along the built-up part of Malibu is a popular private beach, *Paradise Cove*. A $5 entrance fee lands you on a beach with a short pier and a wonderful view of the opposing sandstone bluffs of Point Dume. Much like the beaches of Laguna and La Jolla, the Malibu shoreline is cut with coves, some accessible by stairways and paths. The California Coastal Commission posts signs along the highway that point the way to public beaches. Keep your eyes open for a dozen such spots between Surfrider Beach and Paradise Cove. Also, be prepared to park on the road and deal with hazardous crossings.

Northwest of Point Dume are *Zuma* and *Leo Carrillo* state beaches. Besides providing the title for one of Neil Young's better albums, Zuma is a broad, exhilaratingly scenic and somewhat dangerous beach plopped in sandy, desertlike wilderness. It is Los Angeles' largest county-owned beach, with no fewer than eight parking lots at which a $4 day-use fee is levied. The hidden danger at Zuma is rip currents, necessitating frequent heroics from the lifeguard stand. Further north, Leo Carrillo State Beach runs for over a mile, right up to the Ventura County line. Named after the TV actor who played the Cisco Kid's sidekick, Pancho, this beach is broken into two parts by Sequit Point. Leo Carrillo offers shallow sea caves and tide pools to explore, good surfing and swimming, and acres of sand to spread out on. On the far side of the road, up toward Sycamore Canyon, is a shaded campground.

From the east end of Leo Carrillo, you can hike to *Nicholas Canyon County Beach*. Hiking in is easier than trying to find the unmarked road leading to Nicholas Canyon from the Coast Highway. Beyond Nicholas Canyon, there's the usual handful of coast-access stairways, plus a small state beach at the foot of the Point Dume headlands called *Westward Beach*. And that is Malibu: 27 miles of unspoiled beaches, more and better scenery than you had any right to expect, and an exclusive colony lodged between rocky cliffs and the rolling sea.

A final Malibu attraction worth mentioning is the *J. Paul Getty Museum*. The late oil billionaire created the world's largest endowment for a privately funded museum, built a mile north of Sunset Boulevard on the Coast Highway. Admission is free, but because parking is a problem (so what's new?), you are asked to make a "parking reservation" at least one month in advance by calling (213) 458-2003. The museum's broad collection focuses on western art from classical times through the nineteenth century.

Beyond this, you are on your own in Malibu. Sometimes, you can be made to feel as unwanted as a stray dog shuffling along the side of the road. Unless you know someone who lives here—say, Larry Hagman—you'll have a hard time fashioning any kind of vacation on the Malibu coastline other than a camping trip. Motels are few and far between; house rentals, almost prohibitively costly. (How does $25,000 a month grab you, baby?) No, Malibu is mainly for the Hollywood elite, who commute from the brutal paradise/purgatory of Malibu to the artificial fantasyland of Tinsel Town. Celebrities from Shirley MacLaine and Linda Ronstadt to Mel Brooks and the Guru Maharaj Ji live in Malibu. Is it worth it—the risk, the stress, the traffic, the expense? In the words of Michael Landon, one of the Malibu faithful, "You see the ocean and the birds and say, 'Ahhh.'" Malibu, in other words, is an awfully effective tongue depressor.

Accommodations

Malibu's few hotels and motels have been here awhile, long before the film-colony isolationists closed ranks and decided to deny sewer and building permits. Still, there are some decent places to stay, all of them on the Pacific Coast Highway but only a few on the beach side of the racetrack. *Casa Malibu* is the nicest of them all, with relaxed, mission-style architecture, a large sun deck and a back-door beach. Prices range from $65 to $85 a night, which is not unreasonable, given the location and general scarcity of rooms in Malibu.

The *Malibu Surfer* is more typical of what you'll find: an old 16-unit motel with breathtaking views of the mountains behind it and the ocean across the road. The Surfer has been sitting on its hill since the forties. The manager, who's been tending the desk for nigh on 25 years, claims that Malibu has changed only slightly in that time.

An interesting operation is the *Topanga Ranch Motel*, a grouping of 60-year-old cottages that sit in a shaded grove across from *Topanga State Beach* in south Malibu. The Topanga Ranch gets a lot of repeat business from regulars who book for weeks at a time. Given the serenity of the grounds and the affordability ($40 to $60 a night), this is not surprising. Each cottage comes with a refrigerator, and the back patio faces the tawny mountains.

Restaurants

It is almost impossible to get any kind of building permit or license in Malibu, yet this hasn't staunched the arrival of *Kentucky Fried Chicken*, *McDonald's* and *Jack-in-the-Box*. Of course, there are many fine restaurants in Malibu. Just consider who they're catering to. Good restaurants follow money.

One of the best for seafood in Malibu (and maybe all of California) is *Gladstone's 4 Fish Restaurant*. Facing the ocean, Gladstone's is line-out-the-door popular at sunset. The seafood is extremely fresh and well-prepared, and the place is mobbed seven days a week. Gladstone's is very much a Southern California tradition.

Another local landmark specializing in Mexican food is *Carlos and Pepe's Cantina*. *Alice's Restaurant* (not the one Arlo Guthrie made famous back in Massachusetts) sits right by the pier entrance, serving gourmet seafood (e.g., grilled sea bass on papaya and leeks with a ginger and coconut cream sauce) at uptown prices.

The last place we'd like to mention doesn't serve food anymore, but it's worth a gander, especially if you're trying to quell your appetite. The closed-down *Frostie Freeze Hickory Burger* stand has a 20-foot-tall burger boy hoisting a ceramic hamburger the size of a flying saucer. You can stand below it and wonder what it must be like to have a one-ton burger with all the trimmings dropped on you. What is this grotesquerie doing in Malibu? With all the wealth in this town, couldn't they take up a collection and send it south to Venice, where it belongs?

Nightlife

The scuttlebutt is that celebrities guard their privacy so zealously in Malibu that they do little more than wave at each other. Certainly, they don't go out at night looking to get hassled by rambunctious California weirdos at local discotheques. In other words, they lie low—and you will too, if you come to Malibu. The obvious nightlife can be had in Hollywood, Santa Monica and downtown L.A. For this reason, it was almost anomalous to find a club in Malibu called the *Screaming Clam*. Who goes there? The students at Pepperdine University (the college on the hill in Malibu), or the restless children of the rich and famous? Probably some of each.

FOR FURTHER INFORMATION

Malibu Chamber of Commerce
22235 Pacific Coast Highway
Malibu, CA 90265
(213) 456-9025

Central Coast

Oxnard

If a city were really serious about becoming a big financial hub, a vacation mecca and a possible site for the America's Cup competition, you'd think it would be named something, *anything*, other than Oxnard. But Oxnard is Oxnard, and the city is quite intent on realizing those goals. Blessed by a beautiful natural setting, comfortable year-round temperatures and strong prevailing winds, Oxnard is definitely headed for a major upheaval. The only thing holding it back is the name.

Still, the name somehow befits the city. With a population of well over 100,000 and a land area that would make Los Angeles hungry, it is a large city with the ambience of a small town. The city is situated in the middle of the fertile Oxnard Plain, with fields of crops extending as far as the eye can see. Oxnard's "lower forty" is filled with middle-class housing developments and moderate-sized bank buildings—things that one associates with an up-and-coming community.

There are reasons why seemingly incongruous worlds exist side by side in Oxnard. The city is only 60 miles north of Los Angeles and is right on the coast, making it the next logical urban center for frustrated Angelinos to "discover." Actually, Los Angeles is already well along with the process of discovery. The majority of boats docked at Oxnard's Channel Islands Harbor are owned by people who live in L.A., and although they seldom take their toys out for a spin, their very presence lends credence to the theory that the next big land boom will occur here. It makes sense. The Malibu Peninsula, between Oxnard and L.A., is a pain in the rear to live on, however physically stunning it might be. Oxnard, strategically located where the Ventura Freeway meets the Pacific Coast Highway, gets the nod. You can almost hear Dan Loggins singing, "Please come to Oxnard in the springtime…"

Oxnard is also set in the middle of a fertile agricultural delta, right where the once mighty, now trickling Santa Clara River empties into the Pacific Ocean. The river was dammed, the delta be-

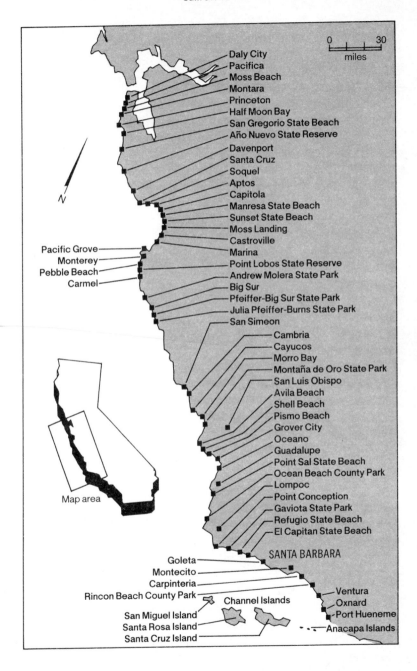

0   30
miles

Daly City
Pacifica
Moss Beach
Montara
Princeton
Half Moon Bay
San Gregorio State Beach
Año Nuevo State Reserve
Davenport
Santa Cruz
Soquel
Aptos
Capitola
Manresa State Beach
Sunset State Beach
Moss Landing
Castroville
Marina
Point Lobos State Reserve
Andrew Molera State Park
Big Sur
Pfeiffer-Big Sur State Park
Julia Pfeiffer-Burns State Park
San Simeon

Pacific Grove
Monterey
Pebble Beach
Carmel

N

Map area

Cambria
Cayucos
Morro Bay
Montaña de Oro State Park
San Luis Obispo
Avila Beach
Shell Beach
Pismo Beach
Grover City
Oceano
Guadalupe
Point Sal State Beach
Ocean Beach County Park
Lompoc
Point Conception
Gaviota State Park
Refugio State Beach
El Capitan State Beach

SANTA BARBARA

Goleta
Montecito
Carpinteria
Rincon Beach County Park
Channel Islands

San Miguel Island
Santa Rosa Island
Santa Cruz Island

Ventura
Oxnard
Port Hueneme
Anacapa Islands

came a plain, and the plain gave way to multicolored fields of crops that run to the foot of the Santa Monica Mountains. Oxnard is the strawberry capital of the world. They take the little ruby-red fruit seriously, holding an annual May festival that's the biggest event of the year. In 1987, the Strawberry Festival ran in the red to the tune of $60,000—a fact that merited a headline in the local paper twice as large as that of the latest chapter in the Iran-Contra affair. Other crops are grown, too—including lemons, corn and broccoli— and trucks and trains can be seen hauling heaping piles of Oxnard's cornucopia off to markets around the globe. Speaking of farming, Oxnard did not derive its name from the mighty ox. No, it was the surname of a mighty sugar-beet mogul, Henry Oxnard, who created an agricultural empire hereabouts back in the days before condos and yachts sailed into port.

Another fortunate accident of geography placed Oxnard's oceanfront at the right angle to receive wind and water currents so vital to an up-and-coming water-sports capital. Channel Islands Harbor was dredged in 1965 and modeled along the lines of a New England village. With 2,000 slips and a bustling restaurant row, Channel Islands Harbor has brought Oxnard the attention it craves. Oxnard has even met the requirements for becoming a host site of the America's Cup. While we were there, the local yacht owners and town boosters were eagerly pushing Oxnard as the dark-horse candidate (facing a formidable foe in San Diego).

A final "accident" gave Oxnard a large chunk of Pacific coastline. For sheer physical beauty, it's hard to beat the drive north from Malibu into Ventura County. The route snakes around a land of barren rock and swings past miles of unobstructed shoreline that's as inviting to look at as it is difficult to reach. Then you come into the verdant farmlands south of Oxnard. One beach along this route is worth singling out. *Point Mugu State Beach* is a small, sandy beach that overlooks a wildlife sanctuary and lagoon. Inexplicable as these things sometimes are, the sanctuary is in the middle of a Navy firing range, off-limits to the non-missile-wielding public. But the beach is a beautiful, quiet place and worth a visit. In the town of Oxnard, a two-mile state beach lies just south of the Santa Clara River. The 295-acre *McGrath State Beach* includes a lake, wildlife refuge and 174 campsites. Camping at McGrath is about as pleasant as it gets at the beach. Large dunes offer protection from the wind, while short trees and tall grasses lend some privacy from neighboring campers. South of McGrath, near a California Edison power plant, is *Mandalay County Park*, with 104 acres of undeveloped dunes, some stretching to the mainland side of the road like vine-covered beasts.

Accommodations

There are less costly places to stay in Oxnard than the *Mandalay Beach Resort*, but none so close to the beach. Mandalay, in fact, is directly on the beach, although even this isn't the resort's chief appeal. The Mandalay Beach Resort goes beyond Oxnard's wildest dreams of upscale. It is constructed along the lines of a Spanish estate, with grottoes and fountains, gardens and waterfalls popping up everywhere. Getting lost on the way to your room is not an unpleasant experience. Buried among all the carefully manicured acreage is the largest free-form swimming pool in Southern California and two tennis courts. After taking a late-day paddle around the deep end, you can retire to the Surf Room, where they offer a free cocktail hour nightly. They also throw in a full breakfast every morning. The cost for all this pampering ranges from $120 to $160 per night.

Restaurants

The best way to check out Oxnard's famed Channel Islands Harbor is from a restaurant window, especially toward sundown when the sailboats head into port. On certain nights, the tall ship *California* honors the assembled multitude by furling and unfurling its sails. And then the games begin...so which restaurant to play them in?

The *Lobster Trap* is a waterside restaurant located on the extensive grounds of the *Casa Sirena Resort*, a 3-story, 274-room luxury hotel and marina overlooking the harbor. Established in 1969, the Lobster Trap flies in live Maine lobsters almost daily to live up to its name. But there are plenty of local seafood items to choose from as well, such as "scalone" and cioppino. The former is a pureed mixture of scallops and abalone, with the scallops acting as a kind of extender for the abalone, a scarce delicacy. It is formed into a pancake then sauteed lightly. Cioppino, on the other hand, is a thick fisherman's stew.

Nightlife

Oxnard and Ventura are so close together that their nightlife intermingles. Because there's no real downtown heart to Oxnard or even a decent mall, the place to go is Ventura. Read on.

FOR FURTHER INFORMATION

Oxnard Convention and Visitors Bureau
325 Esplanade Drive
Oxnard, CA 93030
(805) 485-8833

Ventura

Just north of Oxnard, across the dry bed of the Santa Clara River, lies the modest and attractive town of Ventura. In many ways, Ventura and Oxnard are inseparable, twin peas in the fertile pod of Ventura County. Both have beautiful, uncrowded state beaches, a breezy harbor area and, at the present time, a reasonably sane approach to population growth and development. If one town must be picked over the other, then Ventura would probably get the nod, simply because it is smaller (pop. 75,000), more centralized and historically more interesting. In Ventura, you feel a greater sense of place than in Oxnard, which is certainly a neat and tidy city but suffers from a mild case of new-growth sterility. On the front page of Ventura's only newspaper, for instance, you will find an "Our Yesterdays" column, which looks into the past to recall that "on this day 75 years ago, the Seaside baseball team beat Nordhoff twice in a double-header."

Ventura's full title is San Buenaventura, a name derived from the Catholic mission built here in 1782 by the ubiquitous Father Junipero Serra. The original mission, chapel, grounds and surrounding historic district have all been beautifully restored and maintained with adobe, wood and blue ceramic tile. In fact, the Old Historic District still buzzes with activity today. A five-block area, between Figueroa and California streets, spans the entire spectrum of Ventura County's history. What initially caught our eyes was not history but a row of thrift shops and used bookstores. In two blocks, we counted six different thrift shops, an intimidating prospect for anyone in search of the perfect bowling shirt. This abundance led us to hypothesize that San Buenaventura must have been the patron saint of used clothing.

City Hall, around the corner on Poli Street, is an impressive if not anomalous structure built in 1913 of simulated white marble. Even Ventura's post office is an interesting place. Located three blocks from City Hall on Santa Clara Street, the post office houses a fascinating mural painted by WPA artist Gordon Grant, who spent most of 1936 and 1937 working on it. The resulting mural is a heroic tribute to the common laborer and farmer. Additionally, Ventura County operates a historical museum on Main Street, while the privately run Albinger Archeological Museum delves thousands of years into the past. This is certainly enough to keep anyone busy for a few days.

On top of that, however, Ventura is blessed with a number of beaches. The most accessible of these is *San Buenaventura State Beach*, which runs from the city's 1,700-foot pier south to Marina Park. Protected by breakwaters, this long beach is good for swimming and sunbathing. Behind it sits Promenade Park, with bike paths and a picnic area. Seldom will you find a healthier environment for outdoor recreation.

Wave riders head up to *Surfers Point Park*, at the end of California Street ("C Street" to the locals). The coast bends sharply here, receiving large waves. Another renowned surfing spot is 15 miles north of here, in the middle of nowhere, next to several Mobil Oil platforms. The beach is nonexistent, and the scenery is straight out of futurist fiction, with the surfers doing their thing between two black drilling platforms.

Last but not least, Ventura is where *Channel Islands National Park* has its headquarters. Scattered from 11 to 50 miles off the coast from Ventura Harbor, these five pristine islands make up the 40th and newest of our national parks. On a clear day, you can see *Anacapa* and *Santa Cruz* islands (the two nearest) from the mainland. The park is also a marine and wildlife sanctuary; even the kelp forests in the surrounding waters are protected. Home to sea lions, seals, migrating whales and rare underwater vegetation, the Channel Islands are rugged and windswept. Except for the island of *Santa Rosa*, which is occupied by a privately owned horse ranch, they are uninhabited. If you are seeking primitive pleasures in the great outdoors, a limited number of campsites are available on two of the islands. Permits are obtainable from the National Park Service.

Otherwise, the islands can by visited by boat for the day, either by taking a charter-boat cruise or sailing your own. Be aware, however, that the Santa Barbara Channel is choppy and unpredictable. We were advised to "sit up toward the front of the boat and don't eat breakfast." The day-long, round-trip charters cost about $28 and include landing excursions.

Accommodations

At the north end of San Buenaventura State Beach, a *Holiday Inn* rises like a fortress beside the Ventura Pier, the Ventura Freeway and the railroad tracks. It is the best location on the beach, and the rooms take full advantage with balconies that look over an impressive landscape. It's a high-rise motel, so expect to pay a high-rise dollar ($73-$93) to stay here, but just about every need is met in this city within a city.

Another choice is the venerable *Pierpont Inn*. Set on seven beautifully landscaped acres atop a bluff overlooking Pierpont Bay, the inn has been run by the same family since 1928. The rooms in the original building have been renovated and refurbished but still retain the Old World charm the Pierpont is known for—including working fireplaces for those nights when the winter winds blow. The grounds are thick with flowers, and a path runs down the hill and under the freeway to the beach. A local landmark, the Pierpont attracts a faithful clientele year after year.

Restaurants

Let us again direct your attention to the *Pierpont Inn*, this time for fine dining. The hotel's tradition carries over to the dining room. The windows look out at the gardens and the ocean—a perfect setting for contemplating the enormity of your appetite. The seafood is guaranteed fresh, and though they also serve fine steaks, filet mignon, lamb chops and so forth, how could anyone resist giant prawns stuffed with crabmeat?

For lunch, you might try *Franky's Restaurant*, especially if you're poking around Ventura's Old Historic District. Franky's is filled with artwork. The booths are separated by pieces of sculpture set on pedestals, and the red-brick walls are covered with original oil paintings. The quality of the food is as high as that of the art—and healthy as well. Featuring natural foods with a vegetarian emphasis, Franky's serves pita and croissant sandwiches, heaping salads and a great bowl of homemade soup.

Nightlife

Not a lot happens in Ventura after dinner. If you've come for the right reasons—peace, quiet, contemplation—you really don't want a whole lot to happen. The old folks listen to lounge pianists at the tall hotels, while the younger set gets down at *Club Soda* or knocks 'em back at the *Bombay Bar and Grill*. Bombay offers live bands some nights and amateur contests on others—i.e., the Miss Nissan Hardbody Swimsuit Fashion Competition. Without question, the Bombay Bar and Grill is the hottest ticket in Ventura or Oxnard.

While we were in town, though, we made note of a real entertainment oddity. Donovan, the erstwhile Dylan imitator turned flower child and psychedelic minstrel, was appearing at the Holiday Inn's Top O' the Harbor Room. Twenty-nine dollars got you into Donovan's dinner show, which included salad, a New York strip steak or halibut, potato, vegetable, dessert, "Mellow Yellow," "Sunshine Superman," "Wear Your Love Like Heaven" and "To Susan on the West Coast Waiting."

FOR FURTHER INFORMATION

Ventura Chamber of Commerce
785 Seaward Avenue
Ventura, CA 93001
(805) 648-2075

Rincon Beach County Park

Rincon Point straddles the Ventura and Santa Barbara county lines. It is one of the best surfing spots in California, especially when the big winter swells roll in, and you can expect to find plenty of surfboards bobbing off the point. There's a small county park here, and the beach is reachable from a blufftop lot. Rincon runs all the way up to the town of Carpinteria, lending credence to its reputation as California's hidden Riviera.

Carpinteria

Many a civic group has proclaimed its sandy land grant to be the "world's safest beach," but Carpinteria just might be the first beach to have been so ordained. Way back in 1602, Spanish explorers wrote of it as a *"costa segura de buen gente"*—or, the safest beach on the coast. Nestled against the Santa Ynez Mountains on a fertile plain, Carpinteria is a small town with big assets: beautiful, uncluttered beaches, a pleasing Mediterranean climate and a commanding view of the Channel Islands. The slope of the beach is gentle, with no sudden dropoffs or riptides, making for worry-free swimming.

The original inhabitants of the Carpinteria Valley were Chumash Indians, who plundered the extensive tar pits for pitch to seal their canoes. Carpinteria literally rests on a huge pool of black gold. Beneath the fertile soil of the Carpinteria Valley lies a thick layer of tar, and below that, a sea of oil. Much industry in and around Carpinteria is based on bringing up petroleum products, although horticulture figures in as well.

To a vacationer's eyes, however, Carpinteria's main appeal is that of a quiet town of 11,000 residents, rural in its slowpoke ways, with excellent, naturally protected beaches. Many come to camp at *Carpinteria State Beach*, a 50-acre park with a sandy beach and large dunes, behind which lie 262 made-in-the-shade campsites. If you truly want to get away—and not just to a fake fantasyland of boutiques and yuppie spas—Carpinteria is a delightful spot to put on the brakes. It is arguably the last undiscovered beach town in Southern California.

Accommodations

Most visitors to Carpinteria camp in the state park. The town also gets its modest share of day-trippers who enjoy the "world's safest beach" on summer weekends. Motels are scattered and few, but expect their numbers to increase as word gets around about Carpinteria. Meantime, you can put up overnight at the *Carpinteria Inn*, between the freeway and the beach along Carpinteria Avenue.

Restaurants

The first appearance of scripted red or blue neon in a restaurant window is a harbinger of change, and we did see the handwriting of gentrification glowing on the wall in Carpinteria. *C'est la beach.* Mixed in among the brace of older small-town cafés, delis and sit-down pizza joints is the *Sand Dollar*, a seafood restaurant where you can watch them charbroil the fresh catch that comes in daily, from tuna to swordfish. One can either dine indoors or alfresco on a brick patio.

Nightlife

Over on Santa Claus Lane, a Christmasy retail agglomeration just off the freeway north of Carpinteria, is a restaurant-lounge called *Joh-Bert's*, where you can swing and sway to soft rock and jazz. If you're after something a little livelier, Santa Barbara, with its fecund State Street nightlife, is only 15 minutes away.

FOR FURTHER INFORMATION

Carpinteria Valley Chamber of Commerce
5036 Carpinteria Avenue
Carpinteria, CA 93013
(805) 684-5479

Santa Barbara

At some point in their lives, everyone ought to visit Santa Barbara. All it takes is a day or two's exposure to the beaches, the mountains, the greenery, the Spanish architecture, the abundant culture, and the relaxed ebb and flow of life here to make a convincing case that this is America's most perfect city. If you were to feed all the variables that govern the quality of life into a computer, the city that'd top the list would be Santa Barbara. At least in our book it would. Pittsburgh? No way. We'll take Santa Barbara.

The reasons for Santa Barbara's good fortune are many, and geography is not the least of them. Santa Barbara is encircled by the Santa Ynez Mountains, which act as a cradle, staving off the cold north winds. Twenty miles offshore, the Channel Islands intercept the Pacific swells, affording protection on another front. Santa Barbara is the only city in California facing due south; think of it as the figurative ceiling of Southern California, if you will. The climate is comfortable year-round: cool in the summer, warm in the winter. Located between Los Angeles (100 miles south) and San Francisco (355 miles north), Santa Barbara partakes of the best qualities of north and south.

The 75,000 people who live here are well-to-do. They've made a mission of keeping their city clean and green and out of the hands of those who would turn it into an urban Disneyland at the drop of a bank loan. Consequently, there's always some kind of battle being waged—typically, city-hall caucuses and grassroots crusades to save parks and clamp down on black-hat developers and entrepreneurs. In most communities when such issues arise, the residents sadly fold their newspapers and mutter, "Oh ,well, can't fight progress," before popping open another beer to block out the inevitable portents of progress. In Santa Barbara, they mobilize. They can afford to: they've got the time and money to do so. It is largely a community of wealthy retirees, and these gray panthers sure know how to growl. During our stopover, a sizable group was working overtime to push through a bond referendum enabling the city to purchase 70 acres of coastal real estate before it fell under the knife of development. They posed, smiling, around a bust of an old woman who was identified as Santa Barbara's "patron saint of conservation."

Santa Barbara is an extremely restful city, especially from the point of view of two beachcombers burned out from rambling around the lion's den of Southern California. It is blessed in so many ways we hardly know where to begin, but let's start with the beaches. The main ones, plainly designated *East Beach* and *West Beach*, are separated by Stearns Wharf, the oldest operating wharf on the West Coast. There's really very little difference between East and West, and the beaches run for four unbroken miles. The beach is sandy and broad, kept free of litter and well-lifeguarded. A paved bike path runs along the beach, and congestion is rarely a problem on it. Everyone lopes or cruises at his or her own unhurried pace, buried under a Walkman or smiling as if some cosmic love god has just whispered, "Have a nice day."

Behind the path is a landscaped, grassy ribbon of park with picnic tables and a lawn that's trimmed, weedless and more comfortable than shag carpeting. The only sour note is the presence of oil-drilling rigs offshore, a constant feature of the Southern California seascape. Santa Barbara has done its best to battle the oil companies, but the county has little say about what goes on out at sea beyond the three-mile limit. (They were able to wrangle some concessions out of Exxon in 1986, particularly in the area of emissions standards.) And so the Santa Barbarans grudgingly abide an industry they really don't want or need in their watery front yard.

When you get right down to it, Santa Barbara doesn't need any kind of industry. Most people who live here have made their money elsewhere, relocating in their golden years to enjoy a city that does not tick maniacally to the beat of rush-hour traffic or the shrill sound of the factory whistle. Santa Barbara simply exists in easy harmony with its environment. Even tourism, the closest thing to an industry in Santa Barbara, is spurned in its more ostentatious manifestations. One of the great controversies in recent years was the construction of a 360-room luxury hotel on the waterfront. The man behind the *Red Lion Inn* was Fess Parker, the TV actor whose *Daniel Boone* series made every little boy in America want to trade in his baseball glove for a buckskin jacket. In Santa Barbara, the actor turned real estate investor has practiced a very different kind of trailblazing—i.e., clearing acreage along the ocean so that a sprawling businessman's lodge and conference center could hog the best beachfront view in the city.

A barometer of public opinion on the matter could be read in the artwork etched upon the wall of a local tavern. "Is that a fireplug?" one dog asked another who was relieving himself on some unidentifiable object. "No, it's Fess Parker," was the reply. Crude, yes, but in Santa Barbara no one—neither the elderly activists nor the sizable college-age population at the University of California at Santa Barbara—takes these things lightly.

Still, this is a refined city whose blocks are covered with museums, galleries, theaters, libraries and bookstores. There's a strong public consensus on such matters as town architecture and habitat preservation. Following a devastating earthquake in 1925, the Santa Barbara City Council took the unusual step of establishing an architectural board of review, which drafted a design code mandating that all rebuilding conform to a decreed style. Consequently, Santa Barbara was rebuilt in the appealing Mediterranean mode—vanilla stucco walls, red pipe roofing, arcades and walkways, wrought iron railings, flower- and shrub-filled gardens—that reflect the city's 150-year-old Spanish and Mexican heritage.

The most visible example of this style is the *Mission Santa Barbara*. The "Queen of the Missions" sits on a knoll overlooking the town. At close range, it almost appears two-dimensional, like a Hollywood movie set. The grassy square before it is a greener green, the sky on a clear day, a bluer blue, than can be imagined in a Kodacolor fantasy. The graceful Spanish Colonial facade is executed in modest pink and white tones. The grounds include a flower garden, small cemetery, museum and missionary's quarters—not forgetting the grand, stone-walled church itself, with its twin bell towers. A self-guided tour costs $1, and in the spirit of the place, the postcard stand has an honor box next to it. Of the 21 Franciscan missions established in California, Mission Santa Barbara is the only one still active as a parish church.

Continuing into the hills along Mission Canyon Boulevard, you'll come upon the *Santa Barbara Botanic Garden* and the *Santa Barbara Museum of Natural History*. The botanical garden encompasses 65 acres and 1,000 species of native California trees, flowers, shrubs, grasses and annuals. They are divided into sections (canyon, desert, arroyo, meadow, woodland), each with its own trails. This lovely park will plunge you back into pre-European, precondominium California. And just wait till you discover the redwoods, beneath whose huge boughs everything is stilled to a cathedral-like silence. The natural history museum presents geology and biology exhibits. Praised by the likes of Einstein, it's impossible to miss. Just look for the place with a 72-foot blue whale skeleton out front. Back downtown, a walking tour can be taken of Santa Barbara's "red tile district." Some 20 buildings of historical and architectural interest exist in a 10-block area, and tour maps are available at the Visitors Bureau.

Historically, the Native American presence in the Santa Barbara area dates back many thousands of years to the Chumash Indians, an inventive people wiped out by European diseases. Santa Barbara's colonial history unravels in successive and involved stages of Spanish, Mexican and American occupation. Culturally, Santa

Barbara boasts 28 art galleries and 11 crafts galleries, plus theater, symphony and ballet. Recreationally, there's tennis, golf, polo and yachting, and some of the most competitive volleyball in California is played on the courts of East Beach. We could go on and on....Santa Barbara happens to be one of those towns that defies summarizing in 1,000 words. It is a rich tapestry of a city that begs to be studied and appreciated at length.

But back to the beaches. East and West Beach are by no means the only ones in the area. Just beyond the volleyball courts is *Butterfly Beach*, a hidden fan-shaped cove as delicate as a monarch's wing, reachable either by hiking around the point at East Beach or by taking a remote twist of road known as Butterfly Lane. Next to this, in the shadow of a luxury hotel (formerly the Biltmore, now *Marriott's Santa Barbara Biltmore*) is *Montecito Shores*. Sun worshipers spread out at the foot of the bluffs on a beach that is wide at low tide and narrow at high. Both Montecito Shores and Butterfly Beach belong to the community of Montecito, a suburb of Santa Barbara that is, if anything, even richer.

On the other side of Santa Barbara, past West Beach and the 1,000-slip yacht harbor, the coast gets hillier, and the beaches are tucked into coves like babies into bassinets. *Leadbetter Beach* is within walking distance of the harbor, right off Shoreline Drive. Two miles west lies *Arroyo Burro Beach*, a small county park set around a stream running out of the mountains.

At this point, you are nearly in Goleta, a city of 60,000 you've probably never heard of. Nonetheless, it's closely tied to Santa Barbara. In fact, the University of California at Santa Barbara is located in Goleta. Figure that one out. In any case, the presence of a large student body so close by pumps fresh blood into Santa Barbara, which might otherwise become somewhat stodgy. As it is, there's a balance, which ensures the city's vigor and vitality.

Last of all, we'll mention the courthouse. If the Mission Santa Barbara is the religious symbol of the community, then the Santa Barbara County Courthouse is the most impressive secular landmark in town. Built in the elaborate Spanish-Moorish style, it looks more like a palace than a courthouse. Occupying a full city block, this turreted, muraled, chandeliered, hand-carved, tiled, terracotta'd and stenciled masterpiece must be toured to be believed. It would be an honor to pay a traffic ticket here. The crowning touch is the clock tower ("El Maridor"), atop which an observation deck offers a sweeping panorama of Santa Barbara. Pondering the city from this vantage point, one cannot help but reflect on the perfect yin-yang of the setting: mountains and ocean, warm sun and cool breezes, young folks and old folks, and all the divergent elements that make up Northern and Southern California.

Accommodations

We'll talk about two among many places to stay—one in the hills, the other on the beach. Follow the arrows to the Mission Santa Barbara, then keep curving to the right and soon a sign for *El Encanto* will spring into view. Nestled in the foothills overlooking the city, El Encanto is a European-style inn offering the sort of informal elegance worth driving up a mountain for. The town unfolds below, glimmering at night like a distant field of candle flames. Spread out on the grounds of El Encanto are a number of garden villas. The rooms and suites inside these, each furnished differently, range from cozy to *magnifique* and are priced accordingly ($100 to $300 a night). A large pool and Japanese fish pond are set among a thick, junglelike growth of flowers and shrubs. A touch of class pervades every aspect of El Encanto, where a casually Californian ambience tempers the European formality to a glow as rosy as a Pacific sunset. The view and eucalyptus-scented air are as intoxicating as anything on the restaurant's wine list. You'll find yourself ambling down the zigzag brick-red walkways, lost in the maze but not caring and never wanting to leave.

Down toward the beach, the lodging options are plentiful, from cheap chains to *Fess Parker's Red Lion Inn* and *Marriott's Santa Barbara Biltmore*. The *Santa Barbara Inn* was our second night's choice. Located east of the downtown bustle, where Cabrillo Boulevard hugs the shore in the vicinity of Highway 101 and East Beach, it's quiet over here. The rooms—which range in price from $85 to $148—are spacious and comfortable, and you're only a crosswalk away from the beach and yet another architectural landmark, the Cabrillo Pavilion—a beachfront arts and recreation center dating from 1927.

These are only several of many dozen choices that include bed-and-breakfast inns (our first significant sighting of these along the California coast). For further decision-making assistance, contact the chamber of commerce for a directory or call *Accommodations in Santa Barbara* for free referrals and reservations at (805) 963-9518. And if you're coming in the summer, try to book from four to six weeks in advance.

Restaurants

If you had a dozen mouths and a free month, you still couldn't hope to digest all that Santa Barbara has to offer in the way of restaurants. They publish brochures, flyers and entire magazines about dining in Santa Barbara.

Once again, we'd like to point you to the top of the hill. The dining room at the *El Encanto* boasts the finest view in the city and possibly the best food. The menu is classic French cuisine with a twist of California. The offerings include everything from the house-special crispy duck in a carmelized honey and thyme sauce to half a dozen choices of fresh fish, broiled and served with an appropriately delicate accompaniment (e.g., sea bass with saffron sauce). The restaurant and the hotel are appointed in a dignified color scheme of rose, gray and emerald. Men are asked to wear jackets at dinner. The edible artwork that is laid out before you is so splendidly presented that it's a pity to defile it with a fork. The duck pâté appetizer, for instance, came out formed into the shape of a bird, with pecans for wings, an apple slice for a beak and a sprig of dill for a tail. Bon appetit!

Another Santa Barbara restaurant with a sterling reputation is *Downey's*. Recognized as one of the top 25 restaurants in the state of California, Downey's specializes in "sophisticated California cuisine." It's not inexpensive, nor is the menu predictable, but the standard of quality remains constant.

Joe's Café merits quite a different sort of recommendation. If you can appreciate a saloon with padded booths and a long bar where food and drink are served in large quantities, you'll love Joe's, Santa Barbara's oldest restaurant. Checkered tablecloths cover the tables, and mounted moose and deer heads look down on hungry diners awaiting the arrival of heaping, home-cooked blue plate specials. The torpedo-sized French dip sandwiches are a hot item, but anything here is good, solid, stick-to-your-ribs fare: the combination seafood plate, the brisket of beef, whatever. Take our advice—eat at Joe's.

A strong Mexican influence pervades Santa Barbara, and State, Haley and Milpas streets are lined with Mexican cantinas and eateries. Have at it, amigos, and may the best burrito win. Finally, in the realm of seafood, the *Famous Enterprise Fish Co.* serves mesquite-grilled fish in a cavernous old building with brick walls and exposed steel beams. Everything is cooked with a flourish over the grill in the center. Famous Enterprise is within casting distance of Stearns Wharf on State Street in the funky section of Santa Barbara known as Old Town.

This short list, incidentally, doesn't begin to do justice to the culinary possibilities in this cultured pearl of a town. For a more comprehensive accounting, write the visitors bureau or lay hands on *The Major Guide to Santa Barbara Dining*, sold in area newspaper-vending boxes for a quarter.

Nightlife

After the old folks have donned their stocking caps and trundled off to bed, Santa Barbara reawakens as another city. There are clubs, clubs and more clubs. They line State Street, from Old Town to uptown. You can tap your foot to jazz at a sit-down bistro or rock out till two in the morning. Most young adults of legal drinking age do the latter, keeping the clubs overflowing on weekends. Take your pick: for starters, the *Pacific Coast Dance Company*, the *Bombay Bar and Grill* and *The Club*. "Progressive Top Forty" is deejayed at these late-model dance clubs.

Next stop on the tour is *Rocky Galenti's*—a sports bar, rock club and Italian restaurant rolled into one. Bar-band rock and roll is played in the back room, which fills up with smoke, sweat and bouncing bodies on a good night. Out front, the main activity is the sort of chatty imbibing that's the hallmark of a popular college bar. The walls are covered with caricatures of regulars, there's enough room for a buffalo to roam, and all in all Rocky's is as friendly and lively a place as you'll find in any town. Everyone is welcome. Even a befuddled old man who looked like a cross between Lech Walesa and Meher Baba—and who'd assume sudden, John Travolta-like dance poses for no reason—was humored by the collegians. Every now and then he'd ball his hand into a fist, drop to one knee and shout, "Hey!" Maybe he thought he was at a polka party.

Joe's Café is regarded as a late-night refuge by locals. When the hour is rapidly advancing toward last call, you can always follow the crowd over to Joe's. Middle-aged visitors gravitate to *Don the Beachcomber*, on the third floor of the Santa Barbara Inn. Don serves Polynesian food and large, rummy drinks in a hokey South Seas atmosphere that'll make you feel like you've stumbled into Don Ho's living room. Stumbling back to our room at the inn late one night, we popped into Don the Beachcomber, only to find ourselves face to face with a bulldog of a man seated in a rattan grotto, growling a Kris Kristofferson song to the beat of a Rhythm Ace and glowering at us while we chuckled at his shtick.

At some point during your nighttime wanderings, you should angle out onto Stearns Wharf. This three-block wooden wharf, built in 1872, widens into an over-the-water parking lot for all the people who've come to shop and eat at its restaurants. The best-known place on Stearns Wharf is the *Harbor*, which serves everything from bouillabaisse to coconut fried shrimp. Upstairs, they dispense drinks and soft rock. The Harbor was described to us as a "one-night romance kind of place" by a bellhop who appeared to be in the know. Indeed, we later saw him off in a corner of the Harbor, deep in negotiations for a one-night romance. As for us, we were approached by a girl who insulted our clothes, accused us of being "fake preppies," refused to believe we weren't from the West Coast, asked for some identification to prove otherwise, and then tried to swallow one of our driver's licenses. What's that song Rod Stewart used to sing—"Some Guys Have All the Luck"? We are not those guys.

FOR FURTHER INFORMATION

Santa Barbara Conference and Visitors Bureau
1330 State Street, Suite 200
P.O. Box 299
Santa Barbara, CA 93102
(805) 965-3021

Goleta
Isla Vista

Goleta is a next-door neighbor very nearly equal in size to Santa Barbara that attracts not a fraction of her publicity. Goleta seems to be a repository for those things that Santa Barbara wants to keep outside its city limits, i.e., the University of California at Santa Barbara and the Santa Barbara Airport. Most of Goleta is not coastal but spreads back into the Goleta Valley, pressed against the Santa Ynez Mountains and lined with lemon orchards.

The university overlooks the ocean from high, grassy bluffs, and college kids scuttle down to the beach below to have fun, fun, fun. They also frequent the county and city beaches of tiny Isla Vista, a breath to the west, between Goleta Point and Coal Oil Point. *Goleta County Park* is the largest and most popular beach in the area. Parking is free, and people come to picnic (tables, open-air shelters and hibachis are provided), play volleyball and horseshoes, and frolic in the water. The vast park includes numerous parking lots; a long, thin pier; a wide sand beach; and more green acres than Hooterville. A pierside restaurant, the *Beachside Bar Café*, is reputedly quite good.

Goleta Valley Area Chamber of Commerce
P.O. Box 781
Goleta, CA 93116
(805) 967-4618

El Capitan State Beach
Refugio State Beach
Gaviota State Park

Between Santa Barbara and Point Conception, the coastline runs on a near-perfect east-west axis, and the beaches face due south. This stretch is utterly unaffected by northern swells and protected by the Channel Islands from those rolling up from the south. It makes for ideal ocean swimming, and the state of California has obliged with three beautiful parks along this isolated stretch of Route 1.

The first is El Capitan, about 12 miles north of Santa Barbara. The natural features of this 168-acre park include sea cliffs, tide pools, meadows, marine terraces and canyon lands. Groves of pines, sycamores and palms are spread throughout the park, and 140 rustic campsites sit in their shade. The green rolling hills surrounding El Capitan have the verdant look of Ireland about them. The beach below is reachable by stairs near the concession stand or dirt paths down the bluff. Incidentally, the Reagan ranch is buried in the hills behind El Capitan.

A short hop up the road is Refugio State Beach, which offers more of the same: splendid natural setting, low-angle beach fringed by banana palms, and a happily chirping chorus of birds adding music to the picturesque setting. The surf rolls in a little harder here, and, when we visited, a knot of surfers were getting some long rides up at the western end of the beach. A creek enters the ocean at Refugio, and people were swimming in a cool freshwater lagoon. The smallest of the three parks, Refugio offers 85 campsites. Here, as at El Capitan, the campground had filled to capacity early on a gorgeous summer Saturday.

   Gaviota State Park, 10 more miles up the road, is a large wilderness area that extends into the forested uplands north of Route 1. The beach at Gaviota is striking to see. A railroad trestle carries trains high overhead, spanning the cut between two sheer walls of rock. Gaviota has its own fishing pier, which includes a three-ton hoist, used to launch or haul power boats from the water. The rest of this 2,276-acre park is largely undeveloped. Hikers and backpackers make their way to hot springs in the higher elevations.

Jalama Beach County Park

Jalama Beach is just north of the off-limits Hollister Ranch at Point Conception. Surfers risk the strong currents there because the waves are terrific. Motoring to the point from Gaviota or Jalama in a small boat is commonly done by the fearless surfing set. Otherwise, people surf-cast for everything from perch to halibut and camp on 28 acres of county-park beaches, bluffs and wetlands.

Ocean Beach County Park

Like an adventure? Here's a good one. Above Point Conception, Route 1 curls through the sweet-smelling, flower-filled fields of Lompoc, avoiding the coast. A left turn onto Ocean Avenue in Lompoc will eventually lead through Vandenberg Air Force Base. Thereafter, the road gets narrower, curvier and bumpy as you near Ocean Beach. At last it gives out in a parking lot. Stop, look and listen. Railroad cars sit on a piece of track. The wind whistles across the sandy fields. You are officially in the middle of nowhere.

The beach is a quarter-mile hike over squishy wet sand along the edge of an estuary that's home to several endangered birds and one endangered plant species. Waves break and crash furiously at Ocean Beach, making swimming an impossibility. Even the birds look queasy at the unleashed might of the sea. No one dares brave the waters here, though anglers cast lines into the foaming green from the shore.

Guadalupe

North of Lompoc, sand dunes rise like bare white mountains, paralleling the coastline for 20 miles. They reach their highest peaks west of the tumbledown town of Guadalupe. The highway doesn't go anywhere near the dunes. To reach them, you must take Main Street out of Guadalupe until it ends on the beach at *Rancho Guadalupe County Park*. Main Street passes the town cemetery, a few ragged fields and an open range where cattle graze, unbothered by the wind, chilly temperatures and sand. Sand is everywhere, even blowing over the road and parking lot at the county park. Briefly, we wondered if we'd made a wrong turn and landed at the White Sands missile range.

Somewhere among the tall dunes stands *Mussel Rock*, the highest sand dune on the West Coast. It is all sand—not rock, as the name suggests—and is 450 feet tall, give or take a grain or two due to prevailing winds. An ankle-sinking two-mile hike is required if you wish to see the West's biggest sand heap. The ocean at Rancho Guadalupe is too rough for immersion or recreation. We saw no lifeguards, no surfers, no picnickers, no swimmers. Nothing but sand and, back toward Guadalupe, a few head of cattle.

Much the same holds true for the state beach at *Point Sal*, just above Vandenberg near Guadalupe. Because it is south of the point, the park is protected from the prevailing northwesterly winds, which makes walking the beach possible at other than a 45-degree angle. The ocean, however, churns much too roughly for recreation here.

Pismo Beach
Oceano
Grover City
Shell Beach

North of Santa Barbara, the Coast Highway takes a vacation from the coast, yielding to Vandenberg Air Force Base and swinging inland. For about 50 miles, it passes through some extraordinary interior scenery, from the flower fields of the Lompoc Valley to the charbroiled forest surrounding Guadalupe. In a swooping series of hairpin turns, the road descends toward the plain just north of Arroyo Grande, signaling that Route 1 is once again near the coast.

At this point, you are in Pismo Beach and officially out of Southern California. As evidence, they call this the "central coast," an area that extends all the way north to Monterey. Geographically and spiritually, it is a totally different landscape from Santa Barbara. More western than Californian, Pismo and environs are filled with less body-conscious people: women who wear tentlike checkered dresses and men with lethally pointed cowboy boots. They're more likely to drive falling asunder Pintos than sleek new Porsches, and they live not in swank seaside villas but in mobile homes. Even the mountains that press against Pismo Beach are different—softer in tone and texture, less jagged, and covered with gray-brown whiskers. Looking at them, you can conceive of hiking these large hills on a picnic—*not* the case with the Santa Monica and Santa Ynez ranges down south, which inspire daydreams of backpacking expeditions with Edmund Hillary. Most of all, though, upon entering Pismo Beach you are reminded once again that California is many states rolled into one.

Pismo Beach is the heart of the "Five Cities" region, a group that also includes Oceano and Grover City—less inviting but more populous communities that have recently sprung up like a stray litter just beginning to bark for attention. The area they encompass is referred to with the catchall handle "Pismo Beach." *Pismo* is a Chumash Indian word meaning "blobs of tar that wash up on the beach." By the time the Spanish arrived, the Chumash had been living in the area for 9,000 years. The Spanish had no problem with the Chumash name for the area, because in their language *pismo* allegedly means "a place to fish." Thanks to this semantic twist of fate, the town has been stuck with a name as smile-inducing as "Oxnard."

Today, Pismo has little to do with either tar or fish but lots to do with sand. Lots and lots of sand. Traveling north from Guadalupe on Route 1, one enters Oceano first and then Grover City. Both are larger than Pismo Beach but too slipshod to steal its thunder. Acres of RV parks and trailer encampments roast in the scrub grass like slabs of meat in a smokehouse. Oceano has the distinction of being home to a "family tradition" known as *The Great American Melodrama*, where you can watch a man with a pencil-thin moustache tie a woman to a railroad track while a melodian plays in the background. Oceano is also the home of the *Pismo Dunes Preserve* and the *Pismo Dunes Vehicular Recreation Area*. The preserve is a large area of protected sand dunes set back from the coast and popular with hikers. The recreation area is an 850-acre oceanfront park with tall dunes and hard-packed sand beaches open to vehicular use (that's "use," as in "abuse"). Because these dunes have no vegetative cover, they've been set aside for torture by souped-up dune buggies and all-terrain vehicles—big-wheeled riding lawnmower–type contraptions that churn the sand pointlessly so some red-faced moron in a Cat hat can say he climbed a big hill and almost rolled over in the process. The dunes here are some of the highest and healthiest on the West Coast and are one of the Pismo area's biggest attractions.

Pismo State Beach has an access point in Oceano, one in Grover City and several in Pismo Beach proper. The beach is sandy and wide—so wide, in fact, that cars are allowed on the beach to the south, toward Pismo Dunes. (Think of Pismo Beach as California's answer to Daytona Beach, Florida, without the pretty girls.) North of this access point only pedestrians are allowed, which leaves plenty of unobstructed beach for those who enjoy less noisome pursuits like swimming, tanning, surfing and clamming. Clam-digging is especially rewarding around here. At one time, Pismo Beach

was the Clam Capital of the World, and the town has had a type
of clam named after it. In recent years, surfing has become popular enough to warrant an annual tournament—quite a coup for a
small town on the central coast.

The state beach fronts Pismo Beach's business district and continues north, ending at some chalky white cliffs beneath the smaller,
more well-to-do community of Shell Beach. This town has a minuscule stretch of coarse, dark sand and a slow, gentrified pace all its
own. By comparison, Pismo Beach is cut from plainer cloth. A
cruise through town reveals a number of old motels, a few burger
and taco huts, a chowder house, an old theater that's gone out of
business, a video arcade and a new million-dollar pier that's eerily
devoid of commercial enterprise.

Oh, yes, and there is a municipal parking lot by the pier, around
which the social life of Pismo Beach turns, literally. At night, cars
and trucks circle the parking lot in an endless wagon train. A block
from the pier, on a Sunday afternoon, we spied a group of jumbo
bikers leaning against a row of choppers like walruses sunning on
the rocks. Their jackets announced them as the "Condors From
Bakersfield, CA." No doubt the residents of Pismo Beach would
love to see this type of condor on the brink of extinction, but the
brood from Bakersfield appeared to be doing quite well—big hairy
things with overweight, Morticia Addams saddle mates. Ah, well.

The town of Pismo Beach is not the sort to bill itself as the perfect seaside retreat. It's too modest for that, developmental hype
not yet having migrated this far north. Still, it has the physical
goods and the motels, and it waits on the southern edge of the
central coast at your disposal. Perhaps this quote, taken from a
chamber of commerce brochure, will shed some light on the locals' perspective:

"There is rapture by the lonely shore. There is society where
none intrude by the sea, and music in its roar. I love not man less,
but Nature more." —Lord Byron.

Accommodations

Flanking the main beach in Pismo are two hotels on the upwardly mobile side. The *Sandcastle Inn*, at the southern end, is directly on the beach and within easy walking distance of the pier, in case you brought your fishing tackle. The rooms at the Sandcastle, a hotel condominium, are plush, and the management serves a continental breakfast in the downstairs lobby. Double rooms in season run from $75 to $100—considerably less than you'd pay for similar digs anywhere in Southern California.

The *Sea Crest Motel*, near Shell Beach on the north side of Pismo, ups the Sandcastle's ante with a heated pool and jacuzzi, but you don't get the free breakfast (just complimentary coffee). Situated on a strikingly beautiful cliff, the Sea Crest is a fine perch from which to appreciate the spectacular setting. A long, steep wooden staircase leads to the beach. Also on the grounds are a number of jagged promontories upon which one can repose while the sun slowly sets on you and the rough-and-tumble Pacific.

Restaurants

In the Esperanto of road hunger, *Pismo* means "mediocre." The town really doesn't have much to offer other than burgers and fish 'n' chips, and they didn't even prepare the latter well at a sit-down restaurant where this was the house specialty. The most promising restaurant near the water, from outward appearances, was average at best, their "special of the day" being a ham and swiss sandwich and a cup of clam chowder. The ham was as thinly sliced as that found in plastic envelopes at the grocery store, while the chowder was so bland it could've been made by the clams themselves in an effort to get the locals off this "Pismo clam" shtick. The finest restaurant in town, according to a local consensus, was located in a mini-mall and didn't post a menu, so we won't post an account. (There oughta be a law.) At the *Burger Heaven* in Pismo Beach—presumably where all good beef patties go when they die— the BBQ Chicken Special was devilishly tempting. It's sad to report this was the best we could scare up in Pismo Beach. Once again, we realized we were not in Southern California anymore.

Nightlife

It goes without saying that in a town where the night is ruled by cruising cars and revving motorcycles, the daytime is really the right time. Down by the pier, the parking lot becomes the focal point for the midnight ramblings of the video-game generation. Like fighter pilots on maneuvers, they circle the two-lane lot in customized, casketlike trucks, tape players blaring the same gaping-jaws-of-hell metal machine music, occasionally spiced with a Beastie Boys rap. Whatever their intent or purpose, it did not look the least bit fun.

The liveliest nightclub in town, we were told, was *Harry's*. We made an on-site inspection. The front door had horseshoes for door handles. The sign outside boasted "Live Country Rock Bands 7 Nights a Week." The curb outside boasted a flotilla of Harleys in formation. We'll boast that we stuck around no longer than it took to suffer through a miserable version of "Johnny B. Goode" and stare dumbfounded at a roomful of guys who looked like Johnny B. Bad.

FOR FURTHER INFORMATION

Pismo Beach Chamber of Commerce
581 Dolliver Street
Pismo Beach, CA 93449
(805) 773-4382

Avila Beach

Avila State Beach is around the corner from Shell Beach, on the other side of San Luis Obispo Bay. It is the sun and fun capital of the south central coast. Although the route to and from Avila is more circuitous and rural than the highway junction that leads directly into Pismo Beach, Avila is more popular at certain times of the year—for instance, when school is in session up the road at Cal Poly State University. The college is 10 miles away in San Luis Obispo, the county seat and largest town in San Luis Obispo County. (The entire county has only 200,000 citizens, and they're all in the same phone book.)

Avila Beach is where San Luis Obispo and Cal Poly's well-endowed student body go for the day—before, after and probably during classes. Its status as a day-tripper's haven is confirmed by the absence of motels and surplus of beautiful women. Every one of them was gorgeous. Is this a prerequisite for enrollment at Cal Poly? Anyway, the weather here is the most consistently sunny in the county. It's no wonder that the San Luis Obispans, especially those particular about their tans, come here.

It is a village, of sorts. Avila Beach has a grocery store, a few quick-bite eateries, two piers (one the exclusive property of Union Oil), a mile-long beach, some public facilities and a lifeguard stand. The lovely coeds sun themselves beside the seawall, while the usual troop of shirtless, red-baked young men in knee-length surfer trunks peer down at them and then walk away muttering to themselves: "Gol-dang." Without their surfboards, the guys seem less sure of themselves here than they do elsewhere on the coast. There's probably a good reason for this: these college-educated goddesses are smarter than they are. In any case, Avila Beach was our last glimpse of bikini-clad California girls for many moons.

Montaña de Oro State Park

Just south of Morro Bay, near the small bayside towns of Los Osos and Baywood Park, Montaña de Oro State Park spreads out across an immense land area. Montaña de Oro ("mountain of gold") is a whopper, occupying nearly 7,000 acres and fronting the ocean for 1½ miles from the Morro Sand Spit south. It's a primitive park, with minimal facilities, only 50 campsites and no potable water. The road through the park plunges ever deeper into large groves of eucalyptus trees, with their silvery bark and refreshing fragrance. The beaches here are as wild as an unbroken colt, choked with rocky outcroppings and sea caves and pounded by a frothy, roiling surf. The coarse salt-and-pepper sand is not conducive to sunbathing, but the park is ruggedly beautiful to behold. Indefatigable surfers sometimes hike through the woods to the small beach at Hazard Canyon.

Morro Bay

Driving north along Route 1, we spied a rock looming on the horizon that caused us to do a double take and very nearly swerve off the road. This was no run-of-the-mill boulder. It looked like a bare, brown geodesic dome rising from the landscape.

The mysterious mount happened to be *Morro Rock*. It is the symbol of the town of Morro Bay, the pet rock of the central coast and "Gibraltar of the Pacific." Morro Rock is one of seven volcanic peaks that run in a nearly straight line from San Luis Obispo to Morro Bay, a distance of 12 miles. Collectively known as the Seven Sisters, the range is 21 million years old, long dead and extinct, so you needn't worry about a sudden, Mt. Saint Helens–like eruption spoiling your vacation. Morro Rock is the westernmost peak in the chain. (Actually, there is an eighth further offshore and a ninth off-axis somewhere east of San Luis Obispo, but they don't count.) It looks like a chocolate cake that listed in the oven, and for good reason. Morro Rock lost its sharp peak and some of its elevation through quarrying.

Volcanic talus quarried off Morro Rock in the late 1800s and the 1930s was used in breakwaters here and elsewhere and also built the jetty connecting Morro Rock with the mainland. Unfortunately, it was discovered that Morro's lava rock doesn't hold up against the force of the sea. Moreover, quarrying was beginning to affect the fragile Morro Rock ecosystem. Nesting grounds for the rare and endangered peregrine falcon were being destroyed—as was the rock itself. In 1968, Morro Rock was designated a State Historical Landmark and a Peregrine Falcon Preserve. You can drive up to its base and even halfway around it, but climbing the rock is forbidden.

As surely as Golden Arches mean McDonald's, Morro Rock has become the symbol of Morro Bay. Its likeness has been branded everywhere: on matchbooks, postcards, motel trash baskets. But there's more to Morro Bay than this hazy monolith. It's actually a working village with a sizable sport and commercial fishing fleet operating out of its breezy harbor. Morro Bay has the authentic flavor of a fishing village with no ersatz tourist trappings.

The town is arranged around the *Embarcadero*, where boats dock and retail activity is transacted. The Embarcadero runs for about a mile, from Morro Rock to the boundary for *Morro Bay State Park*. It is a highly walkable mile, passing all manner of bait-and-tackle shops and fish 'n' chips shacks (*local* fish with the chips, they emphasize). Every day, the commercial fleet sails in with fresh catches of salmon, albacore, ling cod, Pacific snapper, Alaskan halibut and thresher shark. For a reasonable charge, an outfit like the colorfully monikered Virg's Fish'n will haul anglers out to deep water to cast lines all day or for a half day. Visitors can also go clamming on the long, sandy spit that protects and very nearly encircles the harbor. The 100-yard crossing to the *Morro Sand Spit* is made via Clam Taxi. For a round trip fee of $3, a ruddy sea salt who looks like he's stared down more gales than Captain Ahab will ferry you across the harbor and deposit you on a sandbank. Once there, you can hike, beachcomb, dig for clams, surf-cast or bird-watch. It's a mite uncomfortable on the spit if "the wind's blowin' like snot," according to the plainspoken skipper, so dress as you would for a tornado. When you want to return, just stand on the spot where you were dropped off, wave at the shoreline and the good captain will pop over in a flash. The "taxi" is caught at the foot of Pacific Street.

Just strolling the Embarcadero is a relaxing way to pass an afternoon. There's the Fisherman's Memorial, a small harborside park with a monster 7,000-pound anchor as its centerpiece. The town's pride and joy is its giant chessboard, an outdoor game board whose dimensions are straight out of Alice in Wonderland, with three-foot-tall chessmen carved from redwood.

Over by Morro Rock are a pair of beaches. The small, crescent-shaped one by the breakwater attracts the sun-worshipers. Spray flies off the top of the breakwater as the waves crash thunderously, but the surf on the beach behind it is as calm as that of a backyard wading pool. If you're tempted to scale the rocks for the view from the top, think twice about it. We hoisted ourselves along a slippery, wet staircase of boulders only to get washed off by an enormous wave that caught us unaware. Wetter than a pair of sea otters but otherwise unhurt, we changed into dry clothes and swore off breakwaters for the rest of the trip. *Atascadero State Beach* is north of Morro Rock, facing due west. Large waves roll lazily toward the shoreline for a good distance, making for long rides.

Looking toward town from Morro Rock, you can plainly see the other dominant symbol of Morro Bay: three 450-foot smokestacks of a Pacific Gas & Electric generating plant. They resemble enormous filter-tipped cigarettes, make a noise not unlike the drone in *Eraserhead* and warm the nearby water by a few degrees.

But on to brighter vistas, like the two state parks close by. *Morro Bay State Park* begins at the south end of Main Street. Immediately, you're driving under a canopy of shade trees. A paved road leads to Black Mountain Lookout—at 865 feet, the highest point in the park—with its sweeping view of the coast. On the grounds of the park are a golf course, a protected great blue heron rookery, 135 campsites and a museum of natural history. The marsh where Los Osos Creek enters Morro Bay is home for 250 species of birds. Canoes can be rented for paddling the quiet waters of the estuary or rowing out to the spit.

All in all, plenty of soul-satisfying, nature-oriented activity can be found in Morro Bay. Like much of the central coast, it is blessed with what is referred to as a Mediterranean climate: mild winters and cool, foggy summers, with the sun burning the gray away by midday and a stiff offshore breeze rippling mainsails. The town is especially attractive when the setting sun drops into the ocean like a glowing orange Alka-Seltzer slipped into a glass of water. As the sun falls, look to Morro Rock, which takes on mysterious hues and auras all its own. One evening around twilight, a small violet cloud hovered over the rock like a halo. Exquisite, yes.

Accommodations

A sudden spurt of inns and motels has filled the Embarcadero and
streets behind it in recent years, as Morro Bay cautiously adapts
to the tourist wave washing north from Los Angeles. But as residents hasten to point out, Morro Bay's charm hasn't yet been buried beneath a human tsunami.

The lodge of first choice is the *Inn at Morro Bay*. Located just
inside the Morro Bay State Park boundary, the inn is set some
distance back from the bustle of the Embarcadero. A luxury resort with a romantic undercurrent, its 100 guest rooms feature
cathedral ceilings, gas fireplaces, country French decor and outdoor decks that overlook the bay. At night, while you're out dining, the housekeeping staff will sneak in like tooth fairies and
turn down the bed, placing roses and chocolates on the pillow
and leaving a small bottle of cognac and two glasses on the bed-
side stand. The suite-sized rooms are filled with heavy, hand-
carved furniture, and the brass-fixtured bathrooms come with a
complimentary assortment of French soap. As lavish as it is, the
Inn at Morro Bay maintains a cozy country-style atmosphere, all
for only $75 to $125 a night.

Another fine choice is the *Embarcadero Inn* ($60 - $90) on the bay
at the south end of the Embarcadero. The rooms are large, the
furniture cushiony, and there are VCRs in the rooms and films at
the front desk. Each room has a gas fireplace and an outdoor balcony, and the inn has a pair of indoor saunas. With its slate-colored,
weathered-wood exterior, the Embarcadero Inn is the most dis-
tinguished lodge on the waterfront.

Restaurants

The *Hungry Tiger* and the *Great American Fish Company* come highly
recommended. The latter's shingle reads "fish, steak and grog."
Both restaurants look out on the harbor. If you're after something
quick and basic, head into *Café Baja* for a hamburger. Make that a
surfburger. They fry up all kinds of special burgers here, such as

the San Miguel Surfburger (topped with bacon and cheddar) and the Rincon Surfburger (guacamole, salsa and Monterey Jack). You can also order fish tacos and red-snapper burgers.

Back on the wharf, albacore and salmon are smoked on the premises at *Bob's Seafood*. The secret of their success is soaking the fish in brine (no sugar), then slow-smoking it over applewood for six hours. The result is a moist, tender and delicately seasoned fish. In addition, Bob's posts a full menu of fried and broiled seafood and serves breakfast till noon.

Moving upscale, the *Inn at Morro Bay* has its own dining room, which serves California-style nouvelle cuisine with a subtle French flair. You can count on fresh ingredients, superb preparation, a respectable wine list, excellent service and a spectacular view over the water. The albacore appetizer had a light, crisp breading and was surrounded by raisins and a creamy beurre blanc. A meaty shark appetizer was accompanied by a sweet, spicy Cajun sauce. The house specialty entrée, Pasta El Encanto, was named after the inn's sister operation in Santa Barbara, where the chef co-created it. Pasta El Encanto consists of two types of pasta combined with a variety of fresh fish and shellfish and tossed with a light cream sauce.

Nightlife

Taking a head count of cocktail lounges in Morro Bay, we came up with seven. You're probably better off retiring to the inn, pressing the switch on the gas fire and popping the cork on a bottle of wine. It's a free world, though, and you are welcome to all the highballs you can drink. For entertainment, angle over to *Rose's Landing*, where you can "dance to the music of Dave Nunes [or someone like him] playing in the Captain's Lounge," if that sort of thing lights your fire.

FOR FURTHER INFORMATION

ʌamber of Commerce

ʌreet

Sʌ

Morro ʌ. ʌ, CA 93442

(805) 772-4467

Cayucos

Cayucos takes its name from the Indian word for "canoe." It enjoys the distinction of being the midpoint between Los Angeles and San Francisco. Each is 225 miles away. The main appeal of Cayucos is that there's nothing to do here. We don't mean this facetiously. In the words of a local booster, "What we offer is peace and serenity from the stresses of big-city life." You can while away time on the long stretches of *Morro Strand State Beach* and *Cayucos State Beach*, along the cove around which Cayucos is built. The turquoise waters of Estero Bay are good for surfing, diving and sailing. Fishing is very popular here, for ocean catches off Cayucos Pier and for steelhead trout at Whale Rock Reservoir.

Cayucos is gradually bracing itself for tourism, building a few more motels, restaurants and—always a telltale sign—gift shops. But they have the right perspective on their town. "There's no other place like it on the central coast," claims a native Cayucan. "If somebody pulls up and asks, 'What can you do here?' they're in the wrong place." You *are* allowed to ask, "Is there any place to stay here?" and there are several answers: the *Seaside Motel* and the *California Unique Ocean View Motel*. (With a name like that, how can you go wrong?) There are others, too, all of them independent, nonfranchised motels, to which we say, "Hooray."

Cayucos Chamber of Commerce
P.O. Box 141
Cayucos, CA 93430
(805) 995-1200

Cambria

Between Cayucos and San Simeon lies the village of Cambria, a shy princess knocking on the back door of the Hearst Castle. A century ago Cambria was a thriving whaling, mining and farming community. With a population of 7,000, it was the second largest township in San Luis Obispo County. Today, its numbers have shrunk to 4,000, and there's little going on but agriculture and a modest tourist trade, mostly the spillover from San Simeon plus enlightened travelers who know a genuinely quaint village from a lousy imitation.

Lately craftsmen, writers and artists have been moving to Cambria in growing numbers, giving it something of the flavor of Laguna Beach without the hectic pace of Southern California. The town is divided into "east" and "west" villages. East is older, with many of its historic houses dating from the days when Cambria was known as "Slabtown," after the rough-hewn boards from which they were built. West Village has been constructed in the image of the tourist town of Solvang (down in the Santa Ynez Valley, near Santa Barbara), with a Danish look to it.

Cambria's often passed-by beachfront might be the most enticing area of all. *Moonstone Beach*, as it's known, runs for miles until it tags up with *San Simeon State Beach* to the north. The coastline is rugged, with gnarled driftwood limbs and tangled mats of seaweed washed ashore. Moonstone Beach takes its name from the polished jade, agate and quartz pebbles that collect in mounds here. On certain parts of the beach there is no sand, just heaps of these pea-sized stones. A dirt trail winds along the short bluffs above the beach. On a raw June morning, with fog blowing off the ocean

and blanketing the land, Moonstone Beach seemed positively ee-
rie. But by 1 p.m., the sun had burned the marine moisture away
to reveal a brilliant blue sky.

This is how it goes in the summertime. On account of coastal
fog, July and August are not the best months to visit the central
coast. September, October and November are usually picture perfect: mild and clear, without the blustery winds and choking fog.
By the way, if you don't want to be pegged a tourist, be sure to
pronounce it *Cam*bria, with a short *a* and the accent on the first
syllable, as in "Camelot."

Accommodations

Some elements in the community, casting a jaundiced eye upon
Southern California's clotted landscape, frown on development.
In the words of a local innkeeper, "Most of the residents have a
slow-growth policy. Some might call it a no-growth policy." A
few bed-and-breakfast inns can be found east of the highway, in
the twin villages that make up the town center. A row of motels,
including the cozy, whitewashed *Sea Otter Inn*, do a steady business along Moonstone Beach Drive. Given the easy beach access
and its location off the highway, this is where wise travelers pull
over. To the west lies the ocean; to the east, golden meadows
and hills. This quiet area is a good place to relax and take beach
walks. It's also a logical base if you plan on visiting Hearst Castle
and the many wineries of nearby Paso Robles.

Restaurants

For its size, Cambria has a surprising number of fine restaurants. The
most celebrated is the *Brambles Dinner House*. Set in an English cottage dating from 1874, the Brambles cultivates an "olde English" atmosphere. Paintings, lithographs, antique plates and glassware are
displayed in curio cabinets and on the walls. The menu looks like a

parchment broadside, and the hearty surf-and-turf fare (steaks, prime rib, seafood) is cooked over an oakwood pit.

Down on Moonstone Beach, the *Moonraker* posts an extensive dinner menu heavy on seafood, from abalone to thresher shark. They also blacken red snapper, prime rib and other menu items at your request. A "moonraker," incidentally, is the small flag at the top of the mast that indicates wind direction. Point your moonraker toward Moonstone Beach and enjoy some Pacific Ocean seafood cooked New Orleans–style.

Nightlife

Like most villages along this tame stretch of coastline, more noise is made by small game than by human beings after 10 p.m. Knock off early and save your strength for a prebreakfast beach hike in the fog.

FOR FURTHER INFORMATION

Cambria Chamber of Commerce
767 Main Street
Cambria, CA 93428
(805) 927-3624

San Simeon

San Simeon is castle country. Everything else—sand, sun, sea and the mountains that roll down to it—takes a back seat to the unfathomable grandiosity of the Hearst Castle, the celebrated palace of newspaperman and art collector William Randolph Hearst. Many Americans are aware of the castle's putative identity as Xanadu in the film *Citizen Kane*. A million people a year visit the castle, which is so large that four completely different tours of the buildings and grounds are offered, none of which overlap. It is the number-one state-operated tourist attraction in California.

Hearst was a very wealthy man when he commissioned work on his castle in 1919. Born in 1863, he was the sole heir to the third largest fortune in America. His father, a rough old cob named George Hearst, made millions speculating in gold and silver mines (including the Comstock Lode) in the West. The elder Hearst began grabbing up ranch land in the 1860s for 65 cents an acre. Purchasing adjoining land grants in the San Simeon area, he amassed a spread of 275,000 acres. In the late 1800s, the family often embarked on summer retreats to San Simeon, living in a tent pitched high atop a 1,600-foot mountain they called Camp Hill.

William Randolph Hearst chose to erect his dream castle on this site. He had not done badly for himself, thanks in no small part to his father's largesse. Hearst was given the *San Francisco Chronicle* on his 24th birthday and went on to inherit the family's $11 million fortune. He oversaw a vast media empire that grew to include 30 newspapers, 15 magazines, 6 radio stations and several film companies. History remembers Hearst as somewhat of a yellow journalist whose hysterical reportage helped start a war and elect a president.

His private passion for art collecting may have been even greater than his public passion for journalism and politicking. Hearst reportedly spent a million dollars a year on artwork for 50 consecutive years. He intended the castle to be a Louvre-like repository for his vast collection of Mediterranean Gothic and Renaissance paintings, tapestries and antique ceilings. Work was begun on the various buildings and gardens in 1919. Hearst persuaded Julia Morgan, a renowned Berkeley-trained architect who completed 800 other commissions in her lifetime, to work for and with him on San Simeon. She consented to devote two weekends a month to the Hearst manse, a project that kept her occupied for the next 20 years.

The crowning glory of the hilltop estate was La Casa Grande, the 115-room main house, which includes an assembly room, two libraries, a movie theater and 31 bathrooms. There's no place like home, especially when it's surrounded by 123 acres of exotic gardens, including a line of 100-foot-tall Mexican fan palms. Three guest houses—Casa del Mar, Casa del Sol and Casa del Monte—adjoin Casa Grande, as do huge indoor and outdoor swimming pools. Hearst, an animal fancier, made a virtual nature preserve of his estate, importing 90 species from around the world and letting them roam the hills and fields. To this day, zebra and Barbary sheep, remnants of this bestiary, wander the grounds.

Relating the dimensions of the Hearst Castle, one can wind up foundering in statistics. There is no end to jaw-dropping facts and tales about the celebrity aristocracy who were Hearst's constant guests during the gilded age of the twenties and thirties. On the guided tours, you can do little more than gape at the Greek and Roman temple relics, the 2,000-year-old sarcophagi, the mille-fleur tapestry from the north of France (purchased for $100,000 in 1920 and priceless today), the Spanish castle ceiling (disassembled, shipped overseas in 100 crates and reassembled at San Simeon). You learn of a storage room filled with fur coats, provided as a courtesy for Hearst's female guests wary of catching a shiver from the cool mountain air after stepping out of the heated, 345,000-gallon outdoor pool.

Some might say that William Hearst only did what any red-blooded American would like to have done—namely, indulge every whim and desire that could be conceived, given virtually bound-less resources. In America, the hoi polloi is fascinated with the big money, and this is what keeps buses chugging up the mountainside day in and day out. Though we don't have a king and queen in the United States, we have a palace and its name is San Simeon.

Seven years after Hearst's death in 1951, the estate was given by his heirs to the state of California to be run as a tourist attraction, in return for $56 million in tax breaks. Today, San Simeon is a state historical monument. Tours run like clockwork from 8:20 a.m. to 3:00 p.m. (later in summer) every day of the year but Christmas, Thanksgiving and New Year's. The first tour takes in the lower floor of the castle, the gardens, pools and one guest house, and is recommended for first-timers. The second tour explores the upper floor of the castle, and the third tackles the "new" wing (finished in the forties) and another guest house. Last is a behind-the-scenes look at hidden wine cellars and terraces, as well as the grounds and gardens of San Simeon. Tickets cost $8 per tour per adult and often fill up well in advance, so make reservations as far ahead as possible. In California, call (800) 952-5580; elsewhere, (619) 452-1950.

The tour might make kids a little fidgety. Think about it—when you were young, did you want to spend your vacation walking around a stranger's house under constant supervision? Each tour lasts about two hours, during which time you are shepherded around the grounds by guides who smile more than TV game-show hosts and remind you not to step off the Sears indoor/outdoor carpet runners that keep tourist hoofprints off the priceless marble, tile and wood floors. If you so much as tiptoe onto one of the antique Persian rugs, an alarm will sound or you will be reprimanded by a security person who won't be smiling. A final opinion: San Simeon is more exciting in the abstract than in the beholding. We'd recommend it to educated adults with an interest in art, architecture and, of course, lifestyles of the rich and famous.

It's worth mentioning that although the castle eclipses everything around it, there are two beaches in San Simeon that'll give you something else to do the rest of the day. *San Simeon State Beach* is a 139-site campground and day-use beach bounded at either end by small creeks. A beach at the foot of Hearst's property has been named after him. The grounds include picnic tables, a 1,000-foot pier and a small, tree-shaded beach, and admission is $3 per car.

Accommodations

The first motel to land in the area was the *San Simeon Lodge*, now 30 years old. When the castle opened as a tourist attraction, a whole Vegas strip of motels appeared to service the million yearly visitors. In San Simeon, proximity has bred uniformity. Motel row, three miles south of the visitors entrance to San Simeon on Route 1, features overnight lodges of roughly equal quality and price, $45 to $80 a night being the general range. A quick scan of the neon horizon turned up a *Holiday Inn*, two *Best Westerns* and a *Friendship Inn*, plus a few independent motels. You can count on an ocean-view or mountain-view room, cable TV and a swimming pool.

Restaurants

Restaurants are attached to most of the motels in San Simeon. Because they have a million mouths to feed, the prevailing culinary philosophy is herd 'em in, feed 'em fast and move along little dogies. They arrive by the busload for an hour of carbohydrate loading before touring the house that Hearst built. One manager bragged to us about her restaurant's ability to feed thousands a day. The secret is to goad them into eating from serve-yourself buffet troughs. "Don't even let 'em see a menu—they might get ideas," she told us.

The *San Simeon Restaurant*, adjoining the San Simeon Inn, has been around the longest. Legend has it that Hearst himself ate here on occasion, back when it was the only restaurant in town. One must heave open a veritable castle door to get inside, then be ushered into a dining room filled with San Simeon memorabilia. The house specialty is prime rib, which suits this meat-and-potatoes crowd just fine.

Optionally, you can dip into "old" San Simeon, a small cluster of buildings on a short spur road off Route 1. There's not much more than an old schoolhouse and the oldest store in the state, *Sebastian's General Store*, but out behind Sebastian's, fish 'n' chips and sandwiches are served at the *Patio Café*. The general store is worth dropping by. It smells of coffee and fresh produce, they sell homemade mustard and deli items, and a barrel near the front contains three-foot-long slabs of Oregon-made beef jerky (the gastrointestinal aftereffects of which would surely kill flies at ten paces).

Nightlife

William Randolph Hearst is dead, and after dark so is San Simeon. Here's how your evening is likely to go, if you go out at all. The motel lounge will feature a guy who smiles like a mannequin while strumming and singing along with tapes and a drum machine. He will perform everything from "Whiskey River" to "The Girl from Ipanema" before you've drained your first drink. While you're chewing the cherry, he will sing "Peaceful Easy Feeling," then take a break. You will stumble back to your room and flip on a late-night talk show and then fall asleep during the monologue.

FOR FURTHER INFORMATION

San Simeon Chamber of Commerce
9190 Castillo Drive
P.O. Box 1
San Simeon, CA 93452
(805) 927-3500

Big Sur

The words "Big Sur" have inspired enough verbiage to fill a dozen Norton anthologies. Poetry, prose, proclamations, propositions, postcards—you name it, and it's been written about Big Sur, one of the last great wilderness areas in the contiguous United States.

Perhaps it's the jagged rocks in the water, the crashing waves flinging cataracts of foam, the portentous fog that hovers over land and sea, or the imposing Santa Lucia Mountains. "Harsh and lovely," wrote local novelist Lillian Bos Ross, "held fast to their ancient loneliness by a sheer drop of 5,000 feet by a shoreless sea." Maybe it's the enticing mystery of nature at its most inhospitable, the oneness of sea, sky and shore. One is never at a loss for words when the subject is Big Sur. Yet in the final reckoning, most attempts to describe it are inadequate.

Still, noble efforts have been made. The wild-eyed poet Robinson Jeffers wrote some of his most heroic verse while living in Big Sur. This is amazing in itself, considering that the highway had not yet been built through here when Jeffers first staked out his literary claim. Despite its obvious magnetism for artists and writers, it was not until the itinerant savant and Brooklyn native Henry Miller moved to Big Sur in the late forties that the region gained any sort of widespread fame. The same man who sparked major obscenity trials with his masterpieces of eroticism wrote this about his newfound Canaan: "At dawn its majesty is almost painful to behold. That same prehistoric look. The look of always. Nature smiling at herself in the mirror of eternity."

Another writer, Jack Kerouac, known as much for his infamous behavior as for his published words, came to Big Sur seeking a solitude similar to Miller's. Briefly, Kerouac bivouacked here in 1960 to escape the war zone of fame that had hounded him ever since the media knocked the stuffing out of the word "beatnik." Battling chronic alcoholism, he lit out for a shack in a Big Sur canyon belonging to poet Lawrence Ferlinghetti (who has also written of Big Sur). In his underrated novel *Big Sur*, Kerouac managed between binges to capture a piece of the rock on paper:

> Big elbows of rock rising everywhere, sea caves within them, seas plollicking all around inside them crashing out foams, the boom and pound on the sand, the sand dipping quick (no Malibu Beach here). Yet you turn and see the pleasant woods winging upcreek like a picture in Vermont. But you look up into the sky, bend way back, my God you're standing directly under that aerial bridge with its thin white line running from rock to rock and witless cars racing across it like dreams! From rock to rock! All the way down the raging coast!

A few years later, Richard Brautigan mythologized the same spot in his *A Confederate General from Big Sur*. Noted photographers Ansel Adams and Edward Weston also spent time here, their visual images of Big Sur gracing many a coffee table.

But enough of artistic inquiry. A few geographic facts are in order to distinguish Big Sur the place from Big Sur the state of mind. A large portion of coastal Big Sur is privately owned, and the town itself is not really a town but a sparsely settled strand of hidden inns, restaurants and residences. "No Trespassing" and "No Beach Access" are two favorite Big Sur mantras, often appearing outside the latter. Roughly, Big Sur stretches from the San Luis Obispo County line to the Monterey Peninsula, a distance of 90 miles. To the east, it extends beyond the Santa Lucia Mountains and the Ventana Wilderness, most of which is watched over by the U.S. Forest Service. All told, Big Sur covers 300 square miles (or 192,000 acres). The population of the region has hovered around the 1,000 mark for decades, a stability that's attributable to the high price of land, the scarcity of water and the near impossibility of getting new structures approved under strict local ordinances.

The name Big Sur is derived from a rare meeting of English and Spanish. *Sur* is taken from *El País Grande del Sur*, which means, "the big country to the south." The name was bestowed by the Spanish upon the impassable region south of the Carmel Mission, established in the late 1700s. Over the years, the name was shortened and partly Anglicized to "Big Sur."

Many moons before the missions were built, the rugged Big Sur region was not found inhospitable by the Esalen Indians. Their villages along the Big Sur Valley (in northern Big Sur) date back 3,000 years. They found a veritable cornucopia of earthly delights at their disposal—plenty of meat and fish, as well as access to hot springs. The Spanish came into the region to convert the contented Esalen, and the Indians died off soon thereafter. By the time the first white settlers arrived, the Esalen were gone. Today, one of the Indians' sacred springs is the centerpiece of the Esalen Institute, an organization that blazes new trails in self-awareness.

The first-time visitor to Big Sur will surely take the Coast Highway (Route 1) in and out. For all intents and purposes, this is the only road through here. Though a few back roads exist, only one—the treacherous but scenic Nacimiento-Fergusson Road—actually pierces the mountains, connecting with Highway 101 to the east. Other roads in the area are little more than dirt tracks, barely large enough for one car and better suited for four-wheel-drive vehicles.

The 90-mile route through Big Sur is as legendary as it is exhilarating. As a driving experience, it is unsurpassed. In 1966, Lady Bird Johnson was moved to proclaim it the nation's first Scenic Highway, and today Big Sur is traveled through by more cars and lumbering RVs than annually visit Yosemite National Park. Like a naturally occurring roller coaster, Route 1 varies in width from 18 to 24 feet, in elevation from 20 to 1,200 feet, and in scenic splendor from "Unbelievable!" and "Oh, wow!" to "Harry, don't get too *close!*"

Before setting out, take a few precautions. Fill the gas tank, and make sure the tires and brakes are in good shape. If you can, drive from north to south. That way, you'll get the most breathtaking views over the edge. Let the passengers do all the ogling, though. If the driver wants to look, make him or her pull over. No less than 300 turnouts have been cut into the roadside for that purpose. En route, the constantly changing land forms will captivate you, as one scenic vista after another rolls into view. A few spots are worth stopping at for a closer look.

Moving from south to north, because that's the direction we were traveling in, both *Jade Cove* and *Willow Creek* offer a good overview of the region's geologic treasures. Willow Creek is primarily a picnic area, while Jade Cove is a wilderness beach. At Jade Cove, we scaled a stepladder over a fence, hiked across a long field and slid down a sloping dirt path to the rocky beach. The mineral jade, specifically nephrite jade, is in the rocks and pebbles on both beaches. Anything below the high-tide line can be taken. In 1971, a team of divers took a 9,000-pound jade boulder, worth $180,000, at Jade Cove.

After 25 miles of hairpin turns that made us carsick (bring Dramamine or Coke and crackers, just in case), we next came upon *Julia Pfeiffer-Burns State Park*. It's a 1,700-acre day-use park (hiking, picnicking) whose chief scenic attraction is Waterfall Cove. A short hike from the parking lot follows McWay Creek, which ends up plummeting 50 feet to the beach below—the only waterfall on the California coast that empties directly into the ocean. Major photo opportunity here.

Five miles north is the renowned Coast Gallery, where successful local artists exhibit their work. Housed in two large redwood barrels, the gallery is a favorite stopping place for bus tours, passengers piling out to rummage through the expensive, tourist-slanted masterworks (bronze sea otters and seagulls costing from $800 to $1,000). One comment, written in the gallery's guest ledger, said it all: "And to think I forgot my Gold Card!" What makes the Coast Gallery special is its extensive collection of original Henry Miller lithographs and watercolors. Miller devotees will also want to visit the Henry Miller Memorial Library, a few hundred yards up the road.

The first of two truly great Big Sur beaches is only five miles farther on. A poorly marked turnoff, Sycamore Canyon Road, leads down to Pfeiffer Beach. The narrow, two-mile dirt road takes you past inhabited Sycamore Canyon. Makeshift homes list among the trees like pine cones, testaments to the rough life still to be found in the wilderness. From the parking lot, a quarter-mile path leads through cypress trees to the beach. Miracle of miracles, Pfeiffer Beach is an actual wide sand beach, bashed by waves that rush through sea caves to the shore in foamy torrents.

Another mile up the highway is *Pfeiffer–Big Sur State Park*, a delightful 821-acre retreat set among the noble redwoods. Overnight visitors can either camp (218 sites) or stay at the lodge (61 cottages). Some of the ancient trees in the park predate the signing of the Magna Carta. Others, long dead, lie like toppled Greek columns in backwood groves. Many miles of trails wind among the hills and redwood groves.

At *Andrew Molera State Park*, five miles farther north, Big Sur's second great beach can be found. The whole park, in fact, is a hidden treasure. No trailers or RVs are allowed in the park, and campers must carry their tents from the entrance lot to a primitive, 50-site campground. The mile-long hike to the beach passes through the campground, a meadow where deer lope unabashedly and a grove of eucalyptus trees. At trail's end a point of land protects the narrow beach from heavy surf. Paths wind through the 2,154-acre park; no day-use fee is charged.

Toward the north end of Big Sur is the Bixby Creek Bridge, one of the most photogenic spans on the West Coast. This concrete arch, a true engineering marvel, is 320 feet long and 260 feet above the creek bed. It was the longest bridge of its kind in the world when built in 1932.

These are just a few of the roadside attractions in Big Sur. A drive through the region will reveal countless others. Finally, a word about the future and possible salvation of Big Sur. It's a topic so hot that locals are burning up over it. At the present time, Big Sur is an untamed wilderness, politically as well as geographically. A large part of the coastal lands are in private hands, while the interior mostly falls under federal and state jurisdiction. Despite controversial efforts to have Big Sur declared a National Seashore or National Park, it is not presently controlled by any governmental entity.

The arguments on both sides of the issue make sense. The locals don't want Big Sur to become another overrun RV playland as so many national parks have. They also don't want to be told what to do with their land by outsiders. Wealthy, well-connected out-of-town liberals like Robert Redford and the late Ansel Adams led a battle on Capitol Hill to annex the land, while the 1,000 powerless Big Sur natives unanimously cried, "Foul play!" They insist they are the best custodians of the land, calling it "private stewardship of the resources." As a show of good faith, they've adopted the stringent guidelines of the California Coastal Commission to ensure that no desecration of Big Sur will take place.

Still, the signs are there—"For Sale" signs, that is—on plots of land in southern Big Sur. The potential for exploitation will exist unless the land is formally and permanently protected by the federal government. Without some sort of governmental intercession, the selling off of land will continue from generation to generation. Benevolence is not hereditary; only greed seems to be. If left in the hands of private citizens, will Big Sur still be smiling at herself in the mirror of eternity a century from now?

Accommodations

Mandated to near invisibility, Big Sur's few accommodations run the gamut from primitive backpacking campsites to an award-winning luxury compound. There are 10 campgrounds in the region, most on federal or state park lands. Two of the largest—*Pfeiffer–Big Sur* and *Andrew Molera*—are close enough to the beach to be considered accessible, by Big Sur standards. Both have much more to offer than exposure to the ocean, however, connected as they are to protected wildlife areas. The Andrew Molera campground is the bargain of all time: $1 per person. All accommodations in Big Sur, campsites included, should be reserved well in advance, especially in summer and on weekends.

For those who don't want to camp but still wish to hike and frolic among nature's trees and mosquitoes, the *Big Sur Lodge* is the answer. The lodge is actually a number of semiprivate cottages scattered among the trees inside Pfeiffer–Big Sur State Park. Clean and comfortable, all rooms come with fireplaces and some have kitchen facilities. The only thing that looks out of place is the big blue swimming pool. Rates are reasonable in-season and drop still lower after September. The best month to visit Big Sur, everyone agrees, is October.

Anywhere but in Big Sur, the *Glen Oaks Motel* would be your typical No-Tell Motel. Its typicality makes it stand out here, though. It's a fairly modern, clean operation, the proprietress a congenial though somewhat scatterbrained matron. We had a hard time getting her to honor our reservation for a room with two beds, since none were left, but she solved the problem after a lot of head scratching with some last-minute room shuffling. The two guys who pulled up after us were not so lucky. Finally, they decided to make do with one bed, vowing to maintain "a dignified and discreet distance" between them. Later, we saw one of them dragging a chaise lounge into the room. No credit cards are accepted; cash only, up front. Across the street, by the way, is the *Glen Oaks Restaurant*, a small gourmet den serving pasta and seafood dishes.

Finally, for those who want nothing but the best, *Ventana* offers "subtle extravagance." At Ventana, you pay dearly for subtlety. Rooms start at $125 a night and go as high as $525 for a suite. *Travel and Leisure*, *Architectural Digest*, the *Los Angeles Times*, the *New York Times* and *Gourmet* have all singled out Ventana for hosannas of praise. Based on sheer aesthetics—the natural, integrative look of the buildings and the staggering setting—it deserves the accolades. Needless to say, Ventana is popular with celebrities, and vice versa.

Restaurants

Straddling different ridges in northern Big Sur are a pair of legendary restaurants, *Ventana* and *Nepenthe*. They are a mile apart in distance but worlds apart in manners. One is known for its exceptional food and high-toned stylings, while the other serves ordinary food in a relaxed, unpretentious atmosphere.

In Spanish, *ventana* means "window," and the windows at Ventana look out upon an 800-acre spread that includes its five-star inn and a rolling meadow. Way off to one side, the ocean is visible in the distance. The food at Ventana is exquisitely prepared and arranged on the dish. It would make a perfect layout for "Platemate of the Month" in *Bon Appetit*. Sample fare: Veal Sauté, served with artichokes, sun-dried tomatoes, pancetta and mustard greens, and Roast Rack of Lamb, with herbed brioche crumbs and Dijon mustard. The main dining room is all varnished-wood walls and exposed beams, pastel throw pillows, Windham Hill background music and, of course, natural lighting through the liberal use of glass. To top it all off, Henry Miller's son Tony tends bar.

Meanwhile, at *Nepenthe*, the Ambrosiaburgers roll out of the kitchen like beer barrels in Milwaukee. Jack Kerouac referred to them as "Heavenburgers" in *Big Sur*. Either way, they are simply large hamburgers served with a special sauce. You do not come to Nepenthe just for the food. You come for the heavenly view, 808 feet above sea level and much closer to the water than Ventana. The place has been run by the same family since 1947, and it reflects their love of the area. The name *nepenthe*, by the way, is derived from the ancient Greek and means "no sorrow." In his poem "The Raven," Edgar Allen Poe cried, "Quaff, oh quaff this kind Nepenthe...." Chances are you will have to quaff, oh quaff a number of drinks while waiting for a table at this kind Nepenthe, because they take no reservations and it is the closest thing to a public meeting spot in this notoriously hermitic community. Folks nurse their drinks on the art-bedecked outdoor patio, warming their hands over the fire (even in July) and enjoying the view.

The food at Nepenthe is not going to make you forget your sorrows—a small selection of steaks, chicken and burgers—but the friendliness of the place might do the trick. The building itself was made of native redwood and adobe by a student of Frank Lloyd Wright. The adjoining café is topped by an angel fashioned from driftwood and mosaic, an alternately moving and frightening image that every visitor should pause to study. All in all, Nepenthe is a total original.

Nightlife

"What in the world is there to do around here?" was the query in the local question-and-answer column. The answer: "In the ordinary sense of resort-area activities, not much, frankly, at least not in the sense of organized social activities." In other words, there are no nightclubs or liquor stores in Big Sur. *Ventana*, *Nepenthe* and *Fernwood* (another restaurant) are where the heavy socializing, such as it is, takes place. Or, as Jack Kerouac put it in *Big Sur*, "There's the laughter of the loon in the shadow of the moon."

FOR FURTHER INFORMATION

Big Sur Chamber of Commerce
P.O. Box 87
Big Sur, CA 93920
(408) 667-2100

Point Lobos State Reserve

Point Lobos calls itself the "crown jewel of the California State Park System," a claim that just might be true. A rugged, almost primeval headland, it juts up and out over a fierce sea south of the village of Carmel. This 1,620-acre tract was, in the 1700s and 1800s, variously used as a livestock pasture, abalone cannery, whaling station and shipping point for coal mined close by. In 1933, Point Lobos (whose name derives from a much longer Spanish name meaning "point of the seawolves") was purchased by the Save the Redwoods League and given to the state to maintain as a park. Today, it is jointly run by the state and the Point Lobos Natural History Association, whose volunteers lead nature walks and staff the reserve's information station. Admission is $3 per car, and trailers and campers are prohibited, as is any kind of camping.

Roads take you only so far into the park, which is fine, since Point Lobos should be explored on foot. A map of the park details 14 nature trails crisscrossing the reserve. Cypress Grove Trail gets

right to the point, leading out to the granite cliffs
nacle Cove. One of two natural stands of Monterey
world grows here. Skittering ground squirrels, fields
ers and offshore rocks crawling with sea lions are ju.
sights.

Beaches are tucked into several coves, and although   water is
ice-cold, folks have been known to swim and dive here. Imagine
our surprise to turn a corner on the Bird Island Trail and catch
sight of *China Cove Beach* 100 feet below, looking like an emerald-
green vision of Tahiti. *Carmel River State Beach*, which runs along
Route 1, is the most popular beach in the vicinity. You needn't
enter the main gate or pay to enjoy this beach; just park along the
side of the road.

Carmel

America is celebrity crazy. People lose their composure at the mere
sight of someone famous and spend much of their time watching
TV and thumbing through magazines for celebrity gossip. But just
what is a celebrity? According to Daniel Boorstin, writing in *The
Image*, a celebrity is someone who is well known for being well
known. The talent or field of endeavor is immaterial. What's important is that the media have flash-carded someone's face in yours
until the image has been branded on your brain.

Among American small towns, Carmel is a celebrity. It can't
travel to Burbank to be on the "Tonight Show," but in every other
respect it fits the definition. Carmel is well known for being well
known. Cars gridlock the streets of this peninsular village and buses
hog-tie it, discharging a cargo of humpbacked sightseers who look
as if they subsist on a diet of chewable Pepto-Bismol tablets. Foreigners descend on the place in droves—Brits, Frenchmen, Ger-
mans, Asians—chattering in heavily accented English or their own
native tongues. The universal truth that binds them is that no one
can figure out what there is to do in Carmel, so they walk around
a lot, munch on treats and pose for pictures in front of fountains,
rocks, trees—anything vaguely scenic.

Of all the towns along the central coast, Carmel has the greatest magnetism for tourists. People include Carmel on their vacation itinerary because they believe they have to. But do they know why? Is it because the travel guides, which condense an entire state into a few familiar reference points, always include Carmel on the short list? Is it that travelers lack the resourcefulness (or the resources) to take less traveled roads that might lead to more enchanting places?

In any case, all roads lead to Carmel. Here's what to expect when you get here. Carmel is a village of 5,000 tucked into the lower left-hand corner of the Monterey Peninsula. These fortunate 5,000 are single-minded about maintaining the quality of life they've paid a king's ransom to enjoy, and catering to busloads of tourists is not their highest priority. Frankly, many Carmelites disdain the locust-like invasions that choke their streets. A guide to Carmel from the local business association states, "You'll find no boardwalks here, no bikini-clad bathers wandering about the town munching hot dogs, and not a semblance of a neon sign anywhere." You'll also find no parking, no sidewalks and no lights on any street in town except Ocean Avenue, the main drag.

Traffic coming into town often backs up to Route 1 as testy drivers inch their way along, engines overheating, looking for parking in an endless game of musical cars. Buses are not allowed past a certain point, so they must wheeze and bellow down a side street to a special bus berthing spot, discharging their blinking passengers into the sunlight to (horrors!) hoof it into hilly Carmel. Wheezing themselves after a few paces, these mostly elderly sightseers troop single-file into the business district, only to discover that the principal diversion in this genteel country village is (drum roll, cymbal crash) *shopping!* Ocean Avenue is a miracle mile of bakeries, bistros and gift shops where you can score anything from gold chains to goat cheese. If you're a compulsive shopper with an itchy finger on the credit card, there are ample ways to indulge yourself in Carmel.

This appears to be the setup: They want you to breeze into town in the morning, spend half a day dropping loot on "gifts" and "antiques" (not to mention "meals"), and then blow out of town before nightfall. This is not meant to reflect badly on Carmel. No malice is intended in this account of how they go about their business. They simply want Carmel to remain a pleasant seaside village. *Theirs.* To that end, Carmel has been buttressing itself against growth and development since day one.

Modern-day Carmel, with its distinctly bohemian, sensitive-intellectuals-in-nature atmosphere, got its start in 1906 as a seaside artists' and professors' colony, populated by academics from Berkeley and Stanford who had been displaced by San Francisco's Great Earthquake. Carmel attracted a literary elite whose ranks included Jack London, Upton Sinclair, Sinclair Lewis and Robinson Jeffers. They were enchanted by the refreshing climate, gossamer sunlight, jagged granite cliffs and powdered-sugar beaches of the peninsula. From the beginning, the citizens of Carmel banded together to ensure that their way of life would be preserved. Restrictive zoning ordinances passed in the twenties outlaw things that are commonplace elsewhere in America, like tall buildings and neon signs. To this day, cutting down a bush in your own yard requires a city hall okay.

Consequently, Carmel has the look (although crowds deny it the feel) of a rural English village. The same early spirit of enlightened preservation endures to this day, perhaps with an even greater twinge of fanaticism, since so much more can go wrong in the modern world. There are no street numbers on houses in Carmel, for instance. No numbers, no addresses and, therefore, no mail delivery. The atavistic Carmelites must personally collect their mail at the local post office. When a small movement to number the homes of Carmel surfaced, an outspoken local newspaper and barometer of community opinion headlined its disparaging editorial, "What, a Subway Next?" When such issues arise, the general outcry is, "Save Carmel from Santa Cruz-itis!"

If you think this is some kind of joke, look who they elected as mayor: Clint Eastwood. Actually, there was concern among some citizens that Eastwood would inevitably side with prodevelopment forces. But Eastwood, who won an election that made national news in 1986, has turned out to be the evenhanded voice of reason his Carmel constituency had hoped for. Thus, you can walk past a bakery and see a sign in the window reading, "Mayor Clint and I love Carmel," next to a drawing of a Monterey cypress. "Maybe the world doesn't allow you to keep things the same," Eastwood told *National Geographic* in a reflective moment. "But we can try."

Carmel is undeniably a beautiful place, nestled among stands of pine and cypress against an indigo sea. It is a smogless village whose only drawback may be that too many people want to share its good thing. The question is, how do you moderate the crowds without creating bad feeling and severing the economic jugular that allows the town to be what it is? If there is a way, Carmel will probably find it.

Carmel's greatest natural blessing is one that the hurry-in, hurry-out crowds seldom see. *Carmel City Beach*, a wide crescent between two forested points, is one of the most striking natural beaches in America. The first glimpse of this dramatic shoreline is unforgetta-ble. As it nears the water, Ocean Avenue slopes sharply downhill, ending at a sandy circle with a Monterey cypress in the center. The beach drops to the sea, forming a kind of sandy amphitheater where people sit and watch the sun set, listen to the crashing breakers (but do not swim in the hazardous surf) and absorb a vista of sun, sea, sky and cypress in all its glory. The Monterey pines and cypress are found nowhere else in the world. The cypress have a distinctive flat-topped, windswept look about them, almost like full-size bonsai.

Though it's nowhere near the beach, the *Carmel Mission* is a worthwhile last stop. Its full name is Mission San Carlos Borromeo del Rio Carmelo (cha-cha-cha), and it's just about the only evidence that Carmel has any history at all prior to this century. Constructed from 1793 to 1797, it is the favorite of the nine missions Father Junípero Serra established in California. He is, in fact, buried here. Architecturally, the mission is notable for its large, arcaded quad-rangle, but there are also interesting gardens, exhibits and a mu-seum on the premises. A donation of $1 is suggested; it is well worth it for the peace to be found inside its walls.

Accommodations

Several enticingly low-key inns can be found in the heart of Carmel. The *Lobos Lodge*, four blocks from the beach on Ocean Avenue, is rustic on the outside and modern on the inside. Each of the 29 units is decorated differently, and all have fireplaces and patios. Even closer to the beach is the *Lamp Lighter Inn*, which is straight out of fairytale land. Its nine cottages have names like "Hansel and Gretel" and are painted to look like gingerbread houses. The owner extends the fantasy by talking about the elves that play in the garden and referring to her associate as an "elf's helper." After half an hour of elf talk, we were not certain she was playing with a full deck, but the Lamp Lighter *is* a charming hideaway. Some units have second-floor lofts, and the location is the best in town. The *Colonial Terrace Inn* occupies another prime spot: on a residential side street, near the beach. The inn's seven buildings are decorated with heritage furnishings and again, no two are alike.

South of Carmel off Route 1, high on a hill overlooking the ocean, is the *Highlands Inn*. This may be the sweetest getaway of all. The inn is a bona fide historic property, built in 1916, renovated and modernized in recent years. It is a smooth-running, first-rate resort popular with honeymooners (a thousand weddings are performed annually) and anyone looking for a great escape in the rural highlands along the central coast. The view of the Pacific from the Grand Lodge is breathtaking; it's as if you're on the bow of a ship suspended above the water. Each room includes a wood-burning fireplace and vista deck. It's a sharp upward climb to the Highlands Inn, both for your car and your pocketbook, but worth it if both are running smoothly.

Restaurants

Carmel is a town of intimate restaurants hidden in off-street alcoves—places like *Le Coq d'Or* and *Sans Souci* that serve fine French cuisine in a romantic atmosphere. Chicken dishes are featured at *Le Coq d'Or*; lamb, quail and veal at Sans Souci. For seafood, try the *Clam Box*, a local institution that doesn't stand on ceremony but doles out memorable dishes like Rainbow Trout Meunière and Prawns Newburg, flavored with sherry.

One night, we stumbled into *Collage*, a high-tech Euro bistro across the street from Carmel's fire station. The menu at Collage *is* a collage of global food items, from sushi to Mexican. You might want to go Italian, for the pasta is homemade and there are seven pasta dishes listed on what is otherwise a scattered menu. If undecided, try the Pasta Collage: a sampler plate of three pastas and three sauces.

The Collage turned out to be an interesting place to eavesdrop on Carmel. Ever wonder what kind of person buys those high-priced gift-shop knickknacks? The blond bombshell at the next table, that's who! "I love those little eggs that come in a basket... oh, God," she cooed to her older male companion. Meanwhile, a seminar in neuroses was being conducted by the bearded gent at a table close by. He was boring his date with a line of chatter that veered wildly from spiritualism to accounting. "I want to get into the position where I can start writing a book," he soberly announced at one point. "Then I'm going to use the proceeds from the book to finance a video." This weighty discussion was interrupted when the maître d' conked a woman he was seating with the warehouse lamp that dangled over her table. All conversation halted until the French-accented maître d' blurted, "I call a doctor," but that proved unnecessary.

If you come to Carmel, you're going to want to eat at the *Hog's Breath*, not because the name is so appetizing but because Clint Eastwood is a prominent co-owner. If you didn't already know this, you'd quickly figure it out from scanning the menu, whose offerings include the Dirty Harry Burger, the Sudden Impact (Polish sausage, Monterey Jack and jalapeños on a French roll), the Eiger Sandwich (roast beef), the For a Few Dollars More steak dinner, and so forth. (Hey, why not "Magnum Forcemeat"?) Come prepared to wait inside the pub or on the outdoor patio for the privilege of feasting on Mayor Clint's movie-titled entrées.

Nightlife

You can order a drink at a restaurant bar or quaff a tall one at Clint Eastwood's latest acquisition, the *Mission Ranch*, which has a piano bar. Honest-to-god *bar* bars are few and far between, and forget about nightclubs in tranquil Carmel. You might drop by *Maxwell McFly's Watering Hole* for a nightcap should you have any life left in you after dinner. It's a real corner pub, with a few tables and a long, stool-lined bar.

Carmel Business Association
P.O. Box 4444
Carmel-by-the-Sea, CA 93921
(408) 624-2522

Pebble Beach

Pebble Beach is a fenced-in community of rich folks, best known for its golf course and the famed *17-Mile Drive*. Set along the western side of the Monterey Peninsula in the heart of the Del Monte Forest, Pebble Beach is private and restricted, accessible only through four gates along the Drive. Chances are if you're coming here, the 17-Mile Drive is penciled in on the itinerary. Everybody does it, believing it is a not-to-be-missed scenic drive "through pine forests and groves of Monterey cypress and along a coastline of singular beauty."

Let's put it simply: You are wasting your time and money if you take the 17-Mile Drive. It would be a time-consuming bore if it were free. The most onerous thing about the 17-Mile Drive (and Pebble Beach, by association) is that they charge $5 for the dubious privilege of driving through their community. This is highway robbery. The money does not get funneled into state or county coffers, or go to some noble nature conservancy. It goes to the Pebble Beach Company.

How this is allowed to happen is beyond us, but year after year, the 17-Mile Drive remains a large draw, recommended as one of *the* things to do on the Monterey Peninsula. The scenery is not nearly as striking as the hundreds of miles of free public roads on California's coastline. For instance, the drive through Big Sur, 90 miles of non-golf-coursed coastal wonder, puts the 17-Mile Drive to shame and doesn't cost a penny.

But let's pay the five bucks, drive through the gate and see what we see. First, you pass mile after mile of what looks like any well-to-do suburban neighborhood in America, trailing smoke-spewing buses and a procession of other hoodwinked motorists looking for the nonexistent sights. Along a short stretch of coastline, they've erected numbered signs with names like "The Restless Sea" and "Point Joe," which are your average waves-slapping-rocks routines and nothing out of the ordinary on the central coast. But because the Pebble Beach Company has given them names, assigned them numbers and charged money, people believe they're experiencing something unique and wonderful. Or maybe they don't, judging from some of the comments we overheard.

The roads are narrow and in bad repair. Eventually, you pass the *Pebble Beach Golf Course and Lodge*, at which point you are supposed to succumb to envy, thinking, "How I wish I could afford to stay here." Unless you're a guest, you can't even park here for more than 15 minutes, another slap in the face. If you've won the California lottery and perchance can afford a room at the lodge (they begin at $190) or a round of golf on its famed course ($95 for lodge guests, $125 for all others), we wish you all the best.

We cruised onward. The sights were getting more sightless by the moment: earth-moving equipment, average-looking suburban homes, charred trees. At this point, 17 miles seemed too many and we couldn't wait to exit. We had a parting taunt ready for the gatekeepers, but a sign said "Do Not Stop At Gate" on the way out, presumably sparing the hired hands a chewing out from hot-headed carloads of tourists now five bucks, two hours and one gallon of gas poorer. To add to the bottomless greed of it all, the brochure we were handed on the way in turned out to be a retail catalog for high-priced golf wear from (where else?) the Pebble Beach Lodge.

The 17-Mile Drive is profiteering at its most pernicious. The lesson seems to be that a roadside attraction can be created from thin air simply by putting up a gate and charging an admission fee. The 17-Mile Drive, though, is not some tawdry wax museum or "hill of mystery" or other trumped-up sideshow. This is the coastline they're charging to see! Perhaps we should start charging them $5 to drive *out* of Pebble Beach.

Pacific Grove

Pacific Grove is the shy but beautiful daughter of
Peninsula. Hidden by trees and buffeted by the s
winds off Monterey Bay, this modest seaside villag   ,0,000 is
content to let her peninsular relations deal with the vagaries and
vulgarity of fame. More of a hometown than a boomtown, Pacific
Grove has a quiet, ascetic way of life dating back to its founding
in 1875, when 100 acres of pine-, oak- and cypress-covered wilderness were given to the Methodist Episcopal Church for the establishment of a "Christian seaside resort."

They intended Pacific Grove to be a camp-meeting retreat, not
a full-fledged city of homes. Thus, when the first camp meeting
was held on August 8th, 1875, the lots were sold in 30- by 60-foot
increments—large enough to accommodate a big tent. Surprisingly,
450 people showed up for the inaugural bash. The sizable turnout
ensured the success of the pious venture and proved that God still
existed in the wild and woolly west. In the ensuing years, the
crowds grew larger and Pacific Grove became a virtual tent city
when summer rolled around. At summer's end, the wooden frames
were left standing but the tents were taken down and stored in
Chautauqua Hall, a utilitarian wood structure built in 1879 for the
"presentation of moral attractions."

Too many people were sticking around, however, for Pacific
Grove to remain a simple religious retreat. In 1889, the 1,300 permanent residents incorporated a square-mile area and the town of
Pacific Grove was born. The tents disappeared, replaced by tiny
board-and-batten cottages—some built directly onto the old 30- by
60-foot tent frames—and larger Victorian homes that praised the
Lord a tad louder. These homes, along with the original churches,
the Chautauqua Hall and the Point Pinos Light Station, still stand
in Pacific Grove, unpretentious reminders of a quieter past. Point
Pinos, incidentally, remains the oldest continuously operating lighthouse on the West Coast.

This is not to imply that Pacific Grove is a dull mausoleum of
dusty hymnbooks and fading memories. On the contrary, the original homes are in good repair and in constant use as residences,
inns and offices. Most have a small wooden plaque nailed to the

ont door, identifying the original owner by name and the year the house was built. A full day can be spent hiking through town, an especially rewarding experience if you follow the instructions for the Pacific Grove Historic Walking Tour, a hoot of a packet provided by the local chamber of commerce. Obtain the necessary documents from their neat little office at Forest and Central avenues, then prepare for a lengthy and entertaining scavenger hunt. To make sure you see it all, the chamber has included a step-by-step quiz. You're supposed to answer each question before moving on to the next site. For example, "What is interesting about the two squid in their bottles?" and "What animal serves to show wind direction at the peak of their roof?" Your efforts will be rewarded with a patch for your shirt and a thorough knowledge of Pacific Grove as a lasting memory.

One interesting stop on the walking tour is the Pacific Grove Natural History Museum. Founded in 1881, it is one of the best of its size in the country. It is also free of charge, although you will be moved to give a donation. Somehow, in two small floors of gallery space, the museum manages to impart every facet of Monterey County's natural history—insects, rodents, birds, fish, reptiles, rocks, fossils, Indians and the town's evocative symbol, the monarch butterfly.

A word about monarchs is in order. A more appropriate mascot could not have been chosen for Pacific Grove, which, when it gets the slightest bit boosteristic, bills itself as "Butterfly Town, U.S.A." Every year, thousands upon thousands of orange and black monarchs migrate to the pine groves of Pacific Grove. They arrive on November 1st and leave by March 1st. On dull winter days, they hang in thick clusters from the trees, but on warm, sunny days they swoop through town. The city protects these lilting creatures, imposing a $500 fine for "molesting butterflies." This same ordinance asks citizens "to protect the butterflies in every way possible from serious harm and possible extinction by brutal and heartless people." If you don't want to meet up with an angry mob wielding antique butter churns, then leave the sweet little things be.

The monarchs are gone by summer and, except when it's sunny, almost undetectable in winter. Their wings fold inward, so that only their neutral-colored undersides are visible. Their distinctively lovely markings are seen only by those with the patience to wait around and look closely. The same is true of the butterflies' hometown. The closer you look at Pacific Grove, the more its coloring will be revealed.

The town is bound by sharp, protruding rocks and churning ocean waters on two sides. *Asilomar State Beach*, located around Point Pinos on the less populous side of town, is a beautiful, west-facing shoreline. No one swims or surfs in Pacific Grove. This is a blessing in disguise, leaving the undeveloped shorefront open to people who like to walk—not run, skateboard, bike, windsurf or any of the other manic pastimes, but walk.

Accommodations

On the Monterey Peninsula, the *Asilomar Conference Center* is the best bargain. Don't let the name put you off. A conference at Asilomar is more likely to be a religious gathering or quiet family retreat than a meeting of business-people frantically tossing figures at one another. Founded in 1913 by the YMCA, the Asilomar Conference Center is now run by the California State Park System. It is spread out on 105 acres of Monterey pines and cypress. Wooden walkways lead to the dunes of Asilomar State Beach, site of some of the most jaw-dropping sunsets in the West. Asilomar's 28 woodsy lodges bear rustic names like "Oak Knoll" and "Willow Inn." Conference facilities are available, but one needn't be part of a group to stay here. A full breakfast, served cafeteria-style in a large hall, comes with your room. It's like being back at camp again.

The rest of Pacific Grove's accommodations seem to take a cue from Asilomar. Most are neat, trim and low-key. Pacific Grove is the ideal place to stay on the Monterey Peninsula. It's centralized, within easy shot of Carmel, Point Lobos, Pebble Beach and Monterey. It's also quiet, residential and affordable. Options range from small motels like the *Larchwood Inn* (beside Asilomar) to the *Pacific*

Grove Plaza, a time-sharing condominium hotel in the heart of town. You can also step back in history at one of the town's Victorian bed-and-breakfast inns. Two of the finest are the *Green Gables Inn* and the *Gosby House*. Managed by the same people, the main difference between them is location. The Green Gables is situated on a quiet cove. The Gosby House is "in the neighborhood," on Lighthouse Avenue, Pacific Grove's main thoroughfare.

Both are ideal places to get away from modern civilization. Offering more privacy than the average bed-and-breakfast, these two inns are declarations of Victorian splendor that the old queen herself could understand. But they're not so stuffy as to be beyond a pair of beach bums like us. The Gosby House has been an inn since it was built in 1887, the earliest visitors being pilgrims to the Chautauqua. It has a quiet garden and courtyard. Inside, it's filled with period furnishings, artwork, a stocked cookie jar in the common area, stuffed bears on the beds and McGuffey's Readers on the fireplace mantels. Some rooms have private baths. Both inns provide a full breakfast buffet, free wine, sherry and hors d'oeuvres in the evening and uncommonly personal attention.

Restaurants

Chances are that dinner will be your evening's highlight, followed by a stroll along Pacific Grove's lovely shoreline. Two fine restaurants—the *Old Bath House* and the *Tinnery*—face each other along Oceanview Boulevard, near Lovers Point on the waterfront. The Old Bath House is the more historic and formal of the two. It's an award-winning restaurant with an extensive wine list and continental menu including such entrées as Duck Merlot and Seafood Cannelloni. The Tinnery leans toward seafood and, though the quality is not as high as that of the Bath House, the meals are well-prepared, the view is beautiful (look for the fishing boats returning to Monterey at sunset), and the staff is as friendly and wholesome as Pacific Grove itself. In this part of the state, by the way, order artichokes whenever possible; they're grown in nearby Castroville. The Tinnery serves a Castroville artichoke appetizer, as do many area restaurants.

Nightlife

A sunset stroll to Lovers Point (originally, Lovers of Jesus Point) should suffice. More by silent agreement than local ordinance, no bars exist in Pacific Grove. Neither do nightclubs, discos, pool halls or beer joints. Monterey County was completely dry until 1972. Now you can order a drink and listen to lounge music at the *Old Bath House* and the *Tinnery*. For anything more than this, you must sidle over to Monterey for some disco arm-twisting with the military boys. We did Pacific Grove one better by passing up an evening of square-dancing at Crocker Hall in the Asilomar Conference Center. It just seemed too wild.

FOR FURTHER INFORMATION

Pacific Grove Chamber of Commerce
Forest and Central Avenues
P.O. 167
Pacific Grove, CA 93950
(408) 373-3304

Monterey

If the Monterey Peninsula were a baseball team, Carmel would lead off and play second base, Pebble Beach would be the over-paid designated hitter, and Pacific Grove would be the utility infielder who rarely gets to play but is kept on the team because it's a stabilizing influence. Monterey would be the cleanup hitter, because that's exactly what it does—it cleans up after the tourists. Whether by design or force of habit, Monterey draws the huddled, restless and hungry masses.

Nothing is wrong with tourism, per se. It gives people something to do two weeks a year and helps keep our temperamental economy afloat. In the case of Monterey, because of its rich history, the restoration of the canneries and the Monterey Bay Aquarium, tourism is unavoidable. Unlike the tour-bus whistle stop of

Carmel, where tourists wander with itchy buns and knitted brows, Monterey actually has something other than shopping and eating to offer. Still, no matter how rich the legacy is around here, you can't escape the nagging feeling of being stuck inside a tourist trap where free will has been reduced to an order of squid 'n' chips and a souvenir seashell ashtray.

First of all, it is hard to find the town of Monterey. Spread out around the curve of a harbor and groping inland toward the county seat of Salinas, Monterey is several towns rolled into one with no discernible center. There is the historic *Old Town*, which can be readily toured with a decent pair of sneakers and a map. This part of Monterey has been taken over by the state-park system, which usually does these things right. They've laid out a walking tour of the area, called the "Path of History." The trail takes you around and inside many restored buildings dating from Monterey's days as a historic seaport.

Discovered in 1542 by Juan Cabrillo (who else?), Monterey has three times been the capital of California. It was also a world trading center, a whaling mecca and a sardine-canning capital. Monterey, you see, is no fly-by-night sideshow. The best place to begin a tour of Old Town is the Pacific House, local headquarters for the park system. They'll give you a map and prep you on what would otherwise be a confusing trek.

En route, you'll see the original Customs House, where all goods were brought ashore and inspected before permission to unload was granted. Many a successful sea captain averted this procedure by unloading on one of the offshore islands, returning later to pick up the untaxed cargo. Also on the tour is California's first theater, which is still putting on performances when it's not serving food and ale under the name of Jack Swan's Tavern. Another highlight is William Tecumseh Sherman's quarters, used from 1847 to 1849, when California was a newborn state and Sherman a man about town. (This was before he torched the South.) Countless other adobe houses and restored structures, some of the oldest in California, are included. Many of the old houses in Monterey's business district can't be entered because they've been commandeered for other functions—investment securities firms, Mexican restaurants, law offices—leading one to suspect, after an hour of solitary wandering, that they've turned an old cliché around. In Monterey, the more things stay the same, the more they change. Still, the old part of Monterey seems oddly devoid of life and movement, popular with neither tourists nor locals.

The two best-known attractions in Monterey have the least historic value, but the tour buses deposit their human cargo here anyway. The *Old Fisherman's Wharf* and *Cannery Row* are separate entities, situated on opposite sides of a Coast Guard facility and 10 minutes apart by foot. They are, however, similar in appeal. Like twin strips of flypaper around which buzzes an endless procession of moderately curious humanity, the Old Fisherman's Wharf and Cannery Row eagerly participate in a game of historical charades.

In truth, they were once the haunts of working men, clanging machines and women of the night. These were raw places, filled with raucous flophouses and saloons. Cannery Row was a row of packhouses where sardines were weighed, sorted, counted and canned by guys and dolls who never dreamed that what they were doing to make ends meet was remotely quaint or romantic. The first canneries were built in the 1890s. By the late 1940s, they were completely shut down, because the bay and ocean were overfished and polluted. This was the place John Steinbeck wrote about in *Cannery Row*, published in 1945. He caught Monterey at its peak: 4,000 workers canned 237,000 tons of sardines that year. Steinbeck saw Cannery Row as "a poem, a stink, a grating noise, a quality of light, a tone, a habit, a nostalgia, a dream. Cannery Row is the gathered and scattered, tin and iron and rust and splintered wood, chipped pavement and weedy lots and junk heaps."

This is not the Cannery Row that exists today, with its upscale gift shops ("Sweet Thursday" being the most egregious appropriation of a Steinbeck title) and overpriced restaurants with names like *Steinbeck Lobster Grotto*. In Cannery Row, a trinket outlet calls itself Steinbeck Jewelers, while the Coast Gallery sells depictions of "Steinbeck's Cannery Row" by Hawaiian artists who weren't around when the canneries were open and have probably never read a word by the man. The gallery is located in the Monterey Plaza Hotel, an elegant, elephantine lodge totally incongruous with the blue-collar town Steinbeck knew. All visitors to Monterey ought to read *Cannery Row* before coming here to appreciate the extent of the fraud. What was a short and grimly amusing set piece has been turned into Cannery Row Square, Sly McFly's Saloon and the Golf Club Fitting Room. (Hey, fellas, replace all divots on Mr. Steinbeck's grave.)

Thankfully, the trend has reached the saturation point. The American Tin Cannery, a mall of yuppie shops and eateries gratuitously tacked onto the western end of Cannery Row, has fallen on the same hard times the original canneries hit in the forties. Here, the signs most often seen in shop windows are "For Lease," "Sale—40% to 60% Off" and "Going Out of Business."

Things improve considerably at the *Monterey Bay Aquarium*, also west of Cannery Row. This amazing museum of the deep was completed in 1984. With 6,500 animals, 500 species, 23 galleries and 100 exhibits, it is the largest aquarium of its kind in the country. Most of the animals on display can be found in the Monterey Bay, renowned for its rich and varied marine life and its clear, blue-green water. Admission is $7 for adults and $3 for children, and it's worth every dime. Despite the crowds, it is an enriching experience. Even the kids remain studiously in awe, especially around the "petting pools," where they can touch and handle live starfish, anemones and bat rays. The expressed goal of the Monterey Bay Aquarium is "to expand public interest and knowledge and concern for the marine life of Monterey Bay and the ocean environment."

On the way back to to the Old Fisherman's Wharf (you were headed there, weren't you?), you'll want to walk out on the Coast Guard Pier. Sea lions can be observed from behind a protective fence out by the breakwater. These lazy-looking, heavy-lidded beasts lounge around like overfed vacationers on a motel-room bed. Appearances are deceptive, though. The breakwater is a resting place on their migrations between Mexico and Canada. This is as close as humans can get to them on the California coast. Feeding them is frowned upon. They must be allowed to catch their own calamari strips.

Originally built by slave labor as a safe harbor for cargo-laden schooners coming around the Horn from the east, the Old Fisherman's Wharf became the center of the West Coast's whaling industry as well. Ever since the late 1800s, it has been the eminent domain of a fleet of Sicilian fishers, whose groaning labors made Monterey the world's sardine capital. A shrine has been erected at the mouth of the harbor in honor of Santa Rosalia, their patron saint.

Like Cannery Row, the Wharf has always been a rough-and-tumble place. Until now, that is. Today, the Old Fisherman's Wharf is best symbolized by the first thing we saw upon traversing its wooden floorboards: a shuddering monkey dressed in a stiflingly hot bellhop's suit, taking spare change from pitying passersby while a man with tattoos on his arms hung onto its leash and changed the cassette tapes in his phony organ grinder.

Lethargic sea lions float beneath the wharf, living off the fat of the land lubbers who toss food over the side. Overhead, mangy pelicans and seagulls dive-bomb for crumbs and dispatch white projectiles on the tourists. Most of the restaurants and squid shacks on the Wharf have Sicilian names like *Domenico's*, *Rappa's* and *Abalonetti*. The food is only fair, but that is immaterial to the tourists. They pay for the view of the pelicans, sea lions and fishing boats. All in all, it's a fairly unexceptional experience.

This brings us to the final mystery of Monterey: the beaches along the bay. The water in this pristine bay is surprisingly rough and is capable of knocking you silly should you try to swim here. Other than the short belts of sand between sea walls, where snorkelers and skin divers gather, the choices for water sports are slim. The beach is wider at *Monterey State Beach*, just north of the municipal wharf (a.k.a. Wharf #2). A stroll along Monterey's waterfront is invigorating, though the wind can blow you to pieces. Don't wear the wacky hat you bought on Cannery Row, unless you want to see it wind up on the head of a sea lion.

Accommodations

Most hotels in Monterey are of the monolithic, corporate mold, employing drab camouflage (neutral colors and adobe) to conceal their inappropriate hugeness. At least the *Hotel Pacific*, located in the heart of Old Town, blends in nicely with the neighborhood. There are plenty of cheaper motels out by the highway, but if you want truly special lodgings, there's an authentic bed-and-breakfast inn within four blocks of Cannery Row. It's called the *Jabberwock*, and each of the seven rooms are distinctive—quite a feat for a place that used to be a convent.

Restaurants

The king of the Monterey dining scene is a man named Ted Balestreri. He is the owner of the *Sardine Factory*, a longtime favorite overlooking Cannery Row. He also owns *The Rogue*, another fine seafood restaurant at the Monterey City Wharf, a less touristy harbor-front center. In addition to his ventures in food, he is a real-estate tycoon. Balestreri is one-quarter of the Foursome Company, a formidable outfit that always gets its way. They are responsible for the recent construction of two controversial, view-obstructing hotels smack dab in the middle of historic, picturesque Monterey.

When asked in an interview if his real-estate holdings had become more important than his restaurants, he answered, "Yes and no....No, because we open one Wendy's every four months in Northern California. We own territorial rights for all Wendy's franchises in San Francisco, Santa Clara and Santa Cruz." It was rather disappointing to learn that the king of the Monterey dining scene was a closet hot-and-juicy burger pusher, turning green lots into fast-food stands, giving grease-pit jobs to another 12 teenagers and taking America one step closer to the Holy Dumpster. There is no question that Balestreri's Sardine Factory is one of the finest epicurian palaces on the Monterey Peninsula. We just thought you should know about the Wendy's.

Overall, our treks to the dining meccas of Monterey proved less than enchanting. One of us was served a Styrofoam cup of "World Famous Clam Chowder" on the Old Fisherman's Wharf that almost had us singing "Goodbye, Cruel World." A seemingly innocuous snack, the chowder was dished up by a slow-witted lout who licked his fingers after dolloping the portion into a container. Two sips of liquid confirmed the worst fear as dizziness and nausea began to set in. Death was surely on the way. A search for quick, alternative food—something fatty to absorb the chowder's salmonella—proved fruitless. Hot pretzels the size of sand dollars for a buck. Slices of pizza that were really stale French bread with margarine and mozzarella hardened on them for two bucks. Squid 'n' chips, the *perfect* antidote, for four bucks. A feverish, staggering 10-minute walk to Cannery Row brought no relief. Designer pretzels for more money. "Boston" pizza. Gourmet candy popcorn. Hot and juicy burgers. Finally, the body took matters into its own hands and staved off death, as well as hunger, for the next 24 hours.

The restaurants on Old Fisherman's Wharf have a disturbing sameness about them—the same menus (squid in all its various forms), the same high prices, the same view of the harbor. We finally zeroed in on *Gianni's*, a family pizzeria nowhere near the harbor. It's on Lighthouse Avenue, the street that binds Pacific Grove to Monterey. Family owned and operated, Gianni's smells of fresh pasta, rich sauce and fresh-baked pizza. To the locals, it's an institution.

Nightlife

Monterey will always hold a special place in the hearts of rock and roll fans. The first true American rock festival took place here in 1967. Immortalized in the documentary film *Monterey Pop*, the festival unleashed Janis Joplin and Jimi Hendrix on the world; captured Otis Redding at his most powerful (sadly, only months before his death in a plane crash); and revealed the Who's thunderous promise, as well as their penchant for destruction. Eric Burdon and the Animals later wrote a hit song about it, extolling the virtues of Flower Power two years before Woodstock. The Monterey Pop Festival, oddly enough, was a one-shot deal, the illegitimate offspring of the more celebrated Monterey Jazz Festival. Now past its 30th season, the jazz festival is still going strong. Held in late September at the Monterey Fairgrounds, a 24-acre field surrounded by oak trees, the jazzfest attracts a star-studded cast of performers. A blues festival is also held on the fairgrounds in late June.

As for ongoing nightlife, Monterey plays the role of beacon for the entire peninsula. The easy-listening set can tap their toes at

one of several piano bars; the *Sandbar* on Wharf #2 will do nicely.
Those in the mood for something livelier should head down to *The
Club*. Some nights they have live rock bands; other nights, "Deejay
Donna." Regardless, the Club is popular with locals and Salinas
Valley night-trippers.

Doc Ricketts' Lab is another popular club. Located in the middle
of Cannery Row, it's housed in the bottom of what once was a
marine-life collecting laboratory (one of the few establishments with
a real connection to the Steinbeck legacy). The lab originally belonged to "Doc," the principal character in Cannery Row. Nowadays, Doc Ricketts' Lab is filled with rock and roll, not octopuses.
The happily dancing specimens at the Lab were further proof that
live music reigns supreme over deejay-interruptus tapes and *zzzip-
zzzip* rap 'n' disco voodoo.

A large number of short-haired military men are out after dark
in Monterey. An Army base, Fort Ord, is in the area, the Navy
runs a postgraduate school, and the Coast Guard claims an installation on the harbor. For whatever reason, they are unusually well-
behaved and even sort of polite. We heard one wide-lapeled lad
actually say "yes ma'am" to a waitress.

FOR FURTHER INFORMATION

Monterey Peninsula Chamber of Commerce
380 Alvarado Street
P.O. Box 1770
Monterey, CA 93942
(408) 649-1770

Marina

Just north of Monterey, the complexion of the beach changes
rapidly. The sand is golden brown, the dunes rise gently but impressively, and the rocky outcroppings on and offshore all but dis-
appear. *Marina State Beach* looks more like a Southern California
beach than anything on the Monterey Peninsula or in Big Sur. To

get here, take the Reservation Road exit off Route 1. With Fort Ord close by, Marina is largely a military town. The base's northern boundary actually touches Marina State Beach. In summer, the beach is swamped with sweltering families seeking relief from the 100-degree heat in the valley. A hang-glider launch ramp sits atop a big brown whale of a dune. Fishing and skin diving are popular, too, but forget about swimming in this rough surf. On a gorgeous June afternoon, the wind was whipping the sea into whitecaps and very nearly blew us off the beach.

Castroville
Moss Landing

The Castroville–Moss Landing area is farm country. "What we do here in Castroville is grow artichokes" is how their chamber of commerce puts it. They are devoted to the 'choke, which is a tasty if unusual vegetable (actually, it's a flower). Looking something like a green pineapple, the artichoke's leaves are disengaged one by one and the edible part scraped off with your teeth until you arrive at the heart, which is a small feast and your reward for being patient with the leaves. Between Monterey and Half Moon Bay, we enjoyed many a Castroville artichoke, dunking them in mayonnaise, butter or vinaigrette like green potato chips.

Artichokes aside, there are three state beaches within striking distance of Castroville and its sidekick, the harbor-front community of Moss Landing. The first of these, heading north, is *Salinas River State Beach*. A wooden walkway leads from the no-fee parking lot onto the beach. A sign warns "swimming and wading unsafe," but the beach is broad and sandy, with steep dunes. A few intrepid fishers were braving gale-force winds, while a sailboat was close to capsizing offshore, pitching wildly in the gusts. Salinas River is in a very rural setting, although the smokestacks of a nearby power plant are visible.

Next up is *Moss Landing State Beach*. A $3 day-use fee is charged, although you can park outside the gate and walk in for nothing. A few miles north of Moss Landing is the entrance for *Zmudowski State Beach*. The turnoff from Route 1 is still a fair distance from the water. The road to Zmudowski follows the outside perimeter of fields of artichokes and brussels sprouts. On the beach, a sign warns, "Danger: intermittent waves of unusual size and force." Zmudowski State Beach, like Moss Landing, is good for clamming and surf-casting. The only folks we saw on the beach, though, were a family of five trying to have a picnic while getting sandblasted silly.

Even if you're bypassing the beaches, stop at Moss Landing for a sandwich at *Bob's Crab*. You can't miss it: Bob operates out of a 35-foot orange trailer with a blinking traffic signal attached to it. He gets his Dungeness crabs fresh from Half Moon Bay and spreads his mayonnaisey crab salad between two fat slices of sourdough bread. Accompanied by a jar of chilled apple juice, it's a fine lunch for $4.25. Next door is *Teri's Stop 'n' Eat*, where you can order teriyaki hamburgers and french-fried artichokes. On the same large lot, a huge produce market sells inexpensive, locally grown fruits and vegetables.

FOR FURTHER INFORMATION

Castroville Chamber of Commerce
P.O. Box 744
Castroville, CA 95012
(408) 633-2465

Sunset State Beach
Manresa State Beach

Another new county, more beaches—California marches on, with a surprise around every turn. The beaches of Santa Cruz County are as scenic as any south of here. Sometimes confined to coves, sometimes running for a great distance along a regular shoreline, they are hospitable to surfers, swimmers and sunbathers. And the backdrops are a staggering potpourri of sheer cliff faces and steep, vegetation-covered dunes.

Sunset State Beach has northern and southern entrances, between which lie seven miles of pristine beach. At the south end, better known as *Palm Beach*, parking is free. Palm Beach is reached by taking the Beach Road turnoff from Route 1 and traversing five miles of bumpy road across fertile farmland. The road ends in a beautifully shaded eucalyptus grove, under whose limbs picnic tables are scattered. High, humpbacked dunes protect the trees from the stiff and steady winds. Cross them, and you're on the beach, being blown about like a piece of litter. The trees on top of the dunes bear scars from years of staring down the wind. The beach itself is broad and beautiful.

The northern entrance of Sunset State Beach has more facilities— paved parking, covered picnic tables, campsites—and charges standard state-park entrance fees ($3 for cars, $12 for campers). The road down to the beach hugs the cliffs like a roller-coaster ride. Monstrous silver driftwood logs have washed ashore. The beach is empty wilderness in all directions. Clamming is good from September to April on what is the northern range of the Pismo clam.

North of Sunset is *Manresa State Beach*, reachable from Route 1 by taking the Mar Monte exit to San Andreas Road and following the signs. It costs $3 to get in, and a staircase leads to the beach from a breathtaking cliff overlook. It's often misty in the morning, though the fog generally burns off by midday.

Capitola
Aptos

At first glance, Capitola looks like nothing more than a glued-on suburb of Santa Cruz, a small side dish next to the main course. But don't be fooled—Capitola is a bustling village with a pulse of its own. Capitola begins east of 41st Avenue, a heavily trafficked thoroughfare off Route 1 that's lined with shopping centers and service plazas. When it dead-ends at East Cliff Drive, hang a left and a few curves later you'll be winding down into the artichoke-like heart of Capitola.

The village is built around a broad, sandy cove. The Esplanade runs along the water, and Capitola Avenue parallels it a block away. All the shops, restaurants and action can be found on these two streets. Capitola is an upwardly mobile mélange of cultured book-store and artist types and nouveau riche mods and models sport-ing the latest skimpy sun-bunny fashions on the beach. It's a safe guess that a sizable percentage of the latter drift down for the day from the campus of the University of California at Santa Cruz, while a few more make the 30-mile drive from the inland city of San Jose as well. In any case, the beaches and sidewalks of Capitola are crawling with more apple-cheeked, blond-haired beauties than we'd seen since Los Angeles County.

There's gold in these hills. Our hunch is that folks who work or own businesses in Santa Cruz make their home in Capitola, if they can afford it. Shops display trendy merchandise (designer swim-wear, arts and crafts) and tend to the sweet tooths of the well-to-do. At the Capitola Mercantile mall, a hungry hound can find home-baked cookies, hand-dipped ice-cream bars and cinnamon rolls that could feed a family of five. Two of the stores are Divine Decadence and the Chocolate Bar. Get the idea?

There's only one snag to enjoying this hidden Acapulco on the north-central coast. It's the universal California complaint: park-ing. "Going to Capitola today?" an eavesdropping Santa Cruz mer-chant asked with raised eyebrows. "Good luck finding a parking space." We did not have good luck. First, we entered a caravan of cars circling the Esplanade and Capitola Avenue like a modern-day wagon train. After a fruitless half hour of burning gas, we discovered an alternative: the Capitola Village Beach Shuttle. Fol-low the yellow and blue signs to a parking lot along a frontage road next to the highway. Buses run between the lot and the beach every 10 minutes from 9:30 a.m. to 6:30 p.m. (later on weekends). There's been talk that service might be cut back to weekends only. Seems that people would rather drive around for hours trying to ferret out nonexistent parking than use the shuttle. Oh well.

In addition to its beautiful city beach, Capitola claims a pair of state beaches just south of town. *New Brighton State Beach* is reached via Park Avenue, off Route 1. Signs point into a tree-shaded glen, beyond which lie high, grass-covered dunes and a flat, sandy beach with calm surf. New Brighton, which faces due south, is spared the prevailing winds that mercilessly wrack other stretches of the Santa Cruz coast. This area was originally known as China Cove or China Beach, from a time in the late 1800s when Asian fishers dragged the water with fishing nets. Tall beach grasses and thick, scrubby vegetation hold the steep dunes in place. At the foot of the dunes is a gravel road used by joggers. New Brighton Beach is also frequented by picnicking families and campers, who take their pick of 115 sites in the woods behind the dunes.

Seacliff State Beach is the site of a real curiosity: a cement World War I supply boat, the *Palo Alto*, that never saw active duty. Towed here in the twenties, it served as an offshore amusement pier and dance casino until storms disabled it. The cement ship is now lashed to the end of a fishing wharf. You can mount a few rusty steps onto its deck and toss a line into the water or simply walk around. Seacliff State Beach properly belongs to the town of Aptos, a tidy little village, most of which falls on the dry side of Route 1. The park is heavily used by fishers and picnickers. Commercial facilities include a bait-and-tackle shop and a snack bar that serves "homemade sandwiches." The beach is reached by a long, winding road that hairpins its way downhill. There are 26 trailer hookups right on the beach. Both Seacliff and New Brighton charge $3 day-use and $12 camping fees.

Accommodations

Capitola isn't a tourist town per se; it's more of a day tripper's and resident's beach. Still, there are a few places to stay, two of them side by side near the town's circa-1857 fisherman's wharf, overlooking the beach and bay. Take your pick of the *Harbor Lights Motel* or the *Capitola Venetian Hotel;* we found both equally appealing and comparable in price.

Restaurants

No one should leave the Santa Cruz–Capitola area without dining at the *Shadowbrook*. Without exaggeration, it is one of the most beautiful restaurants in the West. Set along Soquel Creek in a quiet, residential part of Capitola, the Shadowbrook serves delicious food in an elegant, comfortable setting. To get to the restaurant, park on the street and descend the hill via a red cable car that's been a fixture since 1958. The Shadowbrook has four dining rooms, each with its own theme (the Greenhouse, the Fireside Room, the Wine Cellar). We ate in the Garden Room, at ground level, with a bird's-eye view of the ducks waddling past the windows, curiously eyeing diners before pecking their own meals out of the ground. In deference to our feathered friends, we did not order duck.

The menu runs from such hearty standards as prime rib with horseradish sauce (the house specialty) to more far-flung offerings such as Brazilian Seafood Pie (fresh fish, prawns and scallops in pastry with a spicy citrus sauce). Equally irresistible is the Salmon Valencia—a healthy-sized fillet of coho salmon with an herb vegetable stuffing. Don't pass up appetizers—e.g., artichoke fingers in a sauce of garlic, mustard and basil—or dessert, either.

Nightlife

At night, Capitola turns into a small-town carnival, with packs of people wandering the streets and popping in and out of bars. By 9 or 10 p.m., most of the restaurants have made a Clark Kent changeover into dance clubs or packed bars. The hottest action is at the *Edgewater*. Once they clear off the tables and crank up the sound system, all hell breaks loose. They never danced this frantically at Studio 54, even when the Bee Gees were wearing open satin shirts and squealing like chickens about "Stayin' Alive." A mixed bag of party animals with their radar out come to the Edgewater to bop to the latest dance mixes.

There's less aerobic activity at *Margaritaville* (good Mexican food), *Zelda's* and the *Bandstand* and more of a chatty bar scene where talk doesn't get drowned out by music. The Bandstand and Margaritaville both have large outdoor decks on the beach overlooking the water.

Capitola Chamber of Commerce
410 Capitola Avenue
Capitola, CA 95010
(408) 475-6522

Aptos Chamber of Commerce
9010 Soquel Drive
Aptos, CA 95003
(408) 688-1467

Santa Cruz

Santa Cruz, located north of just about any place that serves authentic burritos, is frequently compared with Southern California. Perhaps this is simply because of its wide, sandy, swimmable beaches—a freakish phenomenon along the northern end of Monterey Bay. Still, the Southern California connection is further bolstered by the volleyball scene at *Cowell Beach*, with the nimble-fingered set going for it with a spiky determination that would do their L.A. cousins proud. Meanwhile, surfing not only flourishes but has literally been enshrined in Santa Cruz. Then there's the party atmosphere, the free-for-all on the boardwalk, the endless sea of youthful faces, kids, adolescents, teenagers and young adults, all trying to stave off middle age. The beach is wall to wall with gorgeous women, the younger ones covered in make-up, imitating the older ones who don't need it. Yes, Santa Cruz *is* a lot like Southern California.

But Santa Cruz ("sacred cross") is many other things, too. The city is a patchwork of lifestyles, politics, land forms and roads that converge to make it the largest seaside resort in Northern California. With a population of over 50,000 that's swelled by weekend crowds from Silicon Valley, San Jose and even San Francisco, Santa Cruz has had no choice but to assert its individuality or get buried in the stampede.

From the outset, the town was destined for uniqueness. The original mission built here in 1791, *Mission La Exaltación de la Santa Cruz*, vanished without a trace. All they know is that it was located somewhere near the San Lorenzo River and quite possibly was swallowed up by it. (To this day, the river is subject to destructive flooding.) A replica of the mission has been built outside of town, but few go out of their way to see it.

Turning away from spiritual matters, Santa Cruz built its first public bathhouse on the main beach in 1865 and later added a boardwalk, dance hall and casino. A lucrative logging industry kept Santa Cruz's economy afloat while it made the slow transition from residential town to resort. Then the crowds began arriving, taking a train called the "Suntan Special" from San Francisco and San Jose. Because of Santa Cruz, the coastal railroad was a smashing success and stations were built at short intervals up and down the coastline, paralleling today's Coast Highway. Santa Cruz's original roller coaster and carousel are still in use on the boardwalk, and many of its old Victorian houses have been restored.

Santa Cruz is built around and subdivided by the San Lorenzo River, which snake-dances its way through town before emptying into the ocean just south of the main beach. On the sandy side of this watery axis, Santa Cruz is a beach town. Over by the cliffs, Santa Cruz is peaceful and suburban. Politically and culturally, Santa Cruz is split in a similar way, with businesspeople on one side and "hippies" on the other. (We'll call them hippies because everyone else in Santa Cruz does.) The town's sizable arts community mingles with the large college population from the nearby state university to create a free-thinking, sixties-style atmosphere.

The University of California at Santa Cruz campus is set on a sprawling cattle ranch east of town. The buildings are hidden beneath groves of redwood trees, making it one of the most well-concealed institutions of higher learning on the planet. A tour of the campus reveals it to be a throwback to the sixties in many respects. The sports mascot is a slug, the campus restaurant is called the Whole Earth (and serves dishes like "Thai-style Tofu and Vegetables"), narrative evaluations are given instead of grades, fraternities and sororities are discouraged because they "run the risk of encouraging elitism, racism, sexism and apathy toward academic work," and courses have been known to carry such titles as "the Pursuit of Truth in the Company of Friends." It's worth a sidetrip to see a university with values so different from the status quo business-administration mills.

If Santa Cruz can be said to resemble any one town in Southern California, it would have to be Santa Monica. Open-minded tolerance has led both to become sanctuaries for the downtrodden and those hopelessly confused by life. Santa Cruz is a figurative border town, with the surrounding nations being Woodstock, Altamont, Mexico City, Surf City and Desolation Row. It's a puzzling but intriguing place. One can examine the various strands in the town's fabric for days and still not comprehend the whole rug.

Therefore, maybe it's best at this point to stick to the beaches. Due to the winding of the river and the boa-like bending of the roads, Santa Cruz has many beach-access points. Each is claimed by a different crowd. Starting at the south end, *Pleasure Point* is one of two key outposts for the surfing cult. It is located off East Cliff Drive and 41st Street, uphill and around the corner from Capitola. Things like cliffs, rocks, sharks and kelp don't scare surfers as long as the waves are good, and at Pleasure Point, they most definitely are. If you can, park on a neighborhood street and observe the rites of surfing from a cliff-top overlook.

Continuing up East Cliff and then over to Portola Drive, *Moran Lake Beach* (at 26th Avenue) is next. Because it's a flat sand beach, people come here to sunbathe. *Sunny Cove* (at Portola and 17th Avenue) draws the bodysurfers. *Lincoln Beach* (at 12th Avenue) is a quiet place, attracting contemplative types. Parking on the surrounding residential streets can be a problem, since much of it is by permit only.

Santa Cruz's coast temporarily ends at the Yacht Harbor (near 7th Avenue). The roads freak out totally but eventually order is restored by the time you get to *Twin Lakes Beach*. This is a popular spot with party animals, with some brave souls wading across the

mouth of the San Lorenzo River to get to it. Building twilight bonfires is a favorite pastime, as is watching the Wednesday afternoon
sailboat regattas.

Despite all these options, you'll probably wind up on Santa
Cruz's *Main Beach*. It fronts the famed boardwalk, and most of the
accommodations in town are close to it. The water is as safe and
calm as bathwater (though far, far colder), and a squadron of lifeguards oversees the busy surf. Both Main Beach and the boardwalk should be strolled for the total Santa Cruz experience. A ski-
lift contraption carries riders high overhead, while caterpillar cars
dipsy-doodle on the roller-coaster tracks. A multitude of food stalls
will sell you a fast lunch, and a multitude of rides will help you
lose it. In short, it's a classic boardwalk scene. From a distance—
say Lighthouse Point, to the north—it gives the town an airy, romantic quality.

Up at the north end of the oceanfront is *Cowell Beach*, the most
happening spot in Santa Cruz. Wimps need not apply. This is the
domain of serious volleyballers and, over by some slippery, deadly
rocks, an almost mythological cult of surfers. The Miss California
Beauty pageant used to be held on Cowell Beach but was canceled
because (we believe we heard this correctly) spectators began pelt-
ing the contestants and each other with raw meat. Now, they hold
a surfing tournament out by Lighthouse Point and the Jose Cuervo
Volleyball Tournament on the sands of Cowell Beach. For a half-
mile radius, this is as close as Northern California comes to Southern California.

Some of the best surf that California (north *or* south) has to offer can be found at *Steamer Lane*. This is the unofficial name for
the surf off Lighthouse Point. Only the best and bravest local surfers come here, because the swells reach mountainous heights and
threaten to hurl their fearless riders against the base of the cliffs or
fillet them on the rocks that jut out of the water. The waves wrap
around the far corner of a cliff, and the surfers wait patiently for
their turn to follow the curls along the deadly face of the shoreline. Those who aren't in the water sit on sofas and car seats that
have been tossed onto the rocks. Everyone else stands on the edge
of an unfenced, eroding cliff, watching nervously, taking pictures

and creating an intimate feeling of community based around total fear. Waves slam against the shore, sending spray upward and occasionally causing onlookers to be washed over the edge to their deaths.

The state has allocated funds to create the *Steamer Lane Lighthouse Field State Beach*. An integral part of the complex will be the Surfing Museum, which already exists in the adjoining lighthouse. This is an imperative stop for anyone who wants to understand California. Lovingly displayed photographs adorn the walls—of people with 16-foot boards, of 19 surfers crammed inside a woody— and videos and news clippings document the sport's surprisingly rich history. But the centerpiece is the shrine, where the ashes of an ill-fated surfer are interred beneath a pile of rocks and shells. The 18-year-old victim died after "challenging the sea" and losing.

Finally, if you're not already beached out, follow West Cliff Drive (the road in front of the lighthouse) north until you reach *Natural Bridges State Beach*. In the water are two stone formations that do indeed resemble bridges. Though no lifeguards patrol the tiny beach, we saw small kids wading knee-deep in the water and playing in its foam.

Accommodations

The motel scene in Santa Cruz is a paradox. Although the supply is enormous and seemingly outstrips the demand, the actual number of desirable choices for people who don't sport mohawks or have metal in their front teeth are few. The stories told about Santa Cruz and its oceanfront motels are sobering—tales of crime, degenerate behavior, dangerous overcrowding of rooms, noise, unidentifiable odors, cobwebs and substance abuse. Here's a good one: A teenage boy goes out to get a Coca-Cola one evening. He leaves the motel-room door unlocked and lingers awhile at the boardwalk arcades. He returns to find a derelict passed out in bed next to his grandmother, who's somehow slept through it all. Then there's the tale of the hippie (they use that word a lot around here) who allegedly lived for a month in a motel elevator.

Based on our own cruises along Riverside Avenue near the board-walk, rooms start at a low of $34 and get jacked up to well over $100 at places with letters missing from their signs and an odor like Indian food in the lobby and rooms. The best-known hotel on the beach is the *Dream Inn*, a high-rise overlooking the volleyball courts and pier. It is said that the status of a visiting volleyballer can be gauged by the view from his or her room at the Dream Inn. This is no idle dreamer's hideaway, though; rooms run from $100 to $130.

The best way to enjoy the beach at Santa Cruz is to stay a few blocks away at one of several adequate and clean motels on Ocean Street. The *Motel Continental* and the *Best Inn* will do all right. Both start at around $50 during the week and run higher on weekends. In general, Santa Cruz innkeepers were reluctant to give us a hard-and-fast price range. They charge whatever they can get away with, especially on summer weekends when the town lights up like a pinball machine.

A final option, perhaps the best of all, is the *Riverside Garden Inn*, a modern, European-style hotel on a saner part of Riverside Avenue. It's the new kid on the block and certainly one of Santa Cruz's better kept secrets. Its courtyard is graced by a small garden, a goldfish pond and a large heated pool. A continental breakfast is included in the room rate (which ranges from $55 to $88 a night). Believe it or not, it costs less to stay here than at one of the rat traps near the boardwalk.

Restaurants

Two of the best seafood dens in Santa Cruz are located, appropriately, on the Municipal Pier (winner of the Wide Body Award for ocean piers). The *Ideal Fish Company* sits at the entrance of the pier, where the sidewalk doubles as a skateboard interstate. It has been in business in one form or another since 1917. *Malio's*, at the end of the pier, leans toward Italian dishes like Linguine and Clams. Both are part of the same "enterprise group," whatever that means.

For breakfast, try the *Broken Egg*, downtown in the middle of

Pacific Mall. At the Broken Egg, your omelette comes with a choice
of fresh fruit or home fries. While you're waiting, you can watch
the hippies parade along the mall over the top of your morning
Chronicle.

Nightlife

Santa Cruz is a party town in the grand tradition. People dance to
any type of music—live, taped, synthesized, loud, soft, eighties,
forties, and especially sixties. Current hits. Garage rock. Glenn
Miller. It doesn't matter. It's as if Santa Cruz were trying to make
up for all the empty space between here and Santa Barbara.

Clubs are scattered around suburban Santa Cruz and cater to a
vast cross section of young adults who come with dates on their
arms from as far away as San Jose. The best clubs close to the
water are the *Catalyst* and the *Crow's Nest*, two decidedly different
means to the same end. The Crow's Nest is actually the second
floor of a seafood restaurant on the Santa Cruz Yacht Harbor (reachable via East Cliff Drive and 7th Avenue). After the plates have
been washed and put away downstairs, the volume shoots up on
the amps upstairs. The Crow's Nest draws a good-looking, well-
behaved crowd. The cream of the crop, if you will.

The Catalyst is an untamed version of the same animal. More
collegiate, loose and liberal, it is a cavernous college clubhouse (not
surprising, since it used to be a bowling alley). All strata of Santa
Cruz's social scene wander through the doors of this miniature convention center, looking for a good time. The Friday Night Happy
Hour (from four to six) is a local tradition, but every night is right
at the Catalyst, which books local and national acts. They also sell
deli food and cold beer from all over the planet.

Yet another great place for live rock and roll is *O.T. Price's*, south-
east of Santa Cruz in a town called Soquel. It may be a little out
of the way, but their heart is in the right place—i.e., on the beach.
One night they threw a "Clean the Beach Party and BBQ." You
got in free for bringing a bag of litter. The next night, the Surfaris
played there.

Santa Cruz Chamber of Commerce
Church and Center Streets
P.O. Box 921
Santa Cruz, CA 95061
(408) 423-1111

Red, White and Blue Beach
Bonny Doon Beach

The amazing beaches of Santa Cruz continue all the way north to
the San Mateo County line. *Red, White and Blue* and *Bonny Doon*
are sought out by city dwellers wanting a little more isolation. The
first of these is a private nude beach six miles outside of Santa Cruz
on Route 1. It is recognizable by the mailbox with the patriotic
color scheme; $5 gets you in. Bonny Doon, five more miles up the
road, can be identified by the line of cars parked on both shoulders and the trails leading over the railroad tracks and dunes to the
beach. For the mildly arduous hike in, the reward is a wide, semicircular beach in a sheltered cove.

Davenport

Davenport is a crossroads in northern Santa Cruz County with a
café, a country store, a pottery shop and a population of 200. There
are beach-access points at *Davenport Landing* and at *Scott Creek
Coastal Access*, a few miles north.

Año Nuevo State Reserve

Año Nuevo is a protected breeding ground for the northern ele-
phant seal and, secondarily, a recreation area for humans. Just

inside the San Mateo County line, its southern-facing beach runs along a mile of curving coastline. A $3 day-use fee gets you past the gate; it's a 10-minute hike to the beach from the parking lot. Whale watching, bird-watching, clam digging and surf-casting are the main activities, and surfers have been known to catch a wave off Año Nuevo Point. The reserve is closed during seal breeding season (December to March), although the park service leads guided tours of the peninsula for small groups at this time. For reservations, which are accepted as early as October, call (415) 879-0227.

Pigeon Point

No real beach here, but what a lighthouse. Set on a cliff above a rugged coast, the 115-foot-tall Pigeon Point Light has been guid-ing mariners since 1872. Because so many ships have sunk off the point, including the catastrophic breakup of a Boston ship, the *Car-rier Pigeon* (and the subsequent wreck of the ship dispatched to sal-vage its cargo), the Pigeon Point Light remains a vital navigational aid. Tours are given on Sundays only (at 10:00, 11:15, 12:30, 1:45 and 4:00). Additionally, a youth hostel is located in the bungalows that formerly housed Coast Guard families. The dormitory-style accommodations hold up to 50, who pay from $6 to $9 per night. It's an interesting place to pass an evening, if you don't balk at a little austerity (i.e., shared bathrooms, bunk beds and no compli-mentary avocado body balm). South of the lighthouse, a trail leads to *Gazos Creek Beach*.

Bean Hollow State Beach

A pair of small, free parking lots just above the beach are about all there is at Bean Hollow. A shelf of rocks divides the beach into two broad coves. The rocky surf is bothered with rip tides. We watched people doggedly trying to play volleyball and picnic in

the face of gray skies and pummeling winds. It looked to be a desperate stab at Southern California wish fulfillment. Raw, elemen-
tal wilderness is the main feature at Bean Hollow; come to escape
and meditate.

Pescadero State Beach
Pomponio State Beach
San Gregorio State Beach

No one will ever accuse the California Coastal Commission of lax-
ity. The state's coastline is dotted with so many state beaches it's
a major task just to keep up with the latest acquisitions. Pescadero,
Pomponio and San Gregorio are three that crop up in rapid succes-
sion along the sparsely populated midcoast of San Mateo County.
There's no entrance fee at Pescadero (the largest of them), while
$2 is supposed to be stuffed in an honor box at Pomponio and San
Gregorio.

Pescadero is barely developed, with no facilities and a pair of
rough gravel lots at cliff's edge. Great patches of foamy green ooze
were spinning wildly in the roiling surf. At the point where Pescadero Creek runs into the sea, fishers cast for steelhead trout. The
beach is longer and less rock-choked by the northern lot.

The scenery that unfolds as you continue up Route 1 is a panoramic feast for the eyes: green and gold rolling hills cut with
gulleys to the east, and stout, brush-covered dunes on the beach
side of the road. At Pomponio is a small lot, picnic tables, hibachis and a path descending to a pebbly beach. Just up the road is
San Gregorio, where folks swim and wade in the shallow lagoons
on warm summer days. All three beaches have creek mouths, making for uncommonly good fishing.

Half Moon Bay

Located just 30 miles south of San Francisco on a
of the Coast Highway, Half Moon Bay aims to ?
County's answer to Cape Cod, Massachusetts. The
known as Coastside, consists of four small commun.   ?alf
Moon Bay, Miramar, El Granada and Princeton—surro ?iding a
half moon–shaped cove. Originally, the "Cape Cod" handle was a
marketing device intended to give San Franciscans in need of a
"discovery" a convenient buzzword to latch onto. In some ways,
Coastside does resemble the few corners of Cape Cod that haven't
yet been overdeveloped. El Granada and Princeton, in particular,
are taking on the gray clapboard exteriors and white picket fences
of Hyannis. Princeton has a small, attractive pier and a harbor at
Pillar Point, the northern end of Half Moon Bay, giving it the relaxed, gentrified air of Hyannis Port.

The town of Half Moon Bay, however, marches to a more
Victorian drumbeat. As Coastside's largest town and center of commerce, Half Moon Bay is beginning to march to several other tem-
pos, too. Many of the town's 8,500 residents have moved here in
recent years, braving the commute up Route 1 to San Francisco or
over Route 92 to Silicon Valley. In the process, they've upscaled
the place. Pasta Moon, Main Street Sushi and the McCoffee Shop
have taken up positions next to the Old Fashioned Drug Store,
the Soda Fountain and the Home Cooked Meal diner. So far, it's
a standoff, but as sure as a half moon will rise in the sky, land
values will continue to go up, eventually sending local farmers to
the Half Moon Bay welfare office. Two shopping malls disguised
as "theme villages" now greet travelers as they pass through on
Route 1, giving those who fear they have become unglued from
civilization since leaving Santa Cruz a chance to show their grat-
itude. One banner heralded the imminent arrival of "Main Street
Goldworks." Oh boy!

Luckily, the forces of nature are working in Half Moon Bay's
favor. The Coast Highway takes on a Big Sur–like complexion several miles north of town as it approaches San Francisco. Scenic
and breathtaking though it is, this route would be torture on a daily
basis. Frequently closed due to rock and mud slides during peri-

of heavy rain, it has earned the nickname Devil's Slide. Much of the land along the coast is used for agriculture. Artichokes, brussels sprouts and flowers bloom in various cycles throughout the year, and in October, Half Moon Bay becomes the pumpkin capital of Northern California, with tens of thousands of people taking part in the festival. At other times, cattle graze in rocky fields all the way up to the foothills. The limited water supply is already being overtaxed by newcomers who want it for their lawns. Finally, coastal zoning regulations will make it difficult to wreak dramatic changes on Coastside, making it the only area within a 30-mile radius of San Francisco that won't go suburban. It is still, in fact, out in the country. Stapled onto the notice board in front of the Organic Food Store was a flyer for "Country Western Dancing Instructions. 4 Wk. Session. Partner Not Required." On the same board were notices for a livestock auction and a rodeo.

The beaches along Half Moon Bay have been left alone to do nature's bidding. All are part of the larger entity of *Half Moon Bay State Beach*, with access points at *Francis Beach*, *Venice Beach* and *Dunes Beach*. Located at the south end of the bay, Francis Beach is the most popular of the three. When we visited, cars were backed up waiting to get in. Francis Beach has the added lure of 50 campsites. Camping costs $10, and day use of the beach, $3. Venice and Dunes are smaller beaches, the roads leading to them ending in dirt and gravel parking lots. It costs $2 to park at each of these. All three are calm for this part of the coast, but swimming is still a very tentative proposition.

Accommodations

The old Victorian buildings of Half Moon Bay have been preserved and many put to use as bed-and-breakfast inns. The *Mill Rose Inn* is the pick of the litter, a romantic retreat by the sea with a quiet English country garden on the grounds. The rooms have private baths and entrances. Sherry is served in the evening and champagne accompanies the complimentary breakfast. Honeymooners take note.

Four miles north of Half Moon Bay, just off Route 1 in El Granada, is the *Harbor View Inn*. It's a modern, Cape Cod–style motel overlooking Pillar Point Harbor. There are restaurants across the highway and beaches a short drive to the south.

Restaurants

The *Shore Bird Restaurant* has really taken this Cape Cod thing to heart. Their building is an exact replica of a house on Cape Cod, copied by the architect down to the minutest detail. Overlooking the Pillar Point Harbor and surrounded by a garden and a white picket fence, the Shore Bird looks more like a prosperous sea captain's home than the area's most popular restaurant.

The food at the Shore Bird is given the same meticulous attention that the architect gave the building. "Homemade" is a recurring word in the menu. All dressings, desserts, chowders and sauces are made from scratch. The restaurant specializes in fresh fish, most of which comes off the boats in the surrounding harbor. They have some uncommon items on their menu, like Crabtown Chicken, Scallops Sausalito, Smoked Salmon Fettucine and Poor Man's Abalone (squid steak). They also serve fish in its simplest, and usually best, form: broiled. For dessert, try the Pumpkin Cheesecake, a Thanksgiving hybrid whose time has come.

Nightlife

The *Miramar Beach Inn* is not an inn; it's a popular restaurant and bar with slightly relaxed morals. After the dinner plates are cleared on Thursdays, they showcase comedy acts and special events. (How does a Jim and Tammy Bakker look-alike contest grab you?) On Fridays and Saturdays, they charge a hefty cover to see bar bands do Creedence Clearwater Revival covers. The *Half Moon Bay Inn*, a dimly lit palace in the center of town, brings in live rock and roll bands on weekends, and there's no cover charge.

FOR FURTHER INFORMATION

Half Moon Bay/Coastside Chamber of Commerce
225 S. Cabrillo Highway ("The Caboose")
P.O. Box 188
Half Moon Bay, CA 94019
(415) 726-5202

Montara
Moss Beach

Montara (pop. 1,972) and Moss Beach (pop. 400) are the last sea-side hamlets you'll pass before the first signs of San Francisco and its suburbs pop into view. Chances are you *will* pass them, too, because the only signs of either on the Coast Highway are a convenience mart and a ramshackle hotel. For those who want to dig a little deeper, though, these two towns have hidden sides and a few points of interest.

Montara is a would-be artists' colony waiting for the artists to show. The only hotel, the *Farallone*, was built in 1908 and is the architectural equivalent of the Dadaist manifestos of the day. Our otherwise run-down room had a stained-glass window and a ladder and a telephone pole running through it. The town's other lodging is a hostel, with dormitory-style rooms surrounding an old lighthouse. *Montara State Beach* lies just north of the lighthouse. From a short bluff, a steep path leads to the half-mile beach. Just beyond Montara is private *Edun Beach*. This is not Eden, as in the Garden of... This is Edun, as in spell the word backward. A parking fee is charged.

Moss Beach's main point of interest is the *James Fitzgerald Marine Reserve*, a three-mile park renowned for its abundant marine life. On weekends, park rangers conduct tide-pool walks. Displays expound on the diversity of tide-pool life. If you promise not to disturb the sea creatures, you can explore on your own. Be careful, though: the rocks are slippery and the water outside the protective reef is rough.

Pacifica
Daly City

From the south, the entrance into San Mateo's largest beach-front city is far more exciting than anything you'll find within its limits. Don't look now, but you are driving through the Devil's Slide, Northern California's answer to Dead Man's Curve. North of Montara, the highway starts zigzagging crazily, slicing through an area of unstable cliffs that rise above and fall below at equally frightening angles. This stretch of road is closed periodically because the loose rocks have a tendency to slide in wet weather, a phenomenon frequently addressed by road signs. Recently, 400 steel rods were inserted into the road bed to keep the Devil's Slide from becoming the Devil Slid. A bypass has been on the books for years, awaiting approval. As if to escape Beelzebub himself, Route 1 cuts inland, curves twice, plunges downhill and suddenly deposits you in Pacifica.

Pacifica means "peaceful," a description that better suits the small villages south of here. Pacifica was, no doubt, peaceful at one time. In 1769, for instance, the Spanish explorer Gaspar de Portola came ashore, peacefully walking the length of what is now Pacifica and discovering the San Francisco Bay. This sighting took place on Sweeney Ridge, now part of the Golden Gate National Recreation Area.

People have been discovering Pacifica ever since, as the Bay Area continues to expand, gobbling up land in every direction. In 1957, nine separate communities came together to form the incorporated city of Pacifica. Today, the population of Pacifica is 40,000. All nine communities are still alleged to maintain their own identities, but at least from the perspective of the Coast Highway, the town looks like an unplanned sprawl of shoe boxes, heading north and clasping hands with Daly City. These back-door suburbs are unsightly evidence of San Francisco's insatiable need for bedrooms. It is this area that inspired Pete Seeger to write "Tiny Boxes." ("Tiny boxes, little boxes, and they're all made out of ticky-tack....") Not much has changed since Seeger parodied these projects, except more tiny boxes have been built and a verse about cheesy condos could be added.

The beaches of Pacifica are as unspectacular as the boxes. *San Pedro Beach* is the southernmost, appearing soon after the "Welcome to Pacifica" sign. Stretching for half a mile from Pedro Point, it's a black-sand spit favored by landscape artists and surfers. Across from San Pedro Beach is an A&W Root Beer stand, where the surfers linger after their daily exertions. This particular A&W has been acclaimed the "best fast-food place on any California beach" by *Surfing* magazine.

A mile north, separated from San Pedro Beach by six acres of rocky headland, is *Rockaway Beach*. If the Ramones had written about this Rockaway Beach, the song would have been a slow blues. Rockaway Beach Avenue ends at a Tote-A-Shed, and the beach below looks more like black dirt than sand. The last real beach before San Francisco is *Sharp Park State Beach*. It's reached via Clarendon Road, off the Coast Highway. But is it worth the trouble? Like chopsticks, two drainpipes poke the ocean at either end of the black-sand beach, their vile smell adding to the drab setting. A generic cement-slab pier that only an angler could love sits at the north end of the beach.

FOR FURTHER INFORMATION

Pacifica Chamber of Commerce
80 Eureka Square
Pacifica, CA 94044
(415) 355-4122

Northern Coast

San Francisco

To be frank about it, we would just as soon have bypassed San Francisco, simply because there's too much of it. On the East Coast, whenever we hit beachless coastal metropolises like Boston and Baltimore, we simply floored it around them. We could've gotten hung up for weeks trying to properly canvass a city the size of San Francisco, and a nervous look at the road map told us that 400 miles of California coastline still lay north of us, not to mention Oregon and Washington. Gulp.

Yes, we would've preferred to vault over the Golden Gate Bridge and leave this splendid city to the myriad travel writers capable of composing entire books on the subject. How could our paltry thousand words add anything meaningful to the voluminous prose works already in circulation? Point us to the next beach, and fast. But wait... the next beach is in San Francisco. Okay, let's make a deal. We'll scribble our paltry thousand words, sticking to San Francisco's waterfront, provided you keep our errors of omission in perspective. This is a book about beaches, after all. San Francisco is not exactly a beach town. Well, it's not the first thing you think of.

The beach, however, is the first thing to be seen if you're traveling the Pacific Scenic Parkway (a.k.a. Skyline Boulevard) from the south. Just above Fort Funston, about a mile or so inside the San Francisco County line, the road forks, with Skyline Boulevard turning inland and the Great Highway following the ocean for four uninterrupted miles. This lengthy strand is known as *Ocean Beach*. It is part of the *Golden Gate National Recreation Area*, the extensive federal park lands that also flank the Golden Gate Bridge and shoot far up into the headlands of western Marin County.

People come to Ocean Beach to park their cars and watch the sun set. Improved and unimproved turnoffs line the Great Highway, and weary commuters cut their engines and meditate on the cosmic orb in its late afternoon dimming. Unsafe for swimming, the beach is kind of a two-toned oddity: a strip of dark, dirty sand

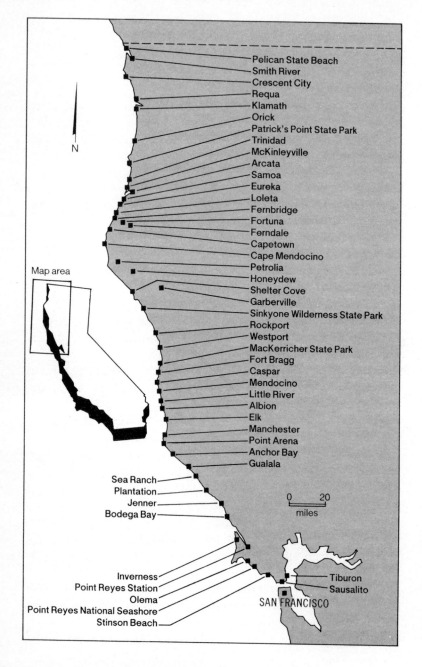

N

Map area

Pelican State Beach
Smith River
Crescent City
Requa
Klamath
Orick
Patrick's Point State Park
Trinidad
McKinleyville
Arcata
Samoa
Eureka
Loleta
Fernbridge
Fortuna
Ferndale
Capetown
Cape Mendocino
Petrolia
Honeydew
Shelter Cove
Garberville
Sinkyone Wilderness State Park
Rockport
Westport
MacKerricher State Park
Fort Bragg
Caspar
Mendocino
Little River
Albion
Elk
Manchester
Point Arena
Anchor Bay
Gualala
Sea Ranch
Plantation
Jenner
Bodega Bay

0   20
miles

Inverness
Point Reyes Station
Olema
Point Reyes National Seashore
Stinson Beach

Tiburon
Sausalito

SAN FRANCISCO

runs parallel to a peanut butter–colored ribbon where the waves rush in. The parking lots, bike paths and access ways are in a state of reconstruction (and have been for years). As you drive north, the road begins to rise, meeting a San Francisco landmark, the Cliff House, before curving right to become Point Lobos Avenue and then Geary Boulevard, which leads into downtown San Francisco. (Note to readers who do not want to be blackballed as tourists: never call it "Frisco"; the natives scoff at this shortening of their beloved city's proper name.)

The wind along Ocean Beach can be murderous, and if its gusting doesn't send a chill through you, the fog will. Several layers of clothing are mandatory in San Francisco, as the weather is changeable from minute to minute and block to block. Generally, the morning fog burns off after ten and returns around three, but no one's promising anything. Because of thermal inversion and other meteorologic phenomena, San Francisco enjoys a natural air-conditioning and air-purifying system. The wind blows the smog south before it has a chance to collect over the city.

Just because it's summertime, don't think you can get away with wearing warm-weather apparel in San Francisco. Winter days are mild, and summer ones, cool. Leave the cutoffs in the suitcase; wear long pants and keep a sweater tied around your neck. Besides being a jaunty affectation in this stylish city, it will come in handy when a sudden gust blows cool air or fog your way. In the words of Mark Twain, "The coldest winter I ever spent was a summer in San Francisco."

A left off Point Lobos Avenue onto El Camino Del Mar will soon have you curving through *Lincoln Park*, with good views of the bay from San Francisco's northwest corner. Trails run along the cliffs at a place called Land's End, one leading to a small beach. Yes, Virginia, there is a swimming beach in San Francisco. It's formally known as *James D. Phelan Beach State Park* (and informally known as *China Beach*). Only a few blocks away from Lincoln Park, China Beach is reachable from a parking lot near the intersection of Sea Cliff and 28th avenues. This small, sandy cove has shower facilities and lifeguards from April to October.

Around the curve from China Beach, the shoreline turns north again, paralleling the Golden Gate Bridge. *Baker's State Beach* runs along this west-facing strip, receiving a full-frontal assault from the Pacific. The surf is rough, but you can picnic in a cypress grove or hike along the windy beach, enjoying one of the best views of the bridge in the city. On a cloudless afternoon in late June, the wind was raising whitecaps on the bay and very nearly blew the hair off our heads, but we diligently snapped a few shots of the copper-colored bridge—the most frequently photographed and rendered symbol in the city and, at 4,200 feet, the second longest single-span bridge in the world. The Golden Gate Bridge turned 50 years old on May 24, 1987, and all of San Francisco showed up to celebrate. In fact, in what sounds like a collegiate stunt turned scary, the whole city tried to get on the bridge at the same time. The unintentional result was a human traffic jam numbering 800,000 strong—half headed in one direction, half in the other and no one moving for hours. The bridge began to sway under the weight of 25 million tons of flesh, blood and bones. Somehow, the pedestrian gridlock disentangled itself and a cataclysm was averted.

In this as well as most other civic crises, the citizens of San Francisco kept their cool. They love their city, its quirks and one another. There is a tangible San Francisco-ness in the air. The city is almost giddily self-satisfied. More than one contented native, taking in our harried countenances, furrowed with the evident stress of growing up tense and serious back east, urged us to relax. Relax? Hell, we thought we were relaxed. But not in the eyes of San Franciscans.

Behind Baker's Beach lurks the Presidio, headquarters for the Sixth Army Division and the least institutional-looking military base in the country. In keeping with the topsy-turvy spirit of San Francisco, the Presidio is more like a quiet, forested park than an army installation. East of the Golden Gate Bridge is Fort Mason, an abandoned army transport and quartermaster's depot that's now park headquarters for the Golden Gate National Recreation Area.

You're now on the very fringe of the multiblock area known as *Fisherman's Wharf*—beloved by tourists, avoided by locals. Mention Fisherman's Wharf to a native, and you'll receive the requisite rolling of the eyes along with an unsolicited down-the-nose comment about how many years it's been since they've driven anywhere *near* Fisherman's Wharf. True, tourists gravitate here in large numbers, but the mood in and around Fisherman's Wharf is that of a lively outdoor bazaar, spiced up with the sort of local color that only a city with as much personality as San Francisco can provide.

Come here to stroll the bay-side wharves and watch the birds circling the fishing boats. Buy a cup of chilled seafood from an outdoor vendor, topped with a tangy dollop of cocktail sauce and a squeeze of lemon. For $2.25, you can grab an impromptu snack of crab, shrimp, lobster or squid, along with a piece of sourdough bread. The protein will fortify you for hiking around *Russian Hill*, *Nob Hill* and *Coit Tower* when you're finished with Fisherman's Wharf. If you're looking for something more substantial, the area is filled with Italian-surnamed seafood restaurants.

There's also shopping, the great American pastime, to be done here. On the high end of the spectrum, visitors with a ready line of credit will want to explore the maze of shops and boutiques at the *Cannery* (a former Del Monte produce-packing plant) and *Ghirardelli Square* (a converted chocolate factory dating from the last century). There's also a low-end aspect to the retail experience. Down on Taylor Street, near the water, we began having unnerving flashbacks of Venice Beach. Sidewalk peddlers hawk their wares here, mostly T-shirts, sweatshirts and sunglasses (the holy trinity of street sales). The main difference is that $10 will purchase four T-shirts in Venice and only three in San Francisco. But they say "San Francisco" and not "Venice Beach" on them, which makes it worth the extra money.

Other Fisherman's Wharf attractions include boat tours and ferry rides. The square rigger *Balclutha*, docked at Pier 43, can be toured for $3. It is one of seven seaworthy vessels belonging to the *National Maritime Museum*. Built in Glasgow in 1886, the *Balclutha* made five round trips from Scotland to San Francisco via Cape Horn in the late 1800s, before making runs up to Alaska for salmon in the early decades of this century. The National Park Service also conducts trips to *Alcatraz*, the island out in the bay on which you can see the former federal penitentiary that housed America's most hardened felons. Al Capone was one of the guests of the house. No one escaped from "the Rock"; this was a grim internment. This highly recommended tour leaves hourly, beginning at 8:45 a.m., from Pier 41 and includes a ranger-led walk around the island and through the main cell block. *Angel Island*, another deserted island in the bay, was notorious as a detainment camp for Asian Americans during World War II. Having long since returned to its natural state, Angel Island can be reached by ferries leaving from Pier 43½. In addition, ferries make frequent crossings from San Francisco to the bay-hugging Marin County villages of Sausalito, Tiburon and Larkspur.

Fisherman's Wharf runs along the bay from Hyde to Stockton streets, ending at the northeast corner of this boxy peninsula, at which point the Embarcadero takes over. Facing east, the 50 piers of the Embarcadero offer deep water berthing in what is one of the world's great natural harbors. And that just about does it for San Francisco's waterfront. Highly recommended to anyone wanting to see it all by automobile is the *49-Mile Drive*. It begins at City Hall (Van Ness Avenue and McAllister Street). Just follow the blue-and-white seagull signs and allow plenty of time. An annotated map of the route can be picked up at the *Visitor Information Center* (on the lower level of Hallidie Plaza, at Powell and Market streets).

In closing, we'd like to mention the neighborhood known as *North Beach*, the seat of Beat Generation solidarity, both because of its literary roots and its name. North Beach was at one time a bona fide beach, right on the water. But then artificial fill was used to extend the booming city, around the time of its forty-niner gold rush, half a mile out to the present-day Fisherman's Wharf and Embarcadero. Nowadays, a mixed cargo of yuppies and bohemians wander the shores of this land-locked beach, which remains a vibrant place with its offbeat boho character intact.

Accommodations

San Francisco is one of the great hotel cities in the world. We could rattle on for pages about this but will confine ourselves to a few choice observations. Along San Francisco's 24 miles of shoreline, the heaviest concentration of hotels and motels is in and around Fisherman's Wharf. No surprise here, as it is the busiest and most picturesque locale in San Francisco. Even the cable cars get their bearings at Fisherman's Wharf, being rotated and pointed in the right direction on a turntable here. All the name-brand hotel chains are present and accounted for, and two of them—*Holiday Inn* and *Sheraton*—rise to a five-story, 500-room salute, with an only slightly smaller *Marriott* crouching nearby. Rooms at these inns generally run from $90 to $165. A break on price can be found at the Fisherman's Wharf *TraveLodge* and *Howard Johnson's*. Alternatively, rows of old hotels and newer motels line Van Ness Avenue, a centrally located street that's convenient to Chinatown, Union Square, Nob Hill, Fisherman's Wharf and Golden Gate Park.

Bed-and-breakfast inns are coming on strong in San Francisco. Given the choice, wouldn't you like to stay in a turn-of-the-century Victorian home with a breathtaking view of the city? If the answer is yes, then San Francisco has a bevy. The same outfit that runs the Gosby House Inn in Pacific Grove, much liked by us, also operates the *White Swan Inn* and *Petite Auberge* on Nob Hill in San Francisco. Rooms start as low as $45, and the inns are warm and intimate—the kinds of places you look forward to returning to at the end of the day.

Just for the record, the top of the line in San Francisco is the *Clift*, a hotel dating from 1915 that's described as "quietly classy." Renovated in the seventies to the tune of $5 million, the Clift is one of the peerless Four Seasons chain. We sampled their wares in Newport Beach and can vouch for any claims made on their behalf. At $135 to $265 a night (and up to $750 for suites), we can, in fact, do everything but afford to stay there.

Restaurants

Great seafood restaurants are as much a San Francisco tradition as cable cars. Considering that Fisherman's Wharf is the main handling and distribution center for seafood in Northern California, how could it miss? The wharf area is chockablock with long-established restaurants and trendy new arrivals.

One of the most venerable oldies is *A. Sabella's*. Their reputation dates back to the twenties, when Antone Sabella opened Sabella's Restaurant on this spot. His father, a poor fisherman who emigrated from Italy, launched the family on their "manifish" destiny with a retail market on the wharf. Sabella's is still run by Antone Sabella (albeit the grandson of the patriarch). Four generations of accumulated wisdom are brought to bear on the matter of fish. The method of preparation is Italian, but with a light hand. The pièce de résistance on the menu is a dish humbly named for and by the founder: Antone. It consists of a piece of swordfish baked in a beurre blanc, stuffed with deviled shrimp and topped with Parmesan cheese and white sauce. Crab is another specialty. The Sabellas pick their crabmeat on the premises and can tell you things about crabs that even marine biologists don't know. Crab legs (sautéed, fried or bordelaise) and Crab Cioppino (simmered with shrimp and shellfish in tomato sauce) are excellent. For that matter, everything on the menu is good enough to recite. Sabella's is tops on Fisherman's Wharf, both for the food and the view— three stories above the hubbub with an unobstructed view of the bay. And don't leave without having a hunk of their world's-best cheesecake.

Another San Francisco institution is the *Cliff House*. Five different structures have occupied the same site since its original construction in 1897. One of the buildings burned down when a boat full of nitroglycerin crashed into the cliff it sits on. The latest edifice is very secure and its culinary reputation improves yearly. The Cliff House boasts two completely different restaurants. Downstairs is more seafood oriented, with an art deco interior. Upstairs is quasi-Italian, with pasta, veal and beef in addition to seafood. Both offer splendid views of the fierce sea spewing tongues of foam on Seal Rocks, just offshore. The windows downstairs look up the coast, toward Marin County. Upstairs, you're peering south, at Ocean Beach. Nationally, the Cliff House is ranked in the top 20 in terms of dollar volume of business. The Cliff House tavern, by the way, is patronized and liked even by native San Franciscans, who voted it their favorite neighborhood bar one recent year. It has a heavy appetizer menu, logs burning in the fireplace and good tunes on the jukebox.

Nightlife

Few would disagree that San Francisco is the most enlightened city in America. It's certainly the most European. Contained within its borders is a little bit of Paris, Rome, Vienna, Sodom and Gomorrah. Everything from ballet to bondage bars can be located on the fog-shrouded streets after dark. In other words, you really don't need us telling you where to go to have a good time in San Francisco.

We'll offer a few stray observations, though. Having grown up as teenagers with a curious eye on the goings-on in Haight-Ashbury in the late sixties, we were more than a little shocked to drive through the area in 1987 and find The Gap (a franchised store selling rugby shirts and prewashed jeans to prep-school types) and a frozen yogurt parlor on the hallowed corner of Haight and Ashbury. Where have all the hippies gone? From the Summer of Love to stock options. Or the gutter.

It's a yuppie world now, and reminders of this turn up in every neighborhood—even in North Beach, a traditionally rough side of town with a literary asterisk attached to it. Latter-day North Beach is a grab bag of shiny, brass-handled cafés, bookstores and poster shops, and strip joints like the *Condor*. Topless dancer Carol Doda performed her famous dance, the Swim, at the Condor in the sixties. When we were in town, "live man and woman love act" was advertised on the outdoor marquee. Since then, they've decided to clothe their dancers. Modesty seems to be on the upswing again.

FOR FURTHER INFORMATION

San Francisco Convention and Visitors Bureau
P.O. Box 6977
San Francisco, CA 94101
(415) 626-5500

San Francisco Visitor Information Center
900 Market Street (Hallidie Plaza)
San Francisco, CA 94102
(415) 391-2000

San Francisco Chamber of Commerce
465 California Street
San Francisco, CA 94104
(415) 392-4511

Sausalito

Driving north across the Golden Gate Bridge is not unlike entering a vast cathedral, the religion therein being pantheism. Everything around you is holy. To the left, you are humbled by the
raging curls of the Pacific and the moss-green humps of the Marin
headlands. To the right, you are comforted by the less fearsome
bay and the romantic city skyline. Overhead rise the coppery orange spires of the bridge. Straight ahead beckons Marin County,
the home of New Age religion.

The first congregation on the right is Sausalito, which is entered
by taking Alexander Avenue after crossing the Golden Gate. Soon,
you will be caught up in a slow-moving line of cars filled with other
wayfaring pilgrims. Another way over to Sausalito is via ferry from
San Francisco, which docks in the heart of the village, sparing you
the headache of traffic. Whether making the passage to Sausalito
by car or ferry, the ride turns out to be more relaxing and scenic
than the destination.

Sausalito dates back to 1869, when 20 San Francisco businessmen formed the Sausalito Land and Ferry Company. The only
note of interest prior to that has to do with the origins of the name.
Though it hasn't been officially documented, legend has it that
Sausalito was given the name "Saucilito" (pidgin Spanish for "willow") in 1775 by Juan Manuel de Ayala, who was impressed by
the trees that grew down to the shoreline. The land Ayala so
admired lay untouched until the ferry company bought up the
waterfront, subdivided it and—presto, change-o!—gave birth to
California's first suburb. The idea behind the ferries was to carry
rich, hermitic San Franciscans—in 1869, already tired of overcrowding—to a "quiet, rural home in a lovely place." By 1880,
only 11 years after the original land purchase, the small town was

growing up into the steep hills surrounding the quiet harbor. The upper crust had a new Canaan. The glue of snobbery that bound them to their promised land still holds fast today.

The setting for a new town could scarcely be more ideal. Unlike San Francisco, with its unpredictable weather, Sausalito is all sunshine and light, free of fog, wind and choppy water. The view across the San Francisco Bay is breathtaking. Given the daily exposure to the islands, bay and city skyline, most early Sausalitans became self-absorbed members of a rigid yacht-club set. The ferries took them back and forth from San Francisco when they needed to venture out of their posh oasis. Over the years, a few "artist types" trickled in—mostly for the landscape-painting opportunities—giving the town a little color. But all in all, Sausalito remained a contented animal, resting on its laurels and its money.

But then, in 1939, the Golden Gate Bridge was built, routing traffic to Marin County and ushering in tourism. This is roughly where Sausalito stands today. Paying the price for its idyllic setting, the lovely bay-side village has become a walking, talking, honking, car-filled, polo-shirted, gold-and-brass-plated tourist trap. Even the bellhops and artisans admit it. They make their bread in Sausalito but live in Mill Valley or San Rafael. Cars shudder in an unmoving line down Bridgeway, the main street, as the occupants search in vain for a parking spot. Do they realize that Sausalito collects more money from parking tickets than from property taxes? The passenger ferries off-load streams of tourists onto Bridgeway in the heart of the shopping district. Fall fashions are already out in June. Leroy Nieman's latest paint-by-numbers hang in gallery windows, as do hundreds of renderings of the Golden Gate Bridge—canvas postcards that go for $2,500 instead of 25 cents. And look, there's a wooden pelican...over there, next to the big brass duck. It is said that when members of Marin County's large art community want to go mainstream, they come to Sausalito.

Less pricey in dollars but ultimately costlier in dental bills are the almost numberless sweet shoppes of Sausalito, which peddle everything from ice cream and cookies to cream cakes and pies (or is it cream pies and cakes?). They beckon newly arrived visitors like sugary sirens, and most succumb to the urge (and not for the first time, judging from the ample rumps dragging down the side-walk). Before noon on a Monday, swarms of people were lined up outside a toothache parlor to get their warclub-sized cones. Many on the streets already had cones glued to their faces. What is it about ice cream and adults on vacation? Is it some kind of Freudian return to childhood?

Be that as it may, Sausalito is a lovely setting. Two or three blocks back from the harbor, up in the hills behind Bridgeway, one discovers gorgeous, tree-shaded streets. It's worth the steep climb to escape the bustle and enjoy a quiet vista. Equally inter-esting to see are the large houses built on the waters of Sausalito Harbor. These are not precisely houseboats but houses built on barges and old ferryboats sunk and secured to the bottom. This watery neighborhood used to be a haven for musicians, artists and societal dropouts like author and Zen philosopher Alan Watts, who lived on a boat here. A prolonged legal battle drove the less wealthy away, and only the "nice" homes survived. Now the development on the water is a mirror image of the development on land. Do the real-estate agents paddle rowboats out here?

None of your strolls around Sausalito is likely to uncover a wealth of history. They're more likely to reveal the brief history of wealth in Marin County. Land values, commercial zoning, condomania and the cardinal rule of real-estate skulduggery—"lo-cation, location, location"—are on display for all to see. It would be nice if Sausalito could swap some of the tourism for a little more peace and quiet. Still, the commotion down on Bridgeway can be ameliorated by the spectacular views of the Bay Area from the heights of Sausalito.

Accommodations

Casa Madrona was born in 1885 as a lumber baron's Victorian man-sion. The original sprawling wooden house sits high on a hilltop above Bridgeway. It is both Sausalito's oldest surviving building and a registered National Landmark. After many incarnations and two near-deaths by landslide, Casa Madrona is now a hotel, hav-ing been expanded, renovated and refurbished all the way down the hillside to the main street. The additions to the original mansion have not diminished Casa Madrona's appeal. In fact, the zigzagging, M.C. Escher–like arrangement of the rooms only adds to their privacy and charisma. The front door opens onto the busy, sometimes noisy thoroughfare, but the rest of the hotel pulls up, up and away onto the hillside. The rooms have been given names like Lord Ashley's Lookout, Le Petit Boudoir and the Artist's Loft (which comes with an easel, brushes and paints), and all are filled with antiques and knickknacks designed to transport you back to the nineteenth century. Rooms in the original Victorian manse start at $65; in the "new Casa," at $120; and in the cottages, at $140. Wine and cheese are laid out in an upstairs parlor around cocktail hour, and a sizable continental breakfast is served every morning.

The *Alta Mira Continental Hotel*, on the quiet, shady street behind Casa Madrona, is our second choice. If you want an even more serene taste of Sausalito, the Alta Mira is your ticket. The "new" Alta Mira was built in 1927 after the first one—built by the original owner, Thomas "Tapeworm" Jackson—burned down. Though the rooms aren't as meticulously appointed as those at Casa Madrona, the Alta Mira has one of the best bay views in town. Come for the legendary Sunday brunch and see for yourself. Rooms of all shapes and sizes are not unreasonably priced, running from $70 to $115.

Restaurants

Like most quaintly dressed bay-side colonies, Sausalito makes you pay a stiff tariff to eat a meal anywhere near the water. With dishes like Pheasant Vladimir, *Ondine* is the choice of the money's-no-object set, while *Houlihan's Old Place* lists a reliable spread of California cuisine, the San Francisco Cioppino being especially good. If you've grown attached to your room at Casa Madrona, you needn't leave the premises for fine food. The top-floor restaurant boasts a glass-enclosed deck for elegant outdoor dining. *Flynn's Landing*, a favorite seafood restaurant in Sausalito, is a few steps away from the lapping of the waves and the trampling of the crowds, on Johnson Street.

Nightlife

At night, Sausalito's social life centers around two olde English-style pubs. Both *Patterson's* and the *No Name Bar* have enough character and ambience to make a British sailor feel welcome. The No Name is purportedly one of the first pubs in America to refer to itself as nothing at all. You can't miss it, though; it's only a block from Patterson's, on the same side of Bridgeway. After the last ferry has taken the daytime crowds back to San Francisco, locals and visitors mingle in a much less frazzled fashion. For anything beyond a few pints of ale, though, you must take the Golden Gate Bridge into San Francisco.

FOR FURTHER INFORMATION

Sausalito Chamber of Commerce
333 Caledonia Street
P.O. Box 566
Sausalito, CA 94966
(415) 332-0505

Tiburon

Up until recently, most of the land on the Tiburon Peninsula belonged to the Southern Pacific railroad. Tiburon was a railroad town, the vital link between the port of San Francisco and the north country. In its heyday, Tiburon was a bustling village with a Victorian Main Street. Much has changed since the decline of the railroad, but Tiburon still mines the "quiet Victorian village" theme, against strong evidence to the contrary.

You can pick up a postcard bearing an artist's rendering of a row of Victorian storefronts and the legend, "I stepped back in time in Tiburon." If you're inclined to believe you've stepped back in time, we can't help but think you've stepped onto the tracks and been hit by the train. First of all, Southern Pacific sold off great chunks of its peninsular uplands to a development firm called the Innisfree Company. The latter group has erected a plague of sterile condominiums on the hills above Tiburon, which look like a stadium full of binoculars trained upon the city of San Francisco across the bay. Longtime residents of the town wish, in hindsight, they'd pooled their resources and snapped up the land, but this is just wishful thinking. Second, the downtown is not at all historic. Rather, it fairly resembles Sausalito's parade of retail shops.

One of the old-time engineers might have derailed his train had he rounded the curve and confronted the spectacle of modern-day Tiburon. The sound of jackhammers and the sight of yellow bull-dozers moving earth around are everywhere on Tiburon Boule-vard. A complex of buildings that look like Japanese greenhouses has gone up on the bay, delivering more architectural inauthenticity to further scuttle any claims to old-world village charm. Every busi-ness with a spare lot has a hand-lettered sign out front reading, "All Day Parking $3.00." Parking, as every greedy tourist hamlet knows, is a foolproof way to nickel and dime the incoming knuckle-heads to death.

Okay. Tiburon has not yet been completely Carmelized. One has to disengage from Highway 101 and drive east on Route 131 to get here, so it is a few miles out of the way. (More commonly, though, people take the ferry from San Francisco, a much shorter distance as the crow flies.) The developmental cannonballs have been whizzing around only in the last five years, so there still are nooks and crannies of tranquility to be found. In Tiburon, you can while away a day in an atmosphere that's less manic than the snow-cone shuffle being danced on the sidewalks of Sausalito. On top of that, Tiburon has one of the finest biking and jogging paths anywhere. It runs for about three miles along the lapping waters of Richardson's Bay, following Tiburon Boulevard out of town. The path is level and wide, the bay view is fantastic, and one passes by a virtual arboretum of greenery.

Tiburon, all in all, is a town in transition, growing to meet the increasing demand for real estate by young, rich San Francisco professionals who want to work in the city and live in the coun-try. Tiburon also has its touristy side, although this is more gen-tly nudged than abrasively urged on visitors. All we dispute is the use of the words "quaint," "remote," "historic" and "Victorian" to describe a village that's slowly being slam-danced down a developmental back alley.

Accommodations

The *Tiburon Lodge and Conference Center* is a modern hotel in a woodsy setting. Actually, you're right on Tiburon Boulevard, half a block from Main Street, but the lodge feels like it's a few wooded acres away from it all. Birds hopscotch around the tree branches that brush the wooden balcony rails, enjoying the warm sun on a typically perfect day. A buffet breakfast is thrown in with the price of your room (which falls in the $75 to $140 range).

The Tiburon Lodge makes a good base if you're exploring Marin County for a few days. Muir Woods, Mount Tamalpais and the beaches of West Marin are all reasonably accessible from Tiburon, as is Angel Island. A state-run ferry to the island costs $4 round-trip, takes 15 minutes, runs hourly for most of the day and leaves from a dock behind the shops along the Main Street waterfront.

Restaurants

Sam's Anchor Café is a favorite gathering place in Tiburon. It's an old-fashioned bar with scuffed linoleum floors, ceiling fans and dim lighting. The menu is basic, ungussied seafood, with a few high-end specials like Red Snapper Picata and Stuffed Prawns Mediterranean thrown in for good measure. The back door opens onto the bay, ensuring an easy, soothing breeze. Sam's even has docking facilities for those arriving by boat—and many do.

Nightlife

Tiny Tiburon actually has more nightlife than Sausalito. *Christopher's* and *The Dock* both book live bands on weekends and are good places to knock back a tall one on weeknights, too. For that matter, you can order full dinners at both.

FOR FURTHER INFORMATION

Belvedere-Tiburon Chamber of Commerce
96 Main Street
P.O. Box 563
Tiburon, CA 94920
(415) 435-5633

Kirby Cove
Rodeo Beach

Much of what used to be Army land in the Marin headlands, north-west of the Golden Gate Bridge, has been turned over to the National Park Service. Camping, hiking, riding and fishing can be done on the sites of Forts Berry, Baker and Cronkite. Rodeo Beach—a small, pebbly cove—is located at the latter. Closer to the bridge is Kirby Cove, which is Marin County's geographic counterpart to Baker's Beach in San Francisco, affording a good view of the Golden Gate Bridge from the other side of the bay. Kirby Cove is a local secret. Getting here involves a locked gate and a hike down a dirt path, so you're better off pressing on to Stinson Beach.

Muir Beach

Not only did he have a stand of redwoods named for him but pioneer environmentalist John Muir rated a beach that bears his name. Signs along Route 1 point to it. A field of rocks and pebbles and a shallow lagoon, bridged with boards and stepping stones, must be crossed to reach Muir Beach from the parking lot. The day we made the trip, sand was blowing in a ghostly stream across the desertlike beach. The setting, with a creek and woods surrounding the beach, was beautiful, but the elements were too harsh to justify spending much time here. Still, it doubtless has its serene days.

Red Rock Beach

Nude sun-worshipers, this one's for you. About a mile and a half south of Stinson Beach there's a dirt parking lot by the side of the road. Fairly sizable though it is, we found it full, with the overflow lining both shoulders of the road. There were no signs around, and the beach was not even visible from the top of the cliff. What gives? We saw a trail leading down, so we took it. Imagine our surprise to round a corner at the bottom and find ourselves face to face with a beach full of naked bodies, frolicking like an R-rated version of a sixties beach flick: women flinging Frisbees, their mammaries bouncing like basketballs, and bearded men with more covering on their faces than on their entire bodies.

Suddenly, we felt self-conscious in our long pants and windbreakers, like the only guests at a Halloween party who show up in street clothes. Unwilling to disrobe merely to go with the flow, we stood a safe distance away like a pair of anxious Adams on the edge of the Garden of Eden. The packed crowd was evidently having fun in their liberated state of undress. There were more people here than at the large public beaches we'd just left. After shuffling around, flummoxed, for a few minutes, we huffed and puffed our way back to the top, thinking, "Maybe next time...."

Stinson Beach

When San Franciscans want to go to the beach, they drive to Stinson Beach. This nearly mile-long strand is part of the National Park Service's vast holdings in San Francisco and Marin counties. Unlike the state beaches, which charge $3 or $4, Stinson is absolutely free.

The crowds turn out when the sun is shining and the air is calm.

Stinson is nestled in a storybook setting about 15 snaking miles beyond the Golden Gate Bridge. To get here, follow Route 1, which leaves the freeway (Highway 101) near Mill Valley. Brace yourself for quite a ride. The road follows the base of Mount Tamalpais, passing west of Muir Woods. The horseshoe curves may make you queasy. You are likely, on any given turn, to meet a snorting Greyhound Americruiser or house-sized RV with a pair of wheels in your lane, so drive carefully.

It's all worth it for the vistas along the cliff edges, from which you can see more ocean than anywhere outside of an airplane window. A long descent brings you into the small town of Stinson Beach, which has one of everything for day-trippers and passers-through: a grocery store, gas station, antique shop, bookstore, surf shop, restaurant, even a small motel. We would say that weekends bring the crowds, except we saw more people bronzing themselves on a Tuesday than a Sunday. The sun was out both days; the difference was the wind, which was relentless on the weekend, forcing beachcombers to seek sanctuary in a picnic area behind a stand of trees. A few days later, it looked like a totally different place. Stinson was packed with a young, college-age crowd enjoying the warmth and even kicking around in the water a little (although no one dared go out to where the waves were crashing with a back-breaking boom). The five enormous lots appear capable of taking on all comers. With golden mountains rising behind it, pure Marin County air to breathe and a wide, white sand beach to play on, Stinson Beach is well worth the curves Route 1 throws in your path to get here.

Point Reyes

The San Andreas fault zone runs vertically through the western part of Marin County. This might explain why people on one side think people on the other side are a bit cracked. We were told by the first person we spoke to that West Marin was different from East Marin, geologically and sociologically. The geologic differences we could see for ourselves. The Point Reyes Peninsula is a

74,000-acre wilderness literally cut off from the mainland by the San Andreas fault.

As for the sociological part, well, what is one to make of this, the headlining news story in the local weekly: "Community Rallies to Save Hurt Horse." Oh, you think, a quiet country town is deeply concerned about a fallen plow mare. How nice. But then you read a little further. The horse was a purebred jumper. When something spooked her in an open field, she sustained the kind of leg injury that usually signals the end of the line and a trip to the glue factory. However, an "animal communicator" was called in from nearby Inverness, and through "conversations" with the fallen horse, the expert concluded that she had a "very positive attitude about her recovery and was determined to walk again." This gave the owner the courage to struggle on. Another expert was brought in to administer acupuncture and herbal salves. As if in a cameo role in a Shakespeare play, another healer strode forth from the wings to administer massage, then took his leave. Hey, why not a witch doctor from Haiti and a handful of leeches?

It's a funny place, California. Just when we thought we'd seen it all, West Marin County and the Point Reyes Peninsula threw us a curve ball.

Point Reyes is a hook-shaped peninsula that is, in essence, a geologic island. Its rock formations do not match those of the mainland it rubs against. Because of the peninsula's startling uniqueness, Congress designated it the West Coast's only National Seashore in 1962, one of seven in the country to be permanently preserved.

The drive from Stinson Beach north to Point Reyes is a stunning one. First you pass Bolinas, an arty little community whose bluffs are eroding into the Pacific, carrying vacation homes even closer to the beach than their owners had in mind. Suddenly, you're in horse and cattle country. The only signs of human life are the tiny rural touchstones of Dogtown (pop. 30), Olema (pop. 55), Inverness (pop. 600) and Point Reyes Station (pop. 200). Olema and Point Reyes Station are good junctions from which to venture into Point Reyes National Seashore. Before leaping into the fray, though, you should visit the Bear Valley Visitors Center in Olema, which can supply you with maps, literature and advice.

Besides being separated from the mainland by the fault, which runs along a narrow valley extending from Bolinas Lagoon to Tomales Bay, Point Reyes is further dislocated by its climate, flora and fauna, means of livelihood and singular history. Continental drift continues to physically isolate the peninsula, which is moving northwest at a rate of three inches a year. Evidence of the fault can be seen in the streams and estuaries cutting through the landscape as the underground foundations creak and grind against each other. Earthquakes and tremors are a way of life around here; as they say, it comes with the territory. In 1906, a devastating earthquake left San Francisco in ruins. Though it's remembered mainly for the damage it did to San Francisco, the quake was actually centered in the Olema Valley, 60 miles north of the city. Point Reyes moved 16.4 feet to the northwest that year.

Inverness Ridge is another of the peninsula's geologic walls. East of the ridge, the weather is the same as that in the valley. West of the ridge, however, the land is frequently blanketed in thick, blinding fog, pelted with rains of biblical intensity and blasted by stiff, chilling winds that blow as high as 100 mph out by the lighthouse, at land's end. It's as if nature were trying to drive people away, screaming, "You've got all that to play with, but this, this is mine!"

Driving along the peninsula on a clear day is a riveting experience, with a fascinating wrinkle in the land materializing around every turn. Forests give way to meadows that yield to dunes and marshlands. Hawks soar above the hills and fields, looking for a rustling in the grass that will signal the presence of a fat mouse. Herons stand like lamps in the marshes. Deer bound nervously out of the shadows. Dairy cows and beef cattle graze stiffly in the buffeting winds. The only signs of human life are the dairy farms, which were allowed to remain after Point Reyes was declared a National Seashore. Basically, the wildest west of all is a mere 60 miles from San Francisco. This is not a theme park. It is the real thing.

The beaches of Point Reyes more than match the majestic surroundings. The peninsula contains 90 miles of coastline. Though much of it is accessible on foot only, the beaches that are reachable by car will be sufficient exposure for most people. If it's a King Lear–type surf you desire, take Sir Francis Drake Boulevard to *Point Reyes Beach*. This 11-mile beach faces west, jutting into the teeth of strong ocean currents. The water here churns like a hellish demon's cauldron, angrily smacking disjointed sets of waves onto the beach. The wind makes the experience even more Shakespearean, blowing in your face like a tempest, carrying sand and salt spray. Caution is advised even if you've only come to hike. To swim on Point Reyes Beach, needless to say, is to shuffle off this mortal coil posthaste.

The violent wrath of the surf reaches its seething pinnacle at Point Reyes Light, on the westernmost tip of the peninsula. In the teeming waters just beyond the rocks lie the carcasses of countless ships that have been wrecked in the smothering fog. The lighthouse was built halfway down the 600-foot cliff in 1870. At this lower level, it was determined, the light could be seen more easily. Visiting the lighthouse means descending 300 steps. You must also wear winter clothing. Wind, fog and sea spray are constant companions on the point. It is said to be the second foggiest spot in America (the first being Cape Disappointment in Washington state). It is arguably the most desolate place on any of our coasts— West, East or Gulf. So relentless is the grayness here, and so overwhelming the isolation, that more than one lighthouse keeper has flipped his lid. On clear days, though, sea lions can be seen from a nearby overlook, and in the winter, the lighthouse is a popular spot for observing migrating California gray whales. The lighthouse is open for tours from ten to five daily, except Tuesday and Wednesday, when it is closed to the public.

For those who desire something a little less dramatic, the beaches along Drakes Bay, cradled in the protected inner side of the peninsula's hook, are just around the corner. We found the sea calmer at *Drakes Beach*, relatively speaking, though it still pounded the shore in huge, hollow tubes. The offshore wind was so stiff that even the shorebirds outside the snack bar were facing into it at an angle. We were advised to move to the right side of the beach, where the white cliffs provide protection from the wind and cold. On good days, Drakes Beach is the most popular swimming and sunbathing area on Point Reyes.

The white cliffs of Drakes Beach are at the heart of an interesting historical controversy. In 1579, Francis Drake (not yet knighted by the queen) was looking for a place to land his *Golden Hind* to

make repairs before setting off to England w
Spanish gold. He found a spot that looked
cliffs reminding him of Mother England. He r
Albion and stayed for a month. All of this is
chaplain's logbook. What isn't certain is the prec
Most scholars believe it was Drakes Beach. Ma
this have been placed here.

The last accessible beach on Point Reyes is *Limantour Beach.* Up
until now, it's been the peninsula's best-kept secret. To get here,
drive all the way back through Inverness and then turn south onto
Limantour Road. In the fifties, Limantour Beach was earmarked
for subdivision. A Carmel-type commercial development was on
the drawing board until distressed conservationists intervened. The
most idyllic beach on the peninsula, Limantour is not bordered by
mountains or bluffs. It is backed by large, smooth dunes and delicate lagoons, making it a perfect location for bird-watchers, sunbathers and swimmers. Again, shielded by the peninsula's hook,
the waters are calmer, and over 350 bird species have been sighted
in the nearby estuary.

Accommodations

San Franciscans come to Point Reyes (and indeed, all of Northern
California) in search of unique getaways from their high-powered
professions. One of the most popular ways to escape the pressures
at home is to spend the night in someone else's. Bed-and-breakfast
inns have become a way of life in Northern California. The Point
Reyes Peninsula has not been left out in the cold. The uniqueness
of the land practically demands unusual places to stay.

Thirty-Nine Cypress in Point Reyes Station is a perfect example
of how far the bed-and-breakfast concept can be taken. This three-
room inn is located just north of the "downtown area" (two stores,
two galleries, two bars, one restaurant and a post office). Overlooking dairy pastures, marshlands and the fringes of Inverness
Ridge, Thirty-Nine Cypress is not a typical renovated turn-of-the-
century manse. It's the actual single-story redwood home of an
energetic West Marin woman who raised her children here. The

...flects the intelligence of the family. Filled with an eclectic ...y of books, cassettes, photographs and artwork, it is more like a home away from home than an inn. A breakfast of fresh fruit, bread and eggs is provided, as is the company of Flora, a truly extraordinary Australian cattle dog who thinks she's a cat. By the way, the owner has worked in the park for years and knows Point Reyes as well as the rangers do.

In addition to Thirty-Nine Cypress, five other B&Bs belong to the Inns of Point Reyes association. For a catalog, write Inns of Point Reyes, P.O. Box 145, Inverness, CA 94937; or call (415) 663-1420. A poster-brochure of some 90 inns across Northern California can be obtained by sending $1 to Bed and Breakfast Innkeepers of Northern California, 2030 Union Street, Suite 310, San Francisco, CA 94123.

Restaurants

Because the median income of Inverness is so high (we were told $50,000) and because many of the townsfolk are meal-buying retirees, the restaurant choices are large over there, spanning the spectrum from country French to Cal-nouvelle. *Barnaby's* is the seafood house of choice. They alter their menu daily according to local availability but always have plenty of mussels and oysters on hand. Both are harvested right out of the Tomales Bay. A bowl of mussels steamed in wine and flavored with garlic goes for $5.95. Barnaby's also employs an applewood-smoking process on chicken and seafood. A sampler platter of their smoked specialties costs $10.95 and serves two.

Vladimir's Czechoslovakian Restaurant, also in Inverness, is interesting because of the man who runs it. A self-proclaimed "mechanical genius" and "extremely hard worker," Vladimir is a Czech expatriate who skied his way to freedom after the Communist coup in 1948. He landed in Inverness in 1960, where he opened his Czech restaurant. Every entrée has Vladimir's name in front of it (e.g., Vladimir's Garlic Lamb Shank, Vladimir's Beef Tongue). Prices are set at $8 for lunch and $12.75 for dinner. No cards.

The most talked-about restaurant in the area is the *Station House* in Point Reyes Station. Almost singlehandedly, it has been credited with uplifting the local cuisine, so much so that *Gourmet* sent one of its gourmands out to investigate. (They raved about it.) Try the Station House if you're in the mood for creative cuisine and don't mind paying big-city prices in a two-horse town. Breakfast and lunch are easier to swallow, monetarily speaking, and the food is just as well prepared.

Nightlife

When the sun is hanging low in the sky, Point Reyes Station resembles the backdrop for a Wyatt Earp movie. Striding diagonally across the street from the post office, one is tempted to draw an imaginary six-gun and fire off a couple of rounds. Don't do it. Instead, go to the *Western Saloon*, one of two bars in town (the other is the slightly more forbidding *Two-Ball Inn*). The Western has a long wooden bar with a rail and a gunmetal cash register, but this is as far as the cowboy motif is carried. Well, we were told that every now and then someone gets drunk and rides a horse into the Western.

There are pool tables and pinball games in the back and a good jukebox up front. Lynyrd Skynyrd and the Beach Boys vie with country and western for most played. A bumper sticker above the cash register reminds you that "Nobody's Ugly After 2 a.m.," and foreign currency is pinned to the wall. They wouldn't add our proffered McDonald's Gift Certificate to the collection of grubstake, but the Western is otherwise a hospitable place.

FOR FURTHER INFORMATION

Point Reyes National Seashore
Bear Valley Road
Point Reyes, CA 94956
(415) 663-1092

Sonoma County:
Bodega Bay
Jenner
Plantation
Sea Ranch

You've heard of ghost towns. Well, Sonoma is a ghost county. The image that will forever remain with us from our passage through Sonoma County is that of a big black cow standing in the middle of the curving Coast Highway. They call it "Dramamine Drive" in these parts, and it's a fair enough nickname. We were comin' 'round the mountain when suddenly we came to a halt. A black cow was standing in our lane, facing us head-on like a Bergman-esque apparition of death. Pea-soup fog was draped around the beast's neck like a shawl, rendering it all but invisible. We stopped our uninsured, rented car inches from its steaming nostrils. The beast appraised the situation carefully, then slowly lumbered into the other lane to let us pass. Had an RV come rumbling around the bend from either direction at that moment, Sonoma County would be one heifer poorer; and the world, one travel book lighter.

More wine country than beach country, Sonoma is blessed with a sunny, rich-soiled interior where grapes grow freely. Most folks come to Sonoma County to visit the valley wineries, merrily tasting their way from one vineyard to another. If you've been gargling too much wine, don't attempt to drive the Sonoma coastline. It is a land of mist and rocks and jagged shore. The highway, once it rejoins the coast past Point Reyes at Bodega Bay, curves up and down and all around the sloping headlands. The lures of this area are its isolation; the coastal plants, trees and wildlife that flourish here; and the fishing opportunities out of Bodega Bay. People who vacation here generally drive pickup trucks and carry shotguns and fishing poles. People who live and work here drive monstrous rigs stacked high with redwood carcasses. One of the most exciting experiences on earth is to play bumper tag with an overloaded logging truck bearing down on you.

Sonoma County's isolation will no doubt remain unaffected for a long time to come, due to the prohibitive difficulty of staking a claim in this remote wilderness. Travelers who are sick of crowds, development and predictable vacations might find the Sonoma coast appealing. But the towns along Route 1—Bodega Bay, Jenner, Plantation—are mere hamlets, with fewer than 500 people each. Restaurants are few and far between, and most are either oyster stands or snack bars attached to country stores. For accommodations, people stay in campers, cabins, tents and boats.

For all the ruggedness of its coast, beaches do exist in Sonoma County. The turnouts along the 13-mile stretch from Bodega Bay to Jenner are collectively known as the *Sonoma Coast State Beaches*. From just north of the unpretentious harbor town of Bodega Bay, where Salmon Creek empties into the Pacific, to the mouth of the Russian River in Jenner, a surprising number of scenic beaches are at your disposal. The emphasis is on "scenic," because you can't swim in these cold, rough and rocky waters. In Sonoma County, you go fishing. It's that simple. Oh, you can also hike, tide-pool and beachcomb for shells and driftwood, but after wandering a few Sonoma beaches, you'll find yourself more inclined to pull the car over and enjoy them from a safe distance. They are beautiful, but they are not habit-forming.

The 13 different Sonoma Coast State Beaches are reachable by steep trails but are separated from each other by impassable rocks. One of the best is *Salmon Creek Beach*, where there's a wide delta at the creek's mouth. *Wright Beach* has some campsites and *Shell Beach* has tide-pools. *Goat Rock Beach* is another large, sandy delta at the mouth of the Russian River. The smelt and steelhead trout fishing is excellent at all of the river mouths.

Northern Sonoma County is a slightly different kettle of fish. The highway begins to rise, curve and then nose-dive unexpectedly. The most interesting sight between Jenner and the Mendocino County line is a Russian fort. Not to worry, Joint Chiefs: Fort Ross has been abandoned since 1841. It was built in 1812 by 40 Indians and 95 Russian fur trappers and has been preserved exactly as it looked when it was abandoned. A small beach, frequented by shell and abalone collectors, sits just beyond the front gate of the fort.

The last 10 miles of coastline in Sonoma County belongs lock, stock and barrel to a development known as *Sea Ranch*. It is a planned community for rich recluses who enjoy a semisolitary country-club existence out of sight of the rest of suffering humanity. After a lengthy and unpleasant battle with the California Coastal Commission, Sea Ranch consented to allow seven coast-access footpaths through their 10-mile oceanfront property. Each is about a quarter mile long and leads to a small cove beach. We walked to the ends of three of them before throwing in the beach towel. Curiously, Sea Ranch has won several awards for architecture and planning. The houses—wooden-shingled and built low to the ground, blending in with the pines and fir trees—all look drearily similar in the cold light of day. The place appears as devoid of life as the surface of the moon. The entire complex, from the golf course on down, is the sort of place you could imagine Big Brother breaking par.

FOR FURTHER INFORMATION

Bodega Bay Area Chamber of Commerce
555 Highway 1
P.O. Box 146
Bodega Bay, CA 94923
(707) 875-3422

Sonoma Valley Chamber of Commerce
453 First Street East
Sonoma, CA 95476
(707) 996-1033

Gualala
Anchor Bay
Point Arena
Manchester
Elk
Albion
Little River

The southern Mendocino County coast is, like that of Sonoma County, rugged and sparsely inhabited. Every 10 miles or so you'll come upon a village with a population of 400 or 500. Virtually all of them are situated on river mouths, with beaches on their banks or tucked into coves. These unincorporated settlements typically have a gas station, post office, small grocery mart, a historic schoolhouse or church and a rambling old hotel or restored inn named after the community (e.g, the *Gualala Hotel*, the *Albion River Inn*, the *Elk Cove Inn* and the *Little River Inn*—the latter boasting a nine-hole golf course).

These towns all saw their better days back when timber was king and outgoing shipments of logs kept the harbors active. Nowadays, the rolling land is patrolled by grazing dairy cattle, and the waterfront is wandered by fishers looking to land trout or salmon. Along Route 1, the elevation rises, and beaches are visible below, though there's rarely access to them. The one beach of note in southern Mendocino County is in the town of Manchester.

Manchester State Beach is reachable from dirt parking lots (no charge) a few well-marked miles west of the highway. Healthy looking dunes, covered with thick grass, serve as the portals to this sizable beach. The sand is dusty and dirty brown in color, but the most notable thing about Manchester State Beach is that it looks like a graveyard for driftwood. The skeletons of dead trees that washed out to sea and then onto the beach line the desertlike expanses of Manchester like fallen soldiers. People use the gargantuan logs as windbreaks. A quarter mile back from the beach is a 48-site campground. Several miles south of Manchester State Beach, the land juts out into the ocean at Point

Arena, whose lighthouse beacon is one of the most powerful on the West Coast.

FOR FURTHER INFORMATION

Fort Bragg-Mendocino Coast Chamber of Commerce
332 N. Main Street
P.O. Box 1141
Fort Bragg, CA 95437
(707) 964-3153

Mendocino

Unless you know what you're looking for, you stand a very good chance of missing Mendocino. Even though it's a famous village, both for its redwood-milling past and artist-colony present, Mendocino is so unobtrusively situated on California's rural north coast that it is more skirted than passed through by Route 1. When it's engulfed in fog, a not infrequent occurrence, Mendocino disappears entirely.

To get a proper handle on Mendocino, it helps to think of it as an impressionistic painting. Perspective is the key. Observed at close range, the town appears to be nothing more than a pleasant rural outpost of scattered wood-frame houses and bed-and-breakfast inns. With a degree of familiarity, though, Mendocino is revealed to be a town with a vision. To understand and share that vision means more than just browsing gift-shop windows on a hurried weekend jaunt from San Francisco. You have to understand the people who live here.

Mendocino dates back to the mid-1800s, when the lumber industry arrived in the area. California's first redwood mill was built on the banks of the Big River, a slow-moving stream that empties into the ocean beneath the green headlands on which the town was built. The cut timber was milled and hauled away by schooners. Mendocino enjoyed nearly a century of prosperity as a lumber town, followed by decades of decline in the wake of the sawmills' closing. Then, in the 1950s, it was discovered by artists.

Artists and artisans were drawn from the burgeoning cities, especially San Francisco. Rising rents, the sudden growth of cities in all directions and the stodgy conformity of the Eisenhower era drove more sensitive souls into the countryside to seek sanctuary. Mendocino became a magnet for societal dropouts. The old, abandoned wood houses came cheaply, the rugged northern coast was quiet and rarely visited, and the natural beauty of Mendocino provided a constant source of inspiration to those who drag paintbrushes across canvas.

The founding of the Mendocino Arts Council in 1959 made it official. Art is such a prevalent force in the life of Mendocino that this unincorporated town of 1,900 lists 1,000 contributing members on its arts-council roster. Its spaces include ceramics, textiles, painting and sculpture studios, three exhibition halls, a theater complex and a magazine production studio. The high points in Mendocino's calendar year are the summer arts and crafts fair and the performing arts festival, although there's always something going on in Mendocino.

Art is a rallying point for the loose-knit townsfolk, who otherwise go about their business quietly, tending organic gardens, soaking in hot tubs and leading a holistic, back-to-nature existence in a place that looks like a setting for a Grape-Nuts commercial. Don't expect to see the latest fashions parading down the sidewalks of Mendocino. There's just not that kind of money up here, and frankly, they don't give a damn. Jeans, flannel shirts and beards are the order of the day. Everyone here looks like a member of the Grateful Dead. Even the women.

There are, for lack of a better word, a lot of hippies burrowed back in the cool green forests and spiny ridge tops behind Mendocino. Their numbers actually include members of the Grateful Dead, we're told. In the sixties, Mendocino was known as a refuge for country-loving hippies who found the grimy streets of Haight-Ashbury too congested for their liking. A lot of marijuana was harvested and smoked in Mendocino and neighboring Humboldt County then and (though some deny it) now. A group called the Sir Douglas Quintet had a Top Forty hit in 1969 with a song called "Mendocino." This shard of lyrics captures the tenor of the times: "Mendocino, Mendocino, where life's such a groove you'll blow your mind in the morning."

Amazingly, things haven't changed much since Sir Doug wrote his soulful, stoned anthem. While the rest of the world is rapidly being cast into a hollow Yuptopian fantasy of the Good Life, Mendocino remains a place where a life of reflection can be lived on modest means. Artists can scrape by without selling out, musicians and film people can seclude themselves in near anonymity, and lesser known cultural aspirants can, at the very least, manage to keep a roof over their head. For instance, we saw a run-down pickup truck by the side of the road whose owner advertised his wares in juvenile hand lettering on the side panels: "Firewood and Donkey Dung."

Mendocino doesn't come to you; you have to go to it. You have to want to be here to make it worth the drive over winding roads, trailing lumber trucks and large recreational vehicles driven by slow-moving tourists unused to the curves. And then there's the weather. Mendocino is frequently shrouded in fog and, in winter, heavy rain. Although virtually no rainfall is recorded in the summer months, fog often blankets the town in the morning and evening. Mendocino coast fogs don't creep in on little cat feet, either; they roll in on heavy cattle hooves.

The Mendocino area is best known as a romantic hideaway. The cool gray days of summer provide a good excuse to stay inside a cozy room and light a redwood fire (provided, of course, there's a fireplace). The readers of the *San Francisco Chronicle* voted Mendocino the number-one spot for a romantic holiday on the North American continent. The phrase is overused, but Mendocino truly is a place to "get away from it all." The distractions are few, and garden-variety tourists push on to Fort Bragg, eight miles north, leaving Mendocino in a state of civilized semisolitude. The town makes a convenient base for exploring the wineries of Mendocino and Sonoma County during the day. But the best thing about Mendocino is that you don't have to do anything at all.

Sports enthusiasts find plenty to do here, including hiking, canoeing, fishing and diving for abalone. Still, the exploration of miles of beach and park lands in and around Mendocino shouldn't be confined to those with fishing poles. Yes, there are beaches up here—especially north of Mendocino, where they run for mile after unbroken mile. Don't get any ideas, though; these are not swimming beaches. The water is prohibitively cold to all but those with a thick-gauge wet suit. Even sunbathers will find themselves thwarted by the changeable weather—foggy one minute, clear the next. Most likely, you and your companion will build a beach bonfire and snuggle close to it after a hard day of getting to know one another better, if you catch our drift.

One needn't stay at a lodge or inn to enjoy Mendocino. There are camping facilities at *Van Damme State Park* (74 sites) and *Russian Gulch State Park* (30 sites). Van Damme spreads inland from its small, sandy beach at the mouth of the Little River, encompassing a sword-fern canyon and a pygmy forest of stunted conifers. Russian Gulch offers serene redwood groves and an open beach where Russian Gulch Creek runs into the ocean. One of the main attractions is the Devil's Punch Bowl, a 100-foot-long and 60-foot-deep blowhole. The force of incoming waves passing through it causes geysers and noisy explosions. Campsites are situated along the creek, inside a canyon forested with second-growth redwoods as well as firs, hemlocks, oaks and laurels. Both Van Damme and Russian Gulch state parks are crisscrossed by miles of hiking trails. As demand is far greater than supply in this splendid neck of the woods, camping reservations are necessary.

Mendocino Headlands State Park runs from the banks of the Big River north, along headlands and terraces. Trails skirt the bluffs, and a sand beach at the river's mouth can be reached via North Big River Road. An outfit called Catch a Canoe will let you do just that. Canoeists can plan their trip to coincide with the tides, wafting upstream with the incoming waters and gently drifting downstream as the tide goes out.

Accommodations

Mendocino is nicely set up with accommodations. There are many bed and breakfast inns in the area, from a few spare rooms in a renovated Victorian to much larger lodges that nonetheless bend over backward to retain that inn feeling. Privacy and intimacy are two reasons people come to Mendocino, and the innkeepers know this. Couples come prepared to spend $100 and $200 a night to light each other's fire. Families and tourists looking for standard-brand motel rooms in the $40 to $60 range press on to Fort Bragg, where there are plenty of them.

The *Stanford Inn Big River Lodge* is a prime spot to lay over in Mendocino. Set high on a hillside overlooking the ocean, it's a perfect compromise between a first-class motel and a bed-and-breakfast inn. The rooms are spacious, with unfinished knotty-pine walls, four-poster beds and wood-burning fireplaces. A complimentary decanter of burgundy from a nearby winery is provided, as well as a couple of Easter egg–size confections from the local *chocolatier*. Redwood logs are stacked by the hearth, accompanied by an eight-step set of instructions on how to build a fire. In the morning, you can trip down to the lobby for a breakfast of hot pastry, juice and coffee, loading up a silver tray and carrying it back to your room. The grounds of the Stanford Inn ramble down the hill to the highway and include a fenced-in enclosure for the owners' horses and llamas. A restaurant is being added, which will serve food grown in an organic garden on the premises.

The restored *Mendocino Hotel*, in the heart of the village, is another fine choice. Your options here range from suites to single rooms with private and shared baths. The more expensive rooms have fireplaces, balconies and/or bay views.

Restaurants

Café Beaujolais is a small restaurant with a big reputation. Dinner is served in season; breakfast and lunch year-round. A highlight of the breakfast menu is the homemade waffle, a tangy, plate-filling treat made from a combination of cornbread, buttermilk and oatmeal. All the beef, pork and poultry served here is organically raised on nearby ranches and is guaranteed chemical-free.

Another tiny temple of California cuisine is the *Little River Restaurant*. It's located in back of the Little River post office, a few miles south of Mendocino. Everything is prepared fresh to order from homemade or homegrown ingredients. There is only seating for 16, so make reservations.

Finally, if you're up for a drive, the *Floodgate Café* on Route 128 east (near the town of Philo) is a wonderful roadside café with a changeable blackboard menu of omelets, salads, pasta dishes and other light, wholesome concoctions.

Nightlife

In the informed opinion of a local innkeeper, the *Heritage House* makes the best drinks on the coast. Along with it, they have one of the best views on the coast. The *MacCallum House*, a century-old mansion that does double duty as an elegant restaurant and a bed-and-breakfast inn, also has a small but sociable bar in a parlor to the left of the main hall as you enter. Called the *Gray Gull Bar*, they post a short menu of burgers and such if you've got hunger pangs but don't want to lay down the long green across the hall or elsewhere in Mendocino.

The hippies and hill dwellers come out of the woodwork to boogie at the *Caspar Inn*, between Mendocino and Fort Bragg. It is the Woodstock-generation equivalent of an army battalion reuniting after the war, except it's enacted on a nightly basis. The group playing when we were in town was the Vicious Hippies, whose specialty is "full-tilt boogie." The crowd was a sociological case study. If the words "roach clip" bring a smile to your face, then check out the Caspar Inn for old time's sake.

The *Seagull Cellar Bar* also has live music. This so-called cellar bar is actually on the second floor of the Seagull Restaurant. Here, we found Mendocino at its mellowest. The band shuffled through some old-time rock and roll at an energy level that wouldn't power a night-light. The only person dancing was handicapped. When the singer asked the crowd if they were having a good time, you could have heard a pin drop. The funny thing is, they were having a good time, in their own mellow way, grooving inwardly and apparently in no hurry to do anything but slow down and veg out.

Fort Bragg-Mendocino Coast Chamber of Commerce
332 N. Main Street
P.O. Box 1141
Fort Bragg, CA 95437
(707) 964-3153

Caspar

Just north of Mendocino, in a little town called Caspar, is *Jug Handle State Reserve*. This park preserves and interprets the phenomenon of marine-cut terraces (or "ecological staircases"). There's no charge for parking and hiking the trails—either the short Headlands Loop, which wanders through fields of grass to sheer bluffs at the edge of the sea, or the Ecological Staircase Trail, a five-mile endurance test that takes in all five steps on this staircase of the millennia.

Fort Bragg

Fort Bragg lies in the middle of the magnificent Mendocino coast like a cow pie on the Yellow Brick Road. It is, with its population of 7,500, a large town for these parts—the largest between San Francisco and Eureka. The focal point as you drive through on Route 1 is the steam-belching Georgia Pacific timber mill, whose stacks generate more fog than Mother Nature does naturally. But your eyes will also be stung by the sight of several miles of liquor stores, motels and burger stands. Fort Bragg is not any worse than the average American city, where these corridors of unzoned straight-line growth are commonplace. It's just that after 150 miles of unspoiled Mendocino-Sonoma coastline, it's a rude jolt to spin into a town that looks like the worst parts of Fayetteville, North Carolina.

We mention Fayetteville because it is the home of America's real

Fort Bragg—the largest Army base in America, and a rotten place to live, work, play in or drive through. Fort Bragg, California, does have that much in common with its East Coast namesake. If you live along the Mendocino coast or farther back in the mountains and valleys, Fort Bragg is the nearest city in which to load up on supplies. But it is no place to take a vacation. It is referred to as "historic" Fort Bragg, though its insignificant history can be summarized in two sentences: A fort was established here in 1857 to keep the Indians in check and was closed down seven years later. Timbering and railroads arrived in 1885 and have been the leading industries ever since.

You can undertake a 28-stop walking tour of the alleged historic district—that is, if you don't mind running the risk of getting flattened by all the pickup truck cowboys whizzing through town. Fort Bragg should be acknowledged for what it really is: the pickup truck capital of the world. The town is overrun with them, and they don't like to slow down for pedestrians.

The only genuine tourist attraction here is the Skunk. It is an authentic re-creation of the logging railroad that ran from Fort Bragg to the inland town of Willits, a distance of 40 miles. The train consists of observation cars hauled by a diesel logging locomotive. It makes several daily one-way and round trips to Willits and Northspur (the halfway point on the line). Our advice is to take the three-hour round-trip to Northspur and forget about Willits. If possible, Willits is even worse-looking than Fort Bragg, and there's nothing to do there. The Fort Bragg–Northspur round-trip costs $16 for adults, $8 for children.

Except for the Skunk, Fort Bragg is little more than a place to fill up on gas and food on your way to points north or south. It's not impossible to imagine Fort Bragg being upgraded into a viable destination. At present, however, it's a town in dire need of a conceptual overhaul.

Accommodations

There are a fair number of nice and new motels in Fort Bragg (along with some not-so-nice and not-so-new ones). The *Best West-*

ern Vista Manor, up at the north end of town, has a swimming pool, clean rooms and a bit of distance from the downtown clamor. The *Quality Inn Seabird*, with 65 units, is another reliable chain motel.

Fort Bragg has its own little beach, where people crouch and scavenge for wave-polished pebbles and glass bits. The nine-room *Glass Beach Bed and Breakfast Inn* sits above it on Main Street. Finally, the *Old Coast Hotel* is a restored street-corner hotel with shared baths that's a good choice for folks seeking a little historic 1800s flavor in Fort Bragg.

Restaurants

The café at the *Old Coast Hotel* serves well-prepared meals with a Cajun-Creole flavor. The *Wharf Restaurant*, on the water, is the place to go for seafood. And for a funky, unpretentious but solid spread of Mexican food, the *El Mexicano* is a local favorite.

Nightlife

You're on your own here. In lieu of nightlife, we watched a documentary film on the life of Jack Kerouac (whose novel *On the Road* indirectly inspired us to ditch our jobs for a life of migratory beachcombing). The film was shown at the local senior citizen's center, where we did not learn much about Fort Bragg's nightlife. To be perfectly honest, by this point in the trip we were beginning to feel like senior citizens ourselves. So on a drizzly Friday night we were content to sit back in stuffed chairs, munching home-made cookies, sipping apple cider and enjoying the film.

For those so inclined, there is no lack of cocktail lounges and taverns haunted by mountain men who lumber down for a drink or ten. We noticed that one of these, a windowless place called the *Tip-Top Lounge*, sat directly across the street from a gun shop. Like we said, you're on your own.

FOR FURTHER INFORMATION

Fort Bragg–Mendocino Coast Chamber of Commerce
332 North Main Street
P.O. Box 1141
Fort Bragg, CA 95437
(707) 964-3153

MacKerricher State Park

North of Fort Bragg, the Mendocino coast opens up for six long miles of sandy beach and dunes at MacKerricher State Park. People ride horses along a shoreline equestrian trail that parallels Georgia-Pacific's private log-hauling road. It's always too cold to swim here, as Mendocino coast waters top off at 54 degrees on a *warm* day, but you can camp, surf-cast for rockfish and ling cod, or throw a line in stocked Lake Cleone. MacKerricher has no RV hookups, but its 143 sites are popular with those who enjoy tent camping at the beach.

Westport
Rockport

A number of beach access points exist at creek mouths on the increasingly remote stretch of Route 1 north of Fort Bragg, before it moves inland above Rockport. Yes, the terrain becomes too much even for the shoreline highway, which makes a cowering northeasterly turn rather than brave the daunting coastline of Cape Mendocino.

Westport and Rockport are the last-chance outposts before Route 1 meets its inglorious end at Highway 101 in Leggett some miles inland. Both of these one-time mill towns have the humble look of New England fishing villages. The best beaches are near Westport. Take your pick of *Westport–Union Landing State Beach*, at the mouth of Dehaven Creek, and *Wages Creek Beach*, at the mouth of (you guessed it) Wages Creek, reachable from a private campground. The creeks and river mouths of northern Mendocino County are good places for netting smelt, surf-fishing and foraging among tide-pools for abalone.

This always-chilly, often-foggy stretch of California's coastline is really best-suited for serious sports enthusiasts. Sunbathing is a no-win undertaking, swimming is out of the question and surfing is only for the seriously deranged, although we're told it's been done.

Sinkyone Wilderness State Park

Sandwiched between the town of Rockport and the *King Range National Conservation Area* are 3,500 acres of state-protected deep wilderness. Occupying the northwest corner of Mendocino County, Sinkyone Wilderness State Park consists of a narrow strip of marine terraces along one of California's remotest stretches of coastline. The steep slopes and benches rise to heights of 1,800 feet and support a diverse variety of plants, from second-growth coast redwoods and California laurels to meadows, shrubs and grasslands. Gray whales can be sighted off the coast here in winter and spring, as can harbor seals and sea lions.

The original inhabitants of this pristine wilderness were Sinkyone Indians, who are thought to have migrated across the Bering Straits and down the West Coast, living off the fat of the land and sea. By the mid-1800s, white pioneers arrived, thinning out the Indians and the forests in short order. Today, the old ranches and lumber camps are abandoned, and the park has returned to its wilderness state. Except for a small visitors center at Needle Rock House, a former rancher's home, the Sinkyone Wilderness Area has little more than trails and a dirt road running through it. Precipitous cliffs rise out of the water along much of the coast. Black sand and coarse gravel beaches lie at the mouths of canyons, reachable from trails at *Whale Gulch*, *Jones Beach*, *Needle Rock* and *Flat*

Rock Creek. These spots yield a bonanza for surf fishers and abalone divers who know about them.

Cape Mendocino

They call it the Lost Coast, and indeed it is so far off the beaten track that few roads and settlements can be found on it. Even the indomitable blacktop of Route 1 turns away from Cape Mendocino, stranding the hardy road warrior who has to continue hugging the shore on an iffy unpaved track called the Usal Road (Route 431). If you are not driving a four-wheel jeep, the next 20 or so miles could mean some serious rattling of your front suspension. The route around the cape is called the Lost Coast Trail Corridor. It explores stunning countryside—grassy marine terraces with grazing sheep and the cool, forested uplands of the King Range—before meeting paved road at a hamlet called Honeydew.

Honeydew is the geographic center of Cape Mendocino. To the northwest, along Route 211, lies the village of Petrolia, after which the road makes a five-mile jog along the coastline before turning inland at Capetown. A short distance further lies Ferndale and the northern terminus of the loop, which rejoins Highway 101 south of Eureka. The scenery is spectacular along Cape Mendocino, which contains some of the last coastal wilderness in Northern California (and, indeed, in the continental United States). The only real beach of note is the resort at Shelter Cove, just inside the Humboldt County line. Shelter Cove is a privately owned tract inside the 54,000-acre *King Range National Conservation Area.* Located 20 miles east of Route 1 and reachable via a paved road out of Garberville, Shelter Cove is the "found" part of the Lost Coast, a protected harbor that's become a vacation and retirement community. A 3,400-foot paved airstrip serves notice that civilization has invaded the wilderness, an impression seconded by the presence of a motel, trailer park, bar, store and restaurant.

With thousands of surrounding acres owned by the government, the footprints of man are likely to be kept to a minimum. There are few roads and many miles of trails within these coastal moun-

tains of the King Range. The four park campgrounds are maintained in summer only. Up the coast, where Route 211 runs along
the coast between Petrolia and Capetown, there are several turnouts and paths to the beach. East of Petrolia, Lighthouse Road follows the Mattole River to a beach at its mouth.

FOR FURTHER INFORMATION

Bureau of Land Management
District Manager
King Range National Conservation Area
555 Leslie Street
Ukiah, CA 95482
(707) 462-3873

Ferndale

All travelers approaching Ferndale should come prepared to set
their time clocks back. Be advised, though: you don't lose an hour,
you lose a century. Back around 1852, the forces of economics,
geography and architecture met in this isolated corner of Humboldt
County to produce the charming Victorian town of Ferndale. Today, it is California's only completely preserved pioneer-era village. The entire town, in fact, is a state historical landmark.

Ferndale originally sprang to life from a transfusion of mixed
European blood: Portuguese, Italian and Scandinavian. The town
became the hub around which their lush farmland circled, a living
testament to its fertility. Dairy farming was the primary source of
income. The creameries became so productive that Ferndale was
nationally known as "Cream City." Although latter-day Ferndale
has succumbed to a modest degree of tourism, the surrounding
area carries on the dairying tradition. Nearby Loleta produces
award-winning cheese, while Fernbridge turns out blue-ribbon beef
jerky.

Because the coastal flatlands were used primarily for dairy farming, Ferndale remained cut off from civilization for years by the

wide greenbelt of surrounding pastureland. The monetary wealth that flowed from the cows' udders built the ornate town and country residences known as "Butterfat Palaces." Constructed in the 1880s, they are fully preserved today.

Ferndale is reached by crossing a 75-year-old bridge over the flood-prone Eel River and then driving another four miles through dairy country. Arriving in Ferndale is like entering another dimension. We fully expected Rod Serling to pop up from the back seat and say, "Two unsuspecting beach bums thought they were making a side trip to an isolated dairy town one early July morning. Instead, they plunged head first into the Twilight Zone." Every single structure in Ferndale looks as it did 100 years ago: cleaned, polished and freshly painted, right down to the elaborate carved woodwork on the eaves, above the doors and around bay windows.

The experience of timelessness is carried even further in Golden Gait Mercantile, a gift shop on Main Street disguised as an old "real goods" store. Antique pill boxes, hair pins, rock candy, lunch biscuits, preserves, post cards and other not so bare necessities of yesteryear are arranged on barrel-heads and peach baskets with original prices listed beside them on index cards. One hundred years recedes quickly, however, when you walk up to the cash register and pay for your "real goods" at today's prices. Still, it's a fun place to poke around.

Like Pacific Grove, the semipreserved Victorian town on the Monterey Peninsula, Ferndale is more than a back-road curio. It is a fully functioning, lived-in community. Because it is so much more isolated than Pacific Grove, though, Ferndale immerses you more completely in its history. But a casual stroll through town will affirm that the folks of Ferndale lead as normal a life as those in the next town down the road. There's a bank, a bar with sports on the TV, a town clock, a rare bookstore, a volunteer repertory theater, a church and an art gallery or two. In Ferndale, they just happen to live in an older, more civilized setting.

Ferndale even has a beach, sort of. It's five miles west of town at an invisible place called Centerville. To get there involves driving a narrow, curving road through old dairy land. Architecture is not the only thing that hasn't changed around here in 100 years; cow pies are very much the same, too. Some of the ancient farmhouses are still standing, although listing would be a better word. We came to a complete stop in front of an abandoned farmhouse, halted in our tracks by a flock of geese that chose that moment to waddle across the road. *Centerville County Beach* begins in a soft sand parking lot. It's isolated out here. Driftwood covers the beach, and the only footprints in the sand were our own.

Many folks visit Ferndale for the day, swinging down from Eureka or Redwood National Park for a quick hit of Victorian charm. Accommodations are limited to a few bed-and-breakfast inns. You can bet the mortgage on your condo, though, that the B&Bs of Ferndale are 100 percent guaranteed Victorian. By general consensus, the nicest one is the *Gingerbread Mansion Bed and Breakfast*. Built in 1859, it has eight rooms and is one of the finest examples of Victorian architecture in town.

FOR FURTHER INFORMATION

Ferndale Chamber of Commerce
P.O. Box 325
Ferndale, CA 95536
(707) 786-4477

Eureka

Eureka is a Greek word meaning "I have found it." It is the state motto of California—one that is fully deserved, we realized after hugging her shore for many months. However, if you were to take Highway 101 north into the city of Eureka without having seen anything else of the state, you might suspect that the word means "They have lost it." The very first thing that pops into view is a gaudy sign announcing, "Burl Slabs 50 Cents." Next follows two miles of ghastly human commerce, the "City of the Redwood Empire" having been all but cleared of trees. What remains standing is a jungle of billboards, guide wires and telephone poles, brand-new malls that already look run-down and motel room after motel room for under $20, although no one but a grizzly bear or a hard-luck trucker would spend the night in such places. We began to think the only fortunate souls in Eureka were those buried six feet under the sod at the Ocean View Cemetery.

The visual madness that greeted us upon entering Eureka from the south was all the more jarring after a calming drive through coastal redwoods and a visit to mannerly Ferndale. As it turns out, though, there's more to Eureka than initially meets the eye. If you round the bend on Broadway (the street name Highway 101 takes in Eureka), you will discover the other Eureka, the one that dates from the 1850s. For a quick orientation, stop off at the Visitors Center on Second Street, which is the best route to take through Eureka's Old Town district. Armed with a Eureka visitors map, you can leave the wheels behind and reenter the age of foot traffic.

Old Town is a diligently restored area, surprising in its size and vitality. One of the principal stops on the tour is the Carson Mansion, two blocks east of the Visitors Center on a hill overlooking the bay. It was the one-time home of William Carson, the lumber baron whose redwood empire opened up the North Coast. A part-Victorian, part-fairy-tale castle, the Carson Mansion was built during lulls in the timbering season by Carson's lumbermen and completed in 1885 after three years of labor. The array of gables, columns and ornamental woodwork is quite impressive, and the restoration as a whole is magnificent. The mansion must be enjoyed from afar, however, since it presently houses a private men's club.

Across the street stands the Pink Lady, another startling example of money's-no-object Victoriana. The gaudiness of this Pepto-Bismol pink structure may give you visual indigestion. Once a residence, it is now home to an accounting firm, a "hypno-therapist" and a massage therapist. Many other structures in and around Old Town claim some historical value. Taken as a whole, the area represents the period when Eureka was "King of the Pacific Northwoods." It got its start in the 1850s as a bare-knuckled brawling, boozing and brothel-crawling lumber town. Tucked away in rugged, isolated landscape, Eureka was forced to fend for itself. The town's primary asset was its location on Humboldt Bay, the second largest enclosed bay in California.

In many respects, Eureka is still the King of the Northwoods.

With a population of 25,000, it is the largest city between San Francisco and Seattle, a distance of a thousand miles. It is the commercial and financial hub of Humboldt and Del Norte counties. Despite the imperilment of the timber trade all over the Pacific northwest, logging has endured in Eureka. But even Eureka hasn't remained immune to the effects of overforesting, cheap lumber from Canada and the setting aside of a significant chunk of Humboldt County timberland as *Redwood National Park*. In recent years, the city has begun turning elsewhere to fill the economic void.

Lately, outsiders have begun moving to Eureka in growing numbers. Their reasons are varied, but most have grown sick and tired of where they came from and simply want to escape the rat race. Eureka, like Mendocino, is a suitably nondistracting place to hammer out an artistic vision. Art galleries, bookshops and cultural events thrive here, thanks, in part, to the enlightened presence of Humboldt State University in nearby Arcata.

"Our community is saved by distance," one recent arrival explained. "We're too far from San Francisco or any other large urban center to be affected or influenced by it. The art community here turns on itself for inspiration." This may be true. Some of the original art on display in the local galleries was good, though much of it was derivative and par for the course for any city. The artistic visions are mainly inspired by Eureka's isolated setting. Transplanted, university-trained artists arrive in redwood country and envision themselves blazing new trails in folk art and landscape painting. All in all, though, the art scene in Eureka is surprisingly healthy. Of course, the native lumberjacks and fishers don't give a hoot one way or the other.

Humboldt County, beyond the streets of Eureka, is an interesting study in and of itself. Occupying a large, ghostly chunk of Northern California, it is inhabited by a strange breed of outcasts. Old hippies, poor Indians, unemployed loggers and renegade marijuana farmers are stuck out in the woods like derelicts in a bus station. Sometimes they straggle in to Eureka, drinking wine out of bags and passing out on the sidewalks.

Water-oriented activities revolve around Humboldt Bay, which is popular with anglers and vital to the commercial fisheries. Thirty million pounds of fish are harvested annually in Humboldt County.

Beaches do not exist in Eureka, though several at Arcata and Trinidad are within easy reach.

Accommodations

In a town with hundreds of structures of historical and architectural interest, you are bound to stay overnight in one of them. A bed and breakfast inn is the logical thing to aim for in Eureka, which has a load of them. Perhaps the most interesting inn in town is the *Carter House*. Built in 1982, it's an exact replication of a beloved Victorian inn, the Murphy House in San Francisco, which was razed to make room for a high-rise. Apparently, the owners of the Carter House couldn't handle this injustice, so they moved north to Eureka and rebuilt the Murphy House from old photographs, paying meticulous attention to detail. The resulting structure defies anyone to tell the difference between it and the original. A four-course gourmet breakfast is included in the price of a stay.

The *Eureka Inn* is a bird of a different feather. This sprawling, English-style inn opened in 1922 as a symbol of the booming community's good fortune. It has since been proclaimed a National Historical Landmark. The anomalous Tudor architecture of the Eureka Inn, set in an otherwise nondescript section of town, only adds to the inn's imperturbable grace. Perennially the last word in luxury accommodations in Eureka, the 150-room inn has aged well. In fact, the constant effort to keep the building in good repair has had the effect of making it appear brand-new. Part of this is due to the fact that the inn has some thoroughly modern amenities: a large heated swimming pool, two saunas, two giant hot tubs, a banquet room and cable TV. The rooms are spacious and comfortable enough for an English lord.

Restaurants

Wherever you dine in Eureka, you'll experience the ambience of the town while eating your meal. The surroundings are as important as the food and are geared to remind you of the town's hard-working past. The last surviving cookhouse in the West is the *Samoa Cookhouse*, located on nearby Samoa Island, the spit of land that pens in Humboldt Bay, holding back the Pacific. Family-style meals are served at the Samoa Cookhouse. As is the case at the average American family's dinner table, you eat what the kitchen serves you. No menu. One set price. One set meal. No à la carte. No wine list. No quiche.

It all starts innocently enough with salad, which you toss yourself in a large metal bowl. This is quickly followed by soup, which is ladled from a black kettle. Gigantic hunks of bread appear next, along with a crock of butter. Then come bowls full of peas, kidney beans, mashed potatoes and gravy, trailed closely by the sliced beef (or whatever the day's entrée happens to be). Order iced tea, and an entire pitcher materializes. Actually, the food at the Samoa Cookhouse is doled out more lumber-camp style than family style, because this is how and where the lumberjacks were served in the heyday of Eureka's timber trade. Lunch costs $4.75, which includes everything mentioned above, and dinner is $8.75, for which you receive two entrées and larger portions of the side dishes, if possible. As one whiskered and suspender-clad old-timer warned, "If you leave here hungry, it's your own dang fault."

Lazio's Seafood is Eureka's other must-try dining experience. It's a family-run institution that's been serving seafood since 1944, though the family's roots in the fishing industry go back as far as 1889, when Lorenzo Lazio started a wholesale fish operation in San Francisco. Today, Lazio's is an interesting place to eat, filled with fishing paraphernalia and attached to an ancient cannery. Take your time poring over the extensive menu, which includes such interesting selections as Crab Legs Lazio and Salmon Cannelloni. But don't be afraid to simply order broiled seafood, as it is fresh enough not to need doctoring with sauces. The broiled salmon is especially fine. For starters, the fried fish appetizer is a veritable mound of Fish McNuggets that could and did feed two starving kids: us. The Pacific oysters on the half shell are plump and gamy (in a good way). They're quite a bit different from their East Coast counterparts and are something of an acquired taste— and we quickly acquired a taste for them.

descript development runs in a rough L shape around the top of the bay and up Highway 101. Arcata has traditionally been a lumber town, and as you drive up from Samoa evidence of its milling past lines the bay shore—warehouses, factories, boarded-up slag heaps, spewing smokestacks and the like. Pulling back, the box-like homes of the vanishing loggers come into view.

At first, Arcata seems to be just another burned-out mill town, but it's actually a city in transition and a fairly impressive oasis of higher learning. Humboldt State University, one of the oldest branches of the California state system, is located here. The school has broadened its scope beyond forestry management to embrace environmental science, marine biology and the liberal arts, making it an oft-imitated model nationwide. The campus is a sparkling jewel set on a large, grassy knoll east of the highway. Its 140 acres afford ample space for 6,000 students to roam without getting distracted by big-city vice. The university pumps new blood and innovative ideas into the town, such as the Arcata Community Forest (a 600-acre preserve of second-growth redwoods that is the only city-owned forest in California) and the Arcata Marsh (a bird sanctuary located on a former garbage landfill and industrial site).

Arcata's social life revolves around its plaza, a substantial midtown renovation. Old buildings have been restored, and new businesses have moved in. On weekends, college students have been known to engage in a colorful ritual known as "Ring around the Plaza." It involves drinking a beer, a margarita or some other libation (ground rules are established beforehand) in each of the bars that surround the plaza, the winner being the one who makes the most cycles, with a consolation prize going to the fastest drinker. Of course, the raised drinking age has greatly reduced the number of legal contestants. In summer, when school's out, the nightlife is nil. "Watch out or they'll roll the sidewalk up over you," a former student warned us.

If you plan on staying overnight, the *Hotel Arcata*—a "recaptured" old inn on the town plaza—is the best place to drop your bags. Opened in 1915, the Hotel Arcata was one of the finest inns of its size on the coast. But then the town hit a financial downturn that reduced its business district to a mere handful of barely subsistent enterprises, and the hotel fell into disrepair. Restored in recent years, the likable three-story structure has a way to go yet but is well on its way to a successful return to grace.

The cultural event of the year in Arcata is the Kinetic Sculpture Race, which takes place in late May. It's difficult to explain the rules or purpose of this extravaganza, but simply put, it is a 35-mile cross-country race that passes over hills and dunes and water. The catch is that the vehicles must be navigable pieces of sculpture; whether pumped, paddled or pushed, it doesn't matter.

The beach nearest Arcata is as hard to fathom as the Kinetic Sculpture Race. It is aptly named *Mad River Beach County Park*. To get there, take the Janes Road exit off Highway 101, then go right, left, right, left and right across a series of narrow farm roads. Try to follow the signs. The thrill of the chase is half the fun. The beach at the end of the road extends in both directions as far as the eye can see. The undertow at Mad River is treacherous, but the fishing is good. Gaggles of anglers were standing around driftwood fires while their spindly poles stood upright in the sand. Oh, yes, be sure to memorize the route you took here, because there are no directional signs leading back out. Otherwise, you'll wind up touring the dairy lands west of Arcata, as we did.

FOR FURTHER INFORMATION

Arcata Chamber of Commerce
1062 "G" Street
Arcata, CA 95521
(707) 822-3619

McKinleyville

Once called Minorsville—after Isaac Minor, owner of the local general store—the town of McKinleyville took its present name in 1901, after President McKinley's assassination. It is the sort of town where horses still have the right of way. One night we went in search of McKinleyville, taking the Clam Beach exit east. After three miles, we finally found some twinkling lights.

Feeling inexplicably patriotic, we were drawn like moths to the American flag in front of *Stanton's Barn* and stopped in for some basic all-American grub. The menu boasted that "we serve only 100% ground beef," as if anything else were the norm. On the wall above our heads was a display of "the barbed wire that fenced the West." Heading back to the car after eating bland patty melts and barbecued-beef sandwiches, we noticed that the Perspirations would be playing that weekend at the cocktail lounge next door. Alas, it was only Tuesday, and we left McKinleyville chagrined at having to miss the Perspirations.

Tiny McKinleyville is blessed with two large beaches. Actually, it is one long beach that's been split into two parts: *Clam Beach County Park* and *Little River State Beach*. Both are just off the highway and free of charge for day use. At Clam Beach, one can dig for razor clams, comb for driftwood and camp in the sand for $5 a night. Clam Beach is an unusually large beach for Northern California, as long as a pasture and as wide as a ball field. Little River is more of the same: dunes, driftwood and hard-packed sand (but no facilities). The Little River trickles through the sand at the north end, creating a natural boundary between it and neighboring *Moonstone Beach*, in Trinidad.

Trinidad

With a population of 300, Trinidad is the smallest incorporated city in California. Were Trinidad to apply for official cityhood today, it would be denied incorporation for being too small. Smallness is a curse more cities should cultivate if this town is any measure of what can be done with it. Trinidad is an ideal seaside village, compacted into a bouillon cube of streets positioned on a headland above a rocky bay. The beaches surrounding Trinidad are some of the most beautiful on the north coast.

From the midvillage promontory, where a red and white lighthouse stands, one can survey the entire scene. For once, the word "picturesque"—that overused warhorse of travel writing—seems entirely appropriate. Anchored boats sway gently in the protected harbor. Pointed rocks jut out of the water, more photogenic than menacing. Minuscule waves lap the craggy shore while a buoy rings solemnly in the distance.

These pure, idyllic visions are doused a little when one discovers the truth about the local beaches: Trinidad is where north coast nudists come to play. On any sunny day, this free-and-easy species can be found frolicking on no fewer than three beaches in town. The most notorious of these is *College Cove*, which adjoins *Trinidad State Beach* just north of the town center. You might have some trouble locating this beach, since its sign is constantly being ripped out of the ground or defaced with spray paint to the point of illegibility. But we were able to find it, rolling into a gravel lot off Stagecoach Road. You're supposed to park, grab a beach towel and walk through the woods to a steep trail that descends a cliff face. Be careful to take the correct trail through the woods; otherwise, you'll get lost in the thick forest. One of us, in fact, became royally disoriented in the tangled growth, scrambling beneath the low-hanging limbs like a blind Natty Bumpo.

There were no nudists at College Cove that afternoon, so it was on to the other two: *Baker's Beach* and *Luffenholtz Beach*. These are closer to the heart of the village, on the calmer bay side. To get to them, follow the Scenic Drive—a decaying chunk of the old Coast Highway that hobbles along in disrepair along the top of the cliff. The beaches are gorgeous, and the view from the bluffs above them is breathtaking. We, however, spied no nudists on a Tuesday in July.

Complaints about nudity are sometimes lodged by unsuspecting visitors who stumble upon them. Generally, a few token arrests are made, and the nudists return en masse to the beaches the next day. Of course, some enjoy the presence of these suitless sun worshipers. "The old men sit up on the bluffs with binoculars," a local businessman explained. "Nobody around here wants to make a big fuss. It's only outsiders that do. To us, it's just people enjoying the sunshine."

Not every beach in Trinidad is clothing-optional. At *Trinidad State Beach*, people keep their private parts covered. It begins in town at Trinidad Head and scoots up the coast for half a mile. The beach can be approached from town by foot or from a parking lot on Stagecoach Road. The latter is the more scenic route, your footsteps carrying you across a jungle of flora atop a majestic bluff. The layers of vegetation passed through are fascinating, from thick pine woods to groves of short, wind-curled trees and umbrella-like shrubs that protect the cliff from erosion. The beach, once you finally reach it, is a large cove broken here and there by tall, climbable rocks.

Like a pot of gold at the end of the rainbow, *Moonstone Beach* lies south of Trinidad at the end of the old Coast Highway. Hunks of driftwood lie strewn around the wide, secluded beach. Surfers reluctantly climb out of the water at sunset, barely able to pull themselves away from this beautiful setting.

To gain a bird's-eye perspective on this bounty of beaches, try climbing Trinidad Head. A circular trail leads to its summit, where there's a Coast Guard station and a granite cross commemorating the town's discovery. Briefly, Trinidad and its natural harbor were first sighted by the Portuguese explorer Sebastian Cermeno in 1595. He did not come close to land for fear of the pointed rocks. The Yurok Indians, who inhabited the area, were probably just as glad to see him go. On June 11, 1775, the Spanish explorer Hezeta anchored in the bay and came ashore. He declared that all his eye beheld belonged to Spain. It was Trinity Sunday when this occurred, thus, the name "Trinidad." The little town boomed in the gold rush, swelling to over 3,000 and serving as the seat of what was then Klamath County. Trinidad boomed again as a mill town in the 1870s and in the 1920s, as a whaling port. When these industries finally bit the dust, so did the town.

Today, Trinidad is home to artists and other lovers of solitude. It is not the sort of town prone to giving the red-carpet treatment to outsiders. What you see—the stunning natural beauty of the beaches, rocks, coves and headlands—is about as much as you're going to get. Of course, that is quite enough.

Accommodations

In the village of Trinidad, a visitor has only one choice for overnight lodging—the *Trinidad Bed and Breakfast Inn*, an attractive, petite Cape Cod home overlooking the harbor. More and varied accommodations can be found north of town on Patrick's Point Drive, fully out of sight of the reclusive townsfolk. Even RVs and trailer camps are allowed out this way, along with a few motels and rental cottages. A fine cottage court can be found at the *Bishop Pine Lodge*, where rustic cottages are spread on shaded grounds. Each unit has a full kitchen and a TV. A card informs you that the management will store your game and fish in their deep freeze. (How often do you find this service offered?) The Bishop Pine Lodge is a restful, out-of-the-way spot, with reasonable rates. Many visitors stay for a week at a time.

Restaurants

Fresh seafood can be found at the *Seascape Restaurant*, beside the pier on the harbor. Reminiscent of a Maine lobster pound, the Seascape may be close to the water but is by no means a tourist trap. Nothing in Trinidad is a tourist trap. The best restaurant in town, in fact, goes out of its way to discourage outsiders in deference to the loyal locals who dine here. Once you've seen the location—above beautiful, secluded Moonstone Beach—you'll understand the attitude at *Merryman's*. They offer "exquisite dining" and enforce a dress code (which, in Trinidad, simply means you must wear clothes). The menu is a short, simple list of fresh seafood, not unreasonably priced. The salmon and halibut entrées, for instance, were under $12. And the view…

The white-columned *Colonial Inn*, on Patrick's Point Drive, is a locally popular dinner house. Resembling an aging mansion in the Virginia horse country, the Colonial offers fine dining in a woodsy setting. It's an institution, and people have been coming from miles around for many years.

Nightlife

Your choices are limited. Have a drink or two at the *Colonial Inn*, or cruise into Arcata to check out the bars rimming the plaza, if you feel like it. Still, if you're staying in or near Trinidad, the very idea of nightlife is faintly blasphemous. Just lie in bed and listen to the crickets through an open window—there's your nightlife.

FOR FURTHER INFORMATION

Greater Trinidad Chamber of Commerce
P.O. Box 356
Trinidad, CA 95570
(707) 677-3698

Patrick's Point State Beach

At 462 acres, Patrick's Point is one of the largest state beaches on the Northern California coast. It is a full-use facility located at the north end of Patrick's Point Drive, just before it rejoins Highway 101. With 125 campsites, hiking trails, overlooks and a museum of natural and Indian history, it is quite a popular place in the summer. A portion of its popularity can be attributed to *Agate Beach*, which falls within its boundaries. Here, along three miles of coastline, one can hunt for small pieces of agate—a translucent, semiprecious stone—as well as jade. The chances of striking it rich fall somewhere between slim and none, but the myriad coves and tide pools stumbled across in the course of beachcombing will amply compensate.

Orick

Weird scenes begin to infiltrate the gold mine of Highway 101 as Orick approaches. Just south of Orick, before the highway moves inland to meet the town, a stretch of road near Freshwater Lagoon has been co-opted by a mile-long wall of trailers and RVs. Something like a modern-day hobo jungle, this roadside camp does not fall under any governmental jurisdiction; thus, it is fair game to anyone who can find an open spot for their gas-guzzling vehicle and a space on the sand for their fishing pole. Some folks have been known to stay for months on end, free of charge, lounging about on lawn chairs and rubber-necking traffic as it runs down the highway, their symbolic front yard.

Orick (pop. 650) is a veritable El Dorado of roadside flotsam, a cluttered little burgh that is as uninviting as a migraine. It is the home of burl souvenirs, both fake and real. "Burls" are the knotty lumps that form on the sides of one out of every 25,000 redwoods. Fake burl is called "hippie burl." Orick is lined with a banged-up string of stands selling burl and "new and used junk and treasures," a heap of trash lobbed in the middle of a beautiful valley. Keep driving.

Just north of Orick is Davidson Road, the turnoff for *Gold Bluff State Beach*. If your vehicle is up to a bumpy, bending, four-mile, one-lane gravel road test, you will be rewarded with a pretty gray-sand beach backed by tan-colored bluffs at both ends. Hey, it's just another fabulous Northern California beach, one more secluded spot for folks who dig clams and solitude in equal proportion. A small campground is located nearby. The day-use fee is $3.

Klamath

One of the fundamental laws of physics has some applicability to the experience of traveling. Heisenberg's uncertainty principle is a statement about the limited precision of scientific measurement. In essence, it says that one can specify either the position of a physical particle or its momentum at any given point in time, but not both. Because one of the variables is unknowable, it's logical to deduce that the value of the unknown variable could be anything. With his equation, the physicist is telling us that nothing is impossible. Or, to put it another way, anything's possible.

Same deal on the road. For instance, on the desolate north coast of California, one would not expect to come upon a 49-foot-tall replica of Paul Bunyan standing in a clearing in the redwoods, with a 17-ton blue ox named Babe beside him. You'd have to smoke all the pot in Humboldt County to hallucinate this pair. But it is no illusion. Paul and Babe are the gatekeepers and world's largest lawn jockeys for a tourist attraction called *Trees of Mystery*. "Trees" celebrates the majesty of the coast redwoods and Sitka spruce that grow to fantastic heights and often phantasmagoric shapes in this neck of the rain forest. It is a worthwhile operation—educational, informative and environmentally sound, which is a winning combination in our book.

Though hard to find, Klamath is a special place. It's everywhere and nowhere—diffused over a seven-mile stretch on both sides of Highway 101, along the Klamath River, up the inland valleys and canyons, atop coastal bluffs, squirreled away in the dark, spooky forests. There is no longer any one place that can be pointed to as the town center. Klamath has a listed population of 1,419. It is difficult to tell if this head count is accurate, if the town is growing or dwindling, whether there is an actual town or just a loose grouping of RV parks, scattered motels, restaurants and redwood shops, and the Trees of Mystery. In the case of Klamath, both position and momentum are unclear.

There's a good reason for this, and the seemingly quiet, salmon-filled waters of the *Klamath River* conceal a terrible secret. Del Norte County is flood country. In the winter, confluence of factors can turn the river into a raging monster that even Paul Bunyan couldn't slow down. In 1964, the wrong combination rang up on the meteorologic slot machine: a cold, wet winter had blanketed the surrounding mountains with a dense pack of snow and ice; a heavy storm front swiftly moved in, inundating the area with rain; and warm, high winds melted 10 feet of frozen precipitation in 24 hours. The net result was a 90-foot wall of water that came rushing down the canyon, with boulders and timber as battering rams, driving the town of Klamath out to sea.

Klamath was born in the mid-1800s during the fevered gold rush that swept California. Mining camps sprang up along the Klamath River. It was a typical story of greed running amok in the wilderness. The miners harassed and depleted the native Yurok Indians' numbers, while the riverbed became so silted in with the detritus of their gold digging that even the salmon stopped running for a time. Klamath City was a thriving lumber port for most of this century, until the virgin forests were cleared. And then the '64 flood came along and wiped the town off the map.

It was a highfalutin town, flush with prosperity when timber was king and the river was kind. In its heyday, 20 bars lined its rough-and-ready Main Street. The December flood left nothing standing but a small church and the massive golden bears that greeted visitors at the edge of town. The original town site is now utterly abandoned, the foundations of homes and businesses overgrown with weeds and reclaimed by nature. The Army Corps of Engineers built a new town site for Klamath, north of the river at an elevation five feet above the river's highest recorded level. But the citizens of Klamath, most of them anyway, never returned. The new town site is occupied only by a fairly grim lotful of mobile homes. As for the bears, a pair guards each end of the rebuilt Highway 101 bridge over the Klamath River.

If Klamath is more of a bear than a bull market these days, it's still a fine place for vacationers with an interest in the wonders of nature. High on the agenda is fishing. The Klamath River is the second largest river in California and one of the best in the world for salmon. The yearly chinook runs draw anglers from all over. From the salmon's point of view, the "anglomania" that follows is not all fair play. The mouth of the Klamath River used to be known as Suicide Row, because the skiff fishers would tie their boats together to form an impenetrable line against which the salmon, returning to spawn in their natal streams, didn't stand a chance.

A big controversy in recent years has been the practice of gill-netting by the Indians. A monofilament net is strung across the river, trapping the returning salmon, whose struggles are considerable to begin with, in a mesh that forces their gills together until they quite literally drown underwater.

Somehow, the fish continue to spawn in sufficient numbers to make their annual run, which begins around mid-July and ends in early October. Many anglers roll into Klamath with little more than a hook and a line, and they have a good time without making a serious dent in the salmon population. Three thousand RV and campsites are hidden around Klamath, and they fill up quickly when word gets out that the run has begun. Nestled around bends in the river, out of sight of the highway, the RV parks become busy fish camps overnight. It's enough to make the nomadism of the RV curiously appealing.

Klamath celebrates the salmon's homecoming with an annual Salmon Festival in early August. But there's more to be caught from these waters than salmon, as any surf-caster can tell you. Shore anglers pull in ling cod, black snapper, cabezon, flounder, perch, smelt and sea trout—not to mention razor clams and Dungeness crabs. There are miles of sand and rocks along the Klamath coast to cast from or hike along. They can also be admired from vista points on the highway. In the words of a man who grew up here, "When the sun's shining, this is one of the most beautiful spots in the world." Unfortunately, the sun is not always shining, especially in the summertime, when the inland temperatures climb, pulling marine air off the ocean and blanketing the coast in a perpetual dome of gray. Sometimes the sun breaks through at midday, and Klamath does indeed look like paradise under its golden rays. The best coastal vista point in the area is Requa Overlook, a turnout off Requa Road, west of Highway 101.

The most accessible beach in the area is *De Martin's Beach* (a.k.a. *False Klamath Cove*), which is one of those rare points where Highway 101 flirts with the ocean's edge on the north coast. The beach falls inside *Redwood National Park*, a 46-mile by 7-mile preserve for *Sequoia sempervirens* that was established in 1968 by an act of Congress and expanded 10 years later. The park has not been an unqualified blessing, as far as the citizens of Del Norte County are concerned. Fully half the county is park land, off limits to logging, and this has taken a painful bite from their already ailing economy. So far, the promised tourism hasn't materialized in sufficient numbers to offset the jobs lost in the timber industry. But the need to preserve the redwoods from their only natural enemy, the chain saw, is indisputable. One of the loftiest stands in the park, the Lady Bird Johnson Grove, commemorates the First Lady whose mission to "beautify America" is one of the better memories of the sixties.

Three state parks lie within the national-park boundaries. *Jedediah Smith*, *Del Norte Coast* and *Prairie* Creek state parks are developed with campsites, hiking trails, information booths, ranger talks, picnic tables and so forth. Though you'll never get wet in the frigid waters of the Pacific, swimming in the creeks that run through these parks is a pleasantly bracing alternative in the summer months.

Before investigating the backcountry trails of Redwood National Park, you'll want to take a crash course on the tall trees at the Trees of Mystery. A $5 admission fee gains you access to this private redwood forest and its "Trail of Mysterious Trees." Redwoods are awesome to contemplate in any setting, but the stand at Trees of Mystery is especially impressive. The Indians believed the area was haunted with evil spirits, causing the trees to grow in crazy ways: twisting, turning, running horizontally, sprouting out of each other. It's really nothing more than Darwinism in overdrive, with the behemoth redwoods and spruces fighting for all the sunlight they can lay their limbs on, employing ingenious adaptive and reproductive techniques in the quiet struggle for survival. A highlight is the Cathedral Tree—nine redwoods growing in a perfect semicircle out of one root structure. As many as 40 weddings a year are held here, and a crackly recording of Nelson Eddy crooning "Trees" plays continuously.

An Indian museum on the premises houses the largest private collection of Indian baskets, pots, ornaments and apparel in the West. The final attraction is the "Trail of Tall Tales," a short walk that retells the myths and legends of Paul Bunyan and his brawny logging crew. Kids, of course, will be in log heaven, but adults too will get something out of the chain-saw sculptures and carvings, completed in a period of six months by a talented local artisan-eccentric named Kenyon Kaiser. There is evidence of primitive genius in his work, which suggests Van Gogh rendering an American epic in wood. His *Pooped Lumberman* is an American classic, kind of a wild-west version of Rodin's *Thinker*.

Accommodations

There are a few places to stay in Klamath that won't have you screaming for a Holiday Inn. Across the street from where Paul Bunyan gives passersby the high five is a neatly kept motor court by the name of *Motel Trees*. Its 23 units are quite comfortable, offering such diversions as cable TV and an adjacent tennis court. You'll sleep like a Babe in this rustic setting, with the only possible disturbance being the odd, wandering bear who decides to leave his pawprints on your bathroom window.

Up on a hill overlooking the Klamath River and the beaches that flank it is the *Requa Inn*, a restored hotel. Done up in 1900s decor, this two-story white wonder is open all year round, except in winter, when it does business on weekends only.

Finally, for those cycling the coast or traveling on a tattered shoe-string, a youth hostel has opened in a turn-of-the-century home across the road from De Martin's Beach in Redwood National Park. For $6.50 a night, you'll share dorm-style, bunk-bedded rooms with a host of fellow travelers, many of them foreign.

Restaurants

For a fine California shore dinner, try the dining room at the *Requa Inn*. Seafood is abundant, with the plump native oysters and fresh-caught salmon and halibut getting high marks. Dinner is less formal at the *Steelhead Lodge*, where the chef of long-standing tends a barbecue pit, grilling salmon, beef and other charbroiled delights. The mountainous margaritas served here are guaranteed to chase away the gray skies, and the rustic lodge atmosphere will have you feeling as fit and full of the outdoors as Euell Gibbons and John Denver put together. The Steelhead Lodge opens around the Fourth of July and shuts down for the winter.

Babe's Iron Tender, named after the blue ox who was Paul's pet, is adjacent to Motel Trees. They serve a standard surf-and-turf menu at night (with a bit more emphasis on the turf—the steaks are great) and sandwiches at lunch. Breakfast is served, too, making Babe's the most convenient place to put on the feedbag between Eureka and Crescent City.

Nightlife

If you've got a thirst for something stronger than canned Coke, head to *Paul's Cannery* for a 50-cent draft and a hunk of salmon jerky, along with a complimentary helping of local color. There's another watering hole just off the highway called *The Club*, but it gets a little rough in there sometimes. Whenever we asked the locals if it was a safe place to drop in (i.e., we wouldn't get scalped or poleaxed), no one could say yes convincingly enough to suit us.

FOR FURTHER INFORMATION

Klamath Chamber of Commerce
P.O. Box 476
Klamath, CA 95548
(707) 482-7165

Redwood National Park
1111 2nd Street
Crescent City, CA 95531
(707) 484-6101

Crescent City

Crescent City is a town of 3,000 that sits near the Oregon border like a tortoise that couldn't quite inch its way over the finish line. In 1970, two-thirds of Del Norte County's meager population of 19,000 lived in Crescent City. By 1980, the town and the county were officially on the skids. The population of both continues to decline from year to year, even though most of the weary-looking souls we saw on the streets were dragging children behind them. The timber industry, priced out of the market by cheaper Canadian imports and reduced to cutting second-growth timber after having cleared the land of its virgin stands, may never recover.

Only a handful of mills still operate in Crescent City. These, along with fisheries and agriculture (mainly dairy cows and lily bulbs) keep the lights on in Del Norte county. Tourism ranks a distant fourth, although it may become a growth industry by default. Actually, Crescent City is banking on something that most communities fight to keep as far away as possible. Yes, it looks like an infusion of convicted felons is going to bail out Crescent City, or at least put some people back on the payroll. A maximum security prison is under construction, and the townsfolk couldn't be happier. You take what you can get in a county where half the annual budget goes to welfare.

Few tourists voluntarily stop in Crescent City. Only sudden nightfall or a driving rainstorm could induce a captive of the road to turn into the cement driveways of the substandard motels that line Highway 101. Younger family members who are given to noisy fits upon sighting golden arches will shout with glee, because Crescent City has every fast-food franchise you can think of. From billboards on down, they do everything short of gillnetting tourists to get them to stop for a meal, fill up on gas or spend the night.

Based on a cursory drive-through, one might surmise that Crescent City is just another "strip town"—i.e., a hodgepodge of businesses laid out to capitalize, like a parasite, on the "host" of Highway 101. Venture off the highway, and you might be surprised to discover a real town of modest dimensions (about a hundred square blocks), arranged around its harbor and the ocean. Used by a commercial fishing fleet and recreational boaters, the Crescent City Harbor is protected by a concrete-reinforced jetty of French design. A broad, grassy park runs along the harbor front, with picnic tables and paths that lead to the water. *Beachfront Park* is a fast-acting antidote to all those bad first impressions of Crescent City. Another dose of pain reliever is provided by a pair of lighthouses that lie off the coast. One of them, Battery Point Lighthouse, is mounted on an offshore bluff reachable only at low tide. The Del Norte Historical Society maintains a museum in the lighthouse, which went out of service in 1965. The other light is six miles out to sea, on a large rock 134 feet above the ocean. The Point St. George Lighthouse remained operative from 1892 to 1975, and though it is unreachable, its lens is on display at the Historical Society's main museum downtown, in an old jail.

Then there are beaches—bunches of beaches. A rocky one, reachable from the ends of the numbered streets, runs for about three-quarters of a mile along the ocean, perpendicular to Beachfront Park's quieter bay-side beach. Continuing on a northwest diagonal out of town, beach access is available at several turnouts along Pebble Beach Drive. On a cool July night, as the sun was setting, a gaggle of surfers braved the waves at *Pebble Beach*. Point St. George forms the northern boundary of this beach. Around the point, Pelican Bay describes a gentle, concave arc along 10 miles of sandy, dune-backed beaches that run all the way up to Smith River.

South of town, the Klamath to Crescent City stretch of Highway 101 turns out of sight of the coast, with the exception of a few overlooks. The old highway had to be moved east due to frequent washouts. There's always something humbugging the highway department up here. When we were driving through, portions of "new" Highway 101 were being worked on because some of the fallen redwoods over which the road was built had rotted through, causing the road to buckle. A short jog of the old Coast Highway remains passable, and it is the road one takes to *Crescent Beach* and *Enderts Beach*. Crescent Beach is accessible from a parking lot at the head of the beach. Enderts, at the end of the road, must be hiked to. The ⅗-mile downhill stroll is well worth it, for at the end of the trail are isolated, driftwood-strewn sands and tidepool–rich rocks to explore. Enderts Beach is, like many north coast beaches, a fine place to observe migrating California gray whales, as well as sea lions and birdlife.

There's also an informative display at Enderts Beach that tells what Yurok and Tolowa Indian money would buy back in the old days. For instance, a brave on the payroll savings plan could purchase a wealthy wife for 10 strings with 12 dentalia (shell money) on each, plus a headband of 50 woodpecker scalps and a fine obsidian blade. The penalty for uttering the name of a dead person was two dentalia strings. This set us to wondering what our publisher's advance would have been worth back in Indian times. One dentalia string, maybe?

Crescent City, like Klamath, is no stranger to natural disaster.

On March 28, 1964, only nine months before the Klamath flood, Crescent City was knocked to its knees by a roundhouse left. A violent earthquake in Anchorage, Alaska, measuring 8.8 on the Richter scale sent a tidal surge toward the Pacific coast. The tsunami that struck Crescent City destroyed 29 city blocks. It was a sad moment, almost the beginning of the end for a town that at one time thought it might be chosen as California's capital city. This was back in 1854, when Gold Rush fever was burning up the north country.

Today, Crescent City is more on the run than in the running, but with its abundance of scenic beauty and some of the best stream and surf fishing in the world, there's always the potential for a comeback. The raw material, at least, is there.

Accommodations

Highway 101 cuts a boomerang-shaped swath through Crescent City, providing motorists with a place to pull over and rest their tired bones. The *Curly Redwood Lodge*, located south of town near Crescent Beach, was constructed from one entire redwood tree. Down along quiet Pebble Beach, the yellow *Pebble Beach Bed and Breakfast Inn* is just steps away from this hikeable beach.

Restaurants

We ordered blue plate specials at one of the few nonfranchise restaurants in town that were still open for business. Told they were out of both items, our second choices—baked turkey and veal patties—arrived after a great deal of confusion. The thinly sliced turkey was smothered in a globular sauce that glowed the color of nuclear reactor waste, and the veal tasted like filet of sole—*shoe* sole, that is. Actually, there's one fine chef in town, and he runs a little dinner house called *Jim's Bistro* right on Highway 101. We guarantee you it's better than the Whopper you were about to settle for.

Nightlife

Look, after fifteen hundred miles, we're almost out of California. Mind if we sit this one out? We'll buy you one in Oregon. Promise.

FOR FURTHER INFORMATION

Crescent City/Del Norte County Chamber of Commerce
Front and "K" Streets
P.O. Box 246
Crescent City, CA 95531
(707) 464-3174

Smith River

California ends with not a bang but a whimper at the town of Smith River. Named for Jedediah Smith, the mountain man who trail-blazed his way across the Sierra Mountains in 1822, Smith River is a small community organized around a grounded motor yacht that serves as the site of an RV park. The salmon and steelhead runs on the Smith River are legendary, with 20-pounders bagged right and left at the height of the late summer and early fall run.

Jedediah Smith Redwoods State Park is only nine miles east of here. Within the park is one of the most magnificent redwood groves on earth. But overall, Smith River and its trailer camps look rather grim under the gray skies of summer, and after nodding at the last beach in California, *Pelican State Beach*, we were excited to cross into Oregon, waving bye-bye to the fruit-quarantine station on the left. Raise your wine glasses with us as we toast California. It's been a long trip from the Mexican border to the top of the state. Next stop, Oregon.

Oregon

Oregon is renowned for its progressive stand on the environment. The wave of ecological concern that swept the nation in the late sixties first took root in Oregon, where far-sighted legislators passed laws and spent money cleaning up the rivers, defouling the air and democratizing the beaches. The result is a state whose coastline is truly public, whose air is truly breathable, whose mountains and rivers truly qualify as unspoiled wilderness.

Anyone with a pair of eyes and a love of nature would have to agree that Oregon possesses the most scenic coastline in America. Grain for grain, this is as striking as it gets at the beach: steep, rocky points and headlands with churning currents and frequent storms lashing their bases; straight stretches of windblown, driftwood-strewn sand; forested hills encircling quiet, hidden coves. Everywhere you look, Stonehenge-like rock formations loom, enhancing the drama of this daunting coastline. Oregon can be an inhospitable place, should you come unprepared. Storms buffet the coastal strip, much of it fir-covered rain forest. Stiff winds whip the beach, causing ghostly streams of hissing sand to scurry around. The marine moisture, cool temperatures and prevailing winds can chill you to the marrow, even in summer. But if you know what you're in for and come bundled up, the experience can be exhilarating.

In temperament, the people of Oregon sometimes seem as chilly as the outdoors. This is a state that, in the sixties and seventies, closed ranks. Originally settled by New Englanders in the mid-1800s, Oregon inherited some of that region's wariness of outsiders. Traditionally, tourists have been tolerated with no great enthusi-

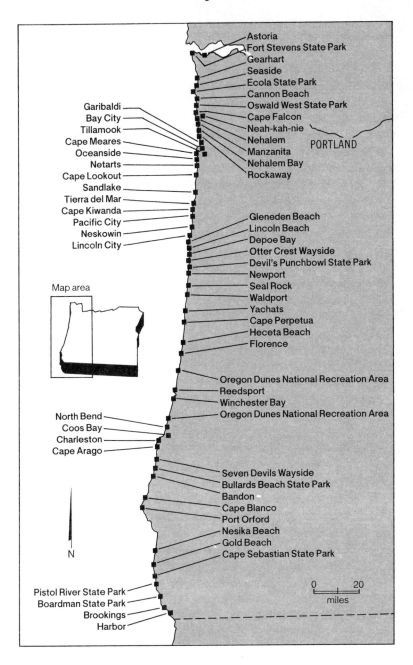

Astoria
Fort Stevens State Park
Gearhart
Seaside
Ecola State Park
Cannon Beach
Oswald West State Park
Cape Falcon
Neah-kah-nie
Nehalem
Manzanita
Nehalem Bay
Rockaway

PORTLAND

Garibaldi
Bay City
Tillamook
Cape Meares
Oceanside
Netarts
Cape Lookout
Sandlake
Tierra del Mar
Cape Kiwanda
Pacific City
Neskowin
Lincoln City

Gleneden Beach
Lincoln Beach
Depoe Bay
Otter Crest Wayside
Devil's Punchbowl State Park
Newport
Seal Rock
Waldport
Yachats
Cape Perpetua
Heceta Beach
Florence

Map area

Oregon Dunes National Recreation Area
Reedsport
Winchester Bay
Oregon Dunes National Recreation Area

North Bend
Coos Bay
Charleston
Cape Arago

Seven Devils Wayside
Bullards Beach State Park
Bandon
Cape Blanco
Port Orford
Nesika Beach
Gold Beach
Cape Sebastian State Park

N

0   20
miles

Pistol River State Park
Boardman State Park
Brookings
Harbor

asm, while immigration has been discouraged in the strongest possible terms. "Welcome to Oregon," former governor Tom McCall, author of many environmental reforms, told a convention in the early seventies. "While you're here, I want you to enjoy yourselves. Travel, visit, drink in the great beauty of our state. But for God's sake, don't move here."

The people of Oregon fret about the "Californication" of their state. They cast a disapproving eye upon anyone who isn't a "native Oregonian," whatever that means. After hearing about the college-educated, progressive-minded citizens of Oregon, however, we were surprised to find an inordinate number of overweight, out-of-work tree-choppers who divide their time between the liquor store, the TV set and the local tavern. We searched in vain for the "native Oregonians," whoever they are.

The scenario has changed drastically since the boom years of the sixties and seventies. After chasing business away and staking their isolationist claim to the woods, Oregon has paid a price for its orneriness. With a cry of "Timber!" Oregon's economy came crashing down. Forty percent of the jobs in the state are tied to the lumber industry. When the national housing market went soft in the early eighties, the demand for wood and wood products declined. The chain saws went silent. The mills shut down. Before long, Oregon was suffering 12 percent unemployment, one of the highest rates in the country.

Even the coast, where tourism should thrive, wears the tattered mantle of the new depression. As beautiful as the beaches might be, the towns around them are often as plain as unbuttered toast. That's not to say they're unattractive, just extremely ordinary. For the most part, they're fishing or lumbering communities, idling their engines at a time when both fishing and timber are down.

Don't come to the Oregon coast expecting luxury resorts, gourmet restaurants and a big night on the town. That's not how it's done up here. Most of the towns are small, with populations from 500 to a few thousand. They are generally spaced about 25 miles apart, because that's how far the stagecoaches could travel in a day. Not much has changed since stagecoach days. Many of the towns—

with the exception of Cannon Beach and Seaside, near the Washington state line—are little more than way stations, places to gas up or bunk down. Between them, mile after mile of forest and field and rugged beach rolls by, nearly empty of humanity.

To its eternal credit, the state of Oregon, in its fervor to preserve the wild country, has marked off no fewer than 64 state parks and waysides along its shoreline. Particularly on the central coast, from Florence to Lincoln City, Highway 101 is one big parkland of picnic tables, turnoffs and vista points. There are crescendos aplenty in this seaside symphony: places like Cape Perpetua, Otter Crest and Ecola Point that are capable of taking your breath away. The magnificence of the coast is dizzying, overwhelming.

You've got to admire Oregon for its conservation ethic in an era when what's good for business is bad for the environment, yet business seems to win every time. They've resisted caving in to the almighty dollar here in the Beaver State. More than that, they've dug in and fought hard when issues concerning the public's right to access have come to the fore. Back in 1966, when a Cannon Beach hotel used a barricade of logs to prohibit beach access to all but registered guests, the state government drafted a piece of legislation that became one of the most far-reaching measures of its kind ever adopted. The "Beach Bill," signed into law on July 6, 1967, recognized public rights to the beach between the vegetation line and the ordinary high-tide line. Moreover, the state's ambitious land-acquisition program has resulted in an unprecedented opening up of the coastline. All totaled, along Oregon's 362-mile coast, 262 miles of beaches and 64 miles of headlands have been set aside for public use.

That's a lot of beach. And while you won't frolic on it as you would in warmer climes—the water's too cold for swimming, and the wind and rain can chase you off in a hurry—it's always open season for photography, hiking, picnicking, camping, fishing and plain old nature appreciation. To drivers of recreational vehicles, Oregon—with its scenic highways and abundant campgrounds— is ranked tops in the country. The state's beaches and streams are a paradise for anglers, although the state fish—the chinook salmon— has been overfished to the brink of being placed on the endangered-

species list. To us, every name on the map brings back memories
of some remarkable topographic wonder: Haystack Rock in Cannon Beach; Face Rock, just offshore in Bandon; Maxwell Point,
the monolithic headland at Oceanside; the towering Oregon Dunes
along the central coast; the triumvirate of headlands known as the
Three Capes. And on and on.

   There's no limit to the beauty of the Oregon coast. If we feel
ambivalent about some of the towns, it is because instead of har-
monizing with the landscape, they are blemishes upon it. We are
thinking of the depressed strip towns along the southern coast, although Lincoln City up north deserves a rap on the knuckles. What
can we say? Like the governor ordered, we traveled, visited and
drank in the great beauty of their state. But we didn't have a lot of
civilized fun after dark, found it difficult to warm up to the people
and can't recall many memorable meals or motels along the way.
Oregon is one place where a sensible dose of the sort of upscaling
we usually deplore would help out. The environment, however,
speaks for itself, and everyone should come to Oregon to see and
experience it firsthand.

Brookings

"Summertime Blues" was playing on the car radio as we drove
across the California border into Oregon. Though it was only July,
the summer seemed to be over. Fog hung low over the highway,
casting a pall on the dark, green hillsides. Nobody told us that
often the worst time of the year on the West Coast is the summer.
From Morro Bay to Crescent City, we'd dealt with morning grayness that frequently burned off by noon, but when it didn't, it
made the Golden State look gloomy. Everywhere we went, we'd
hear that August was the best month to visit, or September, or
October, or November...always some other month. "How can
this be?" we thought. "This is sunny California! This is the West
Coast!" No piece of literature we'd seen—be it brochure, newspaper, magazine or book—mentioned the temperamental summer

weather out here. Okay, enough already.... "Summertime Blues" was playing on the car radio as we drove across the border into Oregon. And it was dark and gray in this new state.

Brookings is the first town in Oregon. It is a place where dented, spray-painted pickup trucks and mufflerless motorcycles are common sights. The men look more like Babe the Ox than Paul Bunyan, and the overburdened women are somewhere in hiding at the laundromat. At one time, Brookings' primary source of income came from the felling of trees. Poor timber management practices and the pointless greed of human enterprise—pointless, in that only the lumber bosses got rich—have reduced the forests around Brookings to a shaven stubble and lumbering to one lonesome mill, belching its steam over the harbor at Brookings.

With a population of 3,375, Brookings is the largest town in Curry County, a narrow, 60-mile corridor that runs along the coast and stops 10 miles inland at the border of the Siskiyou National Forest. With only 16,000 people in the entire county, Curry is home to the largely unseen and unheard citizens of the state, who have a lot in common with the tight-lipped residents of Maine. Brookings is the welcome mat of Curry County, and when the wind's blowing off the water and fog shrouds the town, you may not want to stay for very long.

Combined with an adjacent area known simply as Harbor, Brookings is built around the mouth of the salmon and steelhead-rich Chetco River. It is a small industrial port, with a safe harbor whose mouth is not much larger than a bathtub. Big-bellied anglers flock here like sea gulls, living out of trailers on land and in skiffs at sea.

Away from the harbor, Brookings is a hodgepodge of stores where rural Curry County comes to shop. It is a hard-working town, for those who can find work, though recreationally Oregon is tame compared with California. The most exciting thing to do in Brookings is to go bowling; the county's only alley is here. The other options are to drink at Ken's Tavern, cruise the main drag, scream at passing vehicles, set off fireworks and duck from the occasional squad car. All of the above activities kept us awake the night we were in town.

The most fascinating point of interest in Brookings is *Mt. Emily*.

It is the only spot in the continental United States ever bombed by a foreign power. On September 9, 1942, a Japanese pilot, flying a plane he had assembled on an offshore submarine, dropped an incendiary bomb on Mt. Emily. After the war, the pilot visited Brookings and presented his samurai sword to the city as a gesture of peace and goodwill. It is now on display at City Hall.

There's precious little else to lure you to Brookings. Outside of town, however, a multitude of beaches await you. To reach *Crissy Beach*, the first beach in Oregon, take the second left turn in the state, which will lead you to *Winchuck Wayside Day Park*. From here, it's a hike down a trail to the water. Don't get too hung up on the symbolism of Oregon's first beach, however, because much better ones lie north of here. Some consider the 15-mile stretch of coastline from Brookings to Gold Beach to be the most scenic in Oregon. Two state-park beaches are included in this rugged coastal wedge. *Harris Beach State Park*, one mile north of Brookings, demonstrates just how raw and beautiful the undeveloped Oregon coast can be. Huge islands of rock sit offshore. *Goat Island*, at 21 acres, is the largest island in the state. It has a tiny sand beach, but signs saying, "Unusually high waves, strong outgoing currents, driftlogs roll in surf," warn you away.

Just up the road, stretching for over 11 miles, is the pride of the southern Oregon coast: *Samuel H. Boardman State Park*. Named for the founding father of the state park system, the 1,473-acre facility is a grand and fitting tribute. Numerous viewing points have been cut into the highway's shoulder. Everywhere you look, the massive bluffs are creased with creeks and canyons. Trails lead down to beaches at numerous turnouts. *Whalehead Beach* is typical of the beauty you'll discover here. A creek trickles across the gray sand into the ocean, while two large, offshore rocks perform sentry duty. At high tide, one of the rocks is hit at the right angle, creating a noisy sight not unlike a whale spouting its blowhole. A beach is nestled into Whalehead Cove, at the foot of a 700-foot mount. Clamming, crabbing and beachcombing are popular activities at Boardman, but when the sun comes out it's also plenty warm for sunbathing.

Accommodations

One piece of good news about traveling in Oregon is that motel rooms are dramatically cheaper than in California, even in the summer season. Whether this indicates a depressed tourist industry in Oregon is not ours to reason. We found suitable lodgings in the historic *Chetco Inn* for under $30. Built on a hill in 1915 by the California and Oregon Lumber Company, it was the social center of the community for years. The inn fell on hard times, and not until 1984 was a restoration undertaken. It's still limping along, gamely hanging in there. Some of the 35 rooms face west, looking out on the rocky Oregon coastline.

Restaurants

In Brookings, it seems, they prefer to catch, clean and cook their own fish than have a stranger set a plate in front of them. Most of the dining options seemed geared toward haste and convenience, such as the Mobil Mini-Mart and the Pizza Deli. The exception is the *Chetco River House*, where fresh Oregon seafood is served in an attractive riverside setting.

Nightlife

For us, nightlife meant being kept awake all night by yahoos revving their engines, blowing up firecrackers and scattering at the explosions. The Fourth of July, one of our nation's most frightening holidays, was right around the corner, and not even a small town in Oregon was immune to the pyrotechnics and noisemaking. The rest of the year, those Curry County natives whose cars still run come to Brookings to drink at *Ken's Tavern*, bowl and play video games or just hang out. Many others, of course, forgo nightlife, rising with the dawn to go fishing.

FOR FURTHER INFORMATION

Brookings-Harbor Chamber of Commerce
Shopping Center Avenue
P.O. Box 940
Brookings, OR 97415
(503) 469-3181

Pistol River State Park

North of Boardman State Park lies the Pistol River. The state has provided a few turnouts near its mouth. Hereabouts, the land opens up into dune country, and the big-sky effect that occurs around broad, sandy beaches returns in full force. Between the parking lot and the beach is a shallow lagoon, created periodically when a sand ridge forms, blocking the river where it enters the ocean. We couldn't figure out how to cross the lagoon to the beach without getting wet. A vista point just north of here looks out onto some hulking sea stacks—basaltic extrusions shaped by wave action. Their conical tops bear crowns of green grass. A flat, fan-shaped beach is accessible from the turnout.

Cape Sebastian State Park

Between Brookings and Gold Beach, the land rises to a 700-foot promontory known as Cape Sebastian. Discovered in 1603 by the Spanish explorer Sebastián Vizcaíno and named for the patron saint San Sebastian, it is one of the highest coastal lookouts in southern Oregon. On a clear day, visibility extends nearly 50 miles in either direction. From the summit, a trail winds down to the sea.

Gold Beach

Varoom, varoom. And they're off, sputtering under the bridge and shooting up the river, foaming wake trailing sputtering speedboats in a V for Victory. It's the Fourth of July in Gold Beach, Oregon, and the annual Rogue River Marathon Hydroplane Boat Race has just gotten underway. For two hours, the whine and drone of boat engines will echo across the harbor as they fly up the river to Lobster Point. The racers will make three roundtrip laps in this 60-mile marathon before cutting their engines. From where we're standing, on the deck of the historic Rogue River Bridge, they appear to be locked on a dead heat. There are literally *dozens* of people on the bridge with us, watching with binoculars and milling happily on this festive holiday. The sun has even decided to break through at the last minute. Before you know it, the green hills of God's country have come alive in the golden sunlight, and the river is sparkling like a diamond choker. Everybody's happy on a sunny day in Oregon. And here are the boats again, tearing downriver.

Okay, maybe July 4th on the Rogue River isn't quite the same as celebrating the fiftieth anniversary of the Golden Gate Bridge. But north of San Francisco, you take your fun where you can find it, so we spent our nation's birthday watching guys scoot around the Rogue River in speedboats. All in all, we've had worse Fourths.

Though the town is called Gold Beach, the river is the star of the show. The Rogue, with its headwaters up near Crater Lake, draws people to the area. Three different outfits run daily jetboat trips up the river, exploring the pristine backcountry. The Rogue has been declared a Wild and Scenic River, which means its waters and wildlife, along with the surrounding Siskiyou Mountains and its numerous tributaries, are protected. Some of the wildlife you'll spy through the spray of whitewater includes blacktail deer, black bears, river otters, beavers, mergansers, great blue herons, water ouzels, leaping salmon and steelhead. One can take either a 64-mile, half-day round trip, including a stop for lunch at one of three rustic lodges (your choice) in the upriver town of Agness, or sign on for a longer jaunt back into whitewater country and deep wilderness. Three different operators run the Rogue, one of them the official mail carrier to remote stations on the river. All offer comparable service and prices with $22.50 being the standard adult charge for a half-day river run. The boats make morning trips from May through October, adding an afternoon departure between July 1st and Labor Day.

Gold Beach is largely a quiet town whose 1,500 residents work at the local plywood mill, troll the ocean for a living or ply the small but growing tourist trade. Gold Beach has the heaviest concentration of quality motels and restaurants between Eureka, California, and the town of Newport, halfway up the Oregon coastline. People come here to fish, hike the hills, ride the river and enjoy the solitude. "If you really want to lay back," said a mellow old codger who'd fled San Diego when it started to subdivide alarmingly, "this is the area to come to." The fishing possibilities where the Rogue River empties into the ocean are unsurpassed. To quote a knowledgeable local source, "Gold Beach is one of the few places on earth where you can fly-fish for trout in a wilderness creek in the morning, ocean fish for salmon or bottom fish by noon and cast for migrating steelhead before the sun goes down." Catch a fish and you're sitting on top of the world.

The breakwater extending from the river's mouth is a popular place to surf-cast and lower crab pots. The harbor area is crowded with bait-and-tackle shops, large RV parks and functional motels for anglers who aren't terribly discriminating when it comes to bedding down. South of the harbor, the beach has the look of a lunar landscape, with barren brown dunes tinged gray under often cloudy skies. Beds of cobbles and bleached driftwood logs are strewn in the salt-and-pepper sand. Gold Beach is on the southern edge of Oregon's rain forest. Rainfall averages 80 or 90 inches a year, most of it coming in the winter months, when ferocious storms lash the coast with sheets of rain and high winds.

Gold Beach, like most of Oregon's small coast towns, grows slowly, if at all. Not much has changed since the gold rush drew mad swarms of prospectors west to Oregon in the 1850s, except that the coast is *less* overrun now than it was a century ago. Between towns, one crosses uninterrupted miles of coniferous trees and rolling headlands, with an occasional beach overlook or state park and few signs of civilization.

The stretch of highway from Brookings to Bandon, with Gold Beach at its center, is known as the "Fabulous Fifty Miles." Some claim it is the loveliest part of the coast in Oregon. The scenery really turns striking around Port Orford and Bandon, with their clean, wide beaches and offshore stacks, reefs and blowholes.

Accommodations

For travelers, the Oregon coast—Gold Beach included—is a buyer's market. We stayed at a brand-new *Friendship Inn* on the south bank of the Rogue River for $32 a night and liked everything about it, except the purple doors. The average rate around town is $30 for a single room, and $40 for a double—quite a drop from California. These are decent motels, too, with ocean views, cable TV and heated pools.

If you want to spend a little more, *Jot's Resort* offers a complete vacation within its compound, including a choice of rooms or condominium suites, some with kitchens and fireplaces. The resort has a pool and spa, sports shop, private dock, rental boats and charter fishing on the river or ocean. In season, rooms range from $59 (for a standard waterfront unit) to $145 (for a two-bedroom waterfront condo).

For luxury in a more rustic setting, the *Tu Tu Tun Lodge* lies seven miles out of town on the north bank of the Rogue River. The emphasis is on recreation: heated pool, pool table, pitch-and-putt golf, horseshoes, whitewater rafting trips and so forth. The 16 rooms go for $88 a night; suites on the river cost a little more.

Restaurants

In one respect—dining—Gold Beach is fairly cosmopolitan for being in the heart of lumberjack country. The *Rogue Landing*, for instance, serves high-quality gourmet food. Travelers used to fried fish, french fries and pickle slices can sidestep that rut and order "Escargots aux Champignons" as an appetizer and choose from the likes of "Scallops Sauté à la Bretonne en Casserole" or "Stuffed Shrimp Lafitte" for a main course. We sank our hooks into the Rogue Landing Special: shrimp, scallops and crabmeat, sautéed in butter, lemon, scallions, mushrooms, garlic and wine sauce.

The food's also first-rate at *Chowderhead*. Their Rogue Coast Combo is another pleasing plateful of local catches (halibut, snapper, ling cod). Other selections include the Rocky Mountain Rancher (grilled rainbow trout stuffed with shrimp and crabmeat) or the specialty of the house, the Merry Old Sole (sole stuffed with shrimp, scallops, crab and two kinds of cheese, topped with Newburg sauce). Dinner includes serve-yourself bowls of tomato-based seafood chowder and milk-based clam chowder, both very good.

Jot's Resort has its *Rod 'n Reel Restaurant*, which is big on standard beef and seafood items. Your dinner might be accompanied, as ours was, by country music, sung quietly by two guys who looked like hired hands from the Grand Ol' Opry. Finally, a local favorite is the *Sportsman's Grotto*, which prepares fresh seafood with a minimum of fuss or fanfare. The chinook salmon, razor clams and oysters are all taken from nearby waters. For a sampling of five different types of seafood, order the Chef's Combination Seafood Platter, but first read the fine print. "You'll need to be hungry for this one," it warns.

Nightlife

A once-over of downtown Gold Beach did not turn up a wealth of things to do. Granted, the ill-fated film *Ishtar* was playing at the local theater. Generally, the sidewalks roll up early in Gold Beach. You might poke your head into the *Rogue Room*. Along with its companion establishment, the *Regal Restaurant* (a hash palace that's open 24 hours), it takes up an entire city block and looks like a tobacco warehouse.

Gold Beach Chamber of Commerce
510 South Ellensburg
Gold Beach, OR 97444
(503) 247-7256

Nesika Beach

This little hamlet is hidden away on a coastal loop road six miles
north of Gold Beach. It's just about the only glimpse of the Oregon
coast between Gold Beach and Port Orford, 20 miles up the road.
Nesika Beach is a small community strung out above a long stretch
of sand. The only discernible beach access is at *Geisel Monument
State Wayside*, not far from where the loop reconnects with Highway 101. Here you'll find a parking lot and picnic tables. Past
Nesika Beach, Highway 101 pulls away from the coast for a spell,
but continues the pleasant visual symphony begun back in Gold
Beach: little development, no billboards, lots of dairy cows and
green acres.

But then a sour note is sounded on the left side of the road.
What is that fake-looking *Tyrannosaurus rex* leering at passing motorists over the treetops? Why, it's a fake-looking *Tyrannosaurus
rex*—the official greeter for a place called Prehistoric Gardens. It is
the looniest kind of roadside attraction. The architect behind Prehistoric Gardens sculpted life-size replicas of dinosaurs and distributed them among a patch of woods he refers to as a "rain forest."
His scientific credentials amount to a layman's interest in paleon-
tology augmented by information-gathering visits to natural history museums and a few universities.

The whole idea wouldn't be so laughable, and might even prove
educational for the youngsters, if the dinosaurs looked the slightest bit authentic. But they don't. We've seen more convincing dinosaurs tumble out of cereal boxes—though seldom have we seen
creatures as revolting as those bellying up to the admission window at Prehistoric Gardens, dragging their whining, road-weary

brood behind them. One can only surmise that places like Prehistoric Gardens fill a need for people who can't handle an unbroken
stretch of natural outdoor beauty. The thought of driving unbothered by artificial contrivances is too much for some folks.
Knowing full well they're being taken for the proverbial ride, they'd
rather plop down $3.50 to gawk at wooden, Day-Glo dinosaurs.
Maybe it's fitting, then, that a few miles up the road from Prehistoric Gardens sits Humbug Mountain. It is, incidentally, the second highest peak in Oregon. Within *Humbug Mountain State Park*
lies four more miles of coastline.

Port Orford

Port Orford (pronounced *aw-ferd*) is the westernmost incorporated
city in the contiguous United States. Like Lubec, Maine—its East
Coast counterpart—Port Orford should be visited if you want to
cover America from sea to shining sea, compass point to compass
point. A Beach Boys song was playing on the car radio when we
rolled into town, which only added to our jubilation. Unlike Lubec,
which is located off a pockmarked back road, Port Orford is easy
to reach. In fact, it can't be avoided unless you close your eyes,
because Highway 101 runs right through the center of this quiet
town of 1,080.

The local chamber explains that "Port Orford is geared to a natural style of living. An appreciation and enjoyment of the wonderful outdoors and a dedication to preserve the clean air and pure
water prevails." In other words, for excitement in Port Orford,
they watch the trees grow. Cedar and myrtle are the kinds of trees
that grow in these parts. Myrtlewood carving is a cottage industry
around here, the handcrafted products of this blond wood being
sold at roadside stands—the first we'd seen since leaving the redwood country of Northern California.

The harbor at Port Orford is unique. Open to the ocean, it's
home to a small fishing fleet as well as a few recreational boaters.
None of the boats are docked in the water. When they're not out
at sea, they're berthed right on top of the dock. Two heavy-duty

hoists work overtime lifting the boats from the water and then plopping them back first thing next morning.

Port Orford was founded in 1851 under less than auspicious circumstances. A Captain Tichenor put nine men ashore to establish the first settlement in south coastal Oregon. As soon as he was out of sight, Indians attacked the landing party. History tells how this brave band of Oregonians held their ground against the rampaging Indians from their position atop a large rock. Today, it's known as Battle Rock, and you can climb its steep slope and wonder about what happened there. The beach that faces Battle Rock, in the middle of town, is a nice little spot, perfect for a short stroll after a home-cooked meal at one of Port Orford's several cafés.

Port Orford Head State Park, just north of town, overlooks the beautiful, rugged shore. A stunning vista is just a short hike away from the parking lot, down a cement trail to the point of a wind-whipped headland. To the south, the mouth of Port Orford's harbor is visible. To the north, a constellation of small rocks fills the water. Just one more postcard setting, courtesy of Oregon.

FOR FURTHER INFORMATION

Port Orford Chamber of Commerce
P.O. Box 637
Port Orford, OR 97465
(503) 332-8055

Cape Blanco

The turnoff for Cape Blanco beckons off Highway 101, 11 miles north of Port Orford. It is the westernmost point of land in Oregon, and the second westernmost place in the whole country (after California's Cape Mendocino). Driftwood-covered beaches fold back in either direction, leaving the traveler with an odd sense of finality.

The Cape Blanco Lighthouse rests on a chalky bluff, 245 feet above the ocean. The oldest lighthouse in continuous use in Oregon, it's been warning ships away from the cape since 1870. The waters off Cape Blanco are littered with the skeletons of countless frigates that ran aground prior to the light's construction, when the only signal a ship received was the lantern a good samaritan placed in his Port Orford hotel window. Burning with one million candlepower, the Cape Blanco Lighthouse still uses the same Freenel lens, imported from France, that was installed in 1870.

Cape Blanco State Park is some distance back from the light. Though there are day-use picnic tables and boat ramps here, most people come to camp. A half-mile trail leads from the 58-site campground to a rocky beach. Before 1987, overnight camping fees reflected the Oregonians' attitude toward outsiders. State residents paid $8 a night, while all others were charged $10. Now, everyone pays the same amount.

Bandon

If Stonehenge were placed at the ocean's edge, it might look something like Bandon. Sea stacks—those monoliths of rock formed over the millennia by the action of waves upon basaltic extrusions—are strewn along the beach at Bandon. Some of the rocks are tall spires. Some are humpbacked mounds. One called Table Rock is a nesting place for tufted puffins. (Say that quickly three times.) Some have had caves or tunnels cut through their bases. Some lean together as if square dancing. Some fall into each other as if slam dancing. Others appear to have sculpted, human faces glowering seaward. These ancient formations are more than a random distribution of rocks. Like a surrealist dreamscape by Yves Tanguy or Max Ernst, they seem to possess a magical deeper meaning.

The rocks and the beaches can be found south of the Coquille River mouth, away from the center of Bandon (or Bandon-by-the-Sea, its full name). Much of it falls inside *Bandon State Park*, a large park with four beach accesses spaced about a quarter mile apart. Face Rock Viewpoint overlooks the heart of this rocky landscape. The faint of heart should confine themselves to this promontory.

The trails leading down to the beach are long and steep, making the return trip equivalent to scaling the side of a building.

It should be obvious to anyone who spends more than a few minutes in Bandon that it is the most appealing town on Oregon's south coast, beckoning you to comb its coves and tide pools and walk among the giant sea stacks. The town of Bandon is nearly as unique as its beaches. Perhaps it sticks out among its south coast counterparts because it's been given several chances to better itself. Twice, Bandon has been leveled by fire—in 1914 and 1936— and both times it's bounced back to become an attractive, working community with its Irish essence intact.

The fires, and the will to continue, can be directly traced to the town's Celtic roots. Henry Baldwin was an Irish seaman aboard the *Captain Lincoln* when the schooner went aground on the rocks north of the Coquille River. After struggling to gain shore, Baldwin headed south till he came upon the river. He fell in love with the location. Later, he convinced George Bennett, a fellow Irishman, to help him establish a settlement here. They did so and named it Bandon, after their hometown in Ireland.

At some point in the town's development, a local landowner imported gorse into the area. Gorse is a short, yellow-flowered evergreen native to Ireland. Often, it's used in hedge making. The landowner wanted to use gorse to hold the ocean-whipped bluffs in place. The imported gorse grew even more wildly than it did back in the home country, and soon it overran the town. Gorse is an oily plant that burns easily, even when it's green. Thus, whenever a fire breaks out in Bandon, there goes the neighborhood.

Today, gorse still grows all over Bandon, but the town has learned to live with it. "Boardwalking" is a custom devised by the locals to maneuver around the pesky plant. When someone wants to get through a sticky growth of gorse, they carry two planks, laying one in front of another as they walk.

Bandon's earliest town site is called Old Town, and the businesses on these blocks have been restored to look the way they did before the fires. Only one building, the white-stone Masonic Lodge, survived both blazes. It sits at a back corner of Old Town, looking mighty proud of itself. The expected gift shops and fudge factories are present and accounted for, but Old Town is a working neighborhood, too. The restoration is tasteful, and the streets are built around a pleasant riverfront harbor. More pleasure craft than commercial boats tie up here, though a small fishing fleet does exist. The town has always been a favorite stopping place for boat travelers along the Oregon coast. At one time, before the fires, the steamer lines would dock here on the passage between Seattle and San Francisco, and at Bandon's peak, 9,000 people would be staying here at its hotels.

Times have changed. Most of the 2,770 current residents inhabit a quiet, well-to-do neighborhood away from Old Town. No honky-tonk hand jive is allowed here. What little industry exists is set back from Old Town, in the fertile foothills behind the eastern back streets. Ninety percent of Oregon's cranberries are grown in the bogs behind Bandon. The crop harvested here is sent to an Ocean Spray processing plant in Eugene, Oregon.

Bandon also supports two other clean, innocuous industries. Native myrtle is fashioned by local craftsmen into everything from salad bowls and TV tables to works of sculpture. The hard, deep-grained blond wood is as sturdy as it is beautiful. Cheese is manufactured at the Cheddar Cheese Factory near Old Town. Visitors can drop in and buy a big wheel of Bandon cheddar.

Accommodations

The scenic Beach Loop Drive runs beside the beach and sea stacks south of Bandon. Five decent motels are located within a mile of each other, all of them close to the beach. All other things being equal, the *Sunset Motel* gets our nod simply because of the rates. None of the motels are exorbitant—$55 was the highest rate charged—but a room at the Sunset cost us less than $40. Down the road is the newer and more upscale *Inn at Face Rock*, indisputably the top choice in the area.

Or, heck, why not just move here? Browsing through a local real-estate magazine, we came across home after home going for what appeared to our jaded East Coast eyes to be rock-bottom prices. How about this one: "Three-bedroom home on an acre in good location north of Bandon. Includes fruit trees and outbuildings. Will take good terms on $25,000 or will take $20,000 cash."

Restaurants

Bandon puts its best foot forward in Old Town, a two- by six-block rectangle of small businesses surrounding the Coquille River harbor. It's a calm, attractive area that does not reek of rotten fish and gasoline. The highwater mark of Bandon's cuisine, the *Wheelhouse Restaurant*, has a terrific view of the water, and the seafood's almost as good as the scenery. Grilled and broiled are usually the ways to go, but at the Wheelhouse, deep-fried is nothing to scoff at. They coat their fish and shrimp in a beer batter that doesn't mask the fresh taste of the seafood. For a unique dessert treat, try the peanut butter pie. Another distinctive Bandon eatery is *Andrea's Old Town Café*, which serves "special recipe" seafood and home-grown lamb, among other things.

Nightlife

Two types of watering holes exist in Oregon: the tavern and the lounge. Taverns sell beer and usually have a jukebox or at least a drunk who will burst into song. Lounges sell hard liquor, as well as beer and wine, and sometimes have live music. To us, the tavern is preferable to the lounge, because it seems more connected to the organic cycle of community life—everybody and his grandpappy drops by at some time or another. The lounge, on the other hand, is more often frequented by passers-through: traveling salesmen, businessmen, honeymooning couples, vacationing moms and dads.

Old Town Bandon has representatives of each kind. The *Pastime Tavern* and *Lloyd's Lounge* are located side by side on 2nd Street. The Pastime was built in 1937, right after the second devastating fire. There's cold Rainier beer on tap at 60 cents a glass and 80 cents a pint. At these prices, we had no need or desire to wander elsewhere. Besides, the Pastime had a good jukebox, and we had lots of quarters.

FOR FURTHER INFORMATION

Bandon Chamber of Commerce
P.O. Box 1515
Bandon, OR 97411
(503) 347-9616

Bullards Beach State Park

A mile north of Bandon, just above the Coquille River, is yet another of Oregon's fine, understated state parks. Bullards Beach is reached via a scenic two-mile drive that runs along the snaking river, beside an immaculate campground. The look of the beach is different here. Absent are the stacks and rocks that choke the coastline to the south. Entered through a break in the healthy-size dunes, the beach is a flat, gently sloped plain reminiscent of such windswept East Coast beaches as Cape Hatteras. It's almost a crime the waves are too rough for swimming in Oregon. Anywhere else, Bullards Beach would be invaded by an army of towel-toting beach fanciers. But it was empty on the gorgeous day we visited. Nearby, on a separate side road, is the *Coquille River Lighthouse*, built in 1896. Today, the abandoned light stands in the wind, sand gathering at its base while paint peels away.

Whiskey Run Beach
Agate Beach
Seven Devils Wayside

Signs along Highway 101 between Bandon and Coos Bay note the turnoff to Seven Devils Road, which leads to the seaside village of Charleston and its several state and county beaches. Along the way, one can take a side road down to Whiskey Run Beach, Agate Beach or Seven Devils Wayside. We visited the first of these.

Watch the signs closely, because in Oregon they make them

as inconspicuous as possible. Often, the small, barely readable directional markers for roads and state parks give no advance warning. Indeed, they're posted right at an intersection and are frequently noticed too late, necessitating a U-turn. Do they not want to encourage visitation? Is this an admirable but misguided attempt to keep the environment uncluttered with signage? We'd seen much the same thing in another state, on another coast. Maine, wasn't it?

In any case, Whiskey Run Beach is a lovely but underused beach. On the bluff above it, the Pacific Power & Light Company has erected some experimental wind turbines, a cheap and pollution-free way of harvesting power out of thin air. On the beach itself, Whiskey Run gurgles over a bed of driftwood before meandering into the ocean. It's a broad, flat beach that's usually windy but good for hunting agates or solitary walking.

Just north of here, on Seven Devils Road, is the South Slough National Estuarine Sanctuary. Established in 1974 as the first estuarine sanctuary in the nation, South Slough is primarily a research facility managed by the Oregon Division of State Lands. Recreation in the reserve's 4,400 acres includes hiking, canoeing, fishing and a visitors center with displays and literature about the history and ecology of the estuary.

Charleston

Charleston is an isolated fishing village on the south side of Coos Bay, one of the largest and safest natural harbors on the Oregon coast. Highway 101 misses the town completely and even the big boats get tugged up the bay to the busy port of Coos Bay. This leaves Charleston to make do with a 550-space small boat basin, the Oregon Institute of Marine Biology and a Coast Guard station. And parks, plenty of parks, which is why you'll want to come here.

Charleston and its parks are reachable from Seven Devils Road (if you're traveling north) and the Cape Arago Highway (if you're headed south). Both are marked turnoffs from Highway 101. The

first bead on the chain of beaches and parks out of Charleston is
Bastendorff Beach County Park. Year-round camping under tree-
shaded sites overlooking the beach is the main feature at Bastendorff. Picnic facilities and fish-cleaning tables are provided. The
beach below offers tide pools and access to the large rocks of the
south jetty at the mouth of Coos Bay.

Next up is *Sunset Bay State Park*. Here, we found an extraordinary phenomenon for Oregon: a beach whose waters are warm and
calm enough to swim in. Sunset Bay is shallow and protected from
the wind and waves by steep bluffs that form a sheltering U around
its cove. There were more people gathered at Sunset Bay than we'd
yet seen gathered on any Oregon beach (50, to be exact). Some
were even venturing up to their knees in the water. Close by is a
campground with both tent and trailer sites.

Just a short hop down from Sunset Bay is *Shore Acres State Park*.
Built on land that formerly belonged to the local lumber baron,
Louis J. Simpson, this 600-acre park is notable for its botanic gardens. Both a traditional Japanese garden, built around a 100-foot
lily pond, and a formal English garden can be enjoyed. Simpson
built a three-story summer mansion here in 1906, kind of a scaled-
down, Oregonian version of Randolph Hearst's castle at San Simeon. It burned to the ground in 1921, and a second, smaller
mansion erected on the same site fell into disrepair by the forties,
eventually being razed by the state after it purchased these lands
from the financially ailing Simpson. On these grounds the state
has built a glass-enclosed observation deck from which visitors can
watch waves, whales and sea lions in cold or wet weather. The
gardens contain a hundred varieties of rhododendron, azaleas,
shrubs and trees.

Cape Arago is the third in a string of state parks. Its circular overlook offers an impressive view of the ocean. Just offshore from Cape
Arago's rugged headland is Simpson Reef, a sandstone shelf used
as a beaching area by sea lions. The south cove is visited by fishing
boats that anchor until the tide rises enough to allow safe passage
into the harbors of Coos Bay. Picnicking beneath the leafy boughs
of spruce trees is popular at Cape Arago.

With this bounty of parks and beaches so close by, one might suppose Charleston would be a thriving, attractive village. It is not. The town reeks of fish, and there's nothing to recommend in the way of accommodations or restaurants. Apparently, Charleston cannot hoist itself up the ladder of economic opportunity. The rotting hulks of cars and trucks that barely run sputter through its dusty streets, while hulks of humanity stumble into the local candy stand for carmel corn and cream-and-butter fudge.

A chipper representative of the local visitors bureau sang the praises of the parks with conviction but hit a bum note when it came to the town. "We've got a wonderful gift shop," she enthused, adding in a whisper, "and they leave you alone!" Charleston, like much of the southern Oregon coast, doesn't appear to have any idea how to develop its immense potential for tasteful tourism in a beautiful natural setting. Too bad, because this could help lift Charleston from the morass of poverty in which it sits like a dead oyster in a contaminated bed.

FOR FURTHER INFORMATION

Charleston Information Center
Boat Basin Drive and Cape Arago Highway
P.O. Box 5735
Charleston, OR 97420
(503) 888-2311

Coos Bay

The Coos Bay metropolitan area is the largest on the Oregon coast. Some 30,000 people live in Coos Bay and its neighbor across the bridge, North Bend. Tourism, however, takes a back seat—heck, it's hanging onto the tailpipe for dear life—to shipping and industry. Coos Bay is the largest lumber-shipping port in the world, a reality that will not escape you as miles of lumber mills and shipping docks roll by.

You might accidentally drive off the road should you begin gaping at the mountains of sawdust and wood chips beside the mills,
which loom no less impressively than any of the sand heaps in the
Oregon Dunes National Recreation Area. Most of the motels in Coos
Bay face these industrial work sites from the noisy highway. If
you need a place to stay, you're better off heading up to Reedsport
or down to Bandon.

Very little that could honestly be termed scenic exists in the Coos
Bay/North Bend area. Highway 101 is a nightmare, bordered by
roadside shacks selling "Junque 'n' Whatever," a congestion of run-
down food stands and billboards such as one with a ten-foot-tall
picture of a fat-faced man and the legend, "Leon's—if you can find
a bigger burger, buy it. Biggest, juiciest burger in town." The taverns look like brawling sites, awaiting the five o'clock whistle to
signal the first round. Coos Bay is the kind of town where even
the crime, as in this account clipped from a local newspaper, is
kind of cock-eyed and dull-witted: "A man armed with a rifle de-
manded beer Monday from [a convenience store] then ran into the
woods with a 12-pack under his arm."

A few recreational side trips are possible around here. One can
drive up the Coos River to see myrtle groves and the twin, 200-
foot Gold and Silver Falls. Coos Bay is the heart of myrtle country, for whatever it's worth. More apropos, it is the southern
gateway to the Oregon Dunes National Recreation Area. Horsfel
Road, just north of the North Bend Bridge off Highway 101, is
one of the main entrances into the 41-mile federal park, which
stretches from Coos Bay to Florence.

Coos Bay and North Bend are both working towns, and there's
nothing wrong with that. The few scraps tossed the tourist's way—
the new downtown mall, for instance—have not been picked up.
Though it has the right kinds of shops and would probably do
well anywhere else, the highway swings east of the town center
and, consequently, few are steered in the direction of the mall except by accident.

Coos Bay Area Chamber of Commerce
50 East Central Street
P.O. Box 210
Coos Bay, OR 97420
(503) 269-0215

Oregon Dunes National Recreation Area

At first, we thought our eyes were playing tricks on us. To our
left, looming over the treetops, rose dunes so high it seemed impossible they could be made of sand. But this was no mirage.
The tallest dunes in the United States are found on the mid-
Oregon coast. Some of these steep-sloped sand heaps ascend to
heights of 500 feet.

A combination of factors has created the Oregon dunes over the
past 12,000 years. The process goes something like this: Sand and
sediment washed out to sea by rivers is eventually returned by
waves to the flat, shallow beaches. Prevailing winds pick up the
sand particles exposed at low tide and blow them eastward, where
they accumulate in dune formations. The growing dunes overtake
everything, even trees, in their landward march, which proceeds
at the rate of three to six feet a year. The largest ones, called
oblique dunes, are some distance back from the ocean, with fore-
dunes, hummocks, deflation plains and transverse dunes intervening. Behind these giant, stabilized dunes lie forests and freshwater lakes.

Many come to Oregon Dunes to race dune buggies. Drivers are
advised to use caution when charging up the face of oblique dunes,
but otherwise they tear all over the flat sand plains and sloping
ridges. From a distance, the three-wheeled dune buggies look like
ants scurrying around an anthill. Of course, the ant's work is far
more industrious and useful. It's somewhat maddening to see

bus-sized trailers towing these noisy sand churners into the remote parking lots of the otherwise serene Oregon Dunes. To what great lengths, what waste of fuel, will people go to have fun? But there they are, frolicking in nature's sandbox, kicking up a mess of sand and sound. These contraptions can be rented for about $20 an hour or $100 for all day. Have a ball.

Within the 41-mile park, four paved access roads lead to the beach and dunes, and there are additional trails for four-wheel-drive vehicles only. Sixteen different campgrounds are spread around the park—on the beach, in the woods and by the banks of lakes. The government has provided boat ramps, hiking and horseback-riding trails, parking lots and overlooks, all without compromising the quietude of the dunes.

The main entrance points into the park are the Horsfel Dune and Beach Access, near Coos Bay; County Road 251, out of Winchester Bay; and the Siltcoos and South Jetty Dune and Beach Accesses up north, near Florence. We spent the better part of an afternoon on *Umpqua Beach*, at the park's midsection, where we were out of earshot of the dune buggerers, content simply to walk the beach. The mist kicked up by a roiling surf covered the beach with a gauzy haze on an afternoon when the sun couldn't decide whether it wanted to come out or stay hidden behind the overcast. We thought we saw people further up the beach, but it turned out to be silvery driftwood logs with human-seeming limbs. There was no one else on the beach on a balmy July afternoon. Now, if only the water were warm enough for swimming.

FOR FURTHER INFORMATION

Oregon Dunes National Recreation Area
855 Highway Avenue
Reedsport, OR 97467
(503) 271-3611

Winchester Bay

Winchester Bay—the town and the body of water—sits at the mouth of the Umpqua River. The Umpqua is the largest river between the San Francisco Bay and the Columbia River. Salmon Harbor, dredged out of what was formerly a tidal mud flat, is one of Oregon's finest small harbors for pleasure craft. It's also home to a commercial fishing and charter boat fleet. Clustered around the harbor are a few restaurants, motels and bait shops. This quiet village, a mile or so west of the highway, is one of the gateways to the Oregon Dunes National Recreation Area. Close by is the Umpqua Lighthouse, which has been flashing its red-light warning 19 miles out to sea since 1892.

There's little to do in Winchester Bay but fish and frolic on the dunes. It's a perfect place to unwind, maybe cast the river for rainbow and cutthroat trout or head out to sea for a day of deepwater fishing. If you plan to spend a day in the dune country, you can lay over at the *Winchester Bay Motel*, a 52-unit court facing the bay. *The Oasis*, a 24-hour restaurant and lounge, will see to your dining and entertainment needs, having recently enlarged its dance floor. Their menu of food and fun includes steaks, seafood, salad bar, videogames and pool and Ping-Pong tables. Party!

FOR FURTHER INFORMATION

Lower Umpqua Chamber of Commerce
P.O. Box 11
Reedsport, OR 97467
(503) 271-3495

Reedsport

Reedsport is not on the water but this town of 5,000 is a convenient supply center and resting place for people who have come to enjoy the Oregon Dunes or some of the state parks in the area. It's got the goods and services lined up along Highway 101 in a row that practically insists you stop and do something, even if you only pump a tank of gas.

This strip is the part of town everyone sees, but there's a hidden side of Reedsport as well: the downtown or "Old Town" area. In Reedsport's case, it's not a newfangled Old Town, like so many other towns promote, but the real thing: a string of working-class taverns; retail shops that appear to be holding on by the skin of their teeth; a popular café called the *Downtowner* and other, more fossilized buildings that intimate slowly receding prosperity for this likable burgh. At one of the secondhand stores downtown, we foraged through boxes of used albums before striking paydirt—a pair of classic, out-of-print records for a buck apiece.

If you're stopping over in Reedsport, stay out on the highway but mosey over to Old Town for a meal or a beer to catch the flavor of the town behind the town.

Accommodations

Though the name seems far-fetched here in the rain forests of Oregon, we steered our vehicle into the *Tropicana Motel*. Far from being in the tropics, we were stalled in the middle of a state where the summers are cool and rain is frequent. No, it must have been the AAA sign that drew us to the Tropicana. Basically, wherever you stay in Reedsport, you'll get a basic room with a bed or two, a color TV with a grainy picture and a small bathroom with a stand-up shower stall. Nothing fancy, but Reedsport isn't exactly a resort town. Come to think of it, Oregon isn't exactly a resort state.

Restaurants

Do you crave microwave-heated beef-and-bean burritos from a gas-station mini-mart, or might your palate prefer something from *Pizza Ray and Suzy's?* Perhaps a hearty plate of home-cooked food from *Posey's Bakery and Café*, where the locals come to graze after a long day in the trenches. If you've got fried fish on the brain, point your mainsail to the *Windjammer*, a friendly chowder and seafood house.

Nightlife

Take your pick of three taverns—the *Gang Plank, Ward's Place* (so that's what became of Beaver's dad!) and the *Silver Moon*—or one cocktail lounge, the *Rainbow Inn*, which also serves food. All are directly on or within a block of 4th Street in Old Town.

FOR FURTHER INFORMATION

Lower Umpqua Chamber of Commerce
Highways 101 and 38
P.O. Box 11
Reedsport, OR 97467
(503) 271-3495

Florence
Heceta Beach

Oregon changes for the better at Florence. At least its towns start looking up a little. Though the coast itself is consistently magical in all its various guises, the towns south of Florence (with the exception of Bandon) are not places you'd want to plan a vacation around. Industry may be one of life's unavoidable necessities, but few people can get excited about a motel room looking out on smokestacks and logging trucks.

Florence lies 21 miles north of Reedsport. Between the two towns, the famed Oregon Dunes continue their tireless procession. The dunes end just south of Florence, and a more relaxed approach to coastal living begins. Florence is the last port town in southern Oregon, but the real industry here is retirement. Fully half of

Florence's 5,000 citizens are oldsters who moved here because it's so livable. "Livability" is a word used quite often in Florence. People live here by choice rather than being forced into doing so because it's the only place they could find a job. Those who do work are employed at various low-impact trades, like woodworking, fishing and tourism.

At first glance, the town looks like many others that are simultaneously blessed and cursed with intersecting major highways—car dealerships, shopping centers and a modest string of motels with misleadingly bucolic names—but the difference is that nothing growls at you on the drive through Florence. Overpowered pickup trucks don't pull out within inches of your bumper, and highway smoke and noise are toned down. The biggest problem in Florence is that some of the old folks drive too slow. And so what?

The community seems conscious of its appeal. Ask anyone why they live in or visit Florence, and they'll throw the following facts at you: The area embraces 13 lakes and the Siuslaw River, the Oregon Dunes National Recreation Area, the Siuslaw National Forest, an Old Town district, a harbor, an ocean beach and a partridge in a pine tree. The heart of the town is five miles from the ocean, built on a curve in the Siuslaw River and around the lakes. Florence's Old Town is a bit like Bandon's in that they're here simply because the town is proud of its past.

After 1936, when a bridge and highway were built through Florence, the bypassed Old Town district became a blighted area, as all the new businesses along Highway 101 were more successful at grabbing the motorist's attention than a bunch of dilapidated huts by the river. But in recent years Old Town, capitalizing on America's craving for nostalgia, has been rehabilitated and seems to be doing well now. A few neon signs have crept in—a fancy fashion outlet ("Bonjour!") and a candy shop, too—but Old Town is so compact that this sort of gilding can spread only so far. The Old Town Seafood Company is the most exciting place to go. It's a commercial wholesaler that welcomes visitors to its docks. The river is a pleasant place to stroll after an evening meal.

Florence's beach is three miles north and a few miles west of town. Heceta Beach Road takes you through a thickly vegetated area that has begun, acre by acre, to be cleared for more homes.

Heceta Beach is a quiet development, filled with fancy seaside homes made to look like large cabins. The first high-rise condo we'd seen in Oregon, Driftwood Shores, was on Heceta Beach. The beach itself is accessible only from this "condo resort." Thus, a visit to the beaches south of Florence, at one of the area's two access roads into the Oregon Dunes, might prove more rewarding.

Accommodations

We drove the length and breadth of Florence, quickly realizing that most of the accommodations were directly on the commercial corridor of Highway 101. You simply can't escape the highway here. After ducking into every motel in town, we plopped $36 on the counter at the *Silver Sands Motel*. It was a comfortable place to stay, for the price. The rest of the motels in town were not much more to look at and cost about the same. The only other options are the *Johnson House Bed and Breakfast* in Old Town and the *Driftwood Shores Surfside Resort* on Heceta Beach. Rooms at the latter are rented out by the night for more than anyone should have to pay in Oregon.

Restaurants

The best restaurant in Florence, and probably the southern Oregon coast, is the *Windward Inn*. Steeped in a local dining tradition that goes back to 1935, when it was a gas station and lunch counter, the Windward has been known by many names over the years—Adam's Apple, the Bluebird Café, Danny and Marie's Café—but has always been the pinnacle of Florence's cuisine. Today, as the Windward Inn, it is a casual gourmet restaurant with seafood the main priority. The cut flowers on the table and the restaurant's skylit, attractive wood interior set the stage for the freshly prepared food that follows. Every aspect of our meal was executed perfectly. The salad was crisp and cold, the dressings homemade. The breads were freshly baked on the premises. The charbroiled swordfish was fit for a king, as was the blackened halibut in Cajun cream sauce. And how can we adequately praise the Sea Mussels

Au Gratin Oregon (fresh mussels steamed in wine, then broiled on the half-shell with Oregon hazel nuts, Oregon peppered bacon and Tillamook cheddar cheese)? Entrées are served with wild rice and fresh vegetables. Oh, yes, since there is no nightlife to speak of in Florence, you might as well order dessert at the Windward Inn. Go for the marble cheesecake.

Also worth mentioning, in passing, is *Mo's*, located over the Siuslaw River in Old Town. Mo's is a chain of unpretentious seafood restaurants that are well-loved in this state. Oysters are the house specialty, all of them raised on a 300-acre oyster farm on Yaquina Bay.

Nightlife

Aside from *B.J.'s Ice Cream Parlor*, where you can choose from 48 homemade flavors, the only flicker of life after dark in Florence is in Old Town, where there's a tavern called *Beachcombers* and a restaurant-lounge called the *Fisherman's Wharf*. The latter is open 24 hours a day.

FOR FURTHER INFORMATION

Florence Area Chamber of Commerce
270 Highway 101
P.O. Box 712
Florence, OR 97439
(503) 997-3128

Heceta Head Lighthouse
Sea Lion Caves

The most photographed lighthouse in Oregon lies 10 miles north of Florence, just off the highway at Heceta Head. As is the case with most Oregon state park signs, the directional marker is too near the entrance to do much good to anyone who's barreling up busy Highway 101. Chances are you'll have to U-turn and come back to it. Heceta Head Lighthouse was built in 1894. The white masonry and tall spire give the lighthouse its photogenic quality. It looks the way a lighthouse ought to look. Still in operation, Heceta Head's 1.1 million candlepower beacon can be seen 26 miles out to sea. *Devil's Elbow State Park* (nearly every aspect of Satan's anatomy is saluted somewhere on the Oregon coast) is a popular beach, about a half-mile below the lighthouse at Heceta Head.

Closer to Florence is a roadside attraction called Sea Lion Caves. We'd seen brochures, bumper stickers and signs for it as far back as Northern California, mentally filing it next to Prehistoric Gardens in the "must avoid" category. The overflowing parking lot only fueled our worst fears, especially after having seen the gorgeous beaches south of here completely devoid of people on a beautiful summer day. Apparently, people go to Sea Lion Caves on their vacation, not to the beach.

Still, to be fair, Sea Lion Caves offers an authentic experience in exchange for your money. The largest sea cave in America lies just below the gift shop. For a fee, you can ride an elevator 208 feet down and then walk along the rocky ledges of a 300-foot-wide cavern. Beneath and around you, a multitude of sea lions cavort. The volcanic rock walls echo with the sounds of the sea and the unabashed squeals and yelps of the lions. It's important to note that the sea lions come indoors only in fall and winter. The rest of the time, they frolic outside on the rocks. To fill the entertainment void in the cave during the spring and summer, a host of sea birds—gulls, cormorants, auklets and more—make their nests on the cavern walls.

The management should be credited for not disturbing the animals by allowing visitors too close to them. Interpretive signs are posted along the tour route, so that the tourists learn a thing or two about the wild kingdom before returning to the gift shop.

Cape Perpetua

It's a beautiful drive north from Florence along Highway 101. After the road passes Heceta Head, it begins to rise as it approaches the massive chunk of basalt known as Cape Perpetua. This tree-covered headland shields the beaches to the south from the howling winds that blow year-round. We quickly learned that you can get blown to pieces on Oregon's northern beaches, even during the warmest months of the year.

Cape Perpetua was discovered in 1778 by James Cook, the British explorer. The *Siuslaw National Forest Center*, located nearby, will shed some light on the history of this totally deserted coastal region. Park personnel will also provide maps, directions and advice about the numerous trails that run through Cape Perpetua. The most popular way to see it is to undertake the Auto Tour, a 22-mile loop that circles the headland. You can drive to the top of the cape and then hike the "Trail of the Whispering Spruce" around its 800-foot summit. Another trail leads to the Devil's Churn and Cook's Chasm, two intriguing rock formations where the waves crash with spectacular sound and fury on stormy days and at high tide.

The approach to Cape Perpetua and the nearby town of Yachats is reminiscent of California's Big Sur, albeit scaled down to Oregonian dimensions. At one point, the highway enters a tunnel blasted through the sheer rock of the headland. The road wiggles and snakes its way up, down and around the cape for 25 dizzying miles. It's enough of a roller coaster to send most drivers to the panoramic waysides for a breather.

Several parks and waysides lie in the vicinity of Cape Perpetua. *Carl G. Washburne State Park* has a 66-site campground on one side of the highway and trails that lead down to a two-mile beach on the other. Just north are two turnouts—the *Muriel O. Ponsler Wayside* and the *Stonefield Beach Wayside*—each with paths to a scenic beach. There's a small Forest Service campground along *Rock Creek* and a beach at its mouth. *Neptune State Park* is the largest of the parks, with a 9,300-acre wilderness area that extends back into the hills. Turnoffs at *Strawberry Hill* and *Ocean Beach* offer coast access via short trails.

Yachats

Like Florence and Waldport, the towns nearest to it, the village of
Yachats (pronounced, *yah-hots*) is defined more by the surrounding
countryside. Yachats is so small you practically need a magnify-
ing glass to find it. With a population of either 450 or 560, depending on which city limits sign you believe, Yachats will not
exactly freeze you in your tire tracks. Coming around the final bend
of Cape Perpetua, you pass a restaurant overlooking the water, a
souvenir shop, an art gallery, the Pudgy Pelican ice-cream shop, a
bakery and a deli. Before you know it, a "Yachats Thanks You"
sign is waving bye-bye. Though it's as small as a sand flea, Yachats
yields real treasures to those who take the time to get acquainted.

Yachats is characterized by cool, steady winds and a pounding
surf. Its name is from an Indian word, meaning "roaring river."
From *Yachats State Park* up past *Smelt Sands State Park*, Yachats'
rocky, windblown shore is smacked by an endless barrage of waves,
unimpeded by constructed jetties or natural formations. Waves
crash through the cracks and crevices in the rocks, spewing water
and foam skyward and shaking the very earth beneath your feet.

The biggest human interest story in Yachats—other than the
one about the woman who accidentally drove her Cadillac through
the side of the post office, a tale we heard several times—has to
do with the never-ending battle between private property and
public access. It seems that years ago, after a sweeping beach-
access bill was passed by the Oregon legislature, some stubborn
local property owners decided to keep their fences up. Pedestrians were prevented from crossing the edge of the bluffs on their
land, necessitating a dangerous detour onto slippery rocks for
anyone who wished to continue exploring the lovely coastline.
The property owners, whose initial goal was simply to stem the
human trickle, have lost the battle and may wind up losing the
war. The state is planning to make this section of the shoreline
part of the Oregon Coast Trail, a popular hiking route that will
undoubtedly bring thousands more trekking across the bluffs of
Yachats.

There is a further irony. Because the fences of the property owners currently block the path, one is forced to walk along the wave-

chipped rocks. This detour turns out to be a blessing in disguise. Low tide uncovers a bounty of untouched tide pools, some of the first we'd seen that hadn't been emptied by human hands of their crabs, anemones and starfish. "Look but don't touch" is the unstated rule of tide pool etiquette, but as everyone knows, a determined tourist would steal the pope's underwear if he thought he could get away with it.

Smelt Sands Beach is the only beach that really fits the description in Yachats, and it's just a black-sand baby cove. Its appeal is the rugged setting and the mysterious running of the smelt. These oily little fish run up onto Smelt Sands on certain nights of the lunar calendar, and people with dip nets lie in waiting to snare them. This ritual dates back to Indian times. How do the fish know to come here? How do people figure out when they're coming? Why don't the fish save themselves a lot of grief and run somewhere else for a change? In 1983, they stopped running entirely for a while but have since returned. Every September, they have a major smelt fry in Yachats.

The attraction of Yachats is more spiritual than material, making it popular with sedentary, meditative sorts who come to fill their minds with nature's vast wonder. They sit in big wooden chairs at ocean's edge and stare at the waves, the sea, the sky and the rocks, listening to the roaring surf.

Accommodations

A mile north of Yachats are two motels that have long been favorites with Oregon vacationers. The *Adobe Motel* is a sizable, 58-unit lodge spread across spacious grounds overlooking Smelt Sands Beach. The *Fireside Motel* is practically next door, only a few hundred yards north. Although it doesn't have a gift shop and dining room like the Adobe, the Fireside seems more in tune with the Yachats experience. The management has put together a fine guidebook for visitors to use, pointing out the not always obvious things to do in the surrounding wilderness.

Restaurants

The two waterfront restaurants in Yachats' tiny business district violate our Menu Law, which holds that "all restaurants shall post menus out front." *LeRoy's Blue Whale*, just up from the water, also flouted this law, but in a town of 450 at 9 p.m. Pacific Daylight Time—seconds after the final pitch had been thrown in baseball's midseason all-star game—we were running out of options and hungry as starving grizzlies. Besides, LeRoy's had advertised an "All You Can Eat BBQ Rib Special" for $4.95. We got to LeRoy's one minute after closing. On this particular night, we made our dinner selections from a motel vending machine. One of us had a Snickers bar, while the other went the health-food route with Cheez Puffs.

Seriously, there are two restaurants worth noting in Yachats. The restaurant at the Adobe Motel serves an excellent variety of seafood at lunch and dinner. Breakfast here is good, too. What better way to greet the morn than from a glassed-in dining room only 50 feet from the churning sea? In town, *La Serre* serves a mouth-watering continental menu of steak and seafood items. It's not inexpensive, but true gourmet dining on the Oregon coast is so rare that it's worth splurging when you find it.

Nightlife

Some weather-beaten yokel up in Waldport was going on about a hell-raising tavern in Yachats where, the previous week, he'd seen a man so inebriated that he had ordered—and had been served—a beer while on his knees and ejected from the establishment only after he'd passed out full-length on the floor. At the same bar, he saw a man haul off and wallop someone with a two-by-four and watched yet another guy fire a .357 Magnum beside the ear of a real troublemaker in order to get his attention. In quiet Yachats? Impossible. What was he talking about? Is there a secret saloon in a hollow log somewhere around here?

Beulah's On the Rocks Lounge, attached to her *Sea View Inn Restaurant*, appeared the best place to down a civilized drink in Yachats.

When we looked in Beulah's at 10 p.m., four people were sitting around a table and a gent named Roger Meusal was tickling the ivories.

FOR FURTHER INFORMATION

Yachats Area Chamber of Commerce
2nd Street and Highway 101
P.O. Box 174
Yachats, OR 97498
(503) 547-3530

Waldport

Waldport is built on an ancient Indian burial ground. This curious choice of site gives the town no serious pause, though it probably should, mainly because back in the 1870s, when the local Indian reservation was suddenly reopened to white settlers, nobody paid any mind to small matters like treaties and burial grounds. There was no time for that, you see, because gold had been discovered on the nearby beach. After the gold rush had dwindled to the inevitable golden shower, Waldport became a no-stumps-barred lumber town.

The town's name came from the German *wald*, meaning "forest." The location on the Alsea Bay made it an ideal logging harbor. When the bottom fell out of the pine box business, Waldport had to rely on fishing. This thinned out the population of gold and timber speculators and, in a strange way, salvaged the town.

Except for its historical origins, Waldport today is as ordinary as the blackberry pie that is one of its trademarks. The three-block town center is so anonymous you could mistake it for a highway rest area. Like many of the quietly appealing port towns along Oregon's central coast, Waldport attracts people who have simply seen enough. They come here for the "relative obscurity," a phrase that even the chamber of commerce proudly employs.

Typical of this breed was the cheerful middle-aged woman who was greeting folks at the welcome center beside the Alsea Bay Bridge. She moved to Waldport 12 years ago from Salinas, California, a city of 80,000 near the Monterey Peninsula. It took her only a short while to adjust to not having every convenience store and fast-food franchise at her fingertips. "Now I don't even like to go back down there for a visit," she said.

Then there is the case of the white-haired businessman, a native Oregonian who's seen a bit of the world in his time, having been involved in the resort trade back east before the coast became too over-developed for him. He has returned to Oregon, content to temper his entrepreneurial lust in keeping with the state's less flashy self-image. "Oregon lacks something that is really hard to pinpoint," he admitted almost sadly. "But on the other hand, you have a piece of God's half-acre out here. You can't really say that about too many places anymore." Many are the times he's found himself sitting by the highway in his car, watching the sea from a scenic viewpoint as waves splash on the rocks.

Waldport is built around the Alsea River and the Alsea Bay. The bay is one of the best places in the state to nab Dungeness crabs and is also a hot spot to dig for cockles and clams. Popular with anglers and nature lovers, the river is clear and rich in salmon, despite the town's logging history. (Logging often despoils the salmon's spawning grounds.) Waldport is built around the water at the south end of the Alsea Bay Bridge, which serves as the town's signature. Constructed in 1936, it is one of the most scenic bridges in the state. The signature will soon become a forgery, however. The concrete in its pilings was mixed with the wrong type of sand and is slowly deteriorating. Even now, as a precautionary measure, the speed limit on the bridge is 35 mph and there's a weight limit for trucks. The bridge is scheduled to be rebuilt by 1990.

The beach at Waldport is on the north side of the bridge, at a development known as Bayshore. The neighborhood is mostly residential and the only motel is located on the bay rather than on the ocean, which should give some idea of the town's preference. The surf at Bayshore is too rough for swimming, but the beach is perfectly healthy, as wide as can be and a wonderful place for a leisurely hike. Facing due west, the beach derives the full benefit of sunset over the ocean.

Accommodations

Cottage units outnumber motel rooms in Waldport, proof of the town's long-term, seasonal appeal. The *Bayshore Inn*—located north of the bridge, where it looks across the bay at Waldport—is the most commodious motel in the area. At the time of our visit, rooms with a terrific view of the water were going for $40—more evidence of the bargains that await coastal travelers in Oregon. It's a five-minute walk to the ocean from here and a five-second walk to the bay. A good location at a fair price; you can't ask for more than that. On weekends, the lounge at the Bayshore Inn is packed with locals who come for the live music and the lively possibilities.

Restaurants

For those who like to mix the business of eating with the pleasure of drinking, Waldport is an accommodating town. The two best places to drink are also the best places to eat—"best," in this case, reflecting the town's limited repertoire. *Flounder Inn Tavern* serves a mean plate of broasted chicken and "jo-jo's" for $4.50. Broasting is a pressure-cooked frying process popular at taverns and drive-ins along the West Coast. Jo-jo's are fried potato slices, sometimes cut in curls or circles. To quote the waitress who was helping us decide what we wanted, it makes "quite a delightful meal." A block away, *4J's* is more of a home-style restaurant (e.g., hot roast beef sandwiches, chicken livers and gravy) than a tavern. You can get a ridiculously inexpensive full dinner at 4J's and then wander next door to 4J's Lounge to dance off the mashed potatoes and gravy. Waldport, for the record, has no franchise food joints, a fact that makes the townsfolk swell with pride.

Nightlife

Flounder Inn Tavern is as congenial a bar as you could ever hope to stumble into. The softball trophies are stashed in a glass case, the pool tables occupy a sunken area off to the side, and the casual drinking is kept within civilized bounds. The TV is always on, switched to a sporting event or, when the game has been pre-empted, to a congressional sit-com. (We watched 1987's Iran-Contra hearings all summer long.) The Flounder Inn staff is always in a fine humor, and draft beer costs only 75 cents a glass.

FOR FURTHER INFORMATION

Waldport Area Chamber of Commerce
P.O. Box 669
Waldport, OR 97394
(503) 563-2133

Seal Rock

Four miles north of Waldport is Seal Rock, a group of colorful sandstone formations where seals come to bask in the sun. Human visitors flock to Seal Rock just as they do to Sea Lion Caves down the road, but there is no admission fee charged to see the seals. When the tide is out, people have been known to clamber over to the rocks, scaring the seals away. Maybe they should rename it "Human Intruder Rock."

Newport

The British explorer James Cook, after undertaking his second voyage to the Sandwich Islands (Hawaii, et al.) aboard the *Endeavor*, bumped up against the Pacific northwest on the return trip. He was looking for a passage to the Atlantic. That he didn't find, but he did discover and name two capes on the coast of Oregon during his 1778 visit: Cape Perpetua (after St. Perpetua, an early Christian martyr) and Cape Foulweather. The latter's name is self-explanatory. Winter tempests rage off Cape Foulweather, drowning land and sea in rain and buffeting ships with winds that have been known to reach hurricane force.

Captain Cook and his crew put ashore at Yaquina Bay, a sheltered river mouth between the two capes. Ultimately, Cook did more than just map an uncharted coastline on the far side of the continent from the colonies. His travels gained the attention of Thomas Jefferson, the young nation's third president. Jefferson subsequently brokered the Louisiana Purchase and dispatched Lewis and Clark on their famous expedition. In short, Cook indirectly launched the United States on its westward manifest destiny.

Today, the city of Newport occupies the site of Cook's landing in the "new" New World. It encircles Yaquina Bay and, like a vine, has grown along the highway north of it. The symbol of the city is the grand old bridge that spans the bay. Built during the great depression with WPA funds, Newport Bridge was the final link in Highway 101, the historic route that opened the West Coast to anyone with a car. With its graceful middle arch, it's an impressive point of entry into Newport, and the city lives up to this eloquent introduction. Simply stated, Newport is one of the most appealing towns along the Oregon shore. With a population of 8,800, it is not a big city by any means, but after several weeks in sparsely populated Oregon, Newport looked like San Francisco to us.

Basically, Newport goes about its business without flashing a lot of fool's gold at the tourists. It's the home of one of the largest commercial fishing fleets in the state. Tourists are not unwelcome by any means, but you must find your own fun, whether that means relaxing in a room overlooking the beach; combing the sand for agates, driftwood and colorful Japanese fishing floats; or chartering a boat to go crabbing in the bay, trolling for bottom fish or heading into deep water for some serious sportfishing.

Few towns on the Oregon coast present themselves as tourist destinations with anything resembling enthusiasm. For its size, Newport displays more reticence than usual. Consider its bay front, which hides beneath the bridge like a troll. Along the highway, Newport is a retail area of budget motels, shopping centers, five-and-dimes, banks and convenience stores. In short, it's the usual strip-town corridor of businesses serving people on the road, though considerably more upscale than the Oregonian norm.

The area along the bay, though, is a diamond in the rough that visitors ought to seek out but often miss. This is the site of Newport's Old Town. Nearly every coast community in the Pacific Northwest that hasn't bowed under the weight of poverty has a resurrected Old Town. Signs point the way there, and a transfusion of new money brings in a lot of quaint-looking gift shops, wooden walkways, and restaurants and taverns that mine the theme of an earlier time. In Newport, there has been no such Old Town restoration. That's because it has never stopped being Old Town. It is still a real working district, with the off-loading and processing of fish being the main order of business. Old Town Newport is not a museum of nostalgicized pseudo-folklore for American Express cardholders to browse through while licking ice-cream cones.

Anyone with an appetite for the real thing ought to visit Old Town Newport. The only hitch is that it's fairly hard to find. You'd never even guess it exists, at least from the highway. The only clue is a small green marker reading "Bay Front" that points east at the intersection of Highway 101 and Hubert Street. Several right turns and one downhill plunge deposits you on Bay Boulevard, the heart and soul of Newport. Canneries, packing plants, docks, warehouses and lots stacked high with crab rings and nautical gear line the bay side of the street. Walk-in restaurants, funky bars and stores selling canned Newport seafood occupy the dry side of Bay Boulevard. One can purchase freshly caught and packed albacore or crab at several shops, not to mention bait and tackle, if you're of a mind to catch your own. Walking past the rusting, corrugated-metal storehouses and plants, one is warned by signs to "watch out for loading trucks." This is not, you realize, some Hollywood backlot version of Cannery Row.

Tired fishers and dockworkers march shoulder to shoulder with families who have found their way down here through the bewildering maze of streets. As a concession to tourism, like a bone tossed at a hungry dog to keep him away from the picnic table, there are several standard-brand tourist attractions at the far end of Old Town, including Ripley's Believe It Or Not and a wax museum. We chose not to believe it, and apparently, so does most everyone else, as they were doing slack business.

Close to Old Town is a lighthouse with a curiously brief history. The Yaquina Bay Lighthouse was illuminated in 1871, casting its light for only three years before being taken out of service. It was replaced by the Yaquina Head Lighthouse, erected a few miles north. Unique in Oregon, as it's the only one to combine a keeper's house with a light tower, the original Yaquina Bay Light and its grounds are now a state park. It can be toured for 50 cents; also on the wooded grounds are picnic tables and excellent views of the bay, the bridge and the sea.

Newport is a beach town. That is to say, it has many miles of beaches, not that there are many people out on them. How can there be, when the weather's so awful most of the time? When it rains, it pours, and it pours fully half the year. November through January is the worst, being described as a period of "continual downpour." The remaining months are only subjected to "frequent rainfall." July and August alone offer good weather—and there are no guarantees about that, either.

Checking into our motel on a gray, drizzly July afternoon, we overheard the complaint of an exasperated fellow lodger, who inquired, "Is it always foggy like this?" The desk clerk, trying to be optimistic, replied, "Yes... but it was nice at one o'clock this afternoon!" Even when the sun's shining brightly, the wind can strip the clothes right off your back. Maybe that's why the beach is so deserted.

In any case, on a sunny day the beaches of Newport are gorgeous. For the record, *Newport Beach* runs from the Yaquina River north to *Agate Beach*, on the outskirts of town. A neighborhood called *Nye Beach* is incorporated into this. Nye Beach used to be a summertime tent city, visited by folks from the inland town of Corvallis. Today, it is a village within a city, with its own small shopping district at a turnaround along Beach Drive and such cutesy boutiques as the Peerless Puffin and the Gingham Goose dotting the retail landscape.

Agate Beach is named for obvious reasons. Agates and jaspers are gathered here. These surf-tossed, semiprecious stones roll among the sand and gravel. By the time they tumble ashore, they've been sanded smooth from years of churning in the spin cycle along the ocean's floor. Beachcombers sift through gravel beds at low tide for the rounded stones. At Agate Beach, we saw quite a few amateur gem hunters hunched into the wind on the hard-packed beach. October through April is the best time to find agates, which can be collected on many of Oregon's northern beaches. Gift shops and patient individuals tumble their agates for weeks inside polishing machines until the stones are smooth and shiny.

North of town, the beaches continue. Lighthouse Road leads out to the Yaquina Head Lighthouse, the tallest and second oldest in Oregon. *Moolack Beach* is a state wayside that's popular with kite flyers. All six times we passed by over the course of a week, the sky was filled with multicolored kites, some of which could have passed for UFOs. Seven miles north of Newport is *Beverly Beach State Park*. On the inland side is a large campground (152 tent sites, 127 trailer hookups) in a forested setting. The beach is backed by sandstone cliffs from which 20 million-year-old fossils have been dug.

One Newport-area attraction not to be missed is the *Mark O. Hatfield Marine Science Center*, on the opposite bank of the Yaquina River from Old Town. It's a museum of the sea, with informative exhibits and tanks filled with all sorts of bizarre creatures from the briny deep. For sheer strangeness, nothing could touch the large octopus fanning and flailing its rubbery tentacles all over the sides of its tank. The center conducts nature walks, including birdwatching, tide-pool explorations and beach and estuary hikes.

Across the road is *South Beach State Park*. This one's a whopper, with 257 campsites beside the sea, along with picnic tables and day-use lots. Unlike state parks in California, Oregon parks never charge an entrance fee; the only tariff is for overnight camping, and even there it's $2 to $4 cheaper per night. South Beach is a wide beach with windblown riffles of sand undisturbed by human footprints. But wait, there's more....

South of South Beach lie two more state parks—*Lost Creek* and

Ona Beach. Both are good picnicking spots, with more beautiful shoreline and the only deterrent being the wind. Were we not already accustomed to such beauty from many months of continuous exposure to it, we'd probably be meditating atop an Oregon dune right now.

Accommodations

Along Highway 101, you can pinch a penny at a budget motel like the *Penny Saver*. If you're just passing through, in a hurry to get somewhere else, that would make the most sense. But if you've come to see Newport, you should stay on the ocean. The ocean-view motels are located along Elizabeth Street. The sight of the sea from these cliff-top perches will take your breath away. Forget about cable TV—you'll have your eyes glued to the picture window. Newport Beach is more readily appreciated from a room high above it than at eye level, where you risk wind whipping sand in your eyes.

You can choose from a trio of motels that sit side-by-side on Elizabeth Street. The *Whaler* is the least expensive. The *Windjammer Best Western* offers brand-name dependability. Last of all, the *Aladdin Motor Inn* has recently been renovated and expanded, with a new wing added next to the main building. A final option, on the bay east of Old Town, is the *Embarcadero*, a luxury resort with one- and two-bedroom suites equipped with fireplaces, kitchens and living rooms. There's also an indoor spa and an outdoor crab cooker.

Restaurants

A "nationally famous" restaurant chain by the name of *Mo's* has branches in six towns along the Oregon Coast, from Coos Bay to Lincoln City. They are little more than glorified shacks, but the Oregon seafood is simply and deliciously prepared and the price can't be beat. Started 40 years ago by an Indian named Mohava Niemi, *Mo's* is an Oregon institution, and the original restaurant is located on Bay Boulevard in Old Town Newport. There are, in fact, two Mo's in Newport: *Old Mo's* and, across the street, *Mo's Annex*. The former offers complete dinners of grilled fish, baked oysters, steamer clams and fried calamari for $5.95. At Mo's Annex, the same price scale applies, with the added bonus of a bay view and such interesting entrées as Barbecued Oysters—shelled oysters with a rich barbecue sauce, topped with cheese. Even an item as simple as a tuna fish sandwich has something extra going for it, maybe because the tuna was caught close by and canned next door. The seating is first-come, first-served at picnic tables, and you're urged to crowd on in and enjoy.

Newport is the purported Dungeness crab capital of the world, but there isn't much of a restaurant scene to bolster that claim. The crustacean was not even listed on many menus we surveyed. Stick with Mo's.

Nightlife

Taverns line the length of Bay Boulevard, serving the thirsty men who work on the bay and in the canneries across the street. A sign over the *Barge Inn* proclaims it the "home of winos, dingbats and riffraff," a claim we wouldn't dispute. The largest crowd was gathered down the street at the *Bay Haven Inn*. Every stool was taken and the chatter vied with the jukebox hoo-doo in an atmosphere of hard after-work drinking. The lounge at the *Pip Tide Restaurant* is where the action is after dark—and by action, we mean live rock and roll bands, crowds and a "friendly" form of legalized poker that we still don't understand, even after reading a posted explanation.

FOR FURTHER INFORMATION

Greater Newport Chamber of Commerce
555 Southwest Coast Highway
Newport, OR 97365
(503) 265-8801

Otter Crest Wayside
Devil's Punchbowl State Park

One of the scenic highlights of the Oregon coast is Otter Crest, a
453-foot promontory with a spectacular 30-mile view of the shoreline. Otter Crest and its twin, the Devil's Punchbowl, are reached
via Otter Crest Loop Road, a three-mile spur with junctions along
Highway 101.

At Otter Crest Wayside, the highest point on Cape Foulweather,
you can park in a large paved lot and snap away or visit a gift shop
on the edge of the cliff. South toward Yaquina Head, one gazes
on calm days over gentle rows of whitecaps that leave trails of foam
as they unfurl and break in the shallows of an offshore reef. Basking sea lions and countless gulls and cormorants inhabit the exposed rocks—the protruding heads of ancient lava flows.

At the Devil's Punchbowl, the sea flashes its more temperamental side. The "punchbowl" is a gaping hole formed when the roof
of a sea cave collapsed. Waves funnel in through the arch in the
bowl, swirling violently around the cauldron like a bubbling pot
of clam broth. The effect is especially pronounced at high tide.
Just south of the punchbowl a parking lot and wooden staircase
descends to a flat, sheltered beach. This is one of Oregon's more
tolerable beaches, as the wind is blocked by a wall of sandstone.
Backed by steep cliffs with deep sea caves carved into their bases,
this is a good beach for sunbathing, strolling or poking around the
caves and coves.

Though there's no town out here, Cape Foulweather can be enjoyed at leisure from the *Inn at Otter Crest*, a cushy hilltop resort
with beach access, tennis courts, rec rooms, kitchens, fireplaces
and a fine restaurant.

Depoe Bay

Every town in America, particularly those with a tourist industry
to promote, would love to brag of having the biggest, the best or

the most number of some item. Depoe Bay, however, is a study of superlatives in miniature. This village of 400 claims to have the world's smallest harbor—or, to be precise, the world's smallest natural navigable harbor. It's a pretty dinky harbor, all right. Only six acres in area, it's reachable through a narrow throat of a channel that at its shallowest is barely five feet deep. The world's smallest harbor looks like a child's backyard wading pool from the perspective of the bridge that passes over it.

Not to be outdone in the teeny-tiny sweepstakes, Lincoln City—the next town up the road—is the home of the world's shortest river. It flows a distance of 440 feet to the sea, and has the shortest name as well: the D River. In this Lilliputian part of the Oregon coast, one might think Depoe Bay would have a correspondingly small-scale approach to tourism. Wrong. Depoe Bay draws the tourists into its net in smelt-like swarms. Depoe Bay knows all too well the two things vacationers desire most: places to eat and places to shop. Throw in a little whale-watching on the side, and you've got a captive audience.

Let's stop to consider what's being peddled in the three-block heart of Depoe Bay. The ocean side of the highway is all diagonal parking spaces facing the roiling, agitated sea. Snack stands and gift shops line the other side. When Americans put food at the top of their vacation want list (which is a polled and certified fact), they don't necessarily mean *good* food. They want to stuff themselves with things that are bad for them, because they're on vacation—and isn't that what a vacation is all about? Depoe Bay answers the tourist's call for tooth rot with a full array of shops that dispense caramel corn, 28 flavors of ice cream, cream-and-butter fudge, saltwater taffy, floats and sundaes, and main-course items like foot-long hot dogs. Too much of this sort of thing makes the brain go flaky, which is the only way to explain why people were hanging around the gift shops like flies circling a garbage pail. At this point, we could take off on one of our tirades, but instead we'll simply list the gift items we saw laid out in the shop windows of Depoe Bay and let you make up your own mind. Here goes:

A plaster unicorn rearing up on its hind legs. Gaudy carousel horses mounted on a wood base. A smiling bear in a basket with a soft-sculpture parachute over its head. An ashtray in the shape of a grand piano. Leopard-skin lingerie that would make a whore blush. A pregnant teddy bear wearing a T-shirt that says "Mother-to-Be" on it. Cut-glass wall hangings of roses, robins and sea gulls. Pig figurines in aerobic exercise positions. Worker's caps with sleazy messages on them (e.g., "Ex-Wife for Sale—Take Over Payments" or a runny white smudge and the words, "Those Darn Seagulls!"). Mock Easter bonnets made of lace, crowned with cloth flowers and an arching heart made of beaded glass. "Indian Maid" moccasins. Grotesque scale-model totem poles. Enough printed T-shirts to dress a small nation. Kites and wind socks. Stuffed sea gulls. Rubber octopuses. Tubular wind chimes. Squirt guns. Depoe Bay pennants. More mugs than there are coffee drinkers in the state of Oregon. The Lord's Prayer printed on fake parchment and stood on a miniature easel. Ceramic bums, jesters and gypsies. Salt- and pepper-shaker penguins. Windmill-shaped cornflower-blue napkin holders. Desktop clipper ships. Lighthouse paperweights. Perpetual motion machines. Whales carved out of myrtle. A stone-carved scene of toothless prospectors digging for gold. A dinner plate with a hideous rendering of Dorothy and Toto traipsing the Yellow Brick Road. A wicker basket with a repulsively cute clay poodle in it. Flaming pink conch shells. Disney-character knickknack boxes. Christmas tree ornaments. Fiery Oriental serpents for the mantelpiece. And a glut of merchandise fashioned in the irksomely wry likeness of Garfield the Cat.

This is how gift land looks from where we stand—outside, on the sidewalk. Enter these crackerbox palaces at your own risk. Everything is either hanging precariously from the ceiling or stacked together so tightly that one false move could trigger an avalanche. That familiar rule of the road—"You break it, you bought it"—is the Eleventh Commandment in Depoe Bay. Though we've studied the gift-shop phenomenon at length, we're still baffled by it. Why would anyone wish to browse through mounds of junk rather than enjoy the natural surroundings?

Across the street from the gift shops is *Depoe Bay State Park*, which, we figured, ought to offer some respite from the retail onslaught. Wrong again. The "park" is really just a two-story building with an observation deck and some history and scientific facts about the area. Downstairs (say it ain't so) is a gift shop. A young couple, trying to interest their daughter in the spectacle of the sea, finally yielded to her noisy demands to be taken to the gift shop. "Okay," sighed mom, "let's go look at the junk."

Depoe Bay has been a tourist town almost from the beginning. It really didn't come into being until 1927, when the completed Roosevelt Highway (U.S. 101) made the area accessible to motor traffic. The town took its name from the Indian who originally owned the land. Because he worked at a U.S. Army depot, this Siletz Indian took to calling himself Charles Depot. Later, he amended the spelling to the more fancified and vaguely French "DePoe." The capital "P" was eventually lowercased by the postal service, and it's been Depoe Bay ever since.

Whale-watching is a large draw to the area. From December to May, gray whales can be seen hugging the shore in their annual migration from the Bering Sea to the Baja Peninsula and back. An estimated 16,000 whales make the 12,000 mile round-trip. Depoe Bay is one of the best spots on the West Coast to sit back and scan the waters for the slow-moving whales and their spouting blow-holes. In Depoe Bay, you can either watch whales or become one by overeating.

The sea off Depoe Bay is hazardous and the coast rocky, so there's not much in the way of beaches beyond *Boiler Bay State Park*, a mile north of town. We assumed the name came from the churning, boiling water; waves ricochet off the rocks, meeting incoming swells. In reality, "Boiler Bay" alludes to the 1910 wreck of a small freighter whose boiler still protrudes above the water at low tide. Two miles north of town lies *Fogarty Creek State Park*. A sandy beach flanks the mouth of the creek, and the park is suitable for picnicking and creek or ocean wading. It's also the site of Depoe Bay's Salmon Derby, which isn't a hat made out of fish but an annual picnic that draws out the whole town.

Accommodations

The *Holiday Surf Lodge* is a resort of sorts whose quiet grounds include motel units and detached cabins. In the middle is a building with a spa, sauna, indoor pool, gym and conference center—all under one roof. The location, set a short distance from the edge of the bluffs, is the real bonanza. From your window, you can watch the gray whales pass close to shore—diving, blowing and sometimes even breaching. It's quite a show, and you don't even have to leave dry land. The compound also adjoins an extensive RV park.

Restaurants

In Depoe Bay, the *Sea Hag* is the place to go for "seafood so fresh, the ocean hasn't even missed it yet," according to the menu. Fresh local salmon, oysters and clams (either a heaping bucket of steamers or a plate of razor clams) are featured. The kitchen is unafraid to experiment with more complex entrées, such as Halibut en Papillote (a sizable filet sauced with herb butter, topped with scampi and cooked in parchment) or salmon stuffed with crab and shrimp and baked in wine and herb butter. If you're packing a lumberjack's appetite, the Seafood Hors d'Oeuvres is a main course–sized appetizer with generous samplings of fried whitefish, scallops, and oysters, smoked tuna and boiled baby shrimp. The *Sea Hag* opens at 4 a.m. (you read correctly) and serves breakfast, lunch and dinner.

Nightlife

Anglers frequent a popular tavern called the *Bayside*. The lounge at the *Sea Hag* draws the landlubbers—especially when the portly proprietress accompanies the piano man with a virtuoso performance on the bottles from her post behind the bar. Spoons, whistles, buzzers, empty liquor jugs and Harpo-type horns—if it makes noise, she'll bang it or toot it. If you want a little Fellini-esque after-dinner entertainment in Depoe Bay, the Sea Hag's got your number.

Depoe Bay Chamber of Commerce
P.O. Box 21
Depoe Bay, OR 97341
(503) 765-2889

Lincoln Beach
Gleneden Beach

Lincoln Beach and Gleneden Beach are neighboring hamlets that collectively amount to a few unpaved streets, a mobile-home park and a community center. Gleneden Beach is the site of a wayside with asphalt paths that snake through cool woods to the beach. Short, orange-colored sandstone bluffs serve as the portals to a beach with charred driftwood scattered about. The loudest thing out here is the pounding surf. As usual, there are plenty of picnic tables. Picnicking in the woods behind the beach seems to be the best way to enjoy the beach in Oregon.

Gleneden Beach is also the address of one of the poshest resorts in the northwest, the *Salishan Lodge*. It is a community in itself, with 150 guest rooms in natural-wood lodges. The Salishan Lodge faces the Siletz Bay from the verdant hills behind it. Along the ocean, there's an 18-hole golf course and a 20-shop marketplace. There are no fewer than four dining spots on the lodge premises, the ritziest being the *Dining Room*. Here, you can feast on seasonal northwest delicacies—such as a mixed grill of game sausage, chicken breast, lamb chop and beef liver—and test the boundless knowledge of the wine steward, who presides over a 21,000-bottle cellar. Upon being seated, we were presented not with a simple wine list but a bound, 65-page volume. Do as we did and spring for a bottle of Pinot Noir from one of Oregon's own wineries. Oregon wines are coming into their own on the international wine-tasting scene, having begun to attract attention since the watershed vintage of 1983, and.... But we'll let the wine steward tell you all

about it and direct you to a bottle that will make your dinner a
memorable one.

Dinner for two, including appetizers, soup, entrée, dessert and
wine, will average around $75. A room at the inn starts at $94 a
night. It's expensive, granted, but as a celebration of the best
Oregon has to offer, the Salishan has no peer. They put the "Eden"
in Gleneden Beach.

Lincoln City

Lincoln City is the strip town to end all strip towns. It's eight miles
long and two blocks wide, and the main street is Highway 101.
The raison d'être of Lincoln City is to minister to the needs of
tourists—eating, sleeping, fun seeking, bargain hunting and art,
souvenir and window shopping. No industry other than tourism
exists in Lincoln City, and even as we write, the "For Sale/Zoned
Commercial" signs are going up in the few empty lots along this
overbuilt corridor. The initial nova-like burst of growth was due
to the fact that seven separate towns consolidated here in 1965.
Lincoln City is something the Oregon coast had to get out of its
system, all in one long, ugly strip. There is nothing like it anywhere else in Oregon, a state normally known for its commercial
restraint.

It's really a shame Lincoln City has been so haphazardly developed, because the town has an enjoyable beach—one of the longest and sandiest stretches in the state. It runs for seven miles, nearly
the length of the town itself. For whatever reason, the wind wasn't
blowing as mercilessly in Lincoln City as it did in towns north
and south of here. Maybe this was a fluke, but people were actually out on the beach with pails and shovels and paperbacks or
strolling comfortably in T-shirts like people do in California. The
only difference is that you can't swim in the icy water, and you
won't see anything even vaguely resembling a California girl. If
you do, she is probably from California.

In the interest of fair play, it should be noted that Lincoln City's endless shopping district has some positive points. They call the 25-mile area from Depoe Bay to Lincoln City the "art center of the Oregon coast," with 11 galleries for the art fancier to duck into and out of with a genuine hand-carved duck. Lincoln City alone lays claim to seven galleries. Most of the artwork, however, is the usual placemat–quality seascapes or glazed, lead-weighted coffee mugs. Still, here and there you'll run across something truly unexpected, like a glass blower who will give demonstrations of his technique by appointment only. Lincoln City also has a plethora of bookshops where both new and used books are sold, bought and exchanged. At first, their presence in such large numbers seems rather strange, but when you consider how little there is to do here, the reading bug makes perfect sense. Many a long hour on an Oregon beach (or motel room) can be whiled away with a dog-eared paperback.

Two state parks can be found in Lincoln City. The most interesting is the *D River State Wayside*. From here, you can watch the D River flow into the ocean. Normally, this is nothing to hop up and down about, but the D River happens to be the shortest river in the world. It runs for 440 feet out of Devil's Lake, a large body of water that dominates the eastern edge of town. The water in Devil's Lake is warmer than that of the ocean, which explains why the lake is more popular with the locals than the Pacific. This is probably a good thing, because Lincoln City's oceanfront is beset with severe erosion problems, as winter storms grind at the malleable sandstone cliffs. Signs implore you not to mess with the fragile bluffs—a message that goes unheeded, judging from the many initials carved into the sandstone—and the homes of longtime residents are mere feet from the inevitable seaward plunge. Many people, especially retirees, have begun building their dream home along the 20-mile shoreline of Devil's Lake. The lake, however, is popular with hydroboat racers and water skiers—not exactly the kind of people you want to have around when you're trying to retire in peace.

The other state park in Lincoln City is *Roads End*. The road leading to it passes a shopping center and a quiet residential area, ending in a small park with two picnic tables, some shrubs and driftwood, and a small creek emptying into the ocean.

Accommodations

Lincoln City has over 1,800 motel rooms, easily the largest number of any town on the Oregon coast. Who fills the rooms? The same people who buy the trinkets, the fudge, the ice cream and the wooden ducks. The same people who ride the Go-Karts and the bumper cars. The same people who sit in happy packs on the hard sand beach, basking in the gentle breezes. *Families*. And where families go, motel bargains are sure to follow, especially in a town like Lincoln City, which has a glut of them.

The choices range from acceptable to squalid, one place even stooping so low as to advertise waterbeds and adult movies on its roadside signboard. The *Nidden Hof* and the *Budget Inn* are two decent, economical motels located on the highway in the middle of town. Because they are not directly on the beach but an easy two- or three-block walk away, they keep their prices low—as in under $30. A longtime favorite on the beach is the *Surftides Beach Resort*. At high tide, you can practically leap in the water from the balcony of this rusty orange stalwart. Don't let the word "resort" scare you off. The Surftides is no chi-chi hot-tub haven, and the room rates fall within affordable bounds.

Restaurants

For a town with more restaurants than any other in Oregon, save Portland and Eugene, the food in Lincoln City is achingly mediocre. For instance, we were steered to a place called the *Dory Cove*, a "favorite with the locals." The location certainly was a pleasant surprise—on the residential street that leads to Roads End Wayside on the north side of town. The Dory Cove has apparently been discovered by more than the locals. It was packed, with a line out the door, when we rowed up. Inside, we found a menu filled with cheeseburger variations and fish 'n' chip platters, plus a few broiled seafood entrées that didn't look, from the evidence on neighboring plates, worth the extra money. Still, the Dory Cove is certainly homier than many restaurants we've visited. A sure bet, once again, would be *Mo's*, the Oregon chain whose northernmost franchise is here in Lincoln City.

Nightlife

From all appearances, the wildest place in town is *Cliff's*. At least, we surmised as much from the "Hot Legs Contest" advertised on their marquee. However, based on what we'd seen of the fairer sex in Oregon, the hot-legs contest entrants could easily turn out to be Dungeness crabs. We opted for the *Big "O" Pub and Grub* and the *Old Oregon Tavern*, two fine and funky barrooms in the great northwest tradition—pool tables, foosball, shuffleboard games and a jukebox. Inscribed in Gothic lettering at the entrance of the Old Oregon Tavern was this sobering quote: "There is only one like you this time on earth. This is your time. Do not waste it." Yes, sir, hurry in and start drinking.

FOR FURTHER INFORMATION

Lincoln City Convention and Tourist Bureau
3939 North West Highway 101
P.O. Box 787
Lincoln City, OR 97367
(503) 994-8378

Neskowin

The yin of Lincoln City quickly evaporates into the yang of Neskowin, a small, well-behaved village seven miles north of the end-

less strip town. Neskowin has kept the world at arm's length by
dint of its location on a loop road off the highway. A big factor is
Cascade Head—at 1,770 feet, the highest point on the Oregon coast—
which comes between Lincoln City and Neskowin. From the top
of this dramatic headland, one can look out over the Salmon River,
Lincoln City and points south. This is quintessential rain forest,
getting doused with an average of 100 inches a year.

Neskowin is nestled at the foot of Cascade Head's north face,
against a pretty beach. There are more horse hoofs than tire tracks
along the streets of Neskowin. A favorite diversion is to rent a horse
and ride it along the hard-packed, white-sand beach out to and
around a sea stack known as *Proposal Rock*, which is reachable only
at low tide. The town of Neskowin is as nest-like as its name. Its
homes are charmingly modest wooden structures with a New
England feel to them and are surrounded by plenty of trees. Those
who vacation here speak in whispered tones, hoping those who
chance upon it will keep the secret, too. Despite the community's
reticence, in recent years a 190-room condo complex has crept onto
the beach to join two weather-beaten motels. The *Pacific Sands*, the
larger of the two older motels, looked like the place to stay in
Neskowin.

Pacific City
Cape Kiwanda

Pacific City is one of the few places on the West Coast where a
boat can safely be launched from the shore. For this reason, it is
the home of Oregon's only dory fleet. It is also the southern welcome mat to the "three capes" region. To reach Pacific City, one
must turn off Highway 101 onto the less-traveled Three Capes Scenic Road, a 40-mile-long "blue highway" that takes in a trio of
coastal Oregon's most breathtaking natural wonders: Cape Kiwanda, Cape Lookout and Cape Meares.

The Pacific City Dory Fleet is not as official an institution as it might sound. Rather, it's simply a loose-knit group of anglers who work, independently, from small boats. Using four-wheel-drive vehicles, they tote their wooden, flat-bottomed dories to the sea just south of Cape Kiwanda, release them to the waves, hop aboard and zoom off in search of fish. They've been doing it exactly like this since the twenties, except that modern engines have replaced the heroic, backbreaking oar method.

The launching of the dory fleet is touted everywhere as a colorful spectacle, but there's precious little ceremony or formality to it. Most of the fishers depart in the morning, before the rest of the world is awake, and return at random hours throughout the afternoon. Depending on how the fish are biting, the dorymen may stay out until sunset, when, dog-tired, they will come crashing ashore like a small-scale D-day invasion.

Beyond the dory fleet, there are some natural sights worth investigating around here. The beach at Pacific City runs north to Cape Kiwanda, a distance of five miles. This golden stretch is the *Nestucca Sand Spit*, and it very nearly encloses Nestucca Bay like a locked gate. It is said that people surf here, but the only activity we observed on a warm summer day was some poor schmo trying to get his little three-wheeled Honda out of the soft sand.

The most scenic section of the beach is at the north end, where the spit meets Cape Kiwanda in the vicinity of *Haystack Rock*—a 327-foot-tall basaltic dome a few hundred yards offshore. (There's another, more celebrated monolith with the same name not far up the coast at Cannon Beach.) The sand collects at the foot of the cape, forming a dune so tall that by climbing it you can gain access to the sandstone headland of Kiwanda. This is a beautiful, fragile point of land. People have fallen to their deaths from the top, despite the fences and warning signs.

Hang gliders tempt fate even more than hikers by taking off from the northern side of Cape Kiwanda, leaping to their destiny in the general direction of a town called Sandlake. It and a tiny outpost called Tierra del Mar are the only other human settlements near Cape Kiwanda. The large dune fields around Sandlake, however, are subjected to *Mad Max*–style raids by the dune-buggy crowd.

Tillamook County Chamber of Commerce
3705 Highway 101 North
Tillamook, OR 94141
(503) 842-7525

Cape Lookout

The middle of the Three Capes is Cape Lookout. Its rugged headland extends seaward for 1¾ miles, with a 4-mile sand spit running perpendicular to it and pointing north toward Cape Meares.
On a clear day, from the top of Cape Lookout, visibility extends
all the way up to Tillamook Head, 42 miles away. Clear days are,
however, not all that common along the Oregon coast. Clear hours
of the day, maybe.

You'll likely encounter some rain, fog or drizzle in the course of
a typical summer day. The sun shines most frequently in September and October. If it's only drizzling or raining lightly, you'll
stay relatively dry under the thick canopy of spruce, red cedars
and hemlocks that make up the rain forest and shelter more than
150 types of birds. Facilities at *Cape Lookout State Park* include nearly
250 tent and trailer sites, 100 picnic tables and a marvelous five-
mile round-trip hiking trail out to the point.

Cape Meares
Oceanside
Netarts

Cape Meares was named for Captain John Meares, the British explorer who mapped many points along the Oregon coast in a 1788
voyage. Cape Meares' rocky top is the site of a state park. An out-
of-service lighthouse can be entered and climbed and its eight-sided

light and prismatic crystal lens inspected at close range. It's a stunted nub of a lighthouse set on the edge of a sheer headland 200 feet above the sea. *Cape Meares State Park* is a migratory bird refuge and the site of the oft-photographed Octopus Tree, a huge Sitka spruce with six branching, tentacle-like trunks that meet above the ground.

It's a short downhill drive from the state park into the town of Oceanside. Along the way, you cross Short Creek, where a short trail leads to *Short Beach*. Oceanside is a village with a few small inns and restaurants at sea level and many homes built along the hills that rise steeply behind it. Roads zigzag across the face of the slope, creating a series of tiers with houses built on them—like rows of seats in an arena—each with its own spectacular, unobstructed view of the ocean, sky and offshore stacks. About half the homes are owned by year-round residents who work in Tillamook, and the rest are second homes for wealthy Portlanders.

The town slams to a halt against the imposing rock wall of Maxwell Point—a headland that rises to a staggering height at the ocean's edge like a whale leaping out of a swimming pool. At a small state park here, you can enjoy the beach and the view of Three Arches Rocks. This offshore triumvirate of rounded peaks looks like a neat row of chocolate-covered cherries. It was one of the first designated national wildlife refuges in the country. We have Theodore Roosevelt to thank for that. In 1907, this environmentally-conscious president decided that sea birds and sea lions have rights, too.

Two miles south of Oceanside, on the gentle roller-coaster of Three Capes Scenic Road, the village of Netarts lies along the bay of the same name. Blink and you could miss it. Besides being one of the cleanest bays in Oregon, this broad, shallow bay is a favorite clamming and crabbing spot. We chanced to stay here over a weekend of some of the lowest tides on record—ideal conditions for putting on the waders and digging for razor clams. Windsurfing is also a popular bay activity.

Incidentally, a short but interesting side trip to the site of a now-vanished resort town can be made back at Cape Meares. Turn left coming out of Cape Meares State Park, and a road that is alter-

nately paved and unpaved leads to Bay Ocean Spit, a small settlement of occupied homes on the north side of the cape. From
here, a jetty runs across the bay to a deserted island. It was once
the site of a town whose optimistic founder hoped would become
a "second Atlantic City." That was back in 1912, when T. B. Pot-
ter, a Kansas City real-estate broker, bought land and developed
what was then Bay Ocean Peninsula, christening his fledgling resort Bay Ocean Park. A series of meteorologic misadventures gradually severed the peninsula from the mainland and eroded the
beach, toppling residences and businesses into the ocean. A winter storm in 1953 administered a karate chop that breached the spit
for good. The last building was washed out to sea in 1960.

Accommodations

High atop the Maxwell Point headland sits the *House on the Hill.* A
more panoramic vista could scarcely be imagined. Detached, wood-
shingled, townhouse-style units face the Three Arches Rocks. Rates
run from a modest $45 to $60 a night. (They'd get four times that
amount in California for a view like this one.) Out on unharried
Cape Meares, rooms come cheaply. A perfectly acceptable unit can
be had for a reasonable sum at the *Oceanside Motel* or *Motel Terimore,*
both on Netarts Bay. The *Antler Court Motel* is another bargain: a
homey, unassuming motel with kitchenettes and a funny-looking
dog named Boomer roaming the flowered grounds.

Restaurants

Roseanna's Café in Oceanside is the closest thing to an upscale restaurant on Cape Meares. Fresh seafood and homemade chowder
are featured on a menu whose prices top off at $13.95. The view
of the bay, from the vantage point of the linen and flower-covered
tables, makes for a romantic setting. Over in Netarts, a solid, home-
cooked meal can be had at the *Schooner.* The food is cheap enough
to inspire disbelief. Some of the dinner specials were going for as
little as $2.50—the price of dessert at many restaurants. Appar-

ently, the resort mentality—i.e., "Hey, they've got dough, so let's charge 'em plenty"—hasn't found its way up here yet. One more locally popular spot, especially for grilled crab and cheese sandwiches, is *Wee Willie's*, in the woods along Netarts Highway, between Netarts and Cape Lookout.

Nightlife

The *Anchor Tavern* in Oceanside serves a variety of domestic and imported beer in a quiet, no-frills saloon atmosphere. It's a good place to knock back a few after a day of clamming has left you cross-eyed (or simply cross).

FOR FURTHER INFORMATION

Tillamook County Chamber of Commerce
3705 Highway 101 North
Tillamook, OR 97141
(503) 842-7525

Tillamook

A brief mention is due this inland town, which is a jumping-off point for travelers on their way out to the Three Capes. Tillamook is a town of 2,000 that wants to make you say "cheese." The dairy cows that graze the countless acres of rich, rain-soaked pastureland around Tillamook supply area creameries with enough milk to produce 30 million pounds of Tillamook cheddar a year. The local cheese factory is open for tours, and don't snicker: it is the second most visited attraction in Oregon. Tillamook is cut in half by the cheese slicer of Highway 101. Once in town, follow the signs and you can swing off the conveyor belt onto the Three Capes Scenic Drive. Now you're headed in the right direction: toward the ocean.

FOR FURTHER INFORMATION

Tillamook County Chamber of Commerce
3705 Highway 101 North
Tillamook, OR 97141
(503) 842-7525

Bay City
Garibaldi

These two towns, both on the Tillamook Bay, have sizable commercial and sportfishing fleets, not to mention a few seafood processing plants. Garibaldi is right on the mouth of the bay. It is the nearest point on the coast to Portland, which lies 70 miles east, as the gull flies. Some of the best bottom fishing on the Oregon coast can be found in the ocean waters off Garibaldi, while the bay is an angler's paradise full of salmon, steelhead and cutthroat trout returning to spawn. Garibaldi is a marginally picturesque bay town, worth a lunch stop, maybe—unless you're an Oregon angler, in which case it will probably keep you hooked for days. We, however, were most intrigued by a sign in front of a Garibaldi health-food emporium: "Fungus Under the Nails? Try Tea Tree Oil."

Rockaway

Rockaway is a beach town. It seems odd to put those two words together in Oregon, which lacks beach towns in the sense that California, New Jersey, Frankie, Annette and the rest of the world understand the term. But the beach at Rockaway is large—seven flat and sandy miles—and there's a town running alongside it. Admittedly, it's a fairly generic beach town—no frills, no thrills and as plain as a brown paper sack—but it was nice for a change to romp on a wide, breezy beach.

The capital city of Portland supplies Rockaway with a modest trickle of visitors, and others happen through while driving along the Oregon coast. However, because the road from Portland to Cannon Beach and Seaside, which lie to the north, is more direct, Rockaway winds up playing second fiddle (or is it third?). The whole town looks a bit like something you might examine at a flea market and consider buying until a frayed corner or a stain dissuades you. It just lies there by the side of the highway, like a sleepy garter snake, waiting for unsuspecting tourists to stumble onto it.

After spending the better part of two days here, we still don't know what to say about it, because it leaves no aftertaste and only faint memories: of railroad tracks, of a cavernous brown bowling alley, of humble wood homes with cracked, fading paint. Poking our heads into the Lion's Club Hall one evening, we watched a roomful of senior citizens playing Bingo for a cash prize. Surveying the town from a second floor balcony, we spotted a denim-clad, leather-faced character shuffling down the street. "See that guy?" a Rockaway native said, shaking his head sadly. "Nobody in the world can fry up a mess of fish like he can. He's got a real drinking problem, though."

On the beach, kids were pedaling tricycles all over the vast sand flats. Even with a fair number of people out in the sun and on the sand, it seemed uncrowded. Rockaway Beach is gorgeous. A formation of offshore rocks, one of them a perfect arch, is the town's most recognizable symbol. Sometimes, a west wind blows a curious-looking creature onto the beach. A jellyfish relative, it looks like an oyster shell with a translucent sail attached to it. They're nature's own windsurfers, in other words. They had washed onto the shore by the hundreds, and puzzled beachcombers crouching in the sand were asking one another if they could identify the strange creatures. No one could. The scientific name is velella, though they're more commonly known as by-the-wind sailors.

Generally, people come to Rockaway in the summer to enjoy the beach, while spring and fall bring out the serious anglers. Rockaway is located between two bays, Tillamook and Nehalem, both of which have long jetties that are popular with fishers. Clamming and crabbing are big here, too. It's almost assumed that you've come to Rockaway to fish your blues away, which is why most motel rooms come with kitchenettes. They figure you're going to fry, broil or steam your daily catch.

Seen in this light, Rockaway's unhurried pace and lack of diversions is nothing to get upset about. You'll find no high-octane vacation theatrics here. We fondly recall Rockaway as the first beach in Oregon where we could strip down to swimsuits in the hope of getting something resembling a tan. The sun was shining warmly in a clear blue sky, the sand was golden and the days were long, and it was all a very welcome sight to our sore eyes. Late in the day, the slanting rays of the setting sun bathed the beach in a warm red glow, and all of a sudden, Rockaway seemed a very special place indeed.

Accommodations

Most of the motels on the beach in Rockaway charge around $60 a night, which is high for Oregon and reasonable in any other state. The nicer motels—the *Rockaway Beach Resort* and the *Silver Sands Motel*—are situated right on the beach, look fairly new and come with fireplaces, kitchens, cable TV and pool. If you choose to economize by staying at one of the motels across the highway, you might pay only half as much but you'll be more than twice as uncomfortable. In fact, you might not sleep at all.

Learn from us; we suffered so that you won't have to. We stayed at one place, which shall remain nameless, where the soundproofing was so bad we could hear every trivial utterance in the room next door, not to mention the 4 a.m. clomping of the fishers making their way to the beach to capitalize on the clamming opportunities of a lunar tide. This we could have lived with. But the stench put off by several rooms full of sweat-soaked old furniture, vile disinfectants, and the cumulative BO of the 1,001 Oregon heavyweights who had preceded us was sufficiently noxious to half-convince one of us that he'd actually suffered brain damage during the night. Yes, in Rockaway, it pays to go the extra mile and cough up the extra money.

Restaurants

Though they haul a bounty of seafood from the ocean around here, Rockaway's restaurants prefer to hype their hamburgers, chicken and steaks. At the *Beach Pancake House*, for instance, they promote the specialty of the house in big wooden letters on the front of the place. Curiously, it is not pancakes but chicken 'n' dumplings. And, to tell the truth, they do serve a fair plate of chicken 'n' dumplings, though we're not wild about the dish. At *Lake Lytle Restaurant*, on beautiful Lake Lytle, we heard the cook openly complaining that the clientele didn't order enough of his steaks. At *Kelly's Bar and Grill*, they brag that their omelets are world-renowned. That leaves only *Karla's Krabs*, with its nominal emphasis on seafood, as the place to go for Dungeness crabs and other oceanic delights.

Nightlife

Kelly's is a two-sided complex with a coffee shop and restaurant on one side and a lounge with occasional live entertainment on the other. Beyond this, Rockaway has the usual handful of shotgun taverns. Perhaps illustrative of the correlation between unemployment and drinking, one watering hole was packed full of elbow benders at nine o'clock on a Saturday morning.

FOR FURTHER INFORMATION

Rockaway Beach Chamber of Commerce
P.O. Box 195
Rockaway, OR 97136
(503) 355-8108

Nehalem Bay
Manzanita

Leaving Rockaway, Highway 101 bounces around the backside of Nehalem Bay, passing through a few snoring villages until it pulls into Nehalem, a town of 250 fully awake citizens, judging from the full attendance at the local tavern at ten in the morning. Nehalem Bay is a small, lamb chop–shaped body of water tucked behind a spit of sand. Just west of town, *Nehalem Bay State Park* allows visitors to fully explore both the bay and the ocean. Bay lovers go after crabs all year round, dig for clams in season and fish from skiffs. Though fewer in number around here, ocean partisans have a four-mile beach to play on, which extends from the end of the spit to distant Neah-kah-nie Mountain. The mountain's name is half-Spanish and half-Indian, and no one knows for sure what it means. Perhaps it means "pot of gold," because Spanish sailors supposedly buried some of their plunder here, and never-say-die treasure hunters still search for it.

The setting of Nehalem Bay State Park could not be improved on—unless, of course, the ocean water suddenly reached 75 degrees, the wind died down and the currents weren't poised to drown the heedless swimmer. But with the bay in back of you, the blue-green ocean in front and driftwood and sea oats creating a pastoral effect, who's complaining? Nehalem Beach runs into the beach at Manzanita, a pleasant town half-hidden in the green hills just north of here. The beach is known as *Neah-kah-nie Beach* or, alternatively, *Manzanita Beach*.

Manzanita is a neat, orderly little community, more of a summering haven than a year-round resort town. There's a golf course in the area, a few restaurants, a gas station on the highway, and best of all, one fine motel, the *Sunset Surf*, right on the lovely beach. If we weren't in such a hurry to get to Cannon Beach—the "Queen of the Coast"—we might've lingered in Manzanita for a while. Just north of Manzanita, off Highway 101, you can catch one last blissful look at Nehalem Bay from the *Neah-kah-nie Wayside*. It's one of the most beautiful vista points on the coast. Looking west from this dizzying height, you feel as if you can see all the way to China.

Oswald West State Park

Oswald West State Park could easily serve as a religious shrine for those who worship at the altar of public beach access and an uncluttered shoreline. Stretching north from Neah-kah-nie Mountain to Arch Cape, the five-mile park is named in honor of Oswald West, the governor of Oregon from 1911 to 1915. In 1913, West bulldozed a landmark bill through the Oregon legislature that declared all the state's beaches to be public thoroughfares and prohibited the sale of any land between the high-tide line and low-tide line. This bill was a forerunner of the public-access bills that were passed, up and down the West Coast, in the late 1960s. President Theodore Roosevelt lauded West for being "intelligently alive to the beauty of nature," and the state park named for him is certainly equal to Roosevelt's praise.

Near the park entrance, a posted map clearly illustrates myriad hiking trails for the inveterate wanderer. The shortest and least demanding follows a creek down to *Short Sand Beach*, a wide, protected cove tucked between Neah-kah-nie Mountain and Cape Falcon. If you enjoy camping, there are few more appealing beach campgrounds than the 35-siter just off the beach trail. Protected by and embedded in a thick forest that's off-limits to recreational vehicles, it might be described as semiprimitive. You carry in your camping gear using state-provided wheelbarrows.

Just north of Short Sand Beach is a second monument to a beach-access activist. This one, the Kramer Memorial, is dedicated to, of all things, a writer. Matt Kramer was the Associated Press reporter whose detailed coverage of the 1967 Oregon beach bill caused such a public uproar that the legislature felt compelled to guarantee access to the dry-sand area of the beach (from the high-tide line to the vegetation line). It's more important than it sounds. The law, in effect, ensures the stability of the most fragile layer of the continental shelf. Every American state with a coastline could use a law like it right now, before the whole beach collapses under the weight of one too many Hiltons, Holiday Inns, Sheratons, Marriotts and condominiums.

Cannon Beach

Cannon Beach is the cultured pearl plucked from the hardened shell of the Oregon coast. Here and there along this impoverished state's shoreline we'd noticed tiny pockets of upper crust—flecks of it can be found in Bandon and Manzanita, for instance—but only in Cannon Beach are refinement and good manners allowed to roam freely. Cannon Beach is an arty seaside village filled with galleries, antique shops, bistros, bookstores, wine-and-cheese delis and tasteful, expensive architecture. It is not—nor has it ever been—a logging town, a fishing town, a hunting town or a working-class town.

For the record, Cannon Beach derived its name from a cannon that washed ashore here. The armament came off the *U.S.S. Shark*, a warship that, like many other vessels, ran aground at the mouth of the Columbia River. The area was first spied by a white man's eyes when William Clark (of Lewis and...) moseyed down from Fort Clatsop in 1806 to purchase some whale meat from the Indians. He named the area Ecola, the Indian word for "whale," but the name did not stick—to the town at least. Ecola Point, however, is the name of the headland just north of here.

The year-round population of Cannon Beach is only 1,215, but in the summer it swells tremendously to accommodate Oregonians who want to find the finer things in life laid out for them at the beach. Many visitors travel 80 miles from Portland, a large city with its own growing pains, and expect the same amenities waiting for them in a more relaxed setting. Cannon Beach has done an amazing job of maintaining its high standards while trying to deal with swelling numbers. The result of the human currents that collide here—the year-round residents and the itinerant vacationers—is a well-manicured business district and some quiet residential neighborhoods that zealously guard their privacy. The townsfolk have met the inevitability of growth by keeping the architecture scaled within wood-shingled, Cape Cod–style parameters. Even the local gas station looks like the front of an Aspen ski lodge.

Cannon Beach has been able to grow steadily and maintain a modicum of taste because of its location on a long loop road off

Highway 101. The only traces of the town to be seen from the highway are the directional signs pointing toward it. Because it lies off the beaten track, Cannon Beach has been spared the commercial treadmill. Entering from the south, you'd never guess you were approaching one of Oregon's most popular seaside resorts. From Tolovana Park to the business district of Cannon Beach, the loop passes large homes and toned-down motels for a few miles before reaching town. Even in the heart of downtown, the stores are understated in muted gray and brown tones and weathered wood. The most garish spectacle in Cannon Beach is the Bermuda Triangle of tooth decay that occupies its very heart: Bruce's Candy Kitchen, Osburn's Ice Creamery and the Cannon Beach Cookie Company. All three establishments are chock full of nutty families on the verge of insulin shock from a combination of sugar cones, chocolate chips and "sea foam." If a bartender can legally cut off a customer who's had too much to drink, why can't the same well-meaning courtesy be extended to the 350-pounders in the sweet shoppes who have obviously had too much to eat?

Turning away from the retail world and entering the natural one, a visitor to Cannon Beach will find a wide range of gorgeous settings. The locals, in addition to having saved their town, have saved the land that surrounds it. At the midpoint of the seven-mile beach rises Haystack Rock, the third largest coastal monolith in the world. It shoots 235 feet above the surface of the water and is joined by some shorter, skinnier spires called the Needles. Collectively, these rocks visually anchor the town. Haystack Rock is a protected bird rookery. At low tide, you can climb over the small slime-covered rocks at its base and explore the tide pools. Just after sunset, in the waning minutes of light, Haystack Rock is an impressive sight. The late afternoon winds have died down and the birds demonstrate their takeoff and landing techniques, leaping from nests atop the monolith and hanging in frozen glory among the air currents.

If you really want to walk, wait until low tide and head south. After coming to the end of Cannon and Tolovana beaches, you can, when the tide is out, hike around the next three points—Silver, Humbug and Hug points—and discover a beautiful, secluded cove around every bend. The beaches extend in this manner all the way to the small community of Arch Cape.

People allegedly go swimming at Cannon Beach. There's even a tall, red lifeguard station near Haystack Rock, which would appear to be evidence of this. Really, though, the water is too cold for anything other than wet-suit surfing, and the wind often makes the beach uncomfortable to walk on, even if fully clothed. It's hard to imagine what emerging from the frigid surf in a dripping wet swimsuit might feel like. The paradise of Cannon Beach is slightly diminished by these winds. Rarely letting up, they blow the dry sand landward at such a clip that it actually causes a humming sound. This powdery deluge is known as the "singing sands" effect. In winter, people come to Cannon Beach to watch the storms and listen to the sand—from the warmth of a room with a fireplace and a beach view. Cannon Beach has one of the highest annual rainfalls in the United States—almost 80 inches—which is another debit in the ledger.

Still, people have their fun flying kites on the beach in the summer months. A seemingly innocuous pastime, kite flying is serious business at Cannon Beach. Kites as large as the space shuttle are tugged around the sky, and these aerial contraptions can easily nose-dive directly at your head, so be careful. Sandcastle sculpting is another activity pursued with great vigor here. A sandcastle festival is held each June. Hundreds of contestants and thousands of spectators flock to Cannon Beach to witness the amazing array of shapes and creatures that are sculpted in the hard, wet sand— all of which are washed away by the next high tide. The winning sculpture in the most recent competition was of a large fish playing a piano.

As if to compensate for the weather, Cannon Beach has turned inward, becoming something of a literary and arts center. Each summer, the town opens its doors to students of the Haystack Program of the Arts. This adult-education program brings in nationally known instructors to teach workshops in writing, music and the arts. In December, the entire town participates in a Charles Dickens Festival, which culminates in a dramatic performance at the Coast Theatre, a much-acclaimed venue.

Accommodations

Because Cannon Beach encourages people to visit but not to wear out their welcome, plenty of overnight accommodations are available. They run, at well-spaced intervals, between Tolovana Park all the way up to Ecola State Park. Lodgings are directly on the beach or within an easy walk of it. They range from cute cottages to luxury oceanfront hotels. The *Blue Gull* and the *McBee Motel* are quiet, cozy places, far enough from the traffic flow to ensure privacy but close enough to town to be convenient. The cream of the crop on the oceanfront is the *Surfview Resort*. This luxurious wooden lodge overlooks Haystack Rock. It is a mile from the retail district, its isolation allowing it to harmonize with the splendid setting. The rooms are more like suites, equipped with fireplaces and logs in case the beach is too cold and windy to walk on. The Surfview also operates its own dining room and lounge across the street.

Restaurants

We bypassed the vaunted gourmet restaurants of Cannon Beach and headed straight to *Dooley's West Texas Bar-B-Que* and the *Crab Broiler*, simply because we liked the names. Both are north of town, with the Crab Broiler actually some distance out of town, between Cannon Beach and Seaside on Highway 101. Dooley's can be recognized by the smoke and aroma of its mesquite grill. The restaurant is the product of a marriage (literally) between east Oregon and west Texas, the two partners keeping it all glued together with some tangy barbecue sauce and hearty helpings of ribs, chicken, beef brisket, red-hot chili and Frito pie. The Crab Broiler is a different story. It has been a roadside favorite since 1938. The Barbecued Crab Sandwich (with cheese) is a real crowd pleaser at lunch and dinner. Crabs Au Gratin is a can't-miss item, too. Between local word of mouth and national media attention, the Crab Broiler does a substantial business.

Nightlife

The nightlife in Cannon Beach is as toned down as the architecture. In one bar, taped classical music drowned out the conversation. After surveying a few other enclaves of wine sipping, we found our footsteps leading to *Bill's Tavern*, a friendly pub with a pool table, dartboard, wood stove and "beer garden"—the latter consisting of a few lawn chairs stuck out back for the short summer season. Bill's is large and popular, hosting live rock and roll on weekends. If you missed a meal along the way, you can get homemade chili or a burger at Bill's. You can even combine the two and order one of Bill's personally guaranteed chili burgers.

FOR FURTHER INFORMATION

Cannon Beach Chamber of Commerce
201 East Spruce Street
P.O. Box 64
Cannon Beach, OR 97110
(503) 436-2623

Ecola State Park

At the north end of Cannon Beach, stretching for seven rugged miles up to Seaside, is one of Oregon's most heavily visited state parks. At 1,300 acres, Ecola State Park annually attracts 200,000 visitors. The reasons are obvious. The park lies midway between two of Oregon's most popular beaches, and within a two-hour drive of the Portland area, where over half the state's population resides. Also, the park embraces one of the most beautiful stretches of undeveloped shoreline on the West Coast.

Starting at Ecola Point and moving around the massive headlands at Indian Point and Tillamook Head, the park offers magnificent views and terrific hiking. Most people content themselves with a stroll out to Ecola Point, which yields an incredible view south past Crescent Beach, Haystack Rock, Cannon Beach and

Arch Cape—all the way down to Neah-kah-nie Mountain. Just below the point, snarling waves pound on the rocks, and sea lions
can sometimes be seen basking in the sea spray like woolly vacationers. From this vantage point, one of the most forlorn spectac-
les on the West Coast can be seen. Tillamook Rock is a chunk of
stone jutting out of the water several miles from shore. On top of
it is perched a 100-year-old lighthouse. So rough are the waves
out here that supplies had to be delivered to the lighthouse keeper
on steel cables from a firmly anchored ship. In 1957, the lighthouse was finally abandoned to the harsh realities of the elements.
Now, Tillamook Rock and its lighthouse have been transformed
into the Eternity at Sea Columbarium, from which cremated human remains are scattered.

Crescent Beach is reachable by a trail just south of Ecola Point. It
is far more secluded than Cannon Beach. Even more isolation can
be found along the six-mile stretch of the Oregon Coast Trail between Ecola Point and Seaside. Along the way, you will cross
Indian Beach, a site where Indians once buried precious artifacts.
Today, it is one of the few good surfing spots in Oregon.

Seaside

Seaside is Oregon's only boardwalk town. It is the only boardwalk town north of Santa Cruz, California, for that matter, and
definitely an anomaly in a state that is more boarded up than
boardwalked. Yes, they actually want you to come here, having
spruced up Seaside in a major redevelopment face-lift bent on attracting new convention and tourist business—without compromising the town's character. The welcome mat has been laid out, and
you are invited to shake the sand off your flip-flops and have a
good time.

Unadulterated fun is a rare commodity in Oregon. They may
have launched an "Oregon Comeback" campaign from the governor's office, spouting slogans like "Positively Oregon," but so far
that attitude is more in evidence on the drawing board than on the
beaches. Seaside is different. The entirety of Broadway, the main

drag through town, is devoted to having a good time: buying things, playing games, eating, strolling, browsing and looking at people. It is lined with shopping arcades, indoor malls, game rooms, restaurants, taverns and gift shops—even an aquarium and a museum. The pride and joy of Seaside is its civic center, which hosts concerts, pageants and conventions, pumping up the local economy to a healthy state that no other town on the Oregon coast, save Cannon Beach, even approaches.

Broadway ends at a turnaround that is the heart and soul of Seaside, as its retail district and boardwalk meet here. The circle has been officially designated the end of the Lewis and Clark Trail. In the winter of 1805–1806, William and Meriwether ran out of land here at Seaside. They came down from Fort Clatsop, their winter encampment on the mouth of the Columbia River, 15 miles north. Members of the expedition set up a salt cairn, boiling seawater nonstop for seven weeks to produce four bushels of salt for the trip back east. Imagine what Lewis and Clark might think if they were beamed down for a few moments to see what the end of their trail looks like in the 1980s. The concrete turnaround, facing the boardwalk and seawall that runs along the beach, is a favorite nesting place for urban teenagers on vacation with their parents. A lot of hanging out gets done by what looks like a throng of extras from a music video.

The nicest feature of Seaside is the boardwalk—also called the Promenade, or "Prom" for short—which runs for two miles. The beach is broad and gently sloping, running from the base of Tillamook Head to the mouth of the Columbia River, a distance of 15 miles. One of the few lifeguard stands in Oregon is manned on summer weekends, and people splash around and even surf on warm sunny days. Some playground equipment is also provided on the beach—further evidence of good intentions toward the tourist.

A feeling of vitality pervades this city of 5,000, which continues to generate new ideas for improvement. Under construction is a park along the Necanicum River, which meanders through the center of town and is bridged at numerous points. The half-finished park includes a planked boardwalk, boat docks, benches, shops and restaurants. The canal-like feeling of this lazy river is accented by the presence of brightly colored paddleboats in the water, which can be rented by the hour. Meanwhile, back at the beach, even the Prom has a feeling of newness about it, though it was constructed way back in 1921. The mere presence of a boardwalk was cause for celebration to our fun-starved eyes. Whatever it is they've got here in Seaside, the Oregon coast would do well to catch it.

Accommodations

There's plenty of room in Seaside—something in the neighborhood of 30 hotels and motels where you wouldn't mind laying your head for the night. The choicest of these are right on the beach, with back-door boardwalk access. In this category, the *Hi-Tide Motel* and the *Shilo Inn* are the top contenders for your vacation dollar. The Shilo Inn is a large convention and banquet-style hotel right on the circle, with an indoor swimming pool and an on-premises restaurant. The Hi-Tide Motel is a few blocks south of Broadway on a quiet street. Rooms include kitchenettes, gas fireplaces and an ocean view.

Restaurants

Culinary sophistication is not really Seaside's strong suit. They really like pizza here, as four pizza joints are clustered along Broadway. Sandwich and snack stands abound at the several indoor malls. As Seaside is basically a family town, family-style restaurants predominate, with predictable and affordable menus that lean heavily toward fried seafood. *Dooger's Seafood* is a cut above the norm, preparing Dungeness crab legs, razor and steamer clams, local oysters and sautéed shrimp with a dash more panache than, say, the *Pig 'n' Pancake* (which boasts of serving 35 different types of breakfast 24 hours a day...ecchh). If you want something a bit unusual, seek out *Gran'ma Jeano's "Flutter Bye."* It's run by a wizened old country woman who brought her Kentucky family recipes west and set up a lunch and dinner house in Seaside. She's known for her heapin' helpin's of baked turkey, fried chicken and buttermilk biscuits. Roll over, Colonel Sanders.

Nightlife

Two places in town—the *El Toucan*, a Mexican restaurant with a lounge in back, and the *Filly Lounge*—have live bands on week-ends, mostly Top Forty cover acts with blown-back Van Halen hair and comical rock and roll stud outfits that could have been salvaged from a circus liquidation. The people who prowl these places are mainly local working stiffs and a smattering of party animals from the surrounding boondocks (places with names like Elsie, Jewell and Birkenfeld). Judging from the girth and black-ened teeth of some of these characters, the shift in mood from mirthful to mirthless can transpire in the time it takes to throw back a shot of rotgut and has nothing to do with reason.

The streets are really where the action is, as the healthier look-ing, well-togged teenage progeny walk back and forth, slurping ice-cream cones and trading quips with members of the opposite sex when clumps of each pass one another. Cars rev their engines and circle the circle for no other reason than it's there. A guy who grew up in Seaside volunteered this assessment of the Saturday night rites at the turnaround: "Red car...shiny whitewalls... searchin' for the puss," he explained with a sly grin that revealed missing teeth. "You see, you crank down the top, turn up the mu-sic and sooner or later some pretty kitty comes along, going, 'Oh, what a nice car.'" Guy opens the door, girl climbs in, and as Bryan Ferry once sang, "You can guess the rest."

As for the bars and taverns of Seaside, it's pretty much a stocked pond of losers. At one place, we could almost feel the working-class frustrations mounting to an inevitable crescendo of motive-less fisticuffs. Even the girls were cussing like troopers. One table left behind a half-eaten pizza. Twenty minutes later, two guys with Fu Manchus and scuffed workman's caps happened upon this by-now-cold pizza surprise and acted as if they'd just discovered the

Comstock lode, devouring it hungrily with absolutely no idea who'd been gnawing on it before them. When the pool cues began striking the balls with a little too much force and the conversations took a suddenly ugly turn, we backed out. On the sidewalk, an entire watermelon lay splattered in front of the place. On this, our last night in Oregon, we couldn't resist tempting fate a little. Maybe all those weeks of being around ornery lumberjacks had gotten to us, but we picked up a big, dripping hunk of melon and lobbed it inside the tavern, in the direction of the pool tables. And then ran for our lives.

FOR FURTHER INFORMATION

Seaside Chamber of Commerce
7 North Roosevelt Street
P.O. Box 7
Seaside, OR 97138
(503) 738-6391

Gearhart

Gearhart is a small residential community just north of Seaside, pressed up against the beach like a nursing kitten. The majestic beach that runs for 15 miles without interruption from Tillamook Head to the Columbia River passes in front of Gearhart. There are beach access points in town and at nearby *Del Ray State Beach*. Gearhart is little more than an intersection with a gas station, grocery store, motel and some nice homes spread out among the surrounding streets. It is a peaceful, appealing small town by the sea. Out on the beach, about a mile away from town, a few condominium resorts have gone up along a golf course. Rooms can be rented by the night, as in a hotel, making Gearhart a viable option for anyone laying over in the Seaside/Cannon Beach area.

Fort Stevens State Park

The largest state park in Oregon is located in its northwest corner. Fort Stevens was a military installation built by the Union Army as a defense against Confederate incursions up the Columbia River during the Civil War. (And you thought this was only a war between the north and south.) It saw active duty through 1947. In fact, the Japanese fired upon it during World War II.

Today, this former military reservation is open for civilian inspection. Thirty different batteries, buildings and stations can be walked through, and a museum and interpretive center recount the fort's near-century of service as our nation's sentry along the strategic Columbia River. History aside, Fort Stevens is also a sizable nature park, with 603 campsites, seven miles of paved bike trails, several picnic areas and sandy-shored *Coffenbury Lake*, where people swim and lie out in the sun. There's a whale of an ocean beach out here, too. At the foot of the dunes, spaced about a mile apart, are four lettered parking lots. The beach runs up to the Columbia River bar, a fine fishing spot, and the remains of the *Peter Iredale*, a four-masted schooner that met its end in a winter storm, have been rusting offshore since 1906.

Having made it out to Fort Stevens, we gazed across the four-mile river mouth at Washington State. On the far side of the Columbia River lie some of the longest uninterrupted beaches in the country.

Astoria

Astoria claims to be the first permanent white settlement in the Pacific northwest. This town of 9,600 has roots that date back to the fur-trapping days of the early 1800s. With the signing of the Boundary Treaty of 1846 between the United States and Canada, Astoria became the first city west of the Rocky Mountains with a U.S. post office. Today, it's a thriving port city. Its museums and Victorian neighborhoods, dating from the glory years of the timber and salmon industries, attract their fair share of tourists. As far as we were concerned, though, Astoria was strategically important because of its four-mile bridge, linking Oregon and Washington. Ready to move on, we handed our $1.50 toll to the geezer in the booth and pressed the accelerator to the floor.

FOR FURTHER INFORMATION

Astoria Chamber of Commerce
No. 1 Portway Avenue
P.O. Box 176
Astoria, OR 97103
(503) 325-6311

Washington

Although seemingly self-deprecating, "Welcome to the OTHER Washington" is the slogan used to promote tourism in the West Coast's smallest state. Presumably it is meant to convey the frustration of a state that is sick and tired of being mistaken for our blunder-filled nation's capital. Though we can certainly sympathize with them, we understand the confusion after a lifetime of being bombarded with Washington, D.C., in classrooms, on currency and every night on TV. The White House and the Washington Monument cast a long shadow, all but burying Washington State in semiobscurity. What do most people really know of our northwesternmost state but Seattle, Puget Sound and Mount St. Helens?

We'd be remiss after our travels if we merely stated the advantages of Washington State over Washington, D.C., as a place to vacation. Instead, we feel compelled to sing our praises, shout them from atop Mt. Rainier, send them up in Mount St. Helens smoke signals, if need be. Take our advice. Get out of the crowds, the smog, the heat and the humidity, and take refuge beneath the cool umbrella of an Olympic Peninsula rain forest this summer. Hike the deserted beaches of Washington's underrated Pacific coast. Get lost in the islands of the Puget Sound.

Washington's coastline offers one surprise after another. Have you ever heard of Kalaloch? It's just about the most beautiful, isolated beach in America. How about Long Beach? No, not the Southern California city where the *Queen Mary* is docked. We're referring to Long Beach, Washington. It's only the longest beach in the world: 28 uninterrupted miles of sand along a sparsely pop-

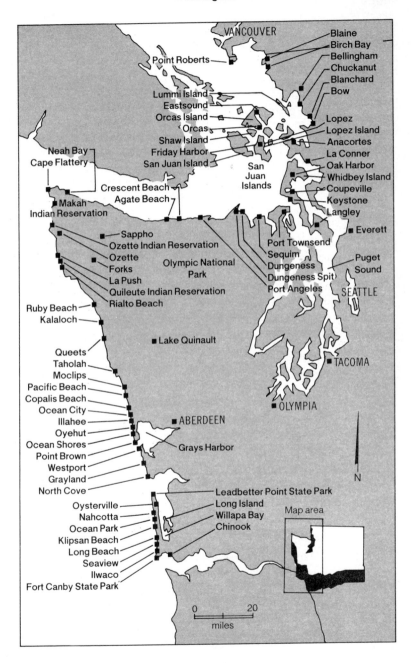

ulated peninsula. Okay then, try the San Juan Islands on for size.
They are not anywhere near Puerto Rico. They lie northwest of
Seattle in the frigid waters of the straits and sounds that divide
the United States and Canada. State-run ferries carry cars and
passengers to four of the largest of them, and if you own a boat,
all 172 of these green gumdrops are fair game for your wandering rudder.

Washington State is a mystery to most people and a fascinating
study in contrasts. Most of the state is rural and, east of the Cascade and Olympic mountain ranges, agricultural. There, the weather is mostly sunny and relatively dry. But despite the climatic
advantages of the state's interior, three-quarters of Washington's
population of 4.4 million choose to live in the foggy, rainy, cool
wedge around Seattle. Certainly, shipping has a lot to do with it;
Puget Sound and the Strait of Juan de Fuca are the closest U.S.
ports to the Far East and some of the most heavily trafficked waterways on the West Coast. Like a mythical giant, Seattle continues to grow in all directions—its skyscrapers shooting upward, its
suburbs sprawling out toward Mt. Rainier and the Canadian border, its piers extending over the waters of Puget Sound. Unlike
most boomtowns, however, Seattle harbors a legacy of enlightened
thinking that has transformed it into something special: a grand
American city as full of vitality and life—and as maddening, too,
in many ways—as the nation itself.

Washington actually owns two shorelines. Along its western
edge, the state faces the Pacific Ocean from the Columbia River to
the Strait of Juan de Fuca. Some of the most remote and extensive
beaches in the world can be found here. Buffeted by cool winds
and often shrouded in fog, they are beautiful and mysterious, ideal
for solitary hiking and other wilderness activities. Various Indian
tribes own about half of Washington's Pacific shoreline, and their
reservation lands are generally off-limits to tourists without prior
permission. Don't wander onto their beaches unless you're certain
it's all right to do so. This is less of a concern on the lower peninsulas, from Long Beach to Ocean Shores.

Washington's other shoreline runs in an east-west direction along
the Strait of Juan de Fuca, between Cape Flattery and Seattle, and
then turns north toward the Canadian border. Following the tor-

tured contours of Puget Sound, it takes in such attractive towns and villages as Dungeness, Port Townsend, LaConner and Birch Bay. Then there are the islands. Parts of Whidbey Island and all of the San Juan Islands are as unsullied and startling to behold as anything we've seen on either coast. They're also spared the extreme rainfall that inundates the Olympic Peninsula, enjoying a mild, moderate climate. In short, they amount to a floating paradise.

Ultimately, the Evergreen State has plenty to offer the traveler with a penchant for the sea and shore—not to mention mountains, valleys, rivers and pristine wilderness. The entire state is an open-air museum, painted from a palette of deep blues and greens. Just be sure when you come here that the plane ticket says Washington the *state* and not Washington the *capital*.

Ilwaco

Ilwaco is the front door to the Long Beach Peninsula. The coast highway (yes, we're still on Highway 101) introduces you to this town as it enters the 30-mile peninsula from the southern end—surprising, in a way, that such a long and heavily traveled sliver of vacation real estate would have but one way in and out. Be that as it may, Ilwaco makes a pleasant front door to the peninsula. It is, and always has been, a fishing community. Founded in 1852 and named after a local Indian chief, Elo Wahka Iim, its rich history includes a period of time known as the Gillnet Wars, during which fishers fought among themselves over the lucrative fishing grounds at the mouth of the mighty Columbia River. Many of the original homes have been preserved.

Despite the solid feeling the old architecture lends the town, Ilwaco has encountered hard times in recent years. Still, it is gamely struggling to keep its head above water, and today the upbeat, best-face-forward tone of Ilwaco can be seen in the murals that line the sides of some of the local businesses. These artistic renderings dramatize the area's history. Ten are already in place, and 20 more are in the works. As for beaches, Ilwaco has none. It is a port whose waterfront dock faces east, toward the Columbia River.

It is, however, a great place to arrange a salmon or steelhead fishing expedition.

Fort Canby State Park

Three miles southwest of Ilwaco, on the bottom tip of the Long Beach Peninsula, is Fort Canby, one of Washington's most interesting state parks. Here you will find not one but two lighthouses, an old fort, 2,000 acres of wilderness, an interpretive center named after Lewis and Clark and four trails that run through forests, marshes, headlands and beaches. You will also find one of the most tragically named points of land in America: Cape Disappointment. The existence of the lighthouses and fort are easily explained by their location—at the mouth of the Columbia River. This massive confluence has long been a graveyard for oceangoing vessels. Either they pass too close to its bar while traveling along the coastline or improperly navigate their way through the mouth en route to Astoria or Portland.

The lighthouses have distinct histories. The North Head Lighthouse was built in 1898, three miles north of the river's mouth, in response to shipwrecks occurring with great frequency along the peninsula. Should you wish to see North Head, you can park your car in a gravel lot and walk an easy quarter-mile trail to the 194-foot bluff upon which it stands. The view toward the river is spectacular, on clear days allowing a glimpse of Fort Stevens, Oregon, and points south.

The Cape Disappointment Lighthouse stands guard directly at the mouth of the river, warning approaching vessels away from the treacherous sandbar. The lighthouse was completed in 1856, but not before meeting every conceivable obstacle and delay that the location could throw in its path. For instance, the boat carrying most of what were to be the original building materials sank just offshore. The trail to Cape Disappointment is, as it should be, longer and more arduous than the little path to North Head. It's worth the extra time, if only to observe firsthand the last powerful gasp of one of the world's truly inspiring rivers. Three separate jetties are required to keep the Columbia River mouth open and navigable. The largest of these is 2.4 miles long and contains 2,946,449 tons of stone. Cape Disappointment, incidentally, is statistically the foggiest spot in America in terms of hours of fog per year.

There is no day-use fee at Fort Canby, which also has 250 campsites. A safe swimming beach can be found here, too. Given the name *Waikiki Beach*, this cold-water cove would get laughed out of the Aloha State.

Seaview

Those vacationers speeding north to Long Beach will not, in all likelihood, notice Seaview, the little town next door to it. At one time, the tables were turned and Seaview was the place to visit on the Long Beach Peninsula. But that was a long time ago—the late 1800s—and Seaview is probably just as glad to keep sight of its gilded past while hanging firmly onto the blessed solitude of the present.

Seaview was planned in 1881 as a real-estate venture for rich speculators from Portland. Not much came of it, but what little did has been preserved for posterity. The most famous of the restored buildings is the *Shelburne Hotel and Inn*, a dark green pleasure palace that was completed in 1896 and has been operating continuously as an inn ever since. On the beachfront, Seaview has the southernmost point of entry for cars on the 30-mile peninsula, at the end of 38th Street.

Long Beach

Long Beach is where the state of Washington comes out to play. It is the proud and self-proclaimed guardian of the world's longest beach. That's right, the world's longest beach—28 miles of driveable, walkable, rideable, runnable sand. Though the beach is state-owned, Long Beach is the only town on the peninsula with the gumption to place a victory arch over one of its beach accesses. With a flourish suitable to such a superlative, the Bolstad Street arch announces, "THE WORLD'S LONGEST BEACH." After driving under this triumphal entranceway, you're on what amounts to a sandy superhighway. Who would have thought that in over three years of wandering two different coastlines, we would stumble on the longest beach of them all in the timber and salmon country of the Pacific northwest?

But it's out here, sure 'nuff—all 28 wide, uninterrupted miles of it—and it's well-appreciated by budget-conscious families who arrive by the station-wagon load. Situated in the southwestern corner of Washington State—where the skies are not cloudy all day (just most of it)—Long Beach is only 15 miles from Oregon, a mere hop over the awe-inspiring Astoria–Megler–Columbia River Bridge. It's also only two hours from Portland and three from Seattle, cities from which it draws much of its business.

The folks of Long Beach are not the least bit hesitant to state their goals and priorities. Tourism is number one in Long Beach, and the way they go after it is as funny, exaggerated and likable as the town itself. The longtime symbol of the community, for example, is the "World's Largest Frying Pan," and it hangs, like some kind of weird metallic manta ray, by its handle from a wooden signpost along the side of the coast highway. "Come and get it!" the goofy pan seems to yodel. In recent years, the town has been cleaning, painting, trimming and streamlining its downtown district. You'll find a brand-new gazebo and a number of carefully rendered wood sculptures. But all the paint in the world can't make a silk purse out of a sow's ear. The new sculptures, in keeping with the town's Disney-esque self-image, are of an impossibly huge octopus, a monstrous sea lion and a sea horse the size of Mr. Ed.

For total immersion in the Houdini tank of Long Beach's unnatural attractions, beat a path to *Marsh's Free Museum* and make the acquaintance of Jake the Alligator Man. We'd seen Jake's likeness on a couple of highway billboards and could scarcely believe our eyes. What the *hell* was that? As it turns out, Jake is the main attraction at Marsh's freak-show museum. It is the most popular hangout in Long Beach. You can catch Jake here anytime, dead and in the (charred) flesh. He's kept inside a Plexiglas casket and is only taken out when they need another photograph for the souvenir postcards. Jake is kind of hard to explain... he's half human and half alligator. He looks like a victim of Pompeii who was sawed in two by an amazingly sick individual and then crazy-glued to the lower half of a charbroiled alligator.

Even the owners of Marsh's Museum claim to know little about Jake beyond the fact that they acquired him from a museum in San Francisco. Our guess is that they got him in exchange for a stillborn, two-headed calf and a lobster child. Really all that matters is that Jake is a favorite with the tourists. For 50 cents, you can have Jake's likeness imprinted onto the head of a stretched penny. For 50 cents more, you can buy a Jake bumper sticker. For another 50 cents you can purchase a button that says, "Jake Is My Friend." And so on. Marsh's "Free" Museum is really just a novelty shop. Though its pretensions about being a museum are as laughable as the oversized frying pan and the wooden octopus, it's still worth visiting. Established in 1921, the "museum" has amassed a fascinating collection of Americana: old bawdy-house music boxes that still work, ancient silver-balled baseball games, shrunken heads, wooden Indians....

Long Beach can be forgiven its excesses. In order to stay afloat in the deep end of the tourist pool, it needs these sorts of diversions. The weather is unpredictable and the ocean surf is dangerous, which eliminates the reasons most families come to the beach. Still, unlike many towns whose community chest is seasonally stuffed with tourist loot, Long Beach hasn't turned its modest amusements into an offensive commercial bombardment. There's a cute "Fun Rides" park for the tots, a carousel, a small Ferris wheel, the obligatory ice-cream and candy outlets, and the *Red Baron* burger hut. All in all, the spirit of highjinks in Long Beach is about on par with that of a small county fair.

Accommodations

The average family budget can easily manage a vacation in Long Beach. Some motels' rates start as low as $17.17, and the vast majority are in the $30 range. But, as one motel owner told us, "There are some real onions out there." Onions? "You know, in some places they compare apples and oranges. Here, in Long Beach, it's apples and onions." Okay, then, our instincts told us the *Shaman Motel* was an apple. It's located near the Bolstad Street beach access, but one block away to avoid the noise of the crowds and the engines.

The *Chautauqua Lodge* is the shiniest apple in Long Beach. Located a mile north of the town center, it is a large, three-story compound geared to conventioneers and vacationers alike. They have an indoor pool, hot tub, sauna, rec rooms and a restaurant and lounge where, on certain nights, wild partying goes on. Better yet, you can walk right out to the beach—a very uncrowded stretch of beach, we might add.

Restaurants

Popular American beach towns normally have restaurants that measure anywhere from 5.5 to 8 on the stomach's Richter scale. You know, fish 'n' chip cheeseburger taco hot-topped potato corndogs with warm cheez-whiz sauce drizzled about and the whole soggy mass rotated continuously inside a bird cage–like rotisserie to the generally slack specifications of the local health department. Well, imagine our surprise and awe to discover first-rate cuisine on the Long Beach Peninsula. In the space of three days, we dined at three of the finest restaurants on the West Coast: the *Sanctuary* (in Chinook), the *Shoalwater Restaurant* (in Seaview) and the *Ark* (in Oysterville, and discussed under that heading).

The historic little village of Chinook, home of the Sanctuary, is seven miles from Long Beach, back toward Astoria. The Sanctuary is housed in what was formerly the Methodist Episcopal Church of Chinook (circa 1906). Consider the extra few miles you'll drive to be a religious pilgrimage and every minute you spend inside the Sanctuary part of a worship service. Maybe a Thanksgiving liturgy. First of all, the setting is unexpectedly conducive to fine dining. Seated in pews at black wooden tables—some situated, like alcoves, beneath stained-glass windows—diners can study the wine list and menu as if they were hymnals. All items—bread, pastries, desserts, soups, sauces—are made on the premises. Since the salmon-choked Columbia River helped make Chinook, in the late 1880s, the richest town per capita in the United States, we sampled the barbecued salmon appetizer. It was the best pure piece of fish we'd had since the Crab Cooker in Newport Beach, California. Fresh, pungent garlic soup arrived soon thereafter. As for our entrées, Snapper Cleopatra (stuffed with shrimp and covered with onions and capers) and Veal Piccata were heavenly. Likewise with the desserts and the service. By meal's end, we were shouting "glory hallelujah!"

The other local dining shrine, the Shoalwater, can be found in Seaview, the sister city of Long Beach. Set on the premises of the Shelburne Inn, a National Historic Landmark, the Shoalwater might be described as relaxed sophistication at its best. When we visited, for instance, the manager on duty was in every way—looks, accent, mannerisms—a dead ringer for George Plimpton, the human hosting machine. Touted by James Beard and courted by publishers for a cookbook, the Shoalwater has been featuring regional cuisine for over 90 years. The menu is inventively adapted to the freshest available vegetables, fish and meat. All breads and pastries are made on the premises, and the menu changes completely every six weeks. Sturgeon was the freshest fish available when we drove through, and because it is rarely seen on menus, we dove for it like drowning sailors. It has the texture of chicken and the taste of, well, sturgeon. In other words, it's a great piece of fish.

In Long Beach itself, there's not much to talk about. The *Cottage Bakery* is a fair place for a casual breakfast or lunch. The massive shop windows are lined with sugar-coated donuts and cream-filled pastries, attracting all the tourists and thus enabling you to sneak over to the great but overlooked sandwich bar and get immediate service.

Nightlife

The taverns in this, the state's most popular beach town, are surprisingly glum places. We expected throngs of wildly attired bozos, some body-building clothes horses, maybe even a pretty gal or two in a miniskirt and sandals. Instead, at the two taverns in the heart of Long Beach, we found a pack of aging, sour-faced regulars who seemed to frequent these places merely to keep daily tabs on each other's drinking problems.

Ah, but there is hope. Even as we fretted, a brand-new tavern, the *Bent Rudder*, was gearing up for its grand opening down the road toward Seaview. The Bent Rudder looked like a sure bet to become the place to go. Large, clean, well-lit and high-spirited, from outward appearances, it was a marked contrast to the other taverns, where folks looked too bummed out even to have a decent fistfight.

For live music, it's slim pickings out here. But again, hope springs eternal. Every Wednesday at the *Potlatch Lounge* (at the Chautauqua Lodge) the local FM radio station stages a two-hour party that leads into some live music. As luck would have it, we were there on a Wednesday. Although we didn't win any door prizes, it was heartening to see a roomful of people—at least four generations' worth and maybe a fifth, if that bump-dancing octogenarian in the bowling shirt survived the evening—having a whale of a good time. So anxious and starved are they for entertainment out here that a two-man band, whose most competent member was a drum machine, got them rocking, standing, stomping and hollering, "Charlie Brown/He's a clown/Whoa, that Charlie Brown/He's a clown...."

FOR FURTHER INFORMATION

Long Beach Peninsula Visitors Bureau
P.O. Box 562
Long Beach, WA 98631
(206) 642-2400

Klipsan Beach
Ocean Park
Surfside

The north end of the Long Beach Peninsula is an altogether quieter place. While Long Beach and Seaview offer shopping, shooting galleries and Jake the Alligator Man, the unincorporated small villages up north tender another commodity: solitude. To put it simply, people come to Ocean Park to get away from it all.

The unofficial boundary distinguishing north from south on the peninsula is Cranberry Road. Right above it is *Loomis Lake*, the largest saltwater lake in the area. It is the focus of a state park on the east side of Route 103 (the road that runs up the peninsula). One can canoe the lake, fish for trout or watch for the trumpeter swans that stop over during their winter migration. The beach side of the park is a day-use area with sheltered picnic tables and trails over the soft dunes to the hard-packed beach.

Next up is Klipsan Beach, a small community of old beach cottages that is the site of a one-time Coast Guard life-saving station. Dating from 1889, the Klipsan Beach Life Saving Station was one of 19 manned outposts that protected and rescued West Coast mariners from Alaska to the Golden Gate of San Francisco. The station and eight adjacent buildings are listed on the National Register of Historic Places.

Ocean Park is the largest town on the peninsula's north end, which is not saying you'll mistake it for Seattle. Founded in 1883 by Methodists as a camp-meeting ground, Ocean Park really hasn't changed in a hundred years. It's still unincorporated, with many cottages and homes dating from its founding. At the intersection of Bay Avenue and Vernon Road by the blinking traffic signal (the only one out here) is a modest commercial buildup: grocery store, liquor store, fish 'n' chips shop, Grannie Annie's Café, and—last but not least—Jack's Country Store. The latter is a cross between a general store and a K mart. It is a huge place; they come damn near close to having one of everything.

A real feel for Ocean Park can be gotten from walking its side streets. Tudor and gingerbread cottages are tucked away beneath the pines, along the green banks of the slough that drains the small lakes on the peninsula. For those who want to point their wheels toward the beach, Bay Avenue runs right out to it, and jeeps and cars are welcome to take their chances on the sandy turnpike. The basic rules of the road are drive slowly and avoid wet spots and soft sand. The intrepid motorist can take the beach route all the way down to Long Beach, rolling along mere feet from the muddy, lapping waves.

Beyond this, most of the activities to be done up here are solitary ones: hiking, jogging, bird-watching, kite-flying and just plain old idle recharging of the inner batteries in a peaceful setting. The last beach access on the 28-mile peninsula is at *Pacific Pines State Beach* near Surfside. This incorporated hamlet is growing up, quickly, with a condo resort and nine-hole golf course laying out a more upscale agenda.

Accommodations

The *Sunset View Resort* in Ocean Park is a fitting place to put on the brakes. Located several blocks off the highway in a sylvan setting of small lakes, a short forest of pines and a broad field of dunes, the resort's six acres also include an enclosed pen, inside which tame Asian fallow deer and pygmy goats wander. Rooms in the rustic-looking lodge are equipped with kitchens and fireplaces and look out on the ocean. A sense of privacy and isolation in a wild, lovely environment keeps people coming back year after year.

Restaurants

Grannie Annie's Café is a popular local spot, judging from the heavy pickup-truck presence outside her canary-yellow establishment. It's the giant T-bone steaks, fried chicken and BBQ ribs that keep her clientele rubbing their ample tummies. For fish and seafood, the *Bay Avenue Fish House* is where you'll want to toss your lunch- or dinnertime net. "Fish is our only reason for being here," they say, and it will be yours, too.

Nightlife

Once again, we hauled in an empty net on the local tavern scene. *Doc's Tavern* looked promising from the outside: a large, friendly corner building with all sorts of sayings painted on the side in large lettering: "Home of the frosty mug," "Where old rockers meet," "Where you get all the truth…and free advice." We got the frosty mug, but we got icy glares as well from a clump of loutish mug-pounders who were hee-hawing and cursing in slurred syllables at one another.

It served to reinforce our conviction that the taverns of the northwest are not particularly hospitable places for anyone but regulars—and even they jump on one another with alarming frequency. By this time, as often as not, we were bringing the bar to us: a six-pack on ice in the motel room, sipped while watching the Atlanta Braves extend an amazing losing streak on WTBS, the Atlanta "superstation" that reaches every corner of this great nation.

FOR FURTHER INFORMATION

Ocean Park Chamber of Commerce
P.O. Box 403
Ocean Park, WA 98640
(206) 665-5090

Nahcotta
Oysterville

These two tiny dots on the map are located at the far northeastern neck of the Long Beach Peninsula, on the Willapa Bay. Both are even quieter than Ocean Park, with a charm that comes from being off the beaten track. It's hard to get any more out-of-the-way than this.

Oysterville didn't used to be so isolated, at least back in the mid-1800s, when record oyster harvests made it something of a boom-town. An old church, a schoolhouse and a courthouse remain, as do many sturdy old homes that date from the 1860s. But there's nothing to suggest that Oysterville once boasted five saloons, two hotels, a newspaper and a college. Hard times began around the turn of the century with declining oyster harvests. The railroad was not extended as far as Oysterville, another death knell, and the courthouse was actually raided in 1893 by a vigilante mob from South Bend, who made off with the records and reestablished the county seat in their town. The only hint of where Oysterville got its name is a ramshackle bayside barn where a hand-lettered sign spells out the going price for oysters—6 for $1, 100 for $13.

Nahcotta looks like Oysterville ought to, with giant heaps of oyster shells rising in Matterhorn-like mountains. Plump oysters are still plucked from the calm waters of the Willapa Bay in large numbers, judging from the active trade on the docks. Plopped among these oyster middens is a celebrated restaurant, *The Ark*. No less an authority than James Beard has paid homage to the Ark, whose cuisine is elegant yet healthful. Among the dishes we would gladly roll over and play dead for are Salmon Filet in Scotch Cream Sauce (made from Scotch and orange juice, laced with Drambuie and garnished with sour cream) and Sturgeon Szechuan (sautéed with garlic, ginger and peppers, then deglazed with sake). Oysters are served several different ways, which is appropriate since the Ark is surrounded by millions of shells. Still, it's not oysters but garlic they pay tribute to, with a nationally publicized Garlic Festival every June. All in all, the Ark is reason enough to visit this end of the peninsula.

Long Island

Directly across from Nahcotta and Oysterville in the Willapa Bay is Long Island, a unique refuge for such winged creatures as the pileated woodpecker and the dusky Canadian goose. Besides being the largest estuarine island on the West Coast, Long Island is also the site of one of the last remaining first-growth stands of red cedar. The 274-acre grove includes trees more than 4,000 years old. Some of these survivors have trunks 11 feet in diameter. Long

Island has been purchased by the federal government and set aside as a National Wildlife Refuge. It can be reached by boat, but there are only primitive campgrounds and few roads. Native wildlife includes bear, deer, elk, beaver, otters and bald eagles.

Leadbetter Point

The tip of the Long Beach Peninsula belongs not to the broad-bellied condominium dweller but to the snowy plover, an endangered shorebird that nests here from April through August. Fittingly, considering its status as a bird sanctuary, Leadbetter Point is shaped like a duck's head. The "head" is off-limits to human intruders during the nesting months, but the "neck" of the park can be visited year-round. This 23,000-acre state park encompasses a variety of terrain—open dunes, grasslands, stumpy forest, salt marshes, bogs and mud flats—all of which are crossed by a 1¾-mile loop trail that circles a portion of the park, from bay to ocean. The principal activities out here are wildlife observation, hiking, photography, bird-watching, beachcombing and waterfowl hunting in season (though for the life of us, we don't know why they allow the latter). We were content to bag some peace and quiet at Leadbetter.

Grayland

North of a town called Raymond, Highway 101 intersects with Route 105, a state road that flares west onto a fist-shaped hunk of land bounded by Willapa Bay and Grays Harbor. Most vacationers stay on 101, heading toward the peninsula north of here where several small beach towns—stretching from Ocean Shores to Moclips—await them. Fishers, however, take Route 105.

What basically happens after the turnoff is—well, nothing at all, at least not right away. We drove through the Shoalwater Indian Reservation, where the only sign of life was a deer loping across the road near a country store called Chief Charley's. The road follows the bay till it rounds Cape Shoalwater, at which point it turns north and runs along the ocean, passing through Grayland and ending at Westport. Visitors who want to see a historic Indian settlement are welcome to detour south to Tokeland, which sits on a nub of land in the Willapa Bay.

The rest of the southern Grays Harbor Peninsula is sparsely settled. The human habitations that do exist are a fairly somber-looking gaggle of country stores with neon beer logos in the windows and trailer parks with rusted car parts tossed around the premises like the aftermath of a mechanical hailstorm. Grayland is aptly named. It's the home of working men and women who have learned to bob and weave with the vagaries of the sea. Some years the catch is good. Some years it isn't. The town is also known for its cranberry bogs, which extend all the way up to the dunes. Grayland's bogs are part of the farmer-owned Ocean Spray cooperative, and the cranberries keep the local economy afloat when the ocean is uncooperative.

Westport

Fishing and drinking. These are the passwords you'll need to know to have a good time in Westport. There are 18 miles of beaches in and around the town, but all the action is at the marina. Chances are you won't even see the beach, except from the stern of your charter boat as it's making its way over the bar into deep water. If you wind up catching the daily limit of salmon—which isn't hard, since current regulations limit each angler's take to two—you'll return to shore and yahoo your way through a bottle of whiskey or a case of beer until you're as pink in the face as a grilled salmon.

Westport is double-billed as the "Salmon Capital" and the "Sport-fishing Capital of the World." There is good reason why this is so. The waters off Westport are teeming with schools of small, snack-sized sea creatures that every hungry salmon loves—anchovies, shrimp and herring—making for some of the richest feeding grounds in the world. Court decisions have shortened the salmon season in recent years, the objective being to save the salmon, whose numbers have been dwindling as the nation's taste for the protein-rich fish soars. In the summer of 1987, the daily limit per angler was two; the season lasted only from June 29th until the mandated quota was reached, sometime around Labor Day; and salmon could only be caught Sunday through Thursday. The state, it seems, decided to give the embattled salmon weekends off.

Even with the restrictions, Westport's charter boats do a brisk business all summer long. Along the waterfront, more than 80 charter boats are tethered to the floating docks that line the protected harbor. The boats range in size from 30 to 65 feet and can carry up to 60 passengers. They shove off in the morning, by dawn's early light, and return after each angler has caught the limit, usually around midafternoon. Not all boats go after salmon. Bottom fish are plentiful, and the daily limit on these is 15 apiece, so you can bait, cast and reel 'em in till your arms give out. With a little luck, even an amateur angler can return to port with a huge haul of red rockfish, flounder, sole and sea bass.

Everything on the harbor front is geared toward fishing. The restaurants and bait shops open at 4 a.m. In season, they hold a daily Salmon Derby. For $2, an angler can sign up to win a $100 prize for the largest salmon and bottom fish caught by the end of the day. A cash prize of several thousand dollars is awarded for the biggest fish of the season.

Our morning in Westport began at 5 a.m., when an amplified voice wafted across the harbor into our motel room. It was urging one and all to come on down and buy a derby ticket at the concession stand. Wiping the sleep from our eyes, we ambled into town to investigate. Boat after boat was pulling away into the gray mist, each with a full load of anglers stoically standing amidships with steaming Styrofoam cups of morning mud. A late riser came charging down to the marina, waving his arms and shouting, "Hey! You forgot me! It says 6:30 on the card! Come back!" But the boat did not come back, and the disappointed straggler had to brood away his morning over a doughy maple bar at *Little Richard's Donut Shop*.

Westport Harbor is built along a sheltered cove, cradled by a large jetty. The town was first settled in 1858. By the gay nineties, it was a bustling maritime center that saw whaling boats, clipper ships, schooners and steamers stabbing their way through the narrow, 30-foot channel. With the widening of the harbor mouth in 1906, Westport became a haven to a growing fleet of fishing boats. Though Westport has seen its share of hard times, the proud townspeople have kept the revitalized waterfront looking tidy. It begs to be browsed and enjoyed, even at the ungodly hour of five in the morning.

Everything takes a back seat to fishing in Westport, but that doesn't mean we can't talk about the goods stashed in the back seat. First, there's a prominent observation deck along the jetty offering a panoramic view of the ocean. Fishers use it to judge whether the bar is passable. Then there's the Westport Maritime Museum, located in a decommissioned Coast Guard building. Photographs and relics document the colorful history of the area, and the building—one of the few Nantucket-style Coast Guard stations in the country—is an attraction in its own right.

The town of Westport occupies the northern tip of the 18-mile peninsula-of-sorts between Grays Harbor and Willapa Bay. This area, known as Twin Harbors, includes Westport and the village of Grayland, on down to Tokeland. Between the two harbors lies 18 miles of driveable shoreline, with three state beaches between Westport and Grayland alone. Surf and jetty fishing are popular at *Westhaven State Park*, a 200-acre facility with 4,000 feet of Pacific Ocean frontage. *Westport Light State Beach* is named after a lighthouse that has been in continuous operation since 1898. It is the tallest light on the Washington coast. Just south is the largest of the parks, *Twin Harbors*, which includes 332 campsites and three miles of shoreline.

Accommodations

The strip of establishments along Westport's South Jetty are not so much motels as fish camps—a place to stash your bags and toss and turn on a lumpy mattress until the morning alarm sends you scurrying for the charter boat. Catering to a sizable market are motels and RV parks less oriented toward satisfying a vacationer's wants than an angler's bare needs. The *Islander* is a notch above the competition. It's not just a motel but a full-service complex including charter boats, an RV park, a restaurant and "java shop" open 18 hours a day, and a cocktail lounge. If you hear the sound of boots stomping pavement at 4:30 a.m., don't lose your cool. Deep-sea fishing is king, and beating the fish out of bed is part of the experience.

Restaurants

Sourdough Lil's claims to be the "only place of its kind in the world." We've never seen anything like it, that's for sure. This unique restaurant was established in 1947 by a woman named Lillian Anderson, who christened it Sourdough Lil's after her special knack at the kneading board. The redoubtable Ms. Anderson, a former Montana poolroom operator, modeled her restaurant after the Klondike honky-tonks of Alaska's Gold Rush days, a place and time she was well acquainted with.

Fresh seafood is brought in daily off the docks: salmon, halibut, oysters, bay scallops. The seafood platter is a good way to sample it all, and you can order it baked, grilled or sautéed in wine. Polish off this feast with a slab of home-made cheesecake, made from a secret recipe handed down by a local cranberry grower's wife. Then shuffle across the floor into Sourdough Lil's 1893 Bar Room if you've got any room left for nightlife, gay nineties–style. Read on.

Nightlife

The 1893 Bar Room at Sourdough Lil's is like a scene out of a Western: sawdust-strewn floor, happy crowd singing along with a banjo and piano-playing duo, liquid gold flowing into frosty mugs and down the hatch. Printed lyric sheets are distributed, and the crowd hollers along to the tune of "Ain't She Sweet," "When Irish Eyes Are Smiling," "I'm Looking over a Four-Leaf Clover" and 97 others. Thousands of dollars in grubstake are glued to the ceiling, a

custom that's survived two ceiling repaintings. The idea is that if
you leave a dollar behind at Sourdough Lil's, you'll never be broke
when you come back to Westport. The bills hang unmolested over
the bar patrons' heads like a sloppy wallpapering job.

Country and western music keeps 'em yee-hawing out here, and
watering holes like *Cowboy Bob's* and the *Knotty Pine Lounge* do as
much business after dark as the Salmon Derby ticket stand does
when morning rolls around. As one Westport native confided, there
are people who never know a sober moment during their week-
long fishing vacation. Like we said, fishing and drinking are all
you need to know about Westport.

FOR FURTHER INFORMATION

Westport-Grayland Chamber of Commerce
1200 North Montesano Street
P.O. Box 306
Westport, WA 98595
(206) 268-9422

Ocean Shores

Under the cover of darkness, Ocean Shores, Washington, could
easily sneak into Orange County, California, and nobody would
notice the difference. It is a completely planned community that's
not so much a town as a territory, occupying the entire peninsula
north of the mouth of Grays Harbor. Ocean Shores was conceived
and built for upper-class and upwardly mobile wage earners with
comfort and privacy in mind. It is spread out over what was, until
1960, a 6,000-acre dairy farm. The year John F. Kennedy was
elected, Ocean Shores was nothing but cows, grassland and prime
USDA-inspected real estate. Then, *Boom*, in the span of a dozen
years, Ocean Shores went from cow pies to condos. The ensuing
land frenzy rivaled anything that happened in Southern California
in the same span of years.

Of course, during the time the land grab went down, so did a lot of shady business. The corporation that bought the peninsula from the Minard family immediately set about divvying the land into "approximate lots." Potential landowners, mostly rich retirees, were chauffeured around the peninsula, and these approximate lots were pointed out to them from the front seat of a moving Jeep. Many of the lots were purchased sight unseen, and when it came time for surveying, zoning, building roads and delivering services, some folks were surprised to find their property was elsewhere than they had been told it would be. So it goes at the beach.

Well, Rome wasn't built in a day, so how can you expect a planned community in the chilly, fog-shrouded Pacific Northwest to perform miracles? Ocean Shores eventually straightened out its act, weeded out the corporate slimeballs and built the roads and sewer lines. The story of Ocean Shores, though short in years, is an interesting study in accelerated development. A locally published history of the community, written in half-sentences and halting newspaper-headline prose, leaves no shell unturned. The following excerpt might help explain the obstacles faced by a high-rolling project set in the not-always-glamorous northwest:

> 1969 started with probably the worst winter in the state's recorded history. There were 21 days of freezing rain, with temperatures as low as 13 degrees, snowdrifts as high as the eaves of some buildings.... The Second Annual February Fog Festival was held, also a "kick the can" contest. An International Crab Relay was scheduled but someone stole the crabs.

It sounds like a plot synopsis for an episode of *Green Acres*.

Today, the wooden, well-spaced dwellings of Ocean Shores serve mostly as second homes, tax write-offs and investments for their owners, many of whom live in Seattle, Olympia, Salem and nearby Hoquiam (a rich suburb of Aberdeen, a Georgia-Pacific mill town). Ocean Shore's multitude of modern residences are spread out unobtrusively over the former grazing land, with a "motel row" set in one clearly defined area, a business district in another, a small convention center elsewhere, and so on. All of them, however, play second fiddle to the predominant residential tone. Marking the entrance to this modern-day rancho are two imposing stone monoliths, emblazoned with a blue seahorse and the words "Ocean Shores." It's all very discreetly done and no doubt a comfort to those who wish to retire out here, but something essential is missing from Ocean Shores. Call it what you will—soul, spirit, vitality, spunk, life. After 27 years of trying, the place is still searching for an identity.

None of this is intended as an insult to the folks of Ocean Shores, most of whom are quite friendly to visitors. Neither is this meant to detract from the area's enviable bounty of natural gifts. Built around Grays Harbor, Ocean Shores boasts 70 miles of waterfront. Six of those miles include some of the widest, flattest and healthiest beach we've seen in our coastal travels. You practically need to hail a cab to get down to the water. After a close survey of local traffic patterns, this is not as far-fetched as it sounds. They drive their cars on the beach here. They don't just park them, pull out the fishing gear and set up shop. They actually drive long distances on the beach.

From Ocean Shores up past Copalis Beach, a distance of over 20 miles, the beach is so healthy and hard-packed it's been designated a public highway. Cars, vans, mopeds, motorcycles and horses create a continuous stream of traffic. Walking down to the water at times is like trying to cross the San Diego Freeway. Fortunately, driving is limited to the middle of the beach, this stipulation mainly intended to prevent rampant destruction of the clam beds nearer the water. The established speed limit on the beach is 25 mph, but without police patrols or warning signs only the horses keep it under the prescribed limit. There are four separate vehicle access ramps in Ocean Shores alone—at Taurus Street, Ocean Lake Way, Pacific Way and Chance a la Mer. Because the beach is so wide and the weather often on the gloomy side, it is easy to understand why people cop a beach buzz from the safety of their vehicles. Not much more than driving and fishing is done on Ocean Shores' beach.

As for strolling, stick to the water and you'll have little trouble. Once out of the pedestrian thicket near motel row, you'll likely have the entire beach to yourself. An occasional van will pass by, its passengers staring with some curiosity at you through their tinted windows. A lone pedestrian is almost as odd to them as the sight of three dead seals was to us. Washed up on the beach, the carcasses appeared to have been speared or shot. They were still bleeding. Upon flagging down a passing van and asking about the dead seals, we were matter-of-factly told, "Oh, the fishermen shoot them on account of because they eat all the fish." The screwball ethics of slaughtering notwithstanding, the sight of three dead seal pups does not make for idyllic late-afternoon strolling. Short of swimming three miles out to the fishing boats, where the murders undoubtedly occurred—the bodies having floated in with the tide—we had no recourse but to flash obscene gestures toward the horizon.

Ocean Shores actually has more than its endless beach going for it. There's an endless bay as well, where sailing and fishing are popular. A passenger ferry bound for Westport leaves from the marina at Grays Harbor. There is a beach access site at the jetty on Point Brown, the southernmost tip of the peninsula. The Ocean Shores Interpretive Center is located near the remnants of an old shipwreck on the harbor. At one time, plans were afloat to turn this new peninsular homeland into the "Venice of the West." Twenty-five miles of canals were planned, but only a portion of them have been dredged. The existing canals blend nicely with the two natural lakes, creating ample waterfront property for future homeowners. And if projected figures actually come to pass, the future looks bright for Ocean Shores. The current year-round population of 2,000 is expected to swell to 12,000 or 15,000 by the year 2000. A hundred new homes are built every year.

Until that residential Canaan comes to pass, though, the convention center will have to remain the centerpiece of the community. Located around the corner from motel row, it's plain and simple. The local economy depends on conventioneers and retirees, because the bulk of Washington's family vacationers still go to Long Beach, where vacation fun of a more conventional sort can be found. Ocean Shores has yet to master the blend of activity and relaxation that makes for a healthy tourist trade, so for now they'll have to content themselves with being one of the "Richest Little Cities" in the Pacific northwest.

Accommodations

With the exception of the nicer lodges on motel row, the majority of places in Ocean Shores weren't faring too well, from the look of it. At two not entirely unsavory motels, for instance, rooms were advertised at $19 and $16.50. For the record, they were the *Vagabond* and the *Ocean Sands Motel*. However, the most comfortable and quietest lodges are the trio of heavy hitters along motel row: the *Polynesian Resort*, the *Canterbury Inn* and the *Grey Gull*. The Canterbury is the oldest of the three and, in our humble opinion, the best. With an indoor pool, comfortable, apartment-style suites and great beach access, it's like staying in someone's home for the night. Actually, you *are* staying in someone's home; the rooms at the Canterbury are owned by absentee investors who allow them to be rented out. The Grey Gull is more like a standard motel. The Polynesian, a four-story wonder, is considered a "resort." Maybe it's the indoor sauna and whirlpool that create illusions of the South Pacific. Any way you look at it, you will pay more to stay at these three, but it's money well spent.

Restaurants

Because Ocean Shores is still, despite the projected yuppie influx, primarily a retirement community filled with well-to-do ex-Boeing execs, the cuisine is like lecture-circuit food: above average in quality but nothing to write home about. After checking around town, we finally dropped anchor at the *Harbor Landing* and were soon ushered into a nearly empty silver and blue dining room. It was the midweek slump, our waiter explained. Weekends are packed and weekdays deserted in summer. The Muzak was blaring unexplainably loudly. The food, however, was quite commendable. Fresh pasta and seafood are the priorities. A combination of the two, Seafood Fettucine, is a good choice.

For a decent quick lunch, try the *Sand Castle Drive-In Restaurant*. It's just a fish 'n' chips and burger joint, but it's a good one.

Mercifully, fast-food franchises are not part of the grand scheme of things out here.

Nightlife

Lumpy's Tavern is located across the street from the convention center in Ocean Shores. No, Wally, Eddie and the Beaver do not play pool here. Lumpy's is the only honest-to-God, all-American beer joint in town. It's the kind of place most conventioneers wouldn't touch with a 10-foot pool cue. They prefer to wander back to motel row, where the lounges service them in the manner to which they're accustomed. *The Ocean Shores Inn* is the oldest and most revered convention hangout. It has a piano lounge where guys with name tags on their sport coats hobnob, glad-hand and gamble. That's right. In Washington, gambling is legal, within certain bounds.

Not to flog a dead seal, but it should be added that driving on the beach after dark is sheer foolishness. The unpredictable sandy surface has toppled many a vehicle and the clam beds have been crushed by late-night yokels who get their jollies playing chicken with the waves. On behalf of the beleaguered bivalve population, we would like to establish a new organization known as CADD: Clams Against Drunk Drivers.

FOR FURTHER INFORMATION

Ocean Shores Chamber of Commerce
P.O. Box 382
Ocean Shores, WA 98569
(206) 289-2451

Oyehut
Illahee

These two microbe-sized communities north of Ocean Shores are
worthy of note only for their extreme cantankerousness. They don't
like outsiders. They can't stand the nouveau riche amenities of their
southern neighbors in Ocean Shores. And though these little towns
sit side by side, it is not even certain that they like each other.
Witness this line from a local publication: "There's nothing more
irksome for an Illaheen than to offer assistance to a lost visitor,
only to find the visitor is looking for a house in Oyehut." The
obvious questions raised by this comment are, (1) How can you
get lost in a pair of towns the size of a K mart parking lot? and
(2) If you happen to get lost, why is it such a big deal to ask
directions?

Local orneriness is partly explained by local history. During the
depression, Finnish fishers settled here, grabbing the land under
the wide interpretation given squatter's rights. Perhaps fearing for
the deal's legality or perhaps simply because it's their natural in-
clination to want to be left alone, the communities have remained
totally aloof over the years. They briefly came out of their shells
in the fifties, when a legal battle raged over their right to the land.
Some residents produced canceled checks to prove they owned their
property. Some had nothing at all to show. Oyehut and Illahee
quickly formed themselves into private corporations and then
crawled back into their crab shells.

Today, they cling to the wide and windy shoreline, two tiny
hamlets full of clam shacks, small homes and sheltered cottages.
Until recent years, many houses didn't have electricity or running water. "Oyehut residents," states the same publication, "take
pride in maintaining a rustic look and outlook." Anyway, we
mention them here because of the beach access at Oyehut. Half
a mile out of Ocean Shores, you can turn west and drive onto
the beach. It is just one more entrance ramp to Washington's
sandy highway.

Ocean City

Ocean City is a quiet, semiprivate community just up the beach from the zip-locked town of Oyehut. Because it is on the older, more traveled Route 109, it has felt the vacationer's footsteps a little more forcefully, but it is far from overrun. The name "Ocean City" seems to imply a big-time beach resort. The reality of Ocean City, however, is "slow down, you move too fast." Development began half a century ago when the road was built north to Moclips, but it was done with relaxation, not commotion, in mind.

Consequently, the only resorts out here are a couple of RV parks with bucolic names—Trail's End and Leisure Time—along with a motel and a few country stores. The only entertainment you'll find is on the shelves of a store called Boredom Beaters, which deals in "Moped Rentals and VHS." South of town is *Ocean City State Park*. For no charge you can park at the beach all day, and a modest $6 will procure a spot at one of 187 overnight campsites. Trails lead to wetlands and ponds.

Copalis Beach

Copalis Beach is billed as the Home of the Razor Clam. Once upon a time, the nickname was the gospel truth. Back in the twenties, when tourists first started coming to this town—just north of Ocean City on Route 109—the razor clams were almost obscenely abundant. For 25 cents, a carload of people could camp in Copalis Beach and spend all day digging those crazy clams. No limit was put on the number that could be taken. Eyes generally being bigger than stomachs, especially with so many clams out here, people took more than they could possibly eat. One longtime resident remembers seeing canvas sacks of clams rotting by the side of the road.

Mills and canneries moved into the area. Bootleg whiskey stills were set up, too, and pistol shots were heard—the telltale sign of a town lost to greed. Eventually, the number of razor clams began to dwindle, both from being collected by overly zealous clam diggers and from being crushed by cars driving over their beds on the beach. Today, Copalis Beach is no longer the Home of the Razor Clam, though they still use the name on their vacation literature. "Graveyard of the Razor Clam" might be a more apt nickname. They make do with a small tourist business, centered around a tavern, a café and a general store that still offers "Clam Shovels for Rent." Nowadays, the take is limited to 15 razor clams in season. That's like being told you can have only one beer at a baseball game.

Pacific Beach
Moclips
Taholah

The lengthy days of summer never seem to end on Washington's western peninsulas. Standing on the beach at Moclips, one of three small villages clustered at the top of the North Beach peninsula, we watched a setting sun color the night sky with a fiery band of purple and orange until long past 10 p.m. These twilight illuminations were reflected in a broad field of glistening wet sand, recently uncovered by the slowly receding tide. All was quiet but for the gentle sound of the surf rolling in. One of us swears he saw a pair of phantom horses and riders galloping along the hard-packed sand at the water's edge. Ghosts. Sufficiently real to cause a distinct twinge of unease. We were now officially in Indian country.

The beaches between the Moclips and Copalis rivers constitute a lost treasure—mostly unvisited and all but unknown to outsiders. Were these same beaches situated on the heavily trafficked East Coast or in Southern California, Moclips and Pacific Beach might look more like Santa Monica and Miami Beach. But, alas, this area is too far off the beaten track to hope a tourist tide will ever start rising.

Moclips and Pacific Beach are cut off from civilization because the Quinault Indians, whose 200,000-acre reservation begins on the north bank of the Moclips River, refuse to allow a road to be built through it. Only eight miles of blacktop is needed to join Route 109 (which skirts Moclips and Pacific Beach, ending at the Indian village of Taholah) with Highway 101 (which resumes its course along the coast at Olympic National Park). Bridging this 8-mile gap using available roads means driving 102 very circuitous miles. There is one mileage-saving alternative—taking an unpaved logging road northeast out of Moclips—but it is a dusty, bumpy ride and still very indirect.

In a sense, one can understand the Indians' reluctance to yield the right of way. Their beaches and reservation lands were open to all until 1969. They closed the gate, some say, because the privilege was abused by obnoxious hippies who lived like free spirits but left behind piles of debris and graffiti-strewn rocks. Then, too, white-red tensions were exacerbated by a local real-estate shyster who apparently burned the Indians in some sort of land deal. In any case, we were told that the Indians retaliated by dynamiting the man's office.

Moclips and Pacific Beach are not well-to-do resort towns. They are dying embers whose gravel streets are strewn with mobile homes, tilting shanties and an undeniable air of poverty. The locals will sit back in their rocking chairs and tell you what thriving places they used to be: how the passenger trains ran out here six times a day, about the prospering canneries and sawmills, about a splendid 250-room hotel right on the edge of the ocean, and (sly wink here) about a red-light district and any number of brawling, pre-Prohibition taverns. The hotel burned down in 1913, and the area has been atrophying ever since. The same slow-talking natives will relate tales about the time John Wayne shot one of his 250 movies here, because it's the most exciting thing that has happened since the hotel burned down.

Lately, the decline of the logging industry in the northwest has cut heavily into in-state tourism, putting an economic choke hold on the beaches. Since 1983, to make matters worse, some sort of bacterial blight has been attacking the razor clams, which have grown scarce. These beaches are the razor clam's ideal habitat, and people from all over the northwest used to descend on the beaches with shovels and clam guns to dig for the sharp-shelled bivalve. The Washington State Fisheries Department closed the season in

1983 and 1984, and it's never been quite the same. Finally, the U.S. Navy shut down its installation in Pacific Beach in October 1987, taking 300 people out of a town that was not much larger than that to begin with.

But then there are the beaches—a resource that no amount of economic hardship can deny and in whose presence there always looms the promise of some sort of renaissance. The two-mile walk from Moclips to Pacific Beach is as idyllic a beach hike as one could want to make. The serenity of so much empty space lifts up the spirits. There's untrammeled beach for as far as the eye can see. The beach is so flat, shallow and gently graded that a few inches of change in the tide level can uncover or swamp 50 feet of beach. Sometimes fog hovers over the beach. Small waves break on the dark, dirty sand, taking on a muddy stain. Brown and gray and blue, like a painting of abstract shapes by Rothko or Motherwell— that's what the beach is like way up here on the far edge of no-where.

On a clear evening, the sunsets are majestic enough to bring you to your knees, to give you religion, to cause you to believe in the supernatural. Did we really see ghosts that night on the beach? There's no doubt about it.

Accommodations

There are two functional motels on the beach in Moclips. One is painted a loud yellow and the other a screaming orange. The yellow one is the *Moclips Motel*, a pleasant place with apartment-style units (living rooms, separate bedrooms, full kitchens) and hard-to-beat prices. Would you believe $29 for two bedrooms on a Saturday night in the heart of the summer? The Moclips Motel has its own little path to the beach, which runs right past the orange rascal, the *Moonstone Beach Motel*. The Moonstone is a few steps closer to the ocean, with a floodlight illuminating the surf at night. Out on Route 109, the *Ocean Crest Resort* is the closest thing to luxury on this part of the peninsula. Units from studios to two-bedroom apartments are available.

Restaurants

Moclips has no restaurants at all, but it has four motels. Two miles away, Pacific Beach has no motels to speak of, but it does have a decent restaurant, the *Lighthouse*. By decent, we mean you'll be served an edible plate of food for a fair price, and you won't leave hungry. Grilled steaks and broiled seafood are served in a spacious dining room that looks like a giant wooden cube from the outside. Compared with what else is available—for instance, a fast-food stand in Taholah called the *Totem Freeze* or the café at a local gas station—the Lighthouse is a palace.

Nightlife

The lounges on the premises of the *Ocean Crest Resort* and the *Lighthouse Restaurant* are the safest bets for a evening cocktail. One tavern by the highway was covered with cabalistic Indian symbols, and it appeared that serious, heavy drinking was transpiring inside. Admittedly, we did not get any closer than the parking lot, fearing a hostile ambush.

FOR FURTHER INFORMATION

Ocean Shores–Olympic Coast Chamber of Commerce
P.O. Box 430
Ocean Shores, WA 98569
(206) 289-4552

Lake Quinault

We stumbled onto the shores of a lake so large and pretty we decided to include it as a bonus to those readers who've borne with us so far. Lake Quinault is a deep blue lake in the lower left-hand corner of *Olympic National Park*. On its south shore is a lodge not unlike the one up the road at Kalaloch. It's worth the two-mile detour off Highway 101, if merely to glance at the lake and its lodge, which is an architectural landmark. Back in 1925, it took only 10 weeks from the turning of the first spadeful of earth till the inaugural guest crossed the threshold. Built of large timbers and rustic in appearance, the *Lake Quinault Lodge* has 54 rooms and a restaurant. Boating, canoeing and fishing can be done on the lake. One of the more esteemed guests of the lodge was Franklin Delano Roosevelt, who was so inspired by his 1937 visit that he put on a full-court press back in Washington, D.C., for the establishment of Olympic National Park. Hats off to FDR, who's probably catching rainbows in that great big trout stream in the sky right now.

Kalaloch

All right now, sharpen your pencils for a pop quiz. Here's hoping you've been boning up on your Indian idioms, because in Washington, they're going to come in handy. The question, if answered correctly, is worth five S&H Green Stamps toward the purchase of a pair of beaded moccasins. Good luck.

Q: The village of Kalaloch, which falls within the boundaries of Olympic National Park, takes its name from an Indian word meaning: (*a*) lots of clams, (*b*) easy living, (*c*) land of plenty, or (*d*) all of the above.

If you answered (*d*), then go to the head of the class. Better yet, if you trust our opinion in these matters, go to Kalaloch on your next vacation and discover one of the loveliest beaches in the nation. Kalaloch is not so much a town as the sole developed outpost along the 57 miles of coastal wilderness that falls within the national park's domain. At this point, it's worth noting that the park is a two-part affair. The vast majority is inland, encompassing many thousands of acres of rain forest and snow-capped mountains. It is the long, narrow strip of coastal park land—which occupies an entirely separate tract—with which we're concerned.

At the Kalaloch compound, you can stock up on necessities (although marshmallows and kites are the big sellers), pump gas at the last filling station for 34 miles, grab a meal, pitch a tent or rent a cabin. Above all, you'll enjoy easy beach access, which is a rare commodity on the Olympic Peninsula. Up in the northwestern corner of the state, Highway 101 turns away from the coast, rubbing against it only for a dozen or so of the park's 57 miles. Above *Ruby Beach*, the road cuts east, following the Hoh River and then turning north toward Forks. South of Kalaloch, it loops around the Quinault Indian Reservation. But between Kalaloch and Ruby Beach is a grand strand of wilderness beaches.

In addition to access points at Ruby Beach, Kalaloch Lodge and the South Beach campground, six numbered beaches are threaded among them. Each has its own small parking lot and a trail leading to the water. It's possible to walk for miles on these pristine beaches without spotting a soul. Even if there are people around, they tend to recede in the fog or are dwarfed by the rocky headlands, the Paul Bunyan-size piles of driftwood and the desertlike expanse of the beach.

The logs are the most memorable feature of the beachscape. Words are incapable of conveying their size or the terrible force that drove them ashore. One finds them stacked against the cliffs, stripped of bark and limbs, bleached gray and sanded smooth by the sea. Some are 20 and 30 feet long—whole, massive tree trunks, lying silently like rows of bleachers above the high tide line. How did these giants get here? The process starts way up in the mountains, when heavy downpours and glacial meltwater floods the narrow creek beds, eroding soil around the root systems of trees close by until they topple into the torrent and are carried out to sea. They bob around in the currents until winter storms drive them ashore, usually some distance from where they washed out. These beach logs are the bones of the rain forest, picked clean by the angry sea.

In winter, the high seas are capable of sending 25-foot waves ashore, and the driftwood logs become battering rams, pummeling the cliff bases, which recede a little farther every year. In the summer, the ocean is gentler and the logs act as bulwarks, protecting the cliffs from wave erosion. It is a process of give and take that has been going on for centuries.

Although more prevalent in the winter months, logs float around in the surf all year long, posing a threat to swimmers, who are already braving hypothermia. We saw a three-word warning—"Beach Logs Kill"—posted in so many places it became a kind of chant. Let the beachcomber beware. Or, as they are fond of saying up here, never turn your back on the ocean. As is the case in any wilderness area, you must be a little more careful here than you would in the womb of civilization. You're warned against getting trapped in a cove by a rising tide or slipping on the rocks. It does help to consult a tide table and plan your beach hike as near to low tide as possible, especially if you intend to amble any distance. After walking this beach, you'll understand why the native Indians regarded Kalaloch as a special, even sacred place.

The sand here is dark brown, being composed of ground pillow lava washed down from the volcanic peaks of the Olympic Mountains. It is fine-grained and dirtier than quartz-based sand—the kind everybody knows and loves. In all respects, though, it behaves like conventional sand—i.e., kids can build castles with it, you'll have to shake it out of your shoes, and it crunches if any winds up in your sandwiches. The beach is hikable all year long, except during violent winter storms. Summer, obviously, is the best time to come here. While the inland valleys are baking with temperatures in the 90s, the mercury might hit 70 degrees at Kalaloch. Offshore breezes keep the air cool and fresh. Kalaloch has been deemed one of the safest places to hole up during a nuclear attack, because of the prevailing winds and the Olympic Mountains' protective wall. We, however, think it's a neat place to go any old time.

Accommodations

People come to the Olympic Peninsula for many reasons. Hunters stalk bear, elk and deer in season. Anglers catch silver smelt, sockeye salmon and freshwater and anadromous trout. Nature lovers seek peace and quiet in the wilderness. Rock hounds scour the beach for semiprecious gemstones and highly prized Japanese fishing floats, though the odds of finding one of these are long. (A woman who's lived in the area for six years says she's never seen one.) RV nomads cool off for a week or two in the summertime.

The park service maintains two campgrounds near the *Kalaloch Lodge*. *Kalaloch Campground* has 180 developed sites, while *South Beach Campground* has 400 primitive tent sites. The campsites are squirreled beneath the moss-hung boughs of tall trees—Sitka spruce, Western hemlock, Douglas fir, big-leaf maple and Western red cedar being the dominant species in the rain forest. Those disinclined to rough it stay at the lodge, whose 87 units include rustic blufftop cabins with an ocean view. Some of the cabins have kitchens and fireplaces, and in the off-season they offer three nights lodging for the price of two, weekends excluded. There are also rooms at the main lodge and the *Sea Crest House Motel*, a separate building in the woods at the far edge of the resort.

Restaurants

The *Galley Restaurant* at the Kalaloch Lodge serves fairly sophisticated fare, including Cajun-blackened salmon, in a fancy dining room overlooking the lagoon at the mouth of Kalaloch Creek. It is one of the most picturesque spots in the park. They serve three meals a day at the lodge, all with a gourmet hand that's a pleasant surprise in Smokey-the-Bear country. This is your only choice for miles around, unless you are cooking over a campfire.

Nightlife

Lodgers, campers and anyone else with a thirst for something stronger than creek water congregate at the *Whaler's Lounge* on the second floor of the Kalaloch Lodge. The real nightlife, however, takes place in the north campground. All the tenters and trailer owners and their children are drawn like moths to the amphitheater for the nightly slide show and program. At these get-acquainted affairs, folks proudly shout out the name of the state they call home, discipline their fidgety offspring (whose attention generally wanes after five minutes) and perhaps learn something about the geology, flora and fauna of the area. Sunset watching is another popular activity, and the crowd at the amphitheater makes a mad dash for the beach to catch the waning rays after the last slide clicks off.

FOR FURTHER INFORMATION

Olympic National Park
600 East Park Avenue
Port Angeles, WA 98362
(206) 452-4501

Ruby Beach

Ruby Beach is a wilderness beach at the mouth of a creek eight miles north of Kalaloch. From the parking lot, a quarter-mile trail leads to the beach. Try not to trip over all the exposed roots. The logs are gargantuan and otherworldly here—fat and round, with enormous knots and limbs flaring off the monstrous main trunks. The beach is covered not with sand but with cobblestones. What little sand there is looks more like topsoil. There are also offshore stacks and islands. Atop Destruction Island, a little lighthouse shines its navigational beacon in a very forlorn setting. The island was originally named Island Dolores ("island of sorrow") because several massacres of Spanish explorers took place here.

At Ruby Beach, Highway 101 turns inland. Just north of here is the Hoh Indian Reservation. Above this, Olympic National Park picks up again for its final push north to Cape Flattery. Roads lead to the beach at La Push, Rialto Beach and Lake Ozette. This stretch of the coast is regarded as the most unspoiled wilderness beach in the contiguous 48 states.

Forks

The town of Forks, though it's 15 miles from the ocean, deserves mention because it's the main supply center of the Olympic Peninsula. With a population of 5,000, it is the largest city for miles around, and it's the jumping-off spot for points along the coast, the bay and the mountains of Olympic National Park. If you are traveling in northwest Washington, you will pass through Forks. There's no way around it.

Forks is merrily described as the "economic hub of the western peninsula, where logging is still king." If logging is king, then the emperor has no clothes. The logging industry has been hit hard since its midseventies peak. A drive anywhere in the vicinity passes miles of barren stump land. Even where there are trees left to cut, labor costs are so high that it is more profitable to ship the raw timber to Japan, have it milled and processed there and shipped back into the United States, incredible as that may sound. As the mills have shut down, unemployment has soared. We could not find such items as "Bakery" and "Car Wash" in the Yellow Pages, but there were six listings under the heading "Alcoholism Treatment Center."

A cross section of an 11-foot, 8-inch Sitka spruce serves as a memorial to happier times, when first-growth spruce covered the countryside. One can, if so inclined, drop by the Forks Timber Museum to learn about the area's logging heritage. But more likely, you'll stop in Forks to patronize its motels, restaurants, grocery stores and gas stations on your way somewhere else. And en route to wherever, you will doubtlessly pass the occasional lumber truck, speeding north to Port Angeles or south to Grays Harbor with a cargo destined for the countries that have become the hot new markets for northwest timber: China and Japan.

Accommodations

Stumbling onto the *Forks Motel* is like finding a Holiday Inn in a town where no one would think to put one. Very nice rooms, very fair prices. There are several other motels close by, but these would have to be considered last resorts. At one, for instance, the Korean manager appeared at his office window after a five-minute wait, shirtless and dripping-wet, complaining of having had his shower interrupted. After hurriedly pulling on a T-shirt, he told us that a two-bedroom unit would cost $55, "but you don't want to pay that kind of money, do you?" Back at the Forks Motel, we grabbed a room with three beds for $50, which we paid gladly.

Restaurants

If you worship salmon, the *Smokehouse* will become your culinary ashram when you're out this way. At the Smokehouse, they smoke it (natch), grill it, charbroil it, bake it and even pack it in plastic for you to take to the folks back home. They slow-smoke their salmon over alderwood the old-fashioned way. On a busy Saturday night, the small kitchen was working overtime to cope with a crowd clamoring for salmon. A pack of 15 German-speaking cyclists traipsed past our table, followed by the contents of an entire Greyhound bus. Then the electricity went out, if you can imagine that.

Nightlife

They might call it Forks, but this town is short on table manners. On Saturday nights, "nightlife" usually means a caravan of pickup trucks caucusing in minimart parking lots. Our slumbers were invaded by the sound of heavy-metal guitar solos blasting from mean machines as they shot down the road, peeling rubber and scattering decibels, their intoxicated occupants hailing one another like Viking conquerors. It made us wonder just what sort of rumble transpires when rednecks meet redskins on the wrong street corner.

FOR FURTHER INFORMATION

Forks Chamber of Commerce
P.O. Box 1249
Forks, WA 98331
(206) 374-2531

La Push
Rialto Beach

One mile north of Forks, a clearly marked, park-service brown-and-white sign points the way down La Push Road. Thirteen miles later, you will pull into La Push, a fishing community belonging to the Quileute Indian tribe. La Push doesn't exactly roll out the red carpet at the sight of an outsider's vehicle, and life here is not one big happy clambake. In fact, the Quileute Days Celebration that was taking place when we passed through looked about as celebratory as a funeral procession. Two bumper stickers seemed to best express the attitude of the desolate, forgotten Indian villages of the far northwest. On the fender of an ancient pickup truck was plastered this message: "We Gave an Inch and They Took 3,000 Miles." The Impala next to it bore this cheerful saying: "Don't Tell ME What Kind of a Day to Have." For whatever reasons—and they are, no doubt, good ones—the residents of La Push don't want you here, and other than sheer curiosity, there really is no reason to come here.

Instead, turn left onto Mora Road, six miles before La Push. It is not clearly marked, but you can use the large country store and gas station that sits on the corner as a landmark. The pockmarked road pierces the heart of stump land—blighted gray-black remnants of a recently logged and not yet replanted area—then turns into smoother blacktop as it crosses the park's boundary. At the end of Mora Road is Rialto Beach, a wild black-sand beach covered with massive, gray drift logs. On an overcast day (which is commonly the case), the logs look like the bones of old dinosaurs. Offshore, beautiful tree-covered stacks thrust upward from the churning water, the basaltic rock withstanding the pounding of the waves. A bundled-up visitor to Rialto Beach sits or leans on drift logs and quietly contemplates the natural acts being performed in this wooden amphitheater.

Cape Flattery
Neah Bay

The northwestern corner of the Great American Jigsaw Puzzle is the hardest one to find. The other three corners—Lubec, Maine; Key West, Florida; and Imperial Beach, California—aren't nearly as elusive as Cape Flattery. Getting there is a modern-day reenactment of the Lewis and Clark expedition. Actually, getting around anywhere on the Olympic Peninsula is no easy hayride, but should you venture out to Cape Flattery, you might wind up taking a hell ride.

Starting from Forks, the only hub of civilization in this neck of the woods, take Highway 101 north toward Port Angeles. Eleven miles out of town, turn left on an unnamed road in the unmarked town of Sappho. This 10-mile shortcut intersects with Route 112 south of Clallam Bay. (All this will make perfect sense with a road map in front of you.) Heading west from Clallam Bay, you are now driving along the Strait of Juan de Fuca. It is one of the widest shipping channels in the world, the West Coast's equivalent of the St. Lawrence Seaway. Route 112 curves and bends along the scenic strait, at times backed by sheer rock cliffs that are, according to the warning signs, prone to sudden rock slides. At other times, there's no shoulder at all—and no guardrail, either. Adding to the excitement of the journey is the knowledge that Canada lies across the mighty strait.

The state route comes to an abrupt end at the town of Neah Bay, and this is where the real fun begins. Neah Bay is the northwesternmost incorporated town in the United States. Not surprisingly, it is an Indian town, the main settlement on the Makah Reservation. Most of what isn't national park on the Olympic Peninsula belongs to the Indians, and the two groups periodically disagree over who has the rights to what, when, why, how, and who cares anyway when you're just trying to find Cape Flattery and your mission is one of goodwill and understanding.

The reality of the situation is that Neah Bay is not much more than an impoverished, windswept village of wooden huts, rickety cinderblock homes and rusted trailers. It is, in anybody's book, a sad testament to the once-strong and wealthy Makah Indians. The legacy of this proud people can be found at the Makah Cultural

Center and Museum, a structure that, because of its modernity, stands out from the harsh realities of the local economy. More than 55,000 artifacts are housed in the museum, some dating back thousands of years. It is a veritable treasure trove for archaeologists the world over.

Today, the Makah people are trying to replace their once-lucrative salmon-fishing industry, which they ironically helped kill off with the indiscriminate use of gill nets and lack of a long-range hatching program. They have also been hit hard by the drop in the logging market, a decline that is understandable once you've seen the surrounding stump land. Where are the trees? The fish? Maybe they should put one of each in the local museum.

Be that as it may, Neah Bay is not a particularly fun place to visit. A sign announces "Makah Tribal Bingo Fri/Sat." It sits close by an abandoned yellow house bearing the crudely spray-painted legend "AC/DC," this being the name of a particularly dead-end heavy-metal band. Some attempt has been made to accommodate outsiders and siphon badly needed dollars into the community, but the boat "resorts" that overlook the strait look more like coin-operated laundromats and the sign for the local motel is twice as large as the building itself. The proud Makah people sulk around Neah Bay, staring defiantly at pale-faced visitors. Only devotion to our mission kept us driving toward Cape Flattery.

On the other side of Neah Bay, one is faced with an interesting dilemma. A hand-carved, barely legible sign points left to something called "Law and Order" and right to "Cape Flattery." We took the rutted gravel road to the right, following it for mile after unmarked mile, grinding the gears and sliding along like warm-weather bobsledders. The road to Cape Flattery crosses Indian land. Either the Indians don't get any money from the government to maintain it or they simply don't give a hoot about the well-being of travelers who, like us, are titillated by the idea of touching every corner in America. We continued driving, but the road worsened, becoming at times navigable only at great risk to the car's chassis. Finally, our mission became secondary to our survival. One too many smacks of the head on the car roof knocked some sense into us, and we turned around on the lip of a ditch.

We never reached Cape Flattery. We know it's out there, somewhere. The road map tells us so. It'd be nice if, one day, the cow-boys and the Indians would settle their differences and work on fixing the road through here. For an area desperately in need of income, the advantages would appear to be obvious.

The Cape Loop Road, reached at the same "Law and Order" intersection, heads southwest. By following a Byzantine set of instructions ("right at T in road..."), you might wind up at *Shi Shi Beach*. It's a beautiful, wild beach, but according to a local publication, not a safe place to leave your car.

For those whose appetite for adventure hasn't been sated by the search for Cape Flattery and Shi Shi Beach, an even wilder chase can be made in search of Ozette. It is another Indian village, located on a separate reservation down the coast from Neah Bay. A road picked up east of Neah Bay runs for 15 miles until it reaches Lake Ozette, Washington's third largest lake. Both the lake, which is quite popular with vacationers, and the beach are part of Olympic National Park. The town of Ozette no longer exists, making the search for it is even more frustrating than that for Cape Flattery. Ozette was one of the main Makah villages when the Europeans first started poking around the Pacific north-west. It was, however, buried by mud slides over 500 years ago. Dubbed the "Pompeii of the Western Hemisphere," it is now a valuable archaeological site. Many normally perishable artifacts were preserved in the mud.

West of Ozette lie some of the most spectacular wilderness beach-es in North America. The only problem is that one must hike three miles to reach them. For lovers of solitude and a healthy walk, this is no problem at all. Safe parking is available at Lake Ozette, and wilderness camping is permitted along the virgin shoreline. The beach at Ozette stretches 18 heavenly miles south to Rialto Beach. If you plan to visit this remote paradise, bring plenty of warm clothing and rain gear, a camera and approximately 9,386 rolls of film.

Agate Beach
Salt Creek Recreation Area

Clallam County has 180 miles of shoreline, an incredible figure. What's more astounding is how remote and difficult to reach much of it is. The county's northern shoreline follows the Strait of Juan de Fuca from Neah Bay to Sequim. Route 112 clings to the edge of the land, offering sweeping views across the bay to Vancouver Island. Often, it is forested right down to the water's edge, and when there's a break in the trees, the clearing is usually composed of loose gravel, hard clay and/or boulders—not ideal beach conditions. Generally inaccessible to cars, the beaches are even dangerous landing places for boats.

Agate Bay, for instance, is the name of a beach near the teeny-tiny settlements of Agate Beach and Crescent Beach. Getting here is a veritable catch-22. "Access is by boat only," says a coast-access guide, with this big *but* attached to it: "CAUTION—boat landing is extremely hazardous." More amenable to motorists and sailors is Salt Creek Recreation Area, west of Port Angeles. Located on the site of Fort Hayden, a World War II harbor defense facility that's reachable from Route 112 via Camp Hayden Road, one can fish, hike and tide-pool here.

Port Angeles

One of the final afternoons of our West Coast trip was spent in Port Angeles. This town of 17,000 will forever stick in our minds not on account of its size, although it was among the largest we'd seen since leaving California, nor because of the majestic Olympic Mountains, which serve as a backdrop. We'll remember Port Angeles because we found a lot of records there. A demanding schedule had not previously allowed us time to scavenge for albums, but we stumbled upon a treasure chest of lost artifacts at an antique store: long out-of-print albums by the Fugs, the Electric Prunes, the Crazy World of Arthur Brown and other sixties weirdos. This, we figured, was our reward for combing 1,500 miles of shoreline, much of it more rural than we'd ever imagined. It was our pot of gold at the end of the sandy rainbow.

We filled a box with acid-rock collectibles, and with the assistance of two bemused shopkeepers, secured our cache with twine and electrician's tape and shipped it back east. And we still had an afternoon and a morning left to explore Port Angeles. The town was given its name—which means "port of the angels"—by a Spanish sea captain in 1791. A large sand spit, the Ediz Hook, protects the harbor, which is the first port of entry to ships steaming up the strait. It is the closest deep-water port in the continental United States to the Orient and the Far East.

The recreational emphasis, though, is not on the waterfront but on the mountains that rise behind it. Port Angeles is the gateway to Olympic National Park. Snow-capped, glacier-cut peaks ascend to heights of just under 8,000 feet. This is the rain forest, or at some elevations, snow forest. Damp air blowing off the ocean is intercepted by the mountains, and cooler temperatures cause the moisture to condense and fall as rain and snow. Mt. Olympus, whose western peak is the highest point in the park, gets blanketed with 200 inches of precipitation a year, most of which falls as snow. Half a dozen active glaciers slowly worm their way down its slopes. So effective a shield are the mountains that little rain falls east of them. The town of Sequim, for example, receives a scant 17 inches of rainfall a year, though it's only 30 miles from Mt. Olympus.

There are three visitors centers and 18 campgrounds scattered throughout the national park's 900,000 acres. Coming out of Port Angeles, a 16-mile uphill drive along Hurricane Ridge Road will carry you to some of the prettiest overlooks in the park. A modern building serves double duty as the Olympic National Park Visitors Center and the Pioneer Memorial Museum. Information and exhibits about the park can be found here. Hurricane Ridge lies at the end of the road, 5,200 feet above sea level.

Just beyond the visitors center, a $3 fee is collected at a guard booth, but it's money well spent. The shift in temperatures and terrain comes quickly. Though it may be balmy and clear in Port Angeles, Hurricane Ridge is another story. We made a 7 a.m. ascent into the mountains, leaving the muggy, sun-dappled town behind. Almost immediately, the air grew chilly. We faced snow-capped peaks, their sides thick with evergreens. By the time we reached Hurricane Ridge, we understood how it got its name. Rain was pouring in wind-driven sheets, and it was impossible to see more than a few feet in the relentless, bone-chilling downpour. It was only August 1st, but it felt like winter up here. Teeth chattering, we glided back down the long incline to Port Angeles, where it was warm and sunny.

Port Angeles is an active mill town, as well as a port. Lumber mills line the harbor area, and the unmistakable aroma of pulp hangs over the town. Pressed against the strait by the mountains, Port Angeles enjoys one of the more stunning natural settings in the west. The town is trying to walk tall despite the economic hardships that have plagued the northwest. The renovated City Pier is a focal point. Flanked by a ferry terminal and the Olympic Peninsula Visitors Center, the public pier houses an observation tower, promenades for strolling and a marine laboratory with aquariums and displays. Visitors can also follow Marine Drive past the Crown Zellerbach paper mill to the end of the Ediz Hook, where there's a picnic area, a boat launch, a beach and a Coast Guard facility.

Downtown, there appear to be as many empty storefronts as there are ones still in business, but the streets are clean and some of the shops are interesting. The center of town is a circle with a fountain and a steep flight of stairs leading from First to Second Street. On the east side, Port Angeles has the usual unsightly smorgasbord of franchises and car lots, but if you can penetrate the congestion, the town rewards the effort you put into getting to know it.

Accommodations

The *Red Lion Bayshore Inn* is in the heart of downtown Port Angeles, within walking distance of the shopping district, one short block from the ferry to Victoria and a five-minute drive to the gates of Olympic National Park. The inn is enormous, even by chain standards, with 187 spacious, clean rooms along the sprawling bayfront.

Restaurants

This is Dungeness crab country, so don't leave the Olympic Peninsula without getting the crabs at least once. The best place to eat Dungeness crab is, logically enough, in Dungeness, at the *3 Crabs*, about 20 miles east of Port Angeles. Close by, the best bets are *Dupuis Seafood*, specializing in cracked crab, on Highway 101 between Port Angeles and Sequim, and *Haguewood's Restaurant*, on the premises of the Red Lion Inn.

Nightlife

There are enough neon Rainier Beer logos on the streets of Port Angeles to illuminate your nighttime footsteps, should you be drawn from the safety of your motel room by some nocturnal urge. If you're hunting up a tavern, let instinct be your guide. The motel lounges are the safest places, while the taverns have all the color. Sometimes, however, the color can be blood red.

FOR FURTHER INFORMATION

Port Angeles Chamber of Commerce
1217 East First Street
Port Angeles, WA 98362
(206) 452-2363

Olympic National Park
600 East Park Avenue
Port Angeles, WA 98362
(206) 452-4501

Sequim
Dungeness

While much of the Olympic Peninsula is inundated with rain, the town of Sequim and the surrounding Dungeness Valley lie in a "rain shadow." By contrast to the 150 or more inches dumped on areas close by, Sequim is a veritable San Diego of sunny bliss, receiving only 17 inches annually. Consequently, people haul boats to Sequim to play in the strait, and some folks even retire here. Sequim (pronounced *squim*) comes from an Indian word meaning "bountiful creature comforts," and indeed, all the trappings of the good life are within arm's reach.

Sequim faces its own bay, which juts down from the strait. Along its shores is a state park where activities from crabbing and clamming to scuba-diving and water-skiing can be enjoyed. To give you an idea of what passes for urgency in these parts, there is a "Red Tide Hotline" with a toll-free number. Give 'em a call if you've got a hot tip on some incoming algae, okay? The state park has campsites and sandy bay beaches. It is also the site of natural clay formations known as "clay babies." Meanwhile, the fertile Dungeness Valley is filled with fields of strawberries and raspberries. And then there's the sun—lots of golden rays pouring over the valley like honey.

One of the most stunning natural features of the Olympic Peninsula is the *Dungeness Spit*, a seven-mile hook that is the longest sand spit in the country. It absorbs the rough ocean waves that funnel in through the Strait of Juan de Fuca, sheltering a quiet bay on its protected eastern side. Inside the hook of Dungeness Strait is a fertile estuary, not to mention some of the most populous nesting grounds on the West Coast for migratory waterfowl. Many different types of ducks nest on the spit, their numbers augmented by cormorants, loons, hawks and herons. The spit is a National Wildlife Refuge, with only a few foot and horse trails passing through it. Spring and fall are the prime bird-watching seasons. You cannot camp or drive around out here, but the park is accessible from Lotzgesell Road, four miles west of Sequim, or from the *Dungeness Recreation Area*, a primitive campground off Highway 101 between Port Angeles and Sequim.

There is, just east of the base of the spit, a little hamlet called Dungeness. This is the village the crab takes its name from. You cannot lose by ordering Dungeness crab in the town of Dungeness, and we did just that at the *3 Crabs*. First, we had sunset for an appetizer: While we waited for a table, a solar light show was flaring over the spit. The range of colors and intensity of hues that warm August night included electric greens and blues, as well as fiery oranges and roses, all dancing around the firmament. Each passing moment brought another turn of the kaleidoscope.

Having been spiritually nourished by this spectacle, we were ready to tear into some crabs. The Dungeness crabs pulled from the strait and the Pacific Ocean all the way up to Alaska are boiled or steamed and served cold. They call it cracked crab because it's been cracked in the kitchen for your dining ease. All that remains is to extract the crabmeat with a small fork. The crabs laid before us were bright red, their legs sprawled over the ends of the plate, which could not contain them. It might be hard to imagine getting full on the meat of a single crab, but these monsters could have held their own in a tag-team match with any two lobsters from Maine. The dipping sauce they are served with has a kind of watery Thousand Island dressing that was a little too sweet for our liking. We simply asked for cocktail sauce and lemon slices and got to work.

Dungeness crab is just one item on a menu that's devoted to local seafood. The Seafood Plate sampler includes prawns, scallops, shrimp, crabmeat, salmon, halibut and geoduck (a tenderized giant-clam steak). For starters, you can order a bucketful of steamers or a platter of chilled oysters. The desserts are out of this world—fruit pies made with peaches and strawberries harvested in the Dungeness Valley and some of the most towering cream pies ever heaped in a pie pan. No trip to the Olympic Peninsula is complete without a hike to the Dungeness Spit and dinner at the 3 Crabs. We can't wait to revisit both.

Port Townsend

Victoriana rules in Port Townsend, a modestly scaled town of 6,000 that serves as the gateway to Puget Sound for ships steaming in from the west. The town was slightly larger a century ago than it is now. At the time, it was projected that Port Townsend would grow by leaps and bounds, but several factors—the emergence of Seattle and Tacoma as inland ports principal among them—kept the lid on growth. As a result, parts of Port Townsend have the look of a town frozen in time. Victorian buildings abound, and even new arrivals maintain the stately bricked and gabled look. The downtown waterfront and a residential neighborhood on the bluffs have been designated National Historic Districts.

Port Townsend is one of the finest examples of a Victorian seacoast town north of San Francisco. Forty different downtown buildings are listed on the National Historic Register, and a 70-stop "historic tour" of the town can be taken. (Pick up a detailed map at the chamber of commerce.) Architecture buffs will be in their glory here, stopping to savor every mansard roof, stained-glass window and square brick facade in town. On the waterfront, ferries make the short passage to Keystone, on Whidbey Island.

Bounded on three sides by bays, Port Townsend offers beach recreation at *Fort Worden State Park*, *North Beach County Park* and *Old Fort Townsend State Park*. Fort Worden faces the strait on the north side of town. In addition to a wide, sandy beach, there are hiking and biking trails, tide pools, an underwater park for divers and the fort itself. Officers' quarters, gun emplacements and other military structures are open to the public. North Beach County Park is quiet and residential, with a terrific view across the strait. Old Fort Townsend is five miles south of town on Route 113. The fort, which served as a defense against hostile Indians, was abandoned in 1895. The park offers seven miles of trails, a bay beach and a memorable view of the distant North Cascade Mountains.

FOR FURTHER INFORMATION

Port Townsend Chamber of Commerce
2437 Sims Way
Port Townsend, WA 98368
(206) 385-2722

Whidbey Island:
Oak Harbor
Coupeville

Depending on which source of information you consult, Whidbey Island is either the first, second or third largest island in the United States. Local boosterism is generally blinder than a pack of bats, so the voices from Whidbey claiming the island is the largest and longest in the country can almost certainly be disputed. Not having our tape measure handy, we chose to rely on the more trustworthy *Washington Public Shore Guide*,* which says that Whidbey is the "second longest island in the contiguous United States," after Long Island. Going the guidebooks one better, we can state without fear of contradiction that Whidbey is the largest island on the West Coast.

It seems odd, at first, that so gargantuan an isle, especially one that's only a joyride away from Seattle, would largely be a secret. We knew very little about Whidbey Island before we visited it, and no one had mentioned it to us during our travels up the coast. Californians exist on a figurative island, seeing little beyond their own borders. Northwesterners speak of the San Juans when the subject of islands is broached. Whidbey is not your basic conversation piece.

A case in point: one afternoon, while hiking around Orcas Island, we came upon a pair of bicyclists from Seattle who were recuperating by the side of the road after climbing a long hill. Taking in our road-weary expressions, they inquired about our itinerary, between deep, athletic breaths. We told them that Friday Harbor and Lopez Island were our next stops, and they nodded approvingly. But when we mentioned Whidbey Island, they didn't nod at all. "Don't bother with Whidbey," they said. "Spend an extra day in the San Juans." They did not expound upon this statement. Having caught their wind, they pedaled off toward their campsite in Moran State Park.

What?! Don't bother with the first, second or third largest island in America? Why, that's sacrilege!

The Washington Public Shore Guide by James W. Scott et al., University of Washington Press, 1986.

Perhaps the Seattleites can be excused on grounds of over-familiarity. Of all the islands in the Puget Sound, Whidbey is the closest to the city. It is also, along with neighboring Camano Island, part of the fifth most densely populated county in the state. Still, this statistic is not as impressive as it sounds, as Washington is not a very populous state. (It ranks twentieth overall.) In the same manner that natives of Manhattan—islanders themselves!—dismiss or ignore Long Island, so it goes with Whidbey. In effect, Whidbey Island is a floating suburb. Instead of wall-to-wall Levittown tract homes, however, Whidbey is covered with vacation houses, retirement havens, farmland and finally, the joyless sprawl of one of our nation's largest naval air stations.

This installation is a dominant force in the county's economy. Luckily, most of the war-game activity is confined to Oak Harbor. With a population of 20,000, it is by far the largest city on the island, occupying a hefty chunk of real estate just south of Deception Pass, the thin strait that separates Whidbey Island from Fidalgo Island. Oak Harbor was chosen as the site for a military base because of the excellent flight conditions. Winds are light, rainfall is half that of Seattle, and the location is relatively isolated. In 1942, when the Navy first landed, the population of Oak Harbor was 375. Today, the booming air station is home of the 13th Naval District Reserve, employing about 9,000 people. Like a cat trying to cover its droppings, the command has posted this sign out front: "Please Pardon Our Noise. It's the Sound of Freedom." The sound of freedom and the surrounding community that caters to the naval noisemakers are what makes Whidbey Island easy prey for a quick dismissal by off-islanders. Beyond the military town of Oak Harbor, however, the island is noticeably free of hysteria.

Whidbey Island is decidedly rural and predominantly agricultural. Rainfall doubles on the southern half of Whidbey, which falls outside the Olympic "rain shadow." Fields give way to more fields, cows and horses roam the fenced-in range, and 135 miles of shoreline lassoes it all. In places, Whidbey enjoys a serenity on par with anything on the San Juans. Much of Whidbey's eastern shore is one huge mud flat at low tide. The same quiet coves fill to capacity (and, sometimes in winter, beyond) at high tide. The western shore of Whidbey is defined by high bluffs above and rocky shores below. Some sand can be found on the southern beaches. Tread softly, though, lest you crush the local razor clams.

The island is reachable by car or ferry. Ferries can be caught from the mainland town of Mukilteo, about 20 miles north of Seattle, and from Port Townsend. Coming from either direction, the ride is barely long enough to let you leave the car and buy a soda topside. Alternatively, one can drive scenic Route 20 south from Anacortes, which passes through beautiful countryside that culminates in a bending, turning, dizzying approach to Deception Pass Bridge.

Deception Pass is the high watermark of any visit to Whidbey Island. The stunningly tall bridge is part of *Deception Pass State Park*, a gorgeous preserve with 1,800 acres of wilderness and eight islands. It is the most heavily visited state park in Washington. The narrow chasm between the islands is fascinating to behold. At maximum tidal runs, water rages through the passage, creating wild eddies along either shore. The park offers many other diversions, most notably nine miles of hiking trails through a virgin forest, four miles of sandy beaches and 254 tent sites. The town of Oak Harbor also has a beach park, offering lagoon swimming on a sand beach a third of a mile long.

An interesting side trip can be made to the often-overlooked southern half of the island. The first stop should be Coupeville, the attractive and unassuming county seat. Although it has been called the "City of Sea Captains," Coupeville is not a city at all but a quiet village of 1,100 built around Penn Cove. Many of its stores and residences date back to the Victorian era. If you're not pitching a tent up at Deception Pass, Coupeville is the place to stay on Whidbey Island.

Other rewarding stopovers can be made at the south Whidbey towns of Greenbank, Freeland and Langley. Greenbank sits on a narrow neck of land between the Strait of Juan de Fuca and Puget Sound. Freeland is a hub for south Whidbey resort hounds. Just north of it is *South Whidbey State Park*, a popular beachfront park with 70 campsites and a steep trail down to the rough waters of the western shore. Langley is the closest thing to an artists' colony on Whidbey Island. (Hey, what would an island be without its reclusive artists?) The pace is slow, the shops are turn-of-the-century charmers, and the scenic surroundings are filled with stands of Douglas fir and Western red cedar, as well as acres of pasture-land.

Accommodations

The *Captain Whidbey Inn* in Coupeville was built in 1907 of madrona logs, but the glue that held it together was the pioneering spirit. The venerable inn was named for the first white man to discover Deception Pass (in 1792), proving that Whidbey was indeed an island. Prior to this, it was considered part of the mainland. The inn is situated on a loop road that runs alongside Penn Cove, on the eastern edge of the island. This road, Madrona Way, ensures that your stay out here will be a quiet one. The main house is virtually unchanged since the day it was built, with a sitting room, fireplace, cove-view dining room and patio, well-stocked library and guest rooms with baths down the hall. A newer annex has been added on an adjoining lagoon. Rooms are equipped with modern conveniences, except for television. When you come to Whidbey Island, the idea is to get away from everything, including *Gilligan's Island.*

In and around Langley are several bed-and-breakfast inns. The king of the hill is the *Saratoga Inn*, nestled atop 25 acres overlooking Puget Sound. For a list of inns in the area, write Whidbey Island Bed and Breakfasts, P.O. Box 259, Langley, WA 98260, or call (206) 321-6272.

Restaurants

Relative to the rest of Whidbey Island, your choice of restaurants in burgeoning Oak Harbor increases in quantity and declines in quality. You practically need a machete to cut a path through all the fast-food marquees. An authentic Mexican family restaurant, *El Cazador,* is where we made our dinnertime stand.

The dining scene improves down the road in Coupeville. The Sea Gull Restaurant is right in the heart of town, on historic Front

Street. The view of Penn Cove and Mt. Baker to the east is one of the best on the island. The food is reasonably good—and reasonably priced, too. For a giant step up in cuisine, hasten to the *Captain Whidbey Inn* to sample their "northwest" style of cooking. Whatever's fresh winds up on the menu, from Penn Cove mussels to wild berry pies.

Nightlife

For a military town, Oak Harbor is a lot less boisterous than many we've seen. In fact, its middle-class neighborhoods are pleasant to drive through, and the retail district looks no worse than that in any other city of 20,000. We saw no cinder-block taverns, no XXX strip clubs, no tattoo parlors or pawn shops. That is to say, a civilian can walk around here without fearing a military reprisal. By the same token, you are wasting a valuable opportunity for rest and relaxation by spending time in Oak Harbor. Dinner in Coupeville, followed by a stroll along its Victorian waterfront, is more appropriate to the spirit of Whidbey Island.

FOR FURTHER INFORMATION

Central Whidbey Chamber of Commerce
P.O. Box 152
Coupeville, WA 98239
(206) 678-5434

North Whidbey Chamber of Commerce
5506 State Route 20
P.O. Box 883
Oak Harbor, WA 98277
(206) 675-3535

Greater Langley Area Chamber of Commerce
220 First Street
P.O. Box 403
Langley, WA 98260
(206) 321-6765

Anacortes

Anacortes, on the northern tip of Fidalgo Island, is the gateway to the San Juan Islands. The state-run ferries to the islands leave from Anacortes, which is the main reason people come here. Another ferry, a county-run operation, makes the seven-minute crossing to tiny Guemes Island for a modest charge.

Anacortes has more going for it than ferry landings, however, and this pretty town of 10,000 merits a closer look. For one thing, Fidalgo Island is covered with parks—13 of them, to be precise. They occupy 900 acres of greenery and scenic vistas, such as the 1,270-foot summit of Mt. Erie. Tulip and daffodil fields fill the island with color, while its waterfront is choked with marinas. In town, there are historic homes to tour, most of them dating from Anacortes's days as a transcontinental shipping hub back in the 1890s. There are also museums and art galleries, mariners' memorials and totem poles to be seen.

The town was named after Anna Curtis Bowman, wife of one of the pioneer founders. Settled in the early 1800s by Croatian and Scandinavian fishermen, it has remained a teeming fishing village with a rugged, old-world feeling about it. In fact, the area is said to look very much like the Dalmatian Coast of Yugoslavia, from which many of the original settlers hailed.

FOR FURTHER INFORMATION

Anacortes Chamber of Commerce
1319 Commercial Avenue
Anacortes, WA 98221
(206) 293-3832

San Juan Islands

Northwest of Seattle, strewn among the icy waters of Puget Sound, lie 172 of the most beautiful islands *not* generally known to man (or woman). These green jewels serve as the final brushstrokes on the watercolor masterpiece of Washington State. Many are owned by the state and have been set aside for the rest and relaxation of the native wildlife.

If you want to get technical about it, the San Juans comprise 172 named islands. The total number of islands in the sound—some, of course, being very small—is 480 at high tide and more than 700 at low tide. Overall, San Juan County has 375 miles of saltwater coastline—more than any other county in America. There are 64 designated nature preserves in the San Juans and 10 under-water marine parks. If you've got a boat and a sense of adventure, you'll be in heaven out here.

Only four of the islands are reachable by ferry, and it is these four—Lopez, Shaw, Orcas and San Juan—to which we'll turn our attention. Some of the other islands—e.g., Stuart, Jones, Waldron, Blakely and Decatur—are inhabited, but they're only reachable by boat and the people who live there generally do not like encroachments on their solitude. Orcas Island is the largest and San Juan the most popular of the ferry-serviced islands.

The ferries themselves are like floating islands, with two decks for cars and trucks and two upper decks for passengers, who relax, read newspapers, sip sodas, snack on cafeteria food, play cards and video games, or just enjoy the view of the islands as they glide by. The ferries leave from the mainland town of Anacortes. You can park your car for $3 a day at the ferry landing or leave it at a free lot four miles away and board a shuttle bus to the ferry. Schedules and fares are not chiseled in stone but change from year to year and season to season. Roughly, the round-trip fare for a car and driver is between $10 and $30, depending on the destination and the time of year. Pedestrians pay from $4 to $6. For up-to-date fare and schedule information, call (206) 464-6400. If you're in Washington State, dial the toll-free number, (800) 542-7052.

The ferries carry about a million people a year to the islands, with a peak-season ridership of 200,000 in August. There are only 2,000 or so rentable rooms spread out among the islands, so if you intend to stay overnight, make reservations well ahead of time. And be aware of the maddening traffic pileups on Sunday evenings, when everyone tries to leave the islands at once.

Lopez Island

By general consensus, Lopez is the friendliest of the San Juan Islands. The first stop for ferries threading the sound, it is a favorite island with people who enjoy the low-key bustle of village life. A permanent population of 1,200 occupies Lopez's 54 square miles, with the numbers swelling in the summer months. The island, third largest in the chain, is particularly attractive to bicyclists and hikers. It is mostly flat, gentle farmland that's not nearly so strenuous to pedal as Orcas Island and not nearly so overrun with cars as San Juan Island.

Upon arriving on Lopez, get your bearings by consulting a chamber of commerce directory at Odlin County Park, about a mile from the ferry landing. Bulletin boards are a way of life around here. News about community events—from meetings to concerts, garage sales and summer rentals—is posted outside both the Village Market (in Lopez Village, the main population center) and Richardson General Store (an old-fashioned market that's listed on the National Register of Historic Places).

There are a few driftwood-strewn public beaches on the island. Two of them—Odlin County Park and Spencer Spit State Park—have campsites, picnic areas, boat ramps and rustic beaches. Overall, Lopez Island sits in the shadow of its more heavily developed neighbors. Though not so well known, it is an amenable island retreat.

Accommodations

A handful of bed-and-breakfast inns and one full-service resort, the *Islander Lopez*, dot the agrarian landscape on Lopez Island. The resort is located on Fisherman Bay. Accommodations include 32 rooms and 4 cabins. If you're arriving by boat, they have a 50-slip marina. With a golf course close by, bikes for the use of guests, and a pool, spa, restaurant and lounge on the premises, there's no lack of things to do here. Room rates are quite reasonable, from $40 to $75 a night in season. As for the B&Bs, *McKaye Harbor Inn* is an appealing four-room Victorian inn right on the beach.

Restaurants

In addition to fine restaurants at the *Islander Lopez Resort* and the *McKaye Harbor Inn*, there are two seafood restaurants in town worth checking out. *Jeanna's Seafood Gallery* is a combination seafood restaurant, art gallery and fresh fish market. The edible artwork served here includes smoked salmon, homemade chowders and vegetarian dishes. With its French Provincial decor indoors and garden terrace outside, *Gail's Restaurant and Deli* is a favorite gathering place. House specialties include alderwood-smoked salmon, Lopez mussels steamed in wine and herbs, and homemade desserts.

Nightlife

The lounge at the *Lopez Islander* resort is one of the livelier haunts in the San Juans, booking a variety of musical talent, some of it nationally known. While solitude is what draws many to Lopez, it's nice to know there's an option should the walls start closing in.

FOR FURTHER INFORMATION

Lopez Island Chamber of Commerce
Village Center
Lopez Island, WA 98261

Shaw Island

Of all the ferry-serviced islands, Shaw has the least to offer the outside world—and the least tolerance of outsiders. It is completely surrounded by three much larger islands—Orcas, San Juan and Lopez—like a hapless swimmer encircled by sharks. Phrases like "strong internal sense of community" and "pursuing their own lifestyle" are frequently used to describe the hermitic island denizens. In terms of nonconformity, Shaw Island is the king of them all. There are no tourist services to be found out here.

Orcas Island

Orcas Island has a curvaceous coastline. On a map, it looks almost like a set of lungs. Because of its unusual shape, Orcas is blessed with a number of safe, deep-water harbors—Eastsound, Westsound, Deer Harbor, Rosario, Olga. This makes it quite popular with yacht-owning aristocrats from Seattle. With the exception of spectacular *Moran State Park*—at 5,174 acres, the largest state park in Washington—most of Orcas Island is privately owned, with the stately second homes of reclusive rich folks set almost invisibly among the forests. Only a golf course offers a hint of their existence, because the island isn't widely developed.

The soil on Orcas isn't fertile enough for commercial farming. The virgin stands of trees haven't been touched by the logging companies. There is no fishing fleet per se on the island. With farming, logging and fishing out of the picture, the 3,000 people who live here year-round either come with money or they work the tourist trade.

Orcas Island, however, is no killer whale when it comes to travelers. A trip here can be as rustic and relaxing as you want to make it. Normally, we don't advise bringing cars to an enchanted isle like Orcas. In addition to the logistical headache and high cost of securing passage, it often seems to defeat the purpose of getting away. Orcas, however, is a large and hilly island with no public transportation. Many people bring bikes with them, but conditions are less than ideal for cycling. There are no bike paths or bike rentals, and the roads are hazardously narrow and curvy. Traipsing the island on foot is out of the question. Eastsound, the island's business and cultural center, is a 20-minute drive from the ferry landing, and Moran State Park is a good half-hour away. Thus, if you wish to see the entire island, you will need a car.

Moran State Park should be required viewing for all visitors to the island. Within its borders are pristine, swimmable lakes and waterfalls, plenty of well-marked hiking trails and 148 tent sites. The crowning touch is Mt. Constitution—at 2,409 feet, the highest peak in the San Juans.

For those who want to hide away in luxury, *Rosario* is the premier resort on the San Juans. Set on a 1,300-acre waterfront estate between Eastsound and Moran State Park, Rosario was fashioned with the comfort of its clientele in mind. There are 179 units, including private haciendas with kitchens and fireplaces on a hill overlooking the bay. The main building on the grounds is the old Moran Mansion, the historic former home of Seattle shipbuilder and mayor Robert Moran. The Orcas Room, on the ground floor of the mansion, is a gourmet restaurant specializing in the cuisine of the Pacific northwest. Also on the premises are a cocktail lounge, indoor and outdoor pools, a spa, tennis courts and a marina. The mansion is listed on the National Register of Historic Places, and the resort spares no expense. Likewise, it is not inexpensive, but if you're aiming high, you can do no better.

Complete solitude can be found at another island hideaway, the *Beach Haven Resort*. The word "resort" is used very loosely. They provide the log cabins and a gentle pebble beach, and you must bring the rest. In other words, plan to come with groceries, books, beer, music and company.

One of the most appealing things about Orcas Island, and the San Juans in general, is the lack of development. Because of its isolation, civilization has a hard time taking root here. In the winter, other than a yacht yacht here and a yacht yacht there, the islands are very deserted places indeed.

FOR FURTHER INFORMATION

Orcas Island Chamber of Commerce
P.O. Box 252
Eastsound, WA 98245
(206) 376-2273

San Juan Island
Friday Harbor

The largest island in the San Juan archipelago is, appropriately, San Juan Island. It is the last stop—after Lopez, Orcas and Shaw—before the state ferry crosses the channel to Sidney, a Canadian town in the province of Victoria. Despite its size, San Juan is in one sense the most compact island. Virtually all the commercial growth is confined to the area surrounding the ferry landing, where the village of Friday Harbor spreads out. For this reason, it's the easiest island to visit for those who choose to leave their cars on the mainland. A visitor can spend the day walking around town or hop a bus bound for the far reaches of the island.

It doesn't take long to gain a feeling for the slowed-down pace of the San Juans. As is the case in most island environments, life is lived a little bit differently here. Friday Harbor was described to us as a party town, a statement that seems ludicrously exaggerated except by the somnambulant standards of the rural northwest. Its reputation as a kind of looser, less straitlaced community is based primarily on the fact that tourists keep the small town buzzing throughout the summer months, culminating in an annual jazz festival. Each July, they present about a dozen groups, from Dixieland to swing, and the ferries ride low under the weight of all the cars that head over for this weekend bash. It's not exactly Woodstock, but for the San Juan Islands, it's a veritable blowout.

The town is geared toward people who pop over for a brief visit on the ferry. Gift shops and restaurants form a multiblock welcome mat that the tourists are only too happy to rub their feet on. "Okay, where do we spend our money?" was one comment overheard from a chirping group. A quick perusal will give you the answer to that: at the upscale stores in the Cannery Landing Mall, at the Cabezon Gift Shop, at the jewelry and crafts stalls tucked into the courtyard off Second Street, at places with names like "C'est Wine" and "King's Toggery." Yes, there are many answers to the question of where to surrender your currency, and all of them appear to be thriving.

Away from this semi-California-ized landscape lies a different San Juan Island, this one inhabited by people who regard themselves as islanders. They're hidden in the cracks and crevices, down dirt and gravel roads, along small coves. Creatures of forest and field who burrow gopherlike into the back pockets of the island, they spurn tourists and revel in their own idiosyncratic islander identity. This gets carried to extremes. There is something of a pecking order, based around license plates. If your plate begins with the letters "SJH," then you qualify for sainthood as an island elder, because that license tag has been affixed to your rusting bumper for a long, long time. If it begins with "SJC," you're grudgingly considered an islander, though a second-generation arriviste. Nowadays, the state of Washington doesn't issue plates with the "SJ" prefix at all, so unless you've already got one, you're out of luck.

An islander can easily be identified as a person who dresses like a scarecrow, grows facial hair in unorthodox ways and affects all sorts of backwoods-savant eccentricities. A parked pickup truck with a large dog in the back is a sure sign there's an islander close by. Sometimes they spell it out, wearing T-shirts that say, "Don't Mess With Me—I'm a Local." As for the tourists...well, we all know what they look like; they've got uniforms of their own. Both sides are easily spotted, and though never the twain shall meet, they bump shoulders without incident during the truce months of June, July and August.

To get an idea of what island life is like, consider the following entries, reprinted from the sheriff's log in the weekly newspaper. What passes for crime on San Juan Island is more like gossip or harmless mischief. To wit: "A San Juan woman said someone stole her motorcycle. A deputy found it was moved as a prank by some of the woman's friends." Case closed. Item no. 2: "A satellite television dish pointed at a liquor store in Friday Harbor was said to be causing a cash register to hum." Finally, this situation comedy plot: "A 17-year-old youth backing his car up in Friday Harbor collided with a parked car. He said he was taking evasive action to avoid a water balloon thrown by another 17-year-old boy."

For the tourists, there's more to do on San Juan Island than buy brass elephants and eat chocolate. Whale-watching from the western side of the island is a popular activity, and buses and cruise boats head out to Whalewatch Park in hopes of sighting a killer whale. A healthy population of black and white Orcas inhabits the offshore waters. Three whale pods, each numbering around 80 whales, make their home here, so the chances of a sighting are excellent.

The National Park Service maintains two park areas—American Camp and English Camp—on opposite sides of the island. The parks were the site of a near war between the United States and Britain over a pig. The so-called Pig War was touched off in 1859 when an American farmer shot and killed a nosy porker caught in the act of rooting through his garden. The offending swine belonged to a British fur-trapping company. Tensions between the American and British inhabitants of the island were already running high. The Oregon Treaty of 1846 had given the United States possession of the Northwest Territory south of the 49th parallel and as far west as "the middle of the channel which separates the continent from Vancouver Island." It was unclear from this directive to which nation San Juan Island belonged, and both sides claimed it. The "sooey"-cide ignited a near skirmish. The two armies set up armed encampments on opposite sides of the island. Troops, threats and armaments escalated until cooler heads prevailed. A British rear admiral stated that he wouldn't "involve two great nations in a war over a squabble about a pig." President Buchanan, who was similarly aghast, said, "It would be a shocking event if... two nations should be precipitated into a war respecting the possession of a small island." One cannot help but think, nearly 130 years later, of Britain's defense of the Falklands or of America's boondoggle in Grenada.

From the American Camp, one can drive or hike to *South Beach*, the largest public beach on the island. South Beach is a good place for bird-watching, whale watching and tide-pooling. Camping is not allowed within the federal park, but there are two private campgrounds on the island as well as sites at *San Juan County Park*. The park service maintains an information office in downtown Friday Harbor, and the staff will answer questions about the park and the island in general.

Accommodations

Because San Juan Island is mostly a haven for summer day trippers, there are only two bona fide motels in Friday Harbor: the *Island Lodge* and the *Friday Harbor Motor Inn*. The latter is a few blocks up Spring Street, away from the ferry landing and marina in a setting quiet enough to allow a good night's sleep yet close enough for an easy stroll into the heart of the bazaar. A double-decker bus that tours the island leaves from the motel parking lot, and mopeds can be rented on the grounds as well. At last count, there were seven bed-and-breakfast inns on San Juan Island, including a 60-foot sailboat that's been turned into a floating B&B. Known as the *Wharfside*, it's docked at the Friday Harbor Marina.

Restaurants

People arrive by the ferryful on a nearly hourly basis, and most of them step off hungry. Friday Harbor answers with a bevy of restaurant choices—everything from deli sandwiches at the *Front Street Café* to fine dining at *Winston's Restaurant*. One of the most popular places in town is *Mojo's*. It's a down-home Texas-style barbecue restaurant where you can scarf down a giant plate of ribs or chicken slathered in tangy homemade barbecue sauce. The house specialty is smoked prime rib, which is delicious. Don't pass up the whole smoked trout as an appetizer, either. Whether you're ordering as a "lone rider" or "riding double," you won't leave hungry. Run by a woman who used to manage a cattle ranch, Mojo's knows how to handle a hungry crowd, and it offers an inviting view of the harbor.

Nightlife

A healthy crew of locals and rowdy out-of-towners gravitates to the *Electric Co.*, the *Turnagain Restaurant* and *Herb's Tavern*. All three places serve food, and both the Turnagain and the Electric Co. offer full-course dinners as well as pizza and snacks. People come in to hang out, eat and drink, discuss boats and the weather, and take a gander at whoever walks in the door. At Herb's, they play pool and tug at paper lottery tabs by the score while downing beer and celebrating the end of another day at the construction trade. A T-shirt sold here says it all: "Herb's Tavern—the Workin' Man's Place." A word to the wise: There's an ordinance against carrying alcohol around in an open container, and most of the arrests on the sheriff's docket, a disproportionate number of them credited to Canadian visitors, are for this offense.

FOR FURTHER INFORMATION

San Juan Island Chamber of Commerce
P.O. Box 98
Friday Harbor, WA 98250
(206) 378-5240

Seattle

After exploring the San Juans, we backtracked to Seattle—way down in the tortured recesses of Puget Sound—in order to prepare for the final hundred-mile push up Interstate 5 to the Canadian border. A week later, we returned to Seattle to get to know the city a little better before catching our flight home.

We thought we'd seen the last great American City back in San Francisco. But then they went and tossed a cement, asphalt and chrome curveball called Seattle at us. For days, we'd passed by the formidable sprawl of Seattle while whizzing all over to catch ferries to the islands. Our casual flirtations had us believing Seattle was a city out of control—traffic flying endlessly past us on 10 lanes of interstate, jet boats spewing oil and gas all over the nearby waterways, airplanes taking off and landing and taking off again at Sea-Tac Airport and Boeing Field like a modern-day version of *Metropolis*. There did not seem to be a perceptible break, other than a few stands of evergreens, between the cities of Olympia, Tacoma, Seattle, Bellevue and Everett—a 75-mile bunker of botched civilization that rivals anything on the East Coast's more viciously maligned "northeast corridor." From the perspective of I-5, these cities are all fairly ugly. Tacoma, we have heard, is ugly from any perspective. *But boy, were we wrong about Seattle!*

We deliberately made Seattle the last stop on our itinerary, visiting all points north and west of here before hanging up the flip-flops and turning in our rental car—10,000 miles and numerous rattles poorer for wear—at the mammoth Sea-Tac Airport. We figured we'd get our toes only moderately wet here—after all, there is no beach in Seattle—and maybe celebrate the end of the road by drinking our body weight in beer for a couple of days. Seattle, we thought, would merely be the backdrop for a joyful, final West Coast binge. On the East Coast several summers previous, we'd ended our travels in Key West. This trip, the last-stop honor went to Seattle. No comparison, we thought. As a finish line, Key West wins hands down. Well, all we can say is that we made a major mistake in forecasting.

Seattle is, in our opinion, among the top five cities in the United States. If the weather were a bit sunnier and the citizens more successful at battling the developers, it could easily move up to Number One. As it is, despite the fact that Seattle suffers a climate so defined by precipitation that major-league baseball must be played indoors—at the arid, sterile Kingdome—the city does astonishingly well for itself.

When we speak of Seattle, we mean downtown Seattle. There are other parts of the city—its hourglass shape is bisected and bordered by the beautiful waters of Lake Washington and Puget Sound, creating innumerable corners and crannies—but most first-time visitors will stay downtown and save the branching out for successive trips. Built on precipitously steep hills that leave the average pedestrian huffing and puffing—and cars with bald tires spinning their wheels on wet pavement—Seattle changes with each turn of the head, each rounding of a corner. The hills lead down to Puget Sound, where tankers, cargo ships and ferries steam in, where tourist-oriented shops and restaurants hold sway, and where the bulk of humanity is content to roam.

This is okay, for the grass *is* greener on this side of the hillside, and you'd be doing yourself a disservice by not exploring these steep streets. Two places, in particular, are worth singling out for praise. First, everyone should visit the much-loved Pike Place Market, an indoor/outdoor pedestrian marketplace built in 1907 that has served as a gathering place for generations. It is the oldest continually operating farmer's market in the country. The countless stalls, shops, restaurants, galleries and sidewalk performers at Pike Place occupy a six-block area—a zone that was declared "protected" when, in the seventies, the unfathomably thick-headed downtown developers tried to have the market torn down to make room for a parking garage. Pike Place is near the wharves at the north end of the downtown area. The fish and produce are as fresh as it gets anywhere in America, the shops are full of interesting things (such as a store called Made in Washington, which sells native food, wine, and basketry), and the human parade is endlessly entertaining.

After an afternoon spent poking around Pike Place, follow the parade south along any of the avenues that parallel the waterfront until you hit Pioneer Square. Seldom will you find a section of a major city so wide-open and free-spirited. Formerly the haunt of hustlers, whores and thieves in Seattle's "colorful" heyday, Pioneer Square was also the home of Skid Road once upon a time. Skid Road was a hilly trail down which logs were rolled to ships waiting on the sound. The name, as you might guess, was shortened to "Skid Row" when the economy slid down the same trail, creating an impoverished thicket of flophouses, missions and dives. Since then, the name has been usurped by every other city in the world to designate their own run-down districts.

The old buildings around Pioneer Square have been restored. Some are fancy turn-of-the-century palaces, some date from the roaring twenties, some are simple row houses. They've also cleaned up the sidewalks and alleys, painted a street lamp here and there, and opened the doors once more to everyone, including the transient tenants. It's a truly great neighborhood, as entertaining a hive of activity as any United States city has to offer. Missions flourish across the street from fabulous bookshops. Wild bars and rocking clubs rub elbows with avant-garde art galleries. Even the street people seem fairly benign and enlightened, in their own way. The closest thing we heard to Manhattan-style nuthouse muttering was one guy who shouted across an avenue, to no one in particular, "Sometimes it's not how long you live, but how you live it." That unsolicited remark finally put Seattle—and a lot of other things, too—in perspective.

Accommodations

The tendency of most Americans who visit an urban metropolis is to avoid the inner city like the drinking water of a third-world nation. This phobia against "going downtown" stems from a paranoid, decades-long movement out toward the country, a suburbanization that, ironically, has created an even more unsightly mishmash of human development than can be found in any downtown in America. It is based on the twofold belief that downtowns are less safe than suburbs, and that motels in the outer environs, like the blue-light specials at K mart, are bargains worth going out of the way for. Granted, some major cities are dangerous places, though the corporate hotels located in them are generally more heavily guarded than an embassy in the Middle East. Yes, the corporate lodges in the major convention cities are ridiculously expensive. Hey, when Messrs. Hilton, Marriott, Sheraton and Hyatt occupy a city, there's really no winning the war of the pocketbook short of armed insurrection.

But there's another side to the story. For instance, in Seattle, you can stay out on Route 99 near the suburban airports and pay less, by a half or a third, than you would downtown. The motels out here are numerous, yet they're as indistinguishable from one another as the channels on their cable TV sets. We, in fact, found ourselves holed up in one of these faceless motels, only because we wanted an early start out of town the next morning. It was not the sort of place we'd want to stay at more than once per beach book, and certainly not something we'd recommend to anyone desiring to see Seattle. Route 99, south of town, is nothing but miles of franchise restaurants, 7-Elevens, car-rental agencies, tire recappers, self-service gas stations and an occasional den of iniquity like Viva's Massage Parlor, which sat across the road from our motel like some kind of mute siren. (Or were we a pair of deaf Ulysses?)

Upon returning to Seattle, we chose to stay downtown our final two nights on the road. By downtown, we mean by Puget Sound, where the waterfront does visual justice to the city and doesn't assault the human spirit like the claptrap of the suburbs. The downtown hotels are, in their own way, just as faceless as the ones out by Sea-Tac, but at least they're *downtown*, which guarantees a parking spot and easy access to everything. Just in case you get tired of walking up and down the hills, by the way, Seattle has the best public transportation system in the United States.

Okay. They also have something like 10,000 motel rooms, most of which are housed inside skyscrapers, where valets flourish like bees buzzing around a honeycomb. We stayed at *Stouffer's* simply because we had a Frequent Flyer coupon a friend had given us. With some fancy altering of the expiration date (sorry, sirs), it gained us a free room for two nights. The good news is that the rooms are comfortable and the view is spectacular. Anything you might desire is on the premises, somewhere in its 27 stories. And you are only seven blocks from the water. The uphill return trip, though, is a killer.

Restaurants

Somehow we managed, between beers, to sniff out a couple of fine Seattle restaurants. In the grand tourist tradition, we did this by sticking close to the crowds and the water. You can't get any closer to either than at *Ivar's Acres of Clams*, a Seattle institution since 1938. Through Ivar's Pier 54 windows you can watch the ferries and the fireboats land next door, but in order to enjoy this spectacle you will probably have to wait for a table with the rest of humanity in the nautically appointed front room. Not to panic, though. Ivar's motto is "Keep Clam," and if you do you will soon be knocking back a Petit Olympic Oysters appetizer or the first of what could easily become an acre of clams. Despite the volume of business, Ivar's manages to produce quality food to match their grand setting. They keep the menu simple and do justice to each item. The salmon steak and Alaskan halibut were both worth the wait, and both worth their weight in precious metal.

Ray's Boathouse, we had heard, was Seattle's other great waterfront seafood restaurant. Unfortunately, it burned down shortly before we hit town. They are, however, in the process of rebuilding, so keep your ear to the ground and maybe Ray will be back in his Boathouse again soon. We hope so.

Pike Place Market is where you'll want to go for lunch or a quick snack. If one of the small eateries is crowded, move on to the next. We chanced in this manner upon *Lowell's*, which turned out to have a great view and good food. It was also a popular daytime watering hole, judging from the nonstop Gatling-gun laughter beside the bar.

Nightlife

It was 2 a.m. in Pioneer Square on a Saturday night. The bars were about to close, but nobody was about to go home. Instead, a crowd of chirping, shouting, laughing, gesticulating college kids began to gather in the triangular 1st Avenue Park. They appeared to be holding an unofficial party outdoors, under the trees and street lamps and stars. A wino cocked a reddened eye at us, gleaning what little he could from our rumpled clothing and dumbfounded expressions. He swayed back philosophically in his bench seat, grinned broadly to reveal a mouthful of metal, and exclaimed in a hoarse croak, "Ya'll oughtta grab a coupla these here foxes and get into some promiscuous activity!"

Welcome to Seattle, where the fun begins at sundown and everyone's invited. After two days, we were so full of positive vibrations about the place that had our plane tickets been refundable, we would have stayed a couple more days. We're talking about two guys who, prior to Seattle, were so road-weary they would've gladly cut a deal with the devil to get home several weeks earlier.

Seattle's nightlife can't be captured in a few sentences. It hops as much as any city we've ever seen. Briefly, though, the best place to go is Pioneer Square, on the south side of downtown—at 1st Avenue and Yesler Way, to be precise. There are too many clubs in this multiblock area for us to mention them all, but every last one was packed, with lines extending out the door. Sometimes, they offer what amounts to a package deal allowing you access to as many bars and clubs as possible. For $5, we got a voucher good for admission to seven different Pioneer Square nightclubs.

The *Old Timer's Café* is a great place for a late-afternoon start, whether you're an old hand or a young whippersnapper. The *Central Tavern*, however, soon became our hands-down favorite. Calling itself "Seattle's only second-class tavern," the Central has live music and cold beer served by female bartenders with spiked hair. You bully your way to the bar, buy the beer in pitchers, then belly your way toward the stage. The Central is a long, wide room, funky and run-down and absolutely wonderful. The band we heard was Moving Parts, a local favorite who have been trying to get a record contract for years. They deserve one. One of their refrains, "We're not going to let it bring us down," was ringing in our ears as we headed back to the hotel somewhere around three in the morning. The only thing bringing us down was the thought of leaving Seattle.

FOR FURTHER INFORMATION

Seattle/King County Convention and Visitors Bureau
1815 7th Avenue
Seattle, WA 98119
(206) 447-4200

Greater Seattle Chamber of Commerce
1200 One Union Square
6th Avenue and University Street
Seattle, WA 98101
(206) 461-7200

Everett

Who ever said this corner of the country was isolated? Uncrowded? Serene? Sandwiched between Seattle (with a population of half a million) and Bellingham (pop. 50,000), Everett is a growing city and home to 50,000 more urban dwellers. Boeing has helped Everett take off; their 747 and 767 jets are assembled here. But the town also has the second largest marina on the West Coast. Only Marina del Rey, way down in Southern California, has a bigger boat basin.

Everett is a port town—apples, logs and aluminum are shipped to the Far East from here—and a resort area with sailing regattas, charter fishing and ferry rides available on the waterfront. Even with Boeing thrusting it into the jet age, there's an honest pioneer heritage in Everett that keeps it from becoming just another sterile city of industry. They have their own public market, for instance, kind of a scaled-down Pike Place. And there are parks galore around here—especially to the east, where the peaks of the North Cascade range rise to heights of nearly 11,000 feet.

FOR FURTHER INFORMATION

Everett Area Chamber of Commerce
1710 West Marine View Drive
P.O. Box 1086
Everett, WA 98201
(206) 252-5181

La Conner

La Conner is an artists' colony on Skagit Bay. It sits on the edge of the Swinomish Indian Reservation and looks out at Whidbey Island, just a few miles across the water. It was brought to our attention by a helpful Washingtonian. Describing the quiet charms of the place, she ticked off the names of a few celebrities encamped there. "Like the guy who wrote *Jonathan Livingston Seagull,* what's his name... Tom Robinson!" She meant, of course, Tom Robbins, the author of *Even Cowgirls Get the Blues.* This cowgirl couldn't get her facts straight, but she was right about one thing: La Conner is a quaint little hideaway (pop. 700), frequently likened to a New England fishing village. Along its flower-lined streets you'll find a row of antique stores, art and craft galleries and a handful of country inns.

FOR FURTHER INFORMATION

La Conner Chamber of Commerce
P.O. Box 644
La Conner, WA 98257
(206) 466-3329

Bellingham

Bellingham is a town of 45,000 built around Bellingham Bay. Remarkable by virtue of its size in so remote a setting, Bellingham has one of the finest natural harbors on the West Coast. It's also the starting point for one of the most scenic coastal drives anywhere: Route 11 (a.k.a. Chuckanut Drive), from Bellingham south to Birmingham. It swoops and hairpins its way around the tree-covered hills high above Puget Sound, which it overlooks. Along the way, you pass such crossroads as Chuckanut, Blanchard and Bow. The road also crosses Larrabee State Park, which offers camping, picnicking and hiking in the mountains and boating, diving and fishing along the bay.

Meanwhile, back in Bellingham, there's plenty to see and do. Old Fairhaven is a restored nineteenth-century neighborhood by the bay. The town has not scrimped on parks, offering several on Lake Whatcom—the long, trout-shaped freshwater lake on the east end—as well as one along the banks of the Squalicum Creek (good fishing here, anglers). The Maritime Heritage Center conducts whale-watching cruises, and visitors can study the life cycle of the salmon at the learning center. Bellingham, the county seat of Whatcom County, has at various times marched to the beat of lumber, coal, gold and oil, never once giving up the ghost. The fatigued or curious traveler, meanwhile, will stop in Bellingham because there are 40 hotels, motels and inns in town.

Just outside Bellingham, incidentally, one can catch a ferry to *Lummi Island*, from the tip of the Lummi Indian Reservation. This long, narrow island has an art gallery, a few inns and restaurants, and an abundance of wild beauty.

Whatcom Chamber of Commerce and Industry
1111 Cornwall Avenue
P.O. Box 958
Bellingham, WA 98227
(206) 734-1330

Birch Bay

Birch Bay possesses the finest sand beach in northern Washington.
It is situated on shallow, moon-shaped Birch Bay, where the sun
warms the sand and the sand warms the calm saltwater sufficiently
to allow swimming. Birch Bay is a resort community complete with
condos, motels, cabins and campsites. The latter can be found at
Birch Bay State Park, a 192-acre wildlife sanctuary and recreation
area on the gentle bay. The park has 150 campsites and nearly
that number of picnic tables. You can come to Birch Bay and build
a beach fire, take a swim, hike along the shore at sunset—in short,
act like you're really at the beach. You can do this because, strange
as it may sound—considering that you're far from the ocean inside
a huge watery horseshoe formed by the Strait of Juan de Fuca and
the Strait of Georgia—you are really at the beach.

Birch Bay Chamber of Commerce
4897 Birch Bay–Lyndon Road
Birch Bay, WA 98230
(206) 332-5888

Blaine

If Blaine were the only American town ever seen by a Canadian,
we would have nothing to be ashamed about. It could be much

worse. It could have been Oakland, California, or Elizabeth, New Jersey, that wound up on the Canadian border, where Blaine resides. Some of our British Columbian neighbors do indeed see Blaine and Blaine alone, and they form their impressions of the American main course from this hors d'oeuvre. Just this side of the international border, Blaine is the last American exit off Interstate 5 and the site of one of the busiest border patrols in the country.

Consequently, the townsfolk get a fair share of business from Canadians, who cross the line for the duty-free liquor stores, the cheap groceries and dairy products, and the state lottery. It is fortunate for our image, then, that Blaine is not a typically deadbeat border town. It is, in truth, a pleasant fishing village built around a well-protected harbor. Formerly enriched by massive salmon runs, Blaine is now enriched by the daily errand runs of its Canadian neighbors.

The character of the town has not been sullied by poverty or lost to bogus upscaling. They have simply spruced up what was already there, making the downtown a relaxing place to stroll and the residential neighborhoods an ideal place to grow up just like Wally and Beaver. The taverns are friendly places, the restaurants are homey and inexpensive (so homey, in fact, that some close at seven in the evening), and the harbor area is a busy beehive of men and women at work. Hey, so what if Canada is less than a mile away. This is Blaine, Washington, U.S.A., and they're doing their jobs just like the hard-working folks anywhere else in America.

The symbol for Blaine is the Peace Arch. This 40-acre state park surprised the heck out of us as we downshifted the last 100 yards for the customs check at the Canadian border. Maintained cooperatively by America and Canada, the Peace Arch commemorates many years of peace between the two giants, a peace that began with the Treaty of Ghent in 1814. At the center of the park stands an impressive, snow-white Doric arch. On one side is inscribed the words, "Children of a Common Mother"; on the other, "Brethren Dwelling in Unity." Pieces of the *Mayflower* are cached in the American side of the pedestal, and remnants of the *Bewer*, the Canadian vessel that opened the passage to Vancouver, are housed in the Canadian side. Flower gardens and picnic tables fill the park on both sides of the border.

New sources of income have trickled into Blaine to replace the losses from the salmon trade—losses the entire Pacific northwest has felt but only a handful of towns have managed to transcend. The money that's arrived in Blaine isn't just nickel-and-dime state-lottery dough, either. It's big bucks, carried in by the golf-cart load and deposited on a spit of land on the other side of Blaine's Drayton Harbor mouth. This newly developed area carries the poetic Indian name *Semi-Ah-Moo*. Until a few years ago, there was nothing out here but the ghosts of Semiahmoo Indians and a few boarded-up cannery buildings. A resort development corporation bought the entire Semiahmoo Spit, as well as a huge chunk of the surrounding Birch Bay headland, and the result is one of the most sophisticated luxury retreats in the northwest, complete with wooded homesites, waterfront condominiums, a world-class hotel-inn and a tournament-level golf course designed by Arnold Palmer. As the sort of folks who court this lifestyle are often heard to say on beer commercials, "Hey, it doesn't get any better than this."

FOR FURTHER INFORMATION

Blaine Chamber of Commerce
P.O. Box 1718
Blaine, WA 98230
(206) 332-4221

Blaine Visitors Information Center
P.O. Box Q
Blaine, WA 98230

Point Roberts

Point Roberts is the end of the road, the apostrophe that hangs over the rest of the West Coast. It enjoys the curious distinction of being the only place in the lower 48 states that you must leave the country to get to. Chances are you've never heard of it, and you've really got to strain your eyes to find it on a map. This is because it hangs down, like a drip on the end of an eave, from British Columbia, about 20 miles due west over water from Blaine.

When the boundary between the United States and Canada was established along the 49th parallel, the peninsular tip upon which Point Roberts rests fell just inside this line. For better or worse, the United States wound up with a 17-square-mile parcel that, although detached from the mainland, is as American as mom and apple pie. Unofficially, though, Point Roberts is Canadian in character. It is their Tijuana, a border crossing on the other side of which lies gambling and drinking and fun (albeit on a considerably more civilized scale).

The permanent population out here is around 1,500. There's an outcropping of modest summer homes, pressed tightly together on Boundary Bay. Lighthouse Park is a day-use recreation area that's free for Whatcom County residents and $2.50 for everyone else. If you continue winding around Point Roberts in a clockwise direction, a gravelly beach materializes on the western edge. A smattering of people come out for the afternoon—everything from Canadian yuppies to Hindu families—to stroll the narrow gravel beach, lazing around on driftwood logs or carrying clam and crab buckets.

From a Canadian's perspective, the real incentive to cross the border is a pair of bars that flank the road where it ends at the beach. The *Reef Tavern* and the *Breakers* have got it all: cheap beer, gambling, pool tables, big-screen TV sets and plenty of room to move. What's more, they take Canadian money at par with United States currency. These warehouse-sized clubs are where British Columbians come to unwind after a week in the trenches. Gambling is a big draw. "$95,800 Gambling Paid Out in May! Free Pool Always," reads the sign outside the Reef.

The gambling going on is the type popular at taverns all over Washington State, mainly "pull tabs" and "punch boards." These are the cheap paper equivalents of Las Vegas's one-armed bandits. You pay a quarter for a cardboard strip, pull the tabs to reveal the panels of animals underneath, and if any rows line up in a perfect match—three mice, three goats—you win whatever cash price that animal signifies. That can be anything from 50 cents to $50. Like the casino players in Vegas who listlessly jack the handles as if in a daze for hours at a time, Washingtonians tear at their pull tabs with all the enthusiasm of broom-pushers.

Americans who want to see Point Roberts, just to say they've set foot on this odd little Q-Tip in the far northwest, will have to endure no fewer than four customs checks in the course of a round-trip. If you're coming from I-5 out of Washington, you will enter Canada and then reenter the United States 45 miles later at Point Roberts. Leaving entails the reverse sequence of customs confrontations. Depending on traffic and the mood of whoever's manning the booth, your passage can be as easy as a breeze or as troublesome as a hurricane.

Coming into Point Roberts was a breeze, and we were genially waved through. Leaving Point Roberts was more like a hurricane. Rain was pouring down in gray sheets that were whipped around by a ferocious wind. Traffic was feeding into the one open lane from three different roads, and had backed up for a half-mile down each. Getting to the front took an hour and a half. And our exultation at having found our way out to land's end dissipated just a little.

Yes, if you're coming to Point Roberts, be advised that you will be crossing international borders, with all the hassles that entails. But for the symbolism of the quest—and to us, it was like grasping the brass ring—a visit to this outer corner of America is a trip well worth making.

FOR FURTHER INFORMATION

Point Roberts Chamber of Commerce
P.O. Box 128
Point Roberts, WA 98281
(206) 945-2313

Directory

Here are the addresses and phone numbers for every hotel, motel, inn, restaurant, café and burger stand mentioned in the text. Also included are those establishments discussed under the heading of nightlife that serve food. Addresses are as complete as we could determine. Sometimes, in Northern California and the rural northwest, nothing more than a street name or route number—for instance, "Hwy. 101"—is given. This is because nothing more specific is available or necessary. When you travel up here, you'll see what we mean. (A) = Accommodations. (R) = Restaurant. (A,R) = Both. Happy trails.

CALIFORNIA

Albion
Albion River Inn, 3790 Hwy. 1, P.O. Box 100, Albion, CA 95410; (707) 937-4044. (A,R)

Arcata
Hotel Arcata, 708 Ninth St., Arcata, CA 95521; (707) 822-6506. (A)

Avalon (see *Santa Catalina Island*)

Big Sur
Big Sur Lodge, Pfeiffer Big Sur State Park, P.O. Box 190, Big Sur, CA 93920; (408) 667-2171. (A,R)

Fernwood Lodge and Park, Hwy. 1, Big Sur, CA 93920; (805)
    667-2422. (A,R)
Glen Oaks Motel, Hwy. 1, Big Sur, CA 93920; (408) 667-2105.
    (A)
Glen Oaks Restaurant, Hwy. 1, Big Sur, CA 93920; (408) 667-
    2623. (R)
Nepenthe, Hwy. 1, Big Sur, CA 93920; (408) 667-2345. (R)
Ventana, Hwy. 1, Big Sur, CA 93920; (408) 667-2331. (A,R)

Cambria
The Brambles Dinner House, 4005 Burton Dr., Cambria, CA
    93428; (805) 927-4716. (R)
Moonraker, 6550 Moonstone Beach Dr., Cambria, CA 93428; (805)
    927-3859. (R)
Sea Otter Inn, 6656 Moonstone Beach Dr., Cambria, CA 93428;
    (805) 927-5888. (A)

Capistrano Beach
Capistrano Surfside Inn, 34680 Coast Hwy., Capistrano Beach,
    CA 92624; (714) 240-7681. (A)
Coach House, 33187 Camino Capistrano, San Juan Capistrano, CA
    92675; (714) 496-8927. (R)
Olamendi's Mexican Cuisine, 34660 Pacific Coast Hwy., Capis-
    trano Beach, CA 92642; (714) 661-1005. (R)

Capitola
The Bandstand, 201 Esplanade, Capitola, CA 95010; (408) 476-
    8205. (R)
Capitola Venetian Hotel, 1500 Wharf Rd., Capitola, CA 95010;
    (408) 476-6471. (A)
Edgewater Club and Restaurant, 215 Esplanade, Capitola, CA
    95010; (408) 475-6215. (R)
Harbor Lights Motel, 5000 Cliff Dr., Capitola, CA 95010; (408)
    476-0505. (A)
Margaritaville, 221 Esplanade, Capitola, CA 95010; (408) 476-2263.
    (R)

Shadowbrook Restaurant, 1750 Wharf Rd., Capitola, CA 95010; (408) 475-1222. (R)

Zelda's, 203 Esplanade, Capitola, CA 95010; (408) 475-4900. (R)

Carlsbad

Carlsbad Inn Beach and Tennis Resort, 3075 Carlsbad Blvd., Carlsbad, CA 92008; (619) 434-7020. (A,R)

Dooley McCluskey's Olde Ale House, 640 Grand Ave., Carlsbad, CA 92008; (619) 434-3114. (R)

Harbor Fish South, 3179 Carlsbad Blvd., Carlsbad, CA 92008; (619) 729-4161. (R)

La Costa Resort Hotel and Spa, Costa Del Mar Rd., Carlsbad, CA 92009; (619) 438-9111. (A,R)

Nieman's (at the Twin Inn Resort Motel), 2978 Carlsbad Blvd., Carlsbad, CA 92008; (619) 729-4131. (R)

Ocean Manor Motel, 2950 Ocean St., Carlsbad, CA 92008; (619) 729-2493. (A)

Carmel

Clam Box Restaurant and Cocktail Lounge, Mission Ave. betw. 5th and 6th Aves., Carmel, CA 93921; (408) 624-8597. (R)

Collage, 5th Ave. betw. San Carlos and Mission Aves., Carmel, CA 93921; (408) 625-9990. (R)

Colonial Terrace Inn, San Antonio St. betw. 12th and 13th Aves., P.O. Box 1375, Carmel, CA 93921; (408) 624-2741. (A)

Highlands Inn, Hwy. 1, P.O. Box 1700, Carmel, CA 93921; (408) 624-3801. (A,R)

Hog's Breath, San Carlos Ave. betw. 5th and 6th Aves., Carmel, CA 93921; (408) 625-1044. (R)

Lamp Lighter Inn, Ocean Ave. and Camino Real, P.O. Box 604, Carmel, CA 93921; (408) 624-7372. (A)

Le Coq d'Or, Mission Ave. betw. 4th and 5th Aves., Carmel, CA 93921; (408) 624-4613. (R)

Lobos Lodge, Ocean Ave. and Monte Verde, P.O. Box L-1, Carmel, CA 93921; (408) 624-3874. (A)

Mission Ranch Hotel and Restaurant, 267270 Dolores Ave., Carmel, CA 93921; (408) 624-3824. (A,R)

Sans Souci, Lincoln Ave. betw. 5th and 6th Aves., Carmel, CA
   93921; (408) 624-6220. (R)

Carpinteria

Carpinteria Inn, 4558 Carpinteria Ave., Carpinteria, CA 93013;
   (805) 684-0473. (A)
Joh-Bert's, 3805 Santa Claus Lane, Carpinteria, CA 93013; (805)
   684-5300. (R)
The Sand Dollar, 5003 Carpinteria Ave., Carpinteria, CA 93013;
   (805) 684-3669. (R)

Catalina Island (see *Santa Catalina Island*)

Cayucos

California Unique Ocean View Motel, 3302 S. Ocean Blvd., Cayucos, CA 93430; (805) 995-2234. (A)
Seaside Motel, 42 S. Ocean Ave., Cayucos, CA 93430; (805) 995-
   3809. (A)

Coronado

El Cordova, 1351 Orange Ave., Coronado, CA 92118; (619) 435-
   4131. (A)
Hotel Del Coronado, 1500 Orange Ave., Coronado, CA 92118;
   (619) 435-6611. (A,R)
McP's Irish Pub, 1107 Orange Ave., Coronado, CA 92118; (619)
   435-5280. (R)
Miguel's Cocina, 1339 Orange Ave., Coronado, CA 92118; (619)
   437-4237. (R)
S&M Submarine Sandwiches, 1025 Orange Ave., Coronado, CA
   92188; (619) 435-2422. (R)

Crescent City

Curly Redwood Lodge, 701 Hwy. 101 S., Crescent City, CA
   95531; (707) 464-2137. (A)
Jim's Bistro, 200 Hwy. 101 N., Crescent City, CA 95531; (707)
   464-4878. (R)

Pebble Beach Bed and Breakfast, 1650 Macken Ave., Crescent City, CA 95531; (707) 464-9086. (A)

Dana Point

Picasso, Mariner's Village Mall, Dana Point, CA 92629; (714) 661-7282. (R)

Del Mar

Bully's Del Mar Mexican Café, 225 1st St., Del Mar, CA 92014; (619) 481-8843. (R)

Bully's North, 1404 Camino Del Mar, Del Mar, CA 92014; (619) 755-1660. (R)

Del Mar Motel on the Beach, 1702 Coast Blvd., Del Mar, CA 92014; (619) 755-1534. (A)

Fish Market Restaurant, 640 Via de la Valle, Solana Beach, CA 92075; (619) 755-2277. (R)

Jake's Oceanfront Restaurant, 1660 Coast Blvd., Del Mar, CA 92014; (619) 755-2002. (R)

Poseidon, 1670 Coast Blvd., Del Mar, CA 92014; (619) 755-9345. (R)

Stratford Inn of Del Mar, 710 Camino Del Mar, Del Mar, CA 92014; (619) 755-1501. (A)

Elk

Elk Cove Inn, 6300 S. Hwy. 1, P.O. Box 367, Elk, CA 95432; (707) 877-3321. (A,R)

Encinitas

Budget Motel, 133 Encinitas Blvd., Encinitas, CA 92024; (619) 944-0260. (A)

Costamar Mex Seafood, 250 N. Hwy. 101, Encinitas, CA 92024; (619) 944-4585. (R)

Lupita's, 830 First St., Encinitas, CA 92024; (619) 436-7097. (R)

Old Town Mexican Café, 937 First St., Encinitas, CA 92024; (619) 436-5895. (R)

Sanderling Place, 85 Encinitas Blvd., Encinitas, CA 92024; (619) 942-7455. (A,R)

TraveLodge, 186 N. Hwy. 101, Encinitas, CA 92024; (619) 944-
0301. (A)

Eureka
Carter House, 1033 Third St., Eureka, CA 95501; (707) 445-1390.
(A)
Eureka Inn, 7th and F Sts., Eureka, CA 95501; (707) 442-6441.
(A,R)
Lazio's Seafood Restaurant, 4 C St., Eureka, CA 95501; (707) 442-
2337. (R)
Old Town Bar and Grill, 327 Second St., Eureka, CA 95501; (707)
445-2971. (R)
Samoa Cookhouse, 445 W. Washington St., Samoa, CA 95564;
(707) 442-1659. (R)

Ferndale
Gingerbread Mansion Bed and Breakfast, 400 Berding St., Ferndale, CA 95536; (707) 786-4000. (A)

Fort Bragg
Best Western Vista Manor, 1100 N. Main St., Fort Bragg, CA
95437; (707) 964-4776. (A)
El Mexicano, 701 N. Harbor Dr., Fort Bragg, CA 95437; (707)
964-7164. (R)
Glass Beach Bed and Breakfast Inn, 726 N. Main St., Fort Bragg,
CA 95437; (707) 964-6774. (A)
Old Coast Hotel, 101 N. Franklin St., Fort Bragg, CA 95437; (707)
964-6443. (A,R)
Quality Inn Seabird, 191 South St., Fort Bragg, CA 95437; (707)
964-4731. (A)
Wharf Restaurant and Lounge, 780 N. Harbor Dr., Fort Bragg,
CA 95437; (707) 964-4283. (R)

Goleta
Beachside Bar Café, 5905 Sandspit Rd., Goleta, CA 93017; (805)
964-7881. (R)

Gualala
Gualala Hotel, 39301 S. Hwy. 1, P.O. Box 675, Gualala, CA 95445; (707) 884-3441. (A,R)

Half Moon Bay
Harbor View Inn, 11 Ave. Alhambra, El Granada, CA 94018; (415) 726-2329. (A)
Mill Rose Inn, 615 Mill St., Half Moon Bay, CA 94019; (415) 726-9794. (A)
Miramar Beach Inn, Magellen Ave., Half Moon Bay, CA 94019; (415) 726-9053. (R)
The Shore Bird Restaurant, 390 Capistrano Rd., Princeton, CA 94018; (415) 728-3036. (R)

Harbor Island
Sheraton Grand on Harbor Island, 1590 Harbor Island Dr., Harbor Island, CA 92101; (619) 291-6400. (A,R)

Hermosa Beach
California Beach Sushi, 934 Hermosa Ave., Hermosa Beach, CA 90254; (213) 374-7758. (R)
Fish Market Café, 20 Pier Ave., Hermosa Beach, CA 90254; (213) 374-9174. (R)
Hennessey's Tavern, 8 Pier Ave., Hermosa Beach, CA 90254; (213) 372-5759. (R)
The Lighthouse, 30 Pier Ave., Hermosa Beach, CA 90254; (213) 372-6911. (R)
Paradise Sushi, 53 Pier Ave., Hermosa Beach, CA 90254; (213) 379-1588. (R)
Sea Sprite Ocean Front Apartment Motel, 1016 Strand, Hermosa Beach, CA 90254; (213) 376-6933. (A)
Sushi Sei, 50 Pier Ave., Hermosa Beach, CA 90254; (213) 379-6900. (R)

Huntington Beach
Best Western Huntington Beach Inn, 21112 Pacific Coast Hwy., Huntington Beach, CA 92648; (714) 536-1421. (A,R)

Café Express, 102 Lake St., Huntington Beach, CA 92648; (714)
    960-9909. (R)
H.B. Charbroiled Chicken, 6th Street and Pacific Coast Hwy.,
    Huntington Beach, CA 92648; (714) 969-8849. (R)
The Hop, 18774 Brookhurst St., Fountain Valley, CA ; (714) 963-
    2366. (R)
Maxwell's Restaurant, 317 Pacific Coast Hwy., Huntington Beach,
    CA 92648; (714) 536-2555. (R)
Regency Inn, 19360 Beach Blvd., Huntington Beach, CA 92648;
    (714) 962-4244. (A)

Imperial Beach
Anthony's Fish Grotto, Hwy. 5 at E Street, Chula Vista, CA
    92010; (619) 425-4200. (R)
Manuel's, 1144 Hollister St., Imperial Beach, CA 92032; (619) 575-
    6829. (R)
Surfside Motel, 800 Seacoast Dr., Imperial Beach, CA 92032; (619)
    424-5183. (A)

Inverness (see Point Reyes)

Klamath
Motel Trees, 15495 Hwy. 101 S., Klamath, CA 95548; (707) 482-
    8205. (A,R)
Redwood Hostel, Hwy. 101 and Wilson Creek Rd., Klamath, CA
    95548; (707) 482-8265. (A)
Requa Inn, 451 Requa Rd., Requa, CA 95561; (707) 482-8205.
    (A,R)
Steelhead Lodge, 330 Terwer Riffle Rd., Klamath, CA 95548; (707)
    482-8145. (A,R)

Laguna Beach
Aliso Creek Inn, 31106 Pacific Coast Hwy., South Laguna, CA
    92677; (714) 499-2271. (A,R)
Beach House Inn, 619 Sleepy Hollow Lane, Laguna Beach, CA
    92651; (714) 494-9707. (R)

Hotel Laguna, 425 S. Coast Hwy., Laguna Beach, CA 92651; (714) 494-1151. (A,R)

Hotel San Maarten, 696 S. Coast Hwy., Laguna Beach, CA 92651; (714) 494-9436. (A,R)

Laguna Reef Motel, 30806 Coast Hwy., Laguna Beach, CA 92651; (714) 499-2227. (A)

Las Brisas, 361 Cliff Dr., Laguna Beach, CA 92651; (714) 497-5434. (R)

Sunshine Cove, 7408 Coast Hwy., Laguna Beach, CA 92651; (714) 494-5589. (R)

White House Restaurant and Tavern, 340 S. Coast Hwy., Laguna Beach, CA 92651; (714) 494-8088. (R)

La Jolla

Avanti, 875 Prospect St., La Jolla, CA 92037; (619) 454-4288. (R)

Carino's Italian Restaurant and Pizza House, 7408 La Jolla Blvd., La Jolla, CA 92037; (619) 459-1400. (R)

Don Juan's Mexican Restaurant, 6990 La Jolla Blvd., La Jolla, CA 92037; (619) 456-2692. (R)

Empress Hotel of La Jolla, 7766 Fay Ave., La Jolla, CA 92037; (619) 454-3001. (A,R)

George's at the Cove, 1250 Prospect St., La Jolla, CA 92037; (619) 454-4244. (R)

Hartley's Restaurant, 5509 La Jolla Blvd., La Jolla, CA 92037; (619) 459-7427. (R)

Marriott Hotel La Jolla, 4240 La Jolla Village Dr., La Jolla, CA 92037; (619) 587-1414. (A,R)

Sea Lodge, 8110 Camino Del Oro, La Jolla, CA 92037; (619) 459-8271. (A,R)

Soup Exchange, 7777 Fay Ave., La Jolla, CA 92037; (619) 459-0121. (R)

Little River

Heritage House, 5200 N. Hwy. 1, Little River, CA 95456; (707) 937-5885. (R)

Little River Inn and Dining Room, Hwy. 1, Drawer B, Little River, CA 95456; (707) 937-5942. (A,R)
Little River Restaurant, 7750 N. Hwy. 1, Little River, CA 95456; (707) 937-4945. (R)

Long Beach
The Breakers Hotel, 210 E. Ocean Blvd., Long Beach, CA 90802; (213) 432-8781. (A)
Casa Sanchez, 3948 E. Anaheim Ave., Long Beach, CA 90803; (213) 494-4156. (R)
555 East Restaurant, 555 E. Ocean Blvd., Long Beach, CA 90802; (213) 437-0626. (R)
Hotel Queen Mary, Pier J, P.O. Box 8, Long Beach, CA 90801; (213) 435-3511. (A,R)
Hyatt Regency, 200 S. Pine Ave., Long Beach, CA 90802; (213) 491-1234. (A,R)
Johnny Reb's Southern Smokehouse, 4663 Long Beach Blvd., Long Beach, CA 90805; (213) 423-7327. (R)
Joe Jost's, 2803 E. Anaheim Ave., Long Beach, CA 90803; (213) 439-5446. (R)
Joe Jost's, 301 Pine Ave., Long Beach, CA 90802; (213) 436-9821. (R)
Legends, 5236 E. 2nd St., Long Beach, CA 90803; (213) 433-5743. (R)
Panama Joe's Café and Bar, 5100 E. 2nd St., Long Beach, CA 90803; (213) 434-7417. (R)
Parker's Lighthouse, 435 Shoreline Dr., Long Beach, CA 90801; (213) 432-6500. (R)
The Pot Holder, 3700 E. Broadway, Long Beach, CA 90803; (213) 433-9305. (R)
Skyroom Restaurant (at the Breakers Hotel), 210 E. Ocean Blvd., Long Beach, CA 90802; (213) 432-8781. (R)

Los Angeles (see Hermosa Beach, Long Beach, Malibu, Manhattan Beach, Marina del Rey, Redondo Beach, Santa Monica, Venice)

Malibu

Alice's Restaurant, Malibu Pier, Malibu, CA 90265; (213) 456-6646. (R)

Carlos and Pepe's Cantina, 22706 Pacific Coast Hwy., Malibu, CA 90265; (213) 456-3105. (R)

Casa Malibu, 22752 Pacific Coast Hwy., Malibu, CA 90265; (213) 456-2219. (A)

Gladstone's 4 Fish, 17300 Pacific Coast Hwy., Pacific Palisades, CA 90272; (213) 454-3474. (R)

Malibu Surfer Motel, 22541 Pacific Coast Hwy., Malibu, CA 90265; (213) 456-6169. (A)

Topanga Ranch Motel, 18711 Pacific Coast Hwy., Malibu, CA 90265; (213) 456-5486. (A)

Manhattan Beach

El Macho Café, 1112 Manhattan Ave., Manhattan Beach, CA 90266; (213) 376-8838. (R)

Radisson Plaza Hotel, 1400 Parkview Ave., Manhattan Beach, CA 90266; (213) 546-7511. (A,R)

Sea View Inn, 3400 Highland Ave., Manhattan Beach, CA 90266; (213) 545-1504. (A)

Shellback Tavern, 116 Manhattan Beach Blvd., Manhattan Beach, CA 90266; (213) 376-7857. (R)

Marina del Rey

Cyrano's, 13535 Mindaneo Way, Marina del Rey, CA 90292; (213) 823-5305. (R)

Edie's Diner, 4211 Admiralty Way, Marina del Rey, CA 90292; (213) 823-5339. (R)

Fiasco's, 4451 Admiralty Way, Marina del Rey, CA 90292; (213) 823-6395. (R)

Marina Beach Hotel, 4100 Admiralty Way, Marina del Rey, CA 90292; (213) 301-3000. (A,R)

Red Onion, 4215 Admiralty Way, Marina del Rey, CA 90292; (213) 821-2291. (R)

Sea Lodge of Marina del Rey, 327 Washington St., Marina del
    Rey, CA 90291; (213) 821-2557. (A)
Stern's Motel, 12664 W. Washington Blvd., Los Angeles, CA
    90066; (213) 306-8243. (A)
Todai Light House, 4676 Admiralty Way, Marina del Rey, CA
    90292; (213) 305-1104. (R)

McKinleyville
Stanton's Barn, Central Ave., McKinleyville, CA 95521; (707) 839-
    3341. (R)

Mendocino (see also Little River and Philo)
Big River Lodge/Stanford Inn by the Sea, Comptche-Ukiah Rd.
    and Hwy. 1, P.O. Box 487, Mendocino, CA 95460; (707) 937-
    5615. (A)
Café Beaujolais, 961 Ukiah St., Mendocino, CA 95460; (707) 937-
    5614. (R)
MacCallum House Inn, 45020 Albion St., P.O. Box 206, Mendo-
    cino, CA 95460; (707) 937-0289. (A)
MacCallum House Restaurant, 45020 Albion St., Mendocino, CA
    95460; (707) 937-5763. (R)
Mendocino Hotel and Garden Cottages, 45080 Main St., P.O. Box
    587, Mendocino, CA 95460; (707) 937-0511. (A,R)
Seagull Restaurant and Cellar Bar, Lansing and Ukiah Sts., Men-
    docino, CA 95460; (707) 937-2100. (R)

Montara
Farallone Hotel, 1410 Main St., Montara, CA 94037; (415) 728-
    7817. (A)

Montecito (see Santa Barbara)

Monterey
Abalonetti, 57 Old Fisherman's Wharf, Monterey, CA 93940; (408)
    373-1851. (R)

Domenico's on the Wharf, 50 Old Fisherman's Wharf, Monterey, CA 93940; (408) 372-3655. (R)

Gianni's Pizza, 725 Lighthouse Ave., Monterey, CA 93940; (408) 649-1500. (R)

Hotel Pacific, 300 Pacific St., Monterey, CA 93940; (408) 373-5700. (A)

The Jabberwock, 598 Laine St., Monterey, CA 93940; (408) 372-4777. (A)

Jack Swan's Tavern, Pacific and Scott Sts., Monterey, CA 93940; (408) 375-5100. (R)

Monterey Plaza Hotel, 400 Cannery Row, Monterey, CA 93940; (408) 646-1700. (A,R)

Rappa's Seafood Restaurant, Old Fisherman's Wharf, Monterey, CA 93940; (408) 372-7562. (R)

The Rogue, Fisherman's Wharf #2, Monterey, CA 93940; (408) 372-4586. (R)

The Sardine Factory, 701 Wave St., Monterey, CA 93940; (408) 373-3775. (R)

Steinbeck Lobster Grotto, 720 Cannery Row, Monterey, CA 93940; (408) 373-1884. (R)

Morro Bay

Bob's Seafood, 833 Embarcadero, Morro Bay, CA 93442; (805) 772-8473. (R)

Café Baja, 980 Main St., Morro Bay, CA 93442; (805) 772-2252. (R)

Embarcadero Inn, 456 Embarcadero, Morro Bay, CA 93442; (805) 772-2700. (A)

Great American Fish Company, 1185 Embarcadero, Morro Bay, CA 93442; (805) 772-4407. (R)

Hungry Tiger, 861 Market St., Morro Bay, CA 93442; (805) 772-7321. (R)

Inn at Morro Bay, 19 Country Club Rd., Morro Bay, CA 93442; (805) 772-5651. (A,R)

Rose's Landing, 725 Embarcadero, Morro Bay, CA 93442; (805) 772-4441. (R)

Moss Landing

Bob's Crab, Hwy. 1, Moss Landing, CA 95039; (408) 633-3127. (R)

Teri's Stop 'n' Eat, Hwy. 1, Moss Landing, CA 95039; (408) 633-3858. (R)

Newport Beach

The Cannery, 3010 Lafayette Ave., Newport Beach, CA 92663; (714) 675-5777. (R)

The Crab Cooker, 2200 Newport Blvd., Newport Beach, CA 92663; (714) 673-0100. (R)

Four Seasons Hotel, 690 Newport Center Dr., Newport Beach, CA 92660; (714) 759-0808. (A,R)

Newport Beach Marriott Hotel and Tennis Club, 900 Newport Center Dr., Newport Beach, CA 92660; (714) 640-4000. (A,R)

Portofino Beach Hotel, 2306 W. Oceanfront, Newport Beach, CA 92663; (714) 673-7030. (A)

Ruby's Diner, 1 Balboa Pier, Newport Beach, CA 92663; (714) 675-7029. (R)

Studio Café, 100 Main St., Newport Beach, CA 92663; (714) 675-7760. (R)

The Warehouse, 3450 Via Osporo, Newport Beach, CA 92663; (714) 673-4700. (R)

Woody's Wharf, 2318 Newport Blvd., Newport Beach, CA 92663; (714) 675-0474 (R)

Ocean Beach

Ocean Beach Motel, 5080 Newport Ave., San Diego, CA 92107; (619) 223-7191. (A)

Oxnard

Casa Sirena Marina Resort, 3605 Peninsula Rd., Oxnard, CA 93030; (805) 985-6311. (A)

Lobster Trap Restaurant (in the Casa Sirena Resort), 3605 Peninsula Rd., Oxnard, CA 93030; (805) 985-6361. (R)

Mandalay Beach Resort, 2101 Mandalay Beach Rd., Oxnard, CA 93030; (805) 984-2500. (A,R)

Pacifica
A&W Root Beer, 5200 Coast Hwy., Pacifica, CA 94044; (415) 368-
3737. (R)

Pacific Beach
Cass Street Bar and Grill, 4612 Cass St., Pacific Beach, CA 92109;
(619) 270-1320. (R)
Club Diego's, 860 Garnet Ave., Pacific Beach, CA 92109; (619)
272-1241. (R)
Crystal Pier Motel, 4500 Ocean Blvd., Pacific Beach, CA 92109;
(619) 483-6983. (A)
Hennessey's Tavern, 4650 Mission Blvd., Pacific Beach, CA 92109;
(619) 483-8847. (R)
Old Pacific Beach Café, 4287 Mission Blvd., Pacific Beach, CA
92109; (619) 270-7522. (R)
Pacific Terrace Inn, 610 Diamond St., Pacific Beach, CA 92109;
(619) 581-3500. (A)

Pacific Grove
Asilomar Conference Center, 800 Asilomar Blvd., P.O. Box 537,
Pacific Grove, CA 93950; (408) 372-8016. (A,R)
Gosby House Inn, 643 Lighthouse Ave., Pacific Grove, CA 93950;
(408) 375-1287. (A)
Green Gables Inn, 104 Fifth St., Pacific Grove, CA 93950; (408)
375-2095. (A)
Larchwood Inn, 740 Crocker Ave., Pacific Grove, CA 93950; (408)
373-1114. (A)
The Old Bath House, 620 Oceanview Blvd., Pacific Grove, CA
93950; (408) 375-5195. (R)
Pacific Grove Plaza, 620 Lighthouse Ave., Pacific Grove, CA
93950; (408) 373-3307. (A)
The Tinnery, 631 Oceanview Blvd., Pacific Grove, CA 93950;
(408) 646-1040. (R)

Pacific Palisades (see Malibu)

Pebble Beach
The Lodge at Pebble Beach, 17-Mile Dr., P.O. Box 1128, Pebble
    Beach, CA 93953; (408) 624-3811. (A,R)

Philo
Floodgate Café, Hwy. 128, Philo, CA 95466; (707) 895-2422. (R)

Pismo Beach
Sandcastle Inn, 1100 Stimson Ave., Pismo Beach, CA 93449; (805)
    773-3422. (A)
Sea Crest Motel, 2241 Price St., Pismo Beach, CA 93449; (805)
    773-4608. (A,R)

Point Reyes
Barnaby's by the Bay, 12938 Sir Francis Drake Blvd., Inverness,
    CA 94937; (415) 669-1114. (R)
Drake Beach Café, Point Reyes National Seashore, Point Reyes,
    CA 94956; (415) 669-1297. (R)
Station House Café, Main St., Point Reyes, CA 94956; (415) 663-
    1515. (R)
Thirty-Nine Cypress, P.O. Box 176, Point Reyes, CA 94956; (415)
    663-1709. (A)
Vladimir's Czechoslovakian Restaurant, Sir Francis Drake Hwy.,
    Inverness, CA 94937; (415) 669-1021. (R)

Princeton (see Half Moon Bay)

Redondo Beach
Blue Moon Saloon, 207 N. Harbor Dr., Redondo Beach, CA
    90277; (213) 374-3339. (R)
Breaker's Seafood Co., 400 Fisherman's Wharf, Redondo Beach,
    CA 90277; (213) 376-0428. (R)
Catalina Grill, 1814 S. Catalina Ave., Redondo Beach, CA 90277;
    (213) 316-7716. (R)
Charley Brown's, 655 N. Harbor Dr., Redondo Beach, 90277; (213)
    318-3474. (R)

Chez Allez, 1718 Pacific Coast Hwy., Redondo Beach, CA 90277; (213) 540-8733. (R)

Chez Melange, 1716 Pacific Coast Hwy., Redondo Beach, CA 90277; (213) 540-1222. (R)

Hennessey's Tavern, 1712 S. Catalina Ave., Redondo Beach, CA 90277; (213) 540-8443. (R)

Palos Verdes Inn, 1700 S. Pacific Coast Hwy., Redondo Beach, CA 90277; (213) 316-4211. (A,R)

Red Onion, 655 N. Harbor Dr., Redondo Beach, CA 90277; (213) 376-8813. (R)

Sheraton Redondo Beach, 300 N. Harbor Dr., Redondo Beach, CA 90277; (213) 318-8888. (A,R)

The Strand Supper Club, 1700 S. Pacific Coast Hwy., Redondo Beach, CA 90277; (213) 316-1700. (R)

Tony's Fish Market and Restaurant, 112 Fisherman's Wharf, Redondo Beach, CA 90277; (213) 376-3416. (R)

San Clemente

Fisherman's Restaurant and Lounge, 611 Avenida Victoria, San Clemente, CA 92672; (714) 498-6438. (R)

San Clemente Inn, 2600 Avenida Del Presidente, San Clemente, CA 92672; (714) 492-6103. (A)

Swallow's Cove, 2600 Avenida Del Presidente, San Clemente, CA 92672; (714) 498-9202. (R)

San Diego (see Harbor Island, La Jolla, Ocean Beach, Pacific Beach)

San Francisco

A. Sabella's, 2766 Taylor St., San Francisco, CA 94133; (415) 771-6775. (R)

Cliff House Seafood and Beverage Company, 1090 Point Lobos, San Francisco, CA 94121; (415) 386-3330. (R)

Fisherman's Wharf TraveLodge, 1201 Columbus Ave., San Francisco, CA 94133; (415) 776-7070. (A)

Four Seasons Clift, 495 Geary St., San Francisco, CA 94102; (415) 775-4700. (A,R)

Holiday Inn Fisherman's Wharf, 1300 Columbus Ave., San Francisco, CA 94133; (415) 771-9000. (A,R)

Howard Johnson's Motor Lodge at Fisherman's Wharf, 580 Beach St., San Francisco, CA 94133. (A,R)

Petite Auberge, 863 Bush St., San Francisco, CA 94108; (415) 928-6000. (A)

San Francisco Marriott Fisherman's Wharf, 1250 Columbus Ave., San Francisco, CA 94133; (415) 775-7555. (A,R)

Sheraton at Fisherman's Wharf, 2500 Mason Ave., San Francisco, CA 94133; (415) 362-5500. (A,R)

White Swan Inn, 845 Bush St., San Francisco, CA 94108; (415) 775-1755. (A)

San Simeon

Best Western Cavalier Inn and Restaurant, 9415 Hearst Dr., San Simeon, CA 93452; (805) 927-4688. (A,R)

Best Western Green Tree Inn, Hwy. 1, P.O. Box 100, San Simeon, CA 93452; (805) 927-4691. (A)

Holiday Inn, 9070 Castillo Ave., San Simeon, CA 93452; (805) 927-8691. (A,R)

San Simeon Lodge, 9520 Castillo Dr., San Simeon, CA 93452; (805) 927-4601. (A)

San Simeon Restaurant, 9520 Castillo Dr., San Simeon, CA 93452; (805) 927-4604. (R)

Sebastian's General Store and Patio Café, Old Hwy. 1, San Simeon, CA 93452; (805) 927-4217. (R)

Silver Surf Friendship Inn Motel, 9390 Castillo Dr., San Simeon, CA 93452; (805) 927-4661. (A)

Santa Barbara

Don the Beachcomber, 435 S. Milpas St., Santa Barbara, CA 93103; (805) 966-2285. (R)

Downey's, 1305 State St., Santa Barbara, CA 93101; (805) 966-5006. (R)

El Encanto Hotel and Villas, 1900 Lasuen Rd., Santa Barbara, CA 93103; (805) 687-5000. (A,R)

Famous Enterprise Fish Co., 225 State St., Santa Barbara, CA 93101; (805) 963-8651. (R)

Fess Parker's Red Lion Resort Hotel, 630 E. Cabrillo Blvd., Santa Barbara, CA 93101; (805) 564-4333. (A,R)

The Harbor Restaurant, 210 Stearns Wharf, Santa Barbara, CA 93101; (805) 963-3311. (R)

Joe's Café, 536 State St., Santa Barbara, CA 93101; (805) 966-4638. (R)

Marriott's Santa Barbara Biltmore, 1260 Channel Dr., Montecito, CA 93108; (805) 969-2261. (A,R)

Rocky Galenti's, 35 State St., Santa Barbara, CA 93101; (805) 963-9477. (R)

Santa Barbara Inn, 435 S. Milpas, Santa Barbara, CA 93103; (805) 966-2285. (A)

Santa Catalina Island

Antonio's Pizzeria, 114 Sumner St., Avalon, CA 90704; (213) 510-0060. (R)

Avalon Seafood, Green Pleasure Pier, Avalon, CA 90704; (213) 510-0197. (R)

Glenmore Plaza Hotel, 120 Sumner St., Avalon, CA 90704; (213) 510-0017. (A)

Pavilion Lodge, 513 Crescent St., Avalon, CA 90704; (213) 510-1788. (A)

Hotel Villa Portofino, 111 Crescent Ave., Avalon, CA 90704; (213) 510-0555. (A)

Ristorante Villa Portofino, 111 Crescent Ave., Avalon, CA 90704; (213) 510-0508. (R)

Santa Cruz

Best Inn, 370 Ocean St., Santa Cruz, CA 95060; (408) 458-9220. (A)

The Broken Egg, 605 Front St., Santa Cruz, CA 95060; (408) 426-0157. (R)

The Catalyst, 1011 Pacific Ave., Santa Cruz, CA 95060; (408) 423-1336.

Crow's Nest, 2218 E. Cliff Dr., Santa Cruz, CA 95062; (408) 476-4560. (R)

Dream Inn, 175 W. Cliff Dr., Santa Cruz, CA 95060; (408) 426-4330. (A,R)

Ideal Fish Company, 106 Beach St., Santa Cruz, CA 95060; (408) 423-5271. (R)

Malio's Seafood Restaurant, Municipal Wharf, Santa Cruz, CA 95060; (408) 423-5200. (R)

Motel Continental, 414 Ocean St., Santa Cruz, CA 95060; (408) 429-1221. (A)

O. T. Price's Music Hall, 3600 Soquel Dr., Soquel, CA 95073; (408) 476-3939. (R)

Riverside Garden Inn, 600 Riverside, Santa Cruz, CA 95060; (408) 458-9660. (A)

Santa Monica

The Breakers Motel, 1501 Ocean Ave., Santa Monica, CA 90401; (213) 451-4811. (R)

Holiday Inn at the Pier, 120 Colorado Ave., Santa Monica, CA 90401; (213) 451-0676. (A,R)

Pacific Sands Motel, 1515 Ocean Ave., Santa Monica, CA 90401; (213) 395-6133. (A)

Ye Olde King's Head, 116 Santa Monica Blvd., Santa Monica, CA 90401; (213) 451-1402. (R)

Sausalito

Alta Mira Continental Hotel, 125 Bulkley Ave., Sausalito, CA 94966; (415) 332-1350. (A,R)

Casa Madrona, 801 Bridgeway, Sausalito, CA 94965; (415) 332-0502. (A,R)

Flynn's Landing, 303 Johnson St., Sausalito, CA 94965; (415) 332-0131. (R)

Houlihan's Old Place, 660 Bridgeway, Sausalito, CA 94965; (415) 332-8512. (R)

No Name Bar, 757 Bridgeway, Sausalito, CA 94965; (415) 332-1392. (R)

Ondine Restaurant, 558 Bridgeway, Sausalito, CA 94965; (415) 332-0791. (R)

Patterson's Bar, 739 Bridgeway, Sausalito, CA 94965; (415) 332-1264. (R)

Winship's, 670 Bridgeway, Sausalito, CA 94965; (415) 332-1454. (R)

Seal Beach

Hennessey's Tavern, 140 Main St., Seal Beach, CA 90740; (213) 598-4419. (R)

Radisson Inn, 600 Marina Dr., Seal Beach, CA 90740; (213) 493-7501. (A)

Walt's Wharf, 201 Main St., Seal Beach, CA 90740; (213) 598-4433. (R)

Sea Ranch

Sea Ranch Lodge, Hwy. 1, P.O. Box 1, Sea Ranch, CA 95497; (707) 785-2371. (A,R)

Shelter Cove

Pelican's Landing Restaurant, Wave Dr., Shelter Cove, CA 95489; (707) 986-7793. (R)

Shelter Cove Beachcomber Inn, 7272 Shelter Cove Rd., Whitehorn, CA 95489; (707) 986-7733. (A)

Shelter Cove Motor Inn, Wave Dr., Shelter Cove, CA 95489; (707) 986-7521. (A)

Solana Beach (see also Del Mar)

Belly Up Tavern, 143 S. Cedros Ave., Solana Beach, CA 92075; (619) 481-9022. (R)

Casa Blanca Motel, 717 S. Hwy. 100, Solana Beach, CA 92075; (619) 755-2707. (A)

Club Diego's, 635 S. Hwy. 101, Solana Beach, CA 92075; (619) 755-4814. (R)

Soquel (see Santa Cruz)

Stinson Beach
Stinson Beach Motel, 3416 Hwy. 1, Stinson Beach, CA 94970; (415) 868-1712. (A)

Sunset Beach
Harbor House Café, 16341 Pacific Coast Hwy., Sunset Beach, CA 90742; (213) 592-5404. (R)
Harpoon Harry's, 16821 Pacific Coast Hwy., Sunset Beach, CA 90742; (213) 592-5216. (R)

Tiburon
Christopher's, 9 Main St., Tiburon, CA 94920; (415) 435-4600. (R)
The Dock, 25 Main St., Tiburon, CA 94920; (415) 435-3559. (R)
Sam's Anchor Café, 27 Main St., Tiburon, CA 94920; (415) 435-4527. (R)
Tiburon Lodge and Conference Center, 1651 Tiburon Blvd., Tiburon, CA 94920; (415) 435-3133. (A,R)

Trinidad
Bishop Pine Lodge, 1481 Patrick's Point Dr., Trinidad, CA 95570; (707) 677-3314. (A)
Colonial Inn Restaurant, Patrick's Point Dr., Trinidad, CA 95570; (707) 677-3001. (R)
Merryman's, Moonstone Beach Dr., Trinidad, CA 95570; (707) 677-3111. (R)
Seascape Restaurant, Trinidad Pier, Trinidad, CA 95570; (707) 677-3762. (R)
Trinidad Bed and Breakfast Inn, 560 Edwards St., Trinidad, CA 95570; (707) 677-0840. (A)

Venice
Cadillac Hotel, 401 Ocean Front Walk, Venice, CA 90291; (213) 399-9602. (A)
Del-Cor Pizza, 1019 Ocean Front Walk, Venice, CA 90291; (213) 392-9619. (R)

Sidewalk Café, 1401 Ocean Front Walk, Venice, CA 90291; (213) 399-5547. (R)

Venice Beach Cotel, 25 Windward Ave., Venice, CA 90291; (213) 399-9914. (A)

Ventura

Bombay Bar and Grill, 143 S. California St., Ventura, CA 93001; (805) 643-4404. (R)

Franky's Restaurant, 456 E. Main St., Ventura, CA 93001; (805) 648-6282. (R)

Holiday Inn, 450 E. Harbor Blvd., Ventura, CA 93001; (805) 648-7731. (A,R)

Pierpont Inn, 550 San Jon Rd., Ventura, CA 93001; (805) 643-6144. (A,R)

OREGON

Bandon

Andrea's Old Town Café and Coffeehouse, 160 Baltimore St., Bandon, OR 97411; (503) 347-3022. (R)

The Inn at Face Rock, 3225 Beach Loop Dr., Bandon, OR 97411; (503) 347-9441. (A,R)

Lloyd's of Bandon, Second St., Bandon, OR 97411; (503) 347-9987. (R)

Sunset Motel, 1755 Beach Loop Dr., Bandon, OR 97411; (503) 347-2453. (A)

The Wheelhouse Restaurant, Chicago and First Sts., Bandon, OR 97411; (503) 347-9331. (R)

Brookings

Chetco Inn, 417 Fern St., Brookings, OR 97415; (503) 469-9984. (A)

Chetco River House, 241 Chetco Ave., Brookings, OR 97415; (503) 469-4031. (R)

Cannon Beach

Bill's Tavern, 188 N. Hemlock St., Cannon Beach, OR 97110; (503) 436-2202. (R)

Blue Gull Motel, 632 S. Hemlock St., Cannon Beach, OR 97110; (503) 436-2714. (A)

Crab Broiler, Hwy. 101 and Hwy. 26, Cannon Beach, OR 97110; (503) 738-5313. (R)

Dooley's West Texas Bar-B-Que, 339 N. Elm St., Cannon Beach, OR 97110; (503) 436-1827. (R)

McBee Motel, 888 S. Hemlock St., Cannon Beach, OR 97110; (503) 436-2569. (A)

Surfview Resort, 1400 S. Hemlock St., Cannon Beach, OR 97110; (503) 436-1566. (A,R)

Depoe Bay

Holiday Surf Lodge, Hwy. 101, P.O. Box 9, Depoe Bay, OR 97341; (503) 765-2133. (A)

Sea Hag, 5757 Hwy. 101, Depoe Bay, OR 97341; (503) 765-7901. (R)

Florence

Driftwood Shores Surfside Resort, 88416 First Ave., Florence, OR 97439; (503) 997-8263. (A,R)

Fisherman's Wharf, 1342 Bay St., Florence, OR 97439; (503) 997-2613. (R)

Johnson House Bed and Breakfast, 216 Maple St., Florence, OR 97439; (503) 997-8000. (A)

Mo's, 1435 Bay St., Florence, OR 97439; (503) 997-2185. (R)

Silver Sands Motel, 1449 Hwy. 101, Florence, OR 97434; (503) 997-3459. (A)

Windward Inn, 3757 Hwy. 101 N., Florence, OR 97439; (503) 997-8243. (R)

Gearhart

Cole's Tyberg Motel, 67 N. Cottage St., Gearhart, OR 97138; (503) 738-7373. (A)

Gearhart by the Sea, Marion Ave. and Tenth St., Gearhart, OR 97138; (503) 738-8331. (A,R)

Gleneden Beach
Salishan Lodge, Hwy. 101, P.O. Box 118, Gleneden Beach, OR 97388; (503) 764-3600. (A,R)
The Dining Room at the Salishan Lodge, Hwy. 101, P.O. Box 118, Gleneden Beach, OR 97388; (503) 764-2371. (R)

Gold Beach
Chowderhead, 910 S. Ellensburg, Gold Beach, OR 97444; (503) 247-7174. (R)
Friendship Inn of Gold Beach, 1010 Jerry's Flat Rd., Gold Beach, OR 97444; (503) 247-4533. (A)
Jot's Resort, 94360 Wedderburn Loop, Gold Beach, OR 97444; (503) 247-6676. (A)
Jot's Rod 'n Reel, 94321 Wedderburn Loop, Gold Beach, OR 97444; (503) 247-6823. (R)
Regal Restaurant and Rogue Room, 319 N. Ellensburg, Gold Beach, OR 97444; (503) 247-2421. (R)
Rogue Landing, 94749 Jerry's Flat Rd., Gold Beach, OR 97444; (503) 247-2711. (R)
Sportsman's Grotto, 185 N. Ellensburg, Gold Beach, OR 97444; (503) 247-2232. (R)
Tu Tu Tun Lodge, 96550 N. Bank Rogue, Gold Beach, OR 97444; (503) 247-6664. (A,R)

Lincoln City
Budget Inn, 1713 N.W. 21st St., Lincoln City, OR 97367; (503) 994-8155. (A)
Dory Cove Restaurant, Road's End, Lincoln City, OR 97367; (503) 994-5180. (R)
Mo's, 860 S.W. 51st St., Lincoln City, OR 97367; (503) 996-2535. (R)
Nidden Hof, 136 N.E. Hwy. 101, Lincoln City, OR 97367; (503) 994-8155. (A)

Big "O" Pub and Grub, 1330 N.E. Hwy. 101, Lincoln City, OR
    97367; (503) 994-2525. (R)
Surftides Beach Resort, 2945 N.W. Jetty Ave., Lincoln City, OR
    97367; (503) 994-2191. (A,R)

Manzanita
Sunset Surf Motel, P.O. Box 458, Manzanita, OR 97130; (503)
    368-5224. (A)

Neskowin
Pacific Sands Resort, P.O. Box 356, Neskowin, OR 97149; (503)
    392-3101. (A)

Netarts (see Oceanside)

Newport
Aladdin Motor Inn, 536 S.W. Elizabeth St., Newport, OR 97365;
    (503) 265-7701. (A,R)
Embarcadero Resort Hotel and Marina, 100 S.E. Bay Blvd., New-
    port, OR 97365; (503) 265-8521. (A,R)
Mo's Annex, 657 S.W. Bay Blvd., Newport, OR 97365; (503) 265-
    7512. (R)
Mo's Restaurant, 622 S.W. Bay Blvd., Newport, OR 97365; (503)
    265-2979. (R)
Penny Saver Motel, 710 N. Coast Hwy., Newport, OR 97365;
    (503) 265-9411. (A)
Pip Tide Restaurant and Lounge, 836 S.W. Bay Blvd., Newport,
    OR 97365; (503) 265-7797. (R)
Whaler Motel, 155 S.W. Elizabeth St., Newport, OR 97365; (503)
    265-9261. (A)
Windjammer Best Western, 744 S.W. Elizabeth St., Newport, OR
    97365; (503) 265-8853. (A)

Oceanside
Anchor Tavern, Pacific St., Oceanside, OR 97134; (503) 842-2041.
    (R)

Antler Court Motel, 4800 Netarts Hwy., Netarts, OR 97143; (503) 842-4003. (A)

House on the Hill, Maxwell Point, P.O. Box 187, Oceanside, OR 97134; (503) 842-6030. (A)

Motel Terimore, 5105 Crab Ave., Netarts, OR 97143; (503) 842-4623. (A)

Oceanside Motel, 1440 Pacific St. N.W., Oceanside, OR 97134; (503) 842-2961. (A)

Roseanna's Café, Pacific St., Oceanside, OR 97134; (503) 842-7351. (R)

Schooner Restaurant and Lounge, Netarts Bay, Netarts, OR 97143; (503) 842-4988. (R)

Wee Willie's Restaurant, 6300 Whiskey Creek Rd., Netarts, OR 97143; (503) 842-6869. (R)

Otter Crest
Inn at Otter Crest, P.O. Box 50, Otter Rock, OR 97369; (503) 765-2111. (A,R)

Reedsport
Pizza Ray and Suzy's, 2165 Winchester Ave., Reedsport, OR 97467; (503) 271-4100. (R)

Posey's Bakery and Café, Umpqua Shopping Center, Hwy. 101, Reedsport, OR 97467; (503) 271-3139. (R)

Rainbow Inn, 262 N. 4th St., Reedsport, OR 97467; (503) 271-4242. (R)

Tropicana Motel, 1593 Hwy. 101, Reedsport, OR 97467; (503) 271-3671. (A)

Windjammer, 1280 Highway Ave., Reedsport, OR 97467; (503) 271-5415. (R)

Rockaway
Beach Pancake House, 202 Hwy. 101 N., Rockaway, OR 97135; (503) 355-2411. (R)

Karla's Krabs 'n Quiche Delight, 2010 Hwy. 101 N., Rockaway, OR 97135; (503) 355-2362. (R)

Kelly's Bar and Grill, 172 S. Hwy. 101, Rockaway, OR 97135; (503) 355-2266. (R)

Lake Lytle Restaurant, 670 Hwy. 101 N., Rockaway, OR 97135; (503) 355-2676. (R)

Rockaway Beach Resort, 615 N. Pacific St., Rockaway, OR 97135; (503) 355-2191. (A)

Silver Sands Motel, 201 S. Pacific St., Rockaway, OR 97135; (503) 355-2206. (A)

Seaside

Dooger's Seafood & Grill, 505 Broadway, Seaside, OR 97138; (503) 738-3773. (R)

El Toucan, 311 Broadway, Seaside, OR 97138; (503) 738-8417. (R)

Gran'ma Jeano's "Flutter Bye," 1021 E. Broadway, Seaside, OR 97138; (503) 738-7571. (R)

Hi-Tide Motel, 30 Ave. G, Seaside, OR 97138; (503) 738-8414. (A)

Pig'n Pancake, 323 W. Broadway, Seaside, OR 97138; (503) 738-7243. (R)

Shilo Inn, 30 N. Prom at Broadway, Seaside, OR 97138; (503) 738-9571. (A,R)

Waldport

Bayshore Inn, 500 Bayshore Dr., Waldport, OR 97394; (503) 563-3202. (A,R)

Flounder Inn Tavern, Hwy. 101, Waldport, OR 97394; (503) 563-2266. (R)

4J's Bridgetender Restaurant, Hwy. 101, Waldport, OR 97394; (503) 563-3717. (R)

Winchester Bay

Winchester Bay Motel, 4th and Broadway, Winchester Bay, OR 97467; (503) 271-4871. (A)

The Oasis Restaurant and Lounge, 8th and Clearlake Sts., Winchester Bay, OR 97467; (503) 271-9976. (R)

Yachats

Adobe Motel, 1555 Hwy. 101, P.O. Box 219, Yachats, OR 97498; (503) 547-3141. (A,R)

Beulah's Sea View Inn Restaurant and On the Rocks Lounge, Hwy. 101, Yachats, OR 97498; (503) 547-3215. (R)

Fireside Motel, Hwy. 101, P.O. Box 313, Yachats, OR 97498; (503) 547-3636. (A)

La Serre, 2nd and Beach Sts., Yachats, OR 97498; (503) 547-3420. (R)

LeRoy's Blue Whale, Hwy. 101, Yachats, OR 97498; (503) 547-3399. (R)

WASHINGTON

Birch Bay

Driftwood Inn Resort, 7394 Birch Bay Dr., Birch Bay, WA 98230; (206) 371-2620. (A)

Edgewater Resort, 7954 Birch Bay Dr., Birch Bay, WA 98230; (206) 371-7533. (A)

Blaine

The Inn at Semi-Ah-Moo, 9565 Semi-Ah-Moo Parkway, Blaine, WA 98230; (206) 371-2000. (A,R)

Chinook (see Long Beach)

Coupeville (see Whidbey Island)

Dungeness

The 3 Crabs, 101 3 Crabs Rd., Dungeness, WA 98382; (206) 683-4264. (R)

Eastsound (see Orcas Island)

Forks

Forks Motel, 432 Forks Ave., Forks, WA 98331; (206) 374-6243. (A)

Smokehouse Restaurant, Hwy. 101 and LaPush Rd., Forks, WA
   98331; (206) 374-6258. (R)

Friday Harbor (see San Juan Island)

Kalaloch
Kalaloch Lodge, Hwy. 101, HC 80, P.O. Box 1100, Kalaloch, WA
   98331; (206) 962-2271. (A,R)

Lake Quinault
Lake Quinault Lodge, S. Shore Dr., P.O. Box 7, Quinault, WA
   98575; (206) 288-2571. (A,R)

Langley (see Whidbey Island)

Long Beach
Chautauqua Lodge, 304 14th St. N.W., Long Beach, WA 98631;
   (206) 642-4401. (A,R)
Cottage Bakery and Delicatessen, Rte. 103, Long Beach, WA
   98631; (206) 642-4441. (R)
O'Connor's Shaman Motel, 3rd St. S., Long Beach, WA 98631;
   (206) 642-3714. (A)
Red Baron Burger Shop, Rte. 3, Long Beach, WA 98631; (206)
   642-2358. (R)
The Sanctuary, Hwy. 101 and Hazel St., Chinook, WA 98614;
   (206) 777-8380. (R)
Shelburne Inn, Rte. 3, P.O. Box 250, Seaview, WA 98644; (206)
   642-2442. (A)
Shoalwater Restaurant (at the Shelburne Inn), Rte. 3, Seaview,
   WA 98644; (206) 642-4142. (R)

Lopez Island
Islander Lopez, Fisherman Bay, Lopez Island, WA 98261; (206)
   468-2233. (A,R)
Gail's Restaurant and Delicatessen, Village Center, Lopez Island,
   WA 98261; (206) 468-2150. (R)

Jeanna's Seafood Gallery, Lopez Plaza, Lopez Island, WA 98261; (206) 468-2114. (R)

McKaye Harbor Inn, P.O. Box 1940, Lopez Island, WA 98261; (206) 468-2253. (A,R)

Moclips

Moclips Motel, Pacific St., P.O. Box 8, Moclips, WA 98562; (206) 276-4228. (A)

Moonstone Beach Motel, Pacific St., Moclips, WA 98562; (206) 276-4346. (A)

Ocean Crest Resort, Sunset Beach, Hwy. 109, Moclips, WA 98562; (206) 276-4465. (A,R)

The Lighthouse Restaurant, Oceanfront, Pacific Beach, WA 98571; (206) 276-4190. (R)

Nahcotta

The Ark Restaurant and Bakery, Dockside, P.O. Box 95, Nahcotta, WA 98637; (206) 665-4133. (R)

Oak Harbor (see Whidbey Island)

Ocean Park

Bay Avenue Fish House, Bay Ave., Ocean Park, WA 98640; (206) 665-5775. (R)

Grannie Annie's Ocean Park Café, Bay Ave., Ocean Park, WA 98640; (206) 665-4323. (R)

Sunset View Resort Motel, Park Ave., P.O. Box 399, Ocean Park, WA 98640; (206) 665-4494. (A)

Ocean Shores

Canterbury Inn, Ocean Shores Blvd., P.O. Box 310, Ocean Shores, WA 98569; (206) 562-6678. (A)

Grey Gull Condominium Motel, Ocean Shores Blvd., P.O. Box 1417, Ocean Shores, WA 98569; (206) 289-3381. (A)

Harbor Landing Restaurant, Pt. Brown Ave., Ocean Shores, WA 98569; (206) 289-3171. (R)

Ocean Sands Motel, Ocean Shores Blvd., Ocean Shores, WA 98569; (206) 289-3585. (A)

Ocean Shores Inn, Ocean Shores Blvd., P.O. Box 639, Ocean Shores, WA 98569; (206) 289-3306. (A,R)

Polynesian Condominium Resort, 291 Ocean Shores Blvd., P.O. Box 998, Ocean Shores, WA 98569; (206) 289-3361. (A,R)

Sand Castle Drive-In Restaurant, Pt. Brown Ave., Ocean Shores, WA 98569; (206) 289-2777. (R)

Vagabond House, Ocean Shores Blvd., Ocean Shores, WA 98569; (206) 289-2350. (A)

Orcas Island

Beach Haven Resort, Enchanted Forest Rd., Orcas Island, East-sound, WA 98245; (206) 376-2288. (A)

Rosario, Orcas Island, Eastsound, WA 98245; (206) 376-2222. (A,R)

Pacific Beach (see Moclips)

Point Roberts

The Breakers Tavern, Marine Dr., Point Roberts, WA 98281; (206) 945-2300. (R)

The Old House Bed and Breakfast, 674 Kendor Dr., Point Roberts, WA 98281; (206) 945-5210. (A)

The Reef Tavern, Marine Dr., Point Roberts, WA 98281; (206) 945-4042. (R)

Port Angeles

Dupuis Seafood, 11 U.S. 101 E., Port Angeles, WA 98362; (206) 457-8033. (R)

Haguewood's Restaurant, 221 N. Lincoln St., Port Angeles, WA 98362; (206) 457-0424. (R)

Red Lion Bayshore Inn, 221 N. Lincoln St., Port Angeles, WA 98362; (206) 452-9215. (A)

San Juan Island

The Electric Co., 175 First St., Friday Harbor, WA 98250; (206) 378-4118. (R)

Friday Harbor Motor Inn, 410 Spring St., P.O. Box 962, Friday Harbor, WA 98250; (206) 378-4351. (A)

Front Street Café, Front and Spring Sts., Friday Harbor, WA 98250; (206) 378-2245. (R)

Herb's Tavern, Spring and First Sts., Friday Harbor, WA 98250; (206) 378-9106. (R)

Island Lodge, 1016 Guard St., Friday Harbor, WA 98250; (206) 378-2000. (A)

Mojo's, 1 Front St., Friday Harbor, WA 98250; (206) 378-5700. (R)

Turnagain Restaurant, 51 Spring St. W., Friday Harbor, WA 98250; (206) 378-4175. (R)

Wharfside Bed and Breakfast, K Dock, Friday Harbor Marina, P.O. Box 1212, Friday Harbor, WA 98250; (206) 378-5661. (A)

Winston's, 95 Nichols St., Friday Harbor, WA 98250; (206) 378-5093. (R)

San Juan Islands (see Lopez Island, Orcas Island, San Juan Island)

Seattle

Ivar's Acres of Clams, Pier 54, 1001 Alaskan Way, Seattle, WA 98104; (206) 624-6852. (R)

Lowell's Restaurant, 1519 Pike Place, Seattle, WA 98101; (206) 622-2036. (R)

Old Timer's Café, 620 1st Ave., Seattle, WA 98104; (206) 623-9800. (R)

Ray's Boathouse, 6049 Seaview N.W., Seattle, WA 98107; (206) 789-3770. (R)

Ray's Downtown, 999 2nd Ave., Seattle, WA 98104; (206) 623-7999. (R)

Stouffer Madison Hotel, 515 Madison St., Seattle, WA 98104; (206) 583-0300. (A,R)

Seaview (see Long Beach)

Sequim (see Dungeness)

Westport
The Islander Motel, Westhaven and Revetment Dr., P.O. Box 488,
    Westport, WA 98595; (206) 268-9166. (A,R)
Little Richard's Donut Shop, Westhaven Dr., Westport, WA
    98595; (206) 268-0733 (R)
Sourdough Lil's, 202 E. Dock Ave., Westport, WA 98595; (206)
    268-9700. (R)

Whidbey Island
Captain Whidbey Inn, 2072 W. Captain Whidbey Rd., Coupeville,
    WA 98239; (206) 678-4097. (A,R)
El Cazador, 6051 60th St. N.W., Oak Harbor, WA 98277; (206)
    675-6114. (R)
Saratoga Inn, 4850 S. Coles Rd., Langley, WA 98260; (206) 221-
    7526. (A)
Sea Gull Restaurant, 10 Front St., Coupeville, WA 98239; (206)
    678-6865. (R)

Appendix:
Beach Facts and
Opinions

State Boards of Tourism and State Park Systems

California

California Office of Tourism, 1121 L Street, Suite 103, Sacramento, CA 95814; (906) 322-1396.

California Department of Parks and Recreation, P.O. Box 2390, Sacramento, CA 95811; (916) 445-6477 (general information), (800) 952-5580 (state-park camping reservations).

Oregon

Oregon Economic Development Department, Tourism Division, 595 Cottage Street N.E., Salem, OR 97310; (800) 233-3306 (inside Oregon), (800) 547-7842 (outside Oregon).

Oregon State Parks, 525 Trade Street S.E., Salem, OR 97310; (503) 378-6305, (800) 452-5687 (state-park campsite information, in-state), (503) 238-7488 (state-park campsite information, out-of-state).

Washington

Department of Trade and Economic Development, Tourism Division, 101 General Administration Building, Olympia, WA 98504; (206) 586-2088.

Washington State Parks and Recreation Commission, 7150 Clearwater Lane, Olympia, WA 98504; (800) 562-0990 (state-park
campsite information, May 1st to Labor Day), (206) 753-2027
(all other times of year).

Mean Monthly Temperatures
(Daily Highs/Daily Lows)

City	May	June	July	Aug.	Sept.	Jan.
San Diego, Calif.	70/57	72/60	76/63	77/65	77/62	65/46
Los Angeles, Calif.	74/56	77/59	83/63	83/63	82/61	65/47
Santa Barbara, Calif.	69/50	72/53	76/56	77/57	76/55	64/43
Monterey, Calif.	66/47	67/49	67/51	69/52	72/52	60/41
San Francisco, Calif.	67/50	70/52	72/54	72/54	74/54	55/42
Mendocino, Calif.	61/47	63/49	64/49	65/50	65/49	56/39
Eureka, Calif.	58/48	60/51	61/52	61/53	62/51	54/41
Newport, Ore.	59/45	63/48	65/50	65/51	64/50	50/38
Cannon Beach, Ore.	61/45	64/50	68/52	68/52	68/49	50/36
Seattle, Wash.	66/49	70/53	75/56	74/56	69/53	44/37

Source: U.S. Weather Bureau

Toll-Free Hotel- and
Motel-Chain Numbers

Best Western, (800) 528-1234
Days Inn, (800) 325-2525
Econo Lodge, (800) 446-6900
Four Seasons, (800) 828-1188
Friendship Inn, (800) 453-4511
Hilton, (800) 445-8667
Holiday Inn, (800) 465-4329
Howard Johnson's, (800) 654-8000
Hyatt, (800) 228-9000
Marriott, (800) 228-9290

Quality Inn, (800) 228-5151
Radisson, (800) 228-9822
Ramada Inn, (800) 272-6232
Red Lion Inn, (800) 547-8010
Sheraton, (800) 325-3535
Stouffer, (800) 468-3571
TraveLodge, (800) 255-3050
Vagabond, (800) 522-1555

Ten Favorite Places
(in alphabetical order)

Big Sur, California
Cannon Beach, Oregon
Kalaloch, Washington
Mendocino, California
Newport Beach, California
Pacific Beach, California
Pacific Grove, California
San Francisco, California
Santa Barbara, California
Seattle, Washington

Honorable Mention
Bandon, Oregon
Hermosa Beach, Manhattan Beach and Redondo Beach, California
Klamath, California
Laguna Beach, California
Long Beach, Washington
Point Reyes, California
San Juan Islands, Washington
Santa Catalina Island, California
Santa Cruz/Capitola, California
Seaside, Oregon

Ten Favorite Hotels, Motels and Inns
(in alphabetical order)

Big River Lodge/Stanford Inn by the Sea (Mendocino, California)
El Encanto Hotel and Villas (Santa Barbara, California)
Gosby House Inn (Pacific Grove, California)
Hotel del Coronado (Coronado, California)
Inn at Morro Bay (Morro Bay, California)
Pacific Terrace Inn (Pacific Beach, California)
Palos Verdes Inn (Redondo Beach, California)
Rosario (Orcas Island, Washington)
Sea Lodge (La Jolla, California)
Surfview Resort (Cannon Beach, Oregon)

Honorable Mention
Big Sur Lodge (Big Sur, California)
Eureka Inn (Eureka, California)
Fireside Motel (Yachats, Oregon)
Highlands Inn (Carmel, California)
Hotel Queen Mary (Long Beach, California)
House on the Hill (Oceanside, Oregon)
The Inn at Semi-Ah-Moo (Blaine, Washington)
Marina Beach Hotel (Marina del Rey, California)
Salishan Lodge (Gleneden Beach, Oregon)
Sea Sprite (Hermosa Beach, California)

Ten Favorite Restaurants
(in alphabetical order)

A. Sabella's (San Francisco, California)
The Cannery (Newport Beach, California)
Cliff House (San Francisco, California)
The Crab Cooker (Newport Beach, California)
The Sanctuary (Chinook, Washington)
Shadowbrook Restaurant (Capitola, California)
Shoalwater Restaurant (Seaview, Washington)

The 3 Crabs (Dungeness, Washington)
Ventana (Big Sur, California)
Windward Inn (Florence, Oregon)

Honorable Mention
The Ark (Nahcotta, Washington)
Beach House Inn (Laguna Beach, California)
Café Beaujolais (Mendocino, California)
El Encanto (Santa Barbara, California)
Ivar's Acres of Clams (Seattle, Washington)
Mo's (Coos Bay, Lincoln City, Newport, and Otter Rock, Oregon)
Pierpont Inn (Ventura, California)
The Shore Bird Restaurant (Princeton-by-the-Sea, California)
Sourdough Lil's (Westport, Washington)
Steelhead Lodge (Klamath, California)

Ten Favorite Bars, Clubs and Hangouts

Acapulco Inn (Long Beach, California)
Belly Up Tavern (Solana Beach, California)
Cass Street Bar and Grill (Pacific Beach, California)
The Catalyst (Santa Cruz, California)
Central Tavern (Seattle, Washington)
Club Diego's (Pacific Beach and Solana Beach, California)
The Hop (Huntington Beach, California)
Joe Jost's Saloon (Long Beach, California)
Kahuna's Surf Bar (Pacific Beach, California)
Red Onion (Marina del Rey, Newport Beach, and Redondo Beach, California)

Honorable Mention
Bill's Tavern (Cannon Beach, Oregon)
Caspar Inn (Caspar, California)
Crow's Nest (Santa Cruz, California)

Hennessey's Tavern (Redondo Beach, Hermosa Beach, Pacific
    Beach, and Seal Beach, California)
La Paz (Manhattan Beach, California)
The Reef Tavern (Point Roberts, Washington)
Rocky Galenti's (Santa Barbara, California)
Rumplestiltskin's (Newport Beach, California)
The Warehouse (Newport Beach, California)
White House Tavern (Laguna Beach, California)

Things We Like about the West Coast and Its Beaches...

fun, fun, fun
sun, sun, sun
watching the sun set over the ocean every night
the wide sand beaches of Southern California
the Pacific Coast Highway (a.k.a., the Coast Highway, P.C.N.
    and Route 1)
surfers, surfboards, surf shops
surf music
surfing as career, lifestyle and religion rolled into one
volleyball on the beach
lifeguards
hot California blonds
permanent suntans
bikinis, monokinis and the flesh parade in the Land of the Flaw-
    less Bod
life lived outdoors with few cares or concerns
needing nothing more to get by than cutoffs, flip-flops and enough
    money for a hot dog or taco
physical fitness
lean California physiques
Corona and lime
drinks at sundown
Happy Hour everywhere you turn
amiable sports bars and taverns where the draft flows like water

the Beach Boys
"California Dreamin'"
the return to the music and style of the fifties and sixties in South-
     ern California
diners and fifties chic
boardwalks and amusement parks
freeways (sometimes)
the California Coastal Access Commission
Oregon's proenvironment philosophy
California wines and wineries
Oregon's Pinot Noirs
the cities of Santa Barbara, San Francisco and Seattle
Spanish architecture (down south)
Victorian architecture (up north)
the rugged Big Sur coast
Morro Rock, Haystack Rock and other offshore monoliths
salmon, steelhead trout, ling cod, Pacific snapper and halibut
fish 'n' chips
Dungeness crab
sea lions, sea otters and the rocks they live on
shorebirds
tide pools
saunas, spas and hot tubs
the lighthouses of the West Coast
the organizations that work to preserve all the nonoperational light-
     houses
solid old fishing piers
the patience of the solitary angler
dory fleets
seafood canneries
creative Cal-nouvelle cuisine
fresh fruits and vegetables
the "old town" districts of many Oregon and Northern California
     coast towns
Oregon's abundant and free state parks
the Oregon Indoor Clean Air Act
a predictable, comfortable climate with relatively little variety
Mexican food, now and then

...And Some Things We Dislike

the "June gloom" no one warned us about

water too cold to swim in a wet suit (and what fun is that?)

the realization that you're paying $145 a night to stay next to an ocean you'll never swim in

stiff prevailing winds along the Oregon coast

skateboard nazis

kamikaze roller skaters

dangerous-looking hippie burnouts who haunt the beaches, bars and back streets

frequently gray skies along the coast from San Francisco to Seattle

torrential rain in the Pacific northwest much of the year

the ever-present specter of earthquakes

a dome of smog that brings you to tears

having to spend more time in your car than anywhere else

four-way stop signs

traffic jams

freeway shootings

parking problems near the beach

rampant overdevelopment across Southern California

"phase two," "models open," "now selling" and other signs of condominium cancer

car culture

drug culture

plastic values and chronic air-headedness

English as a second language

California's offshore drilling platforms

nuclear reactors built along fault lines near population centers

lack of adequate directional markers in Oregon

a bicyclist, six bags dangling from his or her bars, huffing and puffing up a steep Oregon incline in the rain (this is fun?)

bicyclists attempting to share narrow, winding roads with motorists

logging trucks on your tail doing twice the speed limit

oversized recreational vehicles that lumber and snort up the highway

car-rental agencies that sneak all sorts of hidden charges into their
    low basic rates
the strange individual who shouted and pounded on our motel door
    at 4 a.m. one night in Berkeley
$4 day-use fees at many California state beaches
gillnetting salmon
hydroplane races and drunken boat fans
dune buggies
the sad specter of unemployment across the northwest
motels with check-in times later than 2 p.m. and check-out times
    earlier than 11 a.m.
hotels that charge an additional fee for parking on the premises
valet parking and uniformed factotums with their hands stuck out
a predictable, comfortable climate with relatively little variety
Mexican food, now and then

INDEX

Catalog

If you are interested in a list of fine Paperback
books, covering a wide range of subjects
and interests, send your name and address,
requesting your free catalog, to:

McGraw-Hill Paperbacks
11 West 19th Street
New York, N.Y. 10011